BETWEEN IDENTITY AND LOCATION

BETWEEN IDENTITY AND LOCATION

The Cultural Politics of Theory

R. Radhakrishnan

Orient Longman

Grateful acknowledgment is made for permission to reprint the following: chapter 1 from *differences: A Journal of Feminist Cultural Studies*, 2.2 (summer 1990): 126–52, copyright 1990 Indiana University Press, chapter 3 from *The Nature and Context of Minority Discourse*, ed. Abdul R. JanMohamed and David Lloyd (Oxford: Oxford University Press, 1990); chapter 4 from *MELUS* 14.2 (summer 1987): 5–19, copyright 1989, reprinted by permission of the Society for the Study of the Multiethnic Literature of the United States; chapter 5 from *Theory/Pedagogy/Politics: Texts for Change*, ed. Donald Morton and Mas'ud Zavarzadeh, copyright 1991 by the Board of Trustees of the University of Illinois, used by permission from the University of Illinois Press; chapter 6 from *Feminism and Institutions: Dialogues on Feminist Theory*, ed. Linda Kauffman (Oxford: Blackwell, 1989); chapter 7 from *Views beyond the Border Country: Raymond Williams and Cultural Politics*, ed. Dennis L. Dworkin and Leslie G. Roman (New York: Routledge, 1992); chapter 8 from *Callaloo*, 16.4 (1993): 750–71, reprinted by permission of The Johns Hopkins University Press; chapter 9 from *Nationalisms and Sexualities*, ed. Andrew Parker et al. (New York: Routledge, 1991); chapter 10 from *The State of Asian America: Activism and Resistance in the 1990s*, ed. Karin Aguilar-San Juan (Boston: South End Press, 1994); chapter 11 from *Orientations: Mapping Studies in the Asian Diaspora*, eds. Kandice Chuh and Karen Shimakawa (Durham: Duke University Press, 2001).

BETWEEN IDENTITY AND LOCATION: THE CULTURAL POLITICS OF THEORY

ORIENT LONGMAN PRIVATE LIMITED

Registered Office
3-6-752 Himayatnagar, Hyderabad 500 029 (A.P.), INDIA
E-mail : cogeneral@orientlongman.com

Other Offices
Bangalore, Bhopal, Bhubaneshwar, Chennai, Ernakulam, Guwahati,
Hyderabad, Jaipur, Kolkata, Lucknow, Mumbai, New Delhi, Patna

Published by arrangement with the University of Minnesota Press
© The Regents of the University of Minnesota 1996

© Introduction, Orient Longman 2007

First published in 1996 by the University of Minnesota Press
111 Third Avenue South, Suite 209, Minneapolis, MN 55401–2520

First published in India by
Orient Longman Private Limited, India 2007

ISBN 13: 978 81 250 3156 7
ISBN 10: 81 250 3156 1

Printed in India at
Chaman Enterprises
New Delhi

Published by
Orient Longman Private Limited
1/24 Asaf Ali Road, New Delhi 110 002
e-mail: delgeneral@orientlongman.com

For sale in India, Bangladesh, Nepal, Sri Lanka, Maldives, Malaysia,
Indonesia, Singapore, Bhutan and the Middle East.
Not for export to any other country.

For Appa, Amma, Asha, and Surya

Contents

Acknowledgments	ix
Introduction	xiii
1 / The Changing Subject and the Politics of Theory	1
2 / Toward an Effective Intellectual: Foucault or Gramsci?	27
3 / Ethnic Identity and Poststructuralist Differance	62
4 / Culture as Common Ground: Ethnicity and Beyond	80
5 / Canonicity and Theory: Toward a Poststructuralist Pedagogy	96
6 / Negotiating Subject Positions in an Uneven World	119
7 / Cultural Theory and the Politics of Location	133
8 / Postcoloniality and the Boundaries of Identity	155
9 / Nationalism, Gender, and the Narrative of Identity	185
10 / Is the Ethnic "Authentic" in the Diaspora?	203
11 / Conjunctural Identities, Academic Adjacencies	215
12 / Diaspora, Hybridity, Pedagogy	230
Index	247

Acknowledgments

So strange this genre called "Acknowledgments" that invites even as it frustrates the will to narrative. On the one hand, I want to begin at the beginning and thank people, events, and influences in a chronological order. But on the other hand, these very people, events, and influences, as well as my profound indebtedness to them, constitute a simultaneous order that has very little to do with "befores" and "afters." So here I go stumbling through my gratitude: without method, poorly prepared, and inadequately temporalized.

My heartfelt thanks to my friend and editor Janaki Bakhle, who took the initiative in collecting these essays into a single volume, and for her patience with my will to procrastinate. I would like to thank her also for many hours of deep and intense dialogue on matters macro and micro. My thanks to the editorial staff of the University of Minnesota Press, Biodun Iginla, Jeff Moen, Mary Byers, and Anne Running, for their help and cooperation. I extend my sincere appreciation to Mike Sullivan at the University of Massachusetts Computer Center and, in particular, to Asha Radhakrishnan, who transformed a series of low-tech texts into a computer-friendly unit without ever making me feel like a hopeless Luddite. To Bruce Robbins and Kamala Visweswaran, readers of these essays, many thanks for your insightful comments and suggestions.

It feels like just yesterday when I was in graduate school at SUNY-Binghamton working on my dissertation with William V. Spanos. Thank you ever so much, Bill, for your support and generosity and for the intense ethicopolitical passion that you bring to every aspect of your work. The summer of 1982 was a very special time for me at the School of Criticism and Theory at Northwestern University, where I had the privilege of studying with Edward Said and Gayatri Chakravorty Spivak. I thank them for their brilliance, their friendship, and their exemplary groundbreaking intellectual activism. In a similar vein I wish to acknowledge my indebtedness to the Subaltern Studies Group for their tireless and rigorous work.

These essays have been previously published in a variety of contexts over a period of time. In addition to the formal thanks for permission to reprint, I wish to thank a number of colleagues who invited me to contribute these essays: Naomi Schor, Elizabeth Weed, Joseph Skerrett Jr., Bruce Robbins, Masúd Zavarzadeh, Donald Morton, Linda Kauffman, Abdul JanMohamed, David Lloyd, Karin Aguilar-San Juan, Sonia Sahni, Henry Louis Gates Jr., Tejumola Olaniyan, Dennis Dworkin, Leslie G. Roman, Andrew Parker, and Doris Sommer. Several of these essays were rehearsed as talks and presentations at the following venues: University of California–Berkeley, Stanford University, Harvard, Florida State University, University of Rochester, Wesleyan University, Brown, Rutgers University–Newark and New Brunswick, University of Warwick (England), Dubrovnik, Phillips Academy, University of Wisconsin–Milwaukee and Madison, University of Chicago, University of Minnesota, Dartmouth College, University of New Hampshire, University of Alabama, University of California–Santa Barbara, Montclair State University, Institute for the Advanced Study of Humanities at the University of Massachusetts, Amherst, Smith College, Princeton, and the Center for the Critical Analysis of Contemporary Culture at Rutgers University–New Brunswick. I am deeply grateful to my hosts and my audiences for their hospitality as well as their critical engagement with my work.

My grateful appreciation goes out to Gerald Graff, Catherine Stimpson, Richard Ohmann, Brook Thomas, Susan Stanford Friedman, Elizabeth Meese, Barbara Johnson, Donald Pease, Jonathan Culler, George Levine, Andrew Ross, Cornel West, Martin Dillon, Joseph Adams, Chris Fynsk, Ted Norton, and Marsha Abrams for their support and encouragement at different times during these years. It gives me great pleasure to extend a warm and appreciative "Namasthe" to a number of my colleagues in my department: Jules Chametzky, Michael Wolff, Lee Edwards, Arlyn Diamond, Margo Culley, Vincent DiMarco, Don Cheney, and Arthur Kinney. It is with a sense of excitement that I thank the many graduate students who, in course after course and seminar after seminar, kept me honest with their intellectual challenge. My special thanks to Ben Xu, Valerie Traub, Brenda Marshall, Poonam Pillai, and C. Margot Hennessy. It was such fun and excitement working with you.

Putting these essays together amounts to an act of solidarity with a community with whom I share a wide range of themes, issues, crises, and dilemmas, as well as excitement, intellectual pleasures and thrills, and complex epiphanies. Home-Away, Near-Far, Location-Travel: amid these shifting and perennially negotiated signposts and borders, it has been an immensely rich and moving experience to have found a community of "minority" and "diasporan" thinkers who bring to their work an undeniable immediacy of history and lived experience. It is from within this community that I wish to speak, in active advocacy of ever-broadening coalitions based on the reciprocities of ethicopolitical persuasion.

To Sukun, "thank you" is inadequate for your comradeship and for all I have learned from you; to Bhaskar, genuine appreciation for your finely tuned intellect and your capacity to imbibe knowledge under any circumstance. Thank you, Chandrashekar, for communicating to me the passion for critical analysis. I thank my parents with a full heart for letting me follow my own ways: believe me, you are very much a part of my diaspora. Asha, thank you for your friendship and solidarity, and your unique capacity to motivate even as you put up with a never-ending history of lapsed deadlines. I look forward to never being able to get over my indebtedness to you. To Surya, hey, who else can I learn from if not from you?

Introduction

It is ten years now since this book was originally published by the University of Minnesota Press as *Diasporic Mediations: Between Home and Location*. The present edition has two new chapters, a new Introduction and a different title, *Between Identity and Location: The Cultural Politics of Theory*. This work was and continues to be a collection of essays (most of them written between 1985 and 1993), rather than a book with a single thesis or a single object of study. But some rationale does hold the different pieces together within an integral coherence: the flow of a certain way of thinking, what I would call "theoretical thinking," across and beyond the givens of certain themes, issues, and subject matter. So, what is theoretical thinking and how is it different from "theory," or from forms of non-theoretical thinking?

To be able to respond to this question with any cognitive vigor and personal honesty, I need to step back and historicize the institutional production of this strange genre called *"theory"* that was coming into its own around the time I was writing my dissertation at SUNY-Binghamton (1978-83), with William Spanos the founding editor of *boundary2* as my mentor. When I say, "theory" was coming into its own, I mean that the first generation, after the founding generation of Foucault, Barthes, Derrida, Lacan, Althusser, De Man, Fredric Jameson, Edward Said, Gayatri Spivak, Geoffrey Hartman, Hillis Miller, and others, was finding its feet; with each of us wondering all the while if we could get tenure-track jobs in "theory," apprehensive about the longevity of theory as an academic domain. This is not to say that there was no "theory" earlier on: such a claim would indeed be foolishly ahistorical and presentist. So, I must confess that when I say "theory," I mean poststructuralism, in all its variations, as theory. It was the ability of poststructuralist theory to initiate a fundamental quarrel with the very givens of Eurocentric Enlightenment thought that made it exciting and relevant. That such a quarrel had decided to "use the master's tools to dismantle the master's house" made it particularly piquant. To this day I take pride in starting my undergraduate courses in Theory with a flamboyant announcement to my students that Theory is sexy.

So, why and how was theory sexy, that is, when by "sexy," I mean attractive and seductive, liberating and transgressive as well as transformative, and irresistible on multiple levels: affective, cognitive, existential, visceral, aesthetic, historical and ethico-political? What is it that made theory seem like a return to life in all its multifarious and multivalent complexity and profundity? What was it about theory, in the wake of poststructuralism by way of Derrida and deconstruction-Foucault and discourse analysis-Lacanian psychoanalysis and the language like structured-ness of the Unconscious, that made it appear that the plunge into theory was indeed an unconditional immersement in Ek-sistence? Why was the insight so persuasive that it was in theory that the Cogito, with rapture and with excruciating rigor, could avow with dignity and without embarrassment that it was hopelessly "straddled" between living and thinking: indeed that it was richly orphaned between the ontic and the ontological, to borrow from Martin Heidegger and Jacques Derrida, and between the empirical and the transcendental, to avail of Michel Foucault?

It was not at all coincidental that language and literature were the privileged sites where the transformative, dare I say "revolutionary," process of theory was taking place, for after all, it is in language and literature that students of the humanities seek to recognize, identify, legitimate, and valorize what is human. And something "modal" seemed to be happening with the now famous "linguistic turn," and the consequent take over of the innocence of literature by the impurity or the contamination known as theory, and the irreversible inter-disciplinarization of the study of literature. The "linguistic turn," the understanding after Ferdinand de Saussure and Voloshinov-Medvedev, that language was not representative but constitutive of reality, enabled not the tame and domestic textualization of reality, but on the contrary, a rebellious and anti-authoritarian conceptualization of literature as the fierce site of worldly struggles over the interpretation and the meaning of texts. In other words, it wasn't possible, or intellectually or epistemologically respectable or feasible to hold on to an auto-telic theory of the meaning of the literary text. Literary aesthetics could not afford to quarantine the beauty as well as the value of the literary text and shore it up as a necessary strength against the contingency of real life or existence. To avow and to shout from the rooftops of theory that language was constitutive of reality was to let into literary language the messiness, the fragmentariness, the anomie as well as the processual meaninglessness of reality itself. This epistemological paradigm shift that was then known as the postmodern "break" was seen as a decisive rupture from the spatializing aesthetic of modernism and its epiphanic as well as panoptic mastery over the materiality of everyday existence. Literary language or language as literature could no more perpetrate the ideological ruse, in the name of the aesthetic, that form could effect a harmonious alignment between the I am (the ontology of literature) and the I know (the epistemology) of literature. On the contrary, it was in the nature of the postmodern occasion to suggest the possibility that the literary Cogito was the site of a *mise en scene*: the performance of the thesis of the incommensurability between Ontology and Epistemology, between existential verities and literary truths. To recognize a work as postmodern was to suggest that this work was in a relationship of fundamental and radical antagonism with its own tradition, i.e., the hegemonic tradition that was the "given" context for that text.

Was Eliot modern or postmodern? Was Wallace Stevens modern or postmodern? Were Joyce, Samuel Beckett, Virginia Woolf, and Herman Melville modern or postmodern? Was postmodernism periodizable or not? These became fraught issues. What about the suppressed postmodernisms in earlier texts from earlier periods? What about that arch postmodern text *Tristram Shandy*? What about those texts that were really "anti- aesthetic closure" in their linguistic and formal energies, and yet were coercively interpreted and legitimated as texts that celebrated teleology, spatial form and the architectonics of closure? In all these fierce debates about the canonicity or the lack thereof of a number of literary texts, the focal point of attention was the linguistic deportment or the orientation of the work. How did language work in the poem, in the novel: decorously or de-structively (the Heideggerian hermeneutic term) and deconstructively (the Derridean gift)? What was the relationship, within the text, of the rhetoricity of language (grammatology if you wish) to its logocentric burden? In what ways does the text live out symptomatically the tension between its potential for transgressive "becoming" and its tendency towards acquiescence in the law of normative being? How does writing or *ecriture* present itself as the site of the "unconscious" that resists the violent normalization of "be-ing" into meaning? What are the theoretical and self-reflexive and meta-junctures in the text that point towards *other* possibilities and *other* ways of reading that a logocentric aesthetic will just not allow for the very simple reason that a logocentric theory of language forbids and interdicts the revolution of language as such against the hegemony of language as meaning?

Clearly, there is a lot of hype in all this; in particular, in the manner in which literature and language get set up as sites for revolutions and epistemological breaks, but that indeed was part of the radical intellectual *frissons*. What was valuable and worthy of cherishing, and I would say this despite all the subsequent revisionisms that the moment of theory has been subjected to (and I must say I have been part of this movement as well), in all that theoretical extravagance about breaks and transgressions was that an attempt was being made to relate and connect transformations and interrogations happening in the super structural world of literature and interpretation with the destabilization of dominance and authority in the world without. I am not suggesting for a moment that the postmodern break in theory and in literary and cultural analysis was also *ipso facto* a radical or progressive intervention in worldly goings on; but rather a way of thinking was emerging that was interested not in shoring up past and sclerotic forms of authority but rather in deconstructing them from within. Two things were happening simultaneously: the spirited avowal of the non-innocence or the complicity of language and literature in what we now, after Edward Said, call worldliness, and, the dissolution of the authority of literature and literary value within an interdisciplinary continuum: anthropology, sociology, ontological thought and philosophy, a variety of differently grounded feminisms, psychoanalysis, etc. What was remarkable and disruptive about this phenomenon was that it let the world into literature in the name of interdisciplinarity. In other words, this repositioning and reconceptualization of the literary object had real world implications as well.

As best I can recall, the most heady theme was that of the *coupure*, "the epistemological break" in theory that inaugurated the momentum of the post-, without at the same time specifying what did or could or should come after the break? Why such a dedicated and credulous insistence on the "break as such," and what was the necessary connection between "theory" and the "break"? Why could the break not be historical and/or political, and *ergo* theoretical and epistemological? Why did the "post-al" condition have to be epistemological/theoretical? The obsessive focus on epistemology was both much needed and suspect at the same time. Whether it was post-modern, post-structuralist, post-colonial, post-ethnic, post-humanist, or post-marxist, it felt as if a general condition existed that required the articulation of a profound and radical discontinuity from the status quo, from any given regnant regime. It was as though a new epistemology was required so that emergent realities could be talked about on their own knowledge-grounds, rather than be recuperated within the confines of existing knowledge games. The lack of differentiation among the different "posts" would turn out to be as much of a help as it was a hindrance. Discontinuity as such became the general banner under which various singularities and heterogeneities were seeking to historicize themselves in their own particular ways, rather than submit to some totalizing ism or revolutionary platform. The blazing conviction was that new knowledges were indeed emerging and they had to be identified and valorized as such. The break felt real: it was as if one could literally palpate it and experience it as a break. Energized considerably by Foucault, who would then be simplified as no more than the theorist of discontinuity, postmodern theoretical practices sought not only to enfranchise discontinuity as a valid historical and epistemological principle of organization, but also resolutely refused to posit an alternative version of continuity. It was a kind of counter-mnemonic *nirvana* for a number of constituencies for whom the past was a curse, a hex, and a source of oppression and or embarrassment: in other words, a past that demanded divestment.

When did theory become political? Was theory always already political in ways unthought of and undreamt of in conventional cultural politics? Was there a moment when theory was politicized with respect to a definitive range of concerns and questions? What do I mean when I say, "the politics of theory?" What does theory do, and what can one do with theory? Is it absolutely necessary that theory should be available in the form of an immediate set of practices? There are at least two issues here: theory and the classroom, and theory and the world at large. In the classroom it is customary for the student to ask how theory is to be used or applied in a particular interpretive or exegetical context. Now that we have some grasp of deconstruction or Foucauldian genealogy or psychoanalytic theory, how do we perform it as practical criticism in the context of a text? The truly theoretical answer to such a question has to be double-voiced: yes, theory has an obligation to be practical and useful; and no, theory is obliged to produce and celebrate an excess beyond usability. In the humanities, and particularly in the context of literature, theory cannot afford to fetishize instrumental reason or celebrate the necessity of the ends over the contingency of the means. The cultural politics of theory, and mind you I am only talking "the politics of culture," and not *realpolitik*, has to open, first, the experiential space of culture and the professional production of knowledge about such experience, and then secure culture as a negotiable space between identity and location, or in Walter Mignolo's terms, as that precious and open area between "where we live" and "where we think." And this is precisely how, to borrow from Gayatri Chakravorty Spivak, the cultural politics of theory begins to operate "outside, in the teaching machine." It must not be forgotten that in the project of coordinating a creative relationship between the intra-mural politics of the classroom and extra-mural worldliness, the pride of place went to an activity called "reading." There was no more innocent reading, for to read was to read symptomatically and diagnostically within the overarching horizontal relationship between the history of the present and the body of the past sedimented variously as tradition and canonicity. Thanks to Roland Barthes and Jacques Derrida, there was nothing that was not a text which in turn meant that anything and every thing was vulnerable to the perspectival practice called "reading."

All of this brings me, in a meandering sort of way, to the relationship between the title of this collection and "theoretical thinking." I will try to explain this connection and then proceed to summarize each chapter. I must say that the spatio-temporal preposition "between" has taken on enormous semantic significance over the years: to such an extent indeed, that the title of my forthcoming book, to be published by Duke University Press in the USA and Orient Longman in India, is *History, the Human, and the World Between*. My point is simply that all coordinates, despite our attempts to find them in a spirit of positivistic exactitude, are in fact "between": between identity and location, between living and thinking, between theory and practice, between theory as professional and academic expertise and thinking as existential and phenomenological orientation, between ontology as horizon and the ontic as our particular ways of inhabiting that horizon. Thus, in my terms, "theoretical thinking" is a way of acknowledging that whatever is worth thinking about is worth thinking about intrinsically and objectively for the simple reason that the "worldliness" of the world precedes the rationality of the Cogito. But, not so fast: for at the same time, there can be no effective historical "worldliness" but for the fact that thinking makes it so. It is then between a certain pre-given objective identity of the world and the various thinking locations that make up human subjectivity that worldliness is made to happen by way of schools of thought such as realism, idealism, Gandhism, utopianism, postcoloniality, structuralist-Marxism, a variety of feminisms, New Historicism, Poststructuralism, and so on. As you can see these isms function both as macropolitical worldviews and as micropolitical practices of expertise and specialization. What is indeed fascinating is that it is quite unpredictable how the macro picture and the micro angle will come together within the worldly project. In other words, questions such as, "Is postcoloniality the habitation, and poststructuralism the mode of making sense?" cannot be answered *a priori*. The relationship between "where we live" and "where we think" is an ongoing performative rationale, and not the prescriptive instantiation of a preexisting norm. And "theoretical thinking" bears the burden of such an unpredictability. In each of the chapters of this book, there is a project: i.e., a series of questions or concerns, as well as a formation: i.e., a conscious academic choice whereby the project is made sense of, by way of certain epistemologies, isms, schools of thought, practitioners of specialist thought. Theoretical thinking becomes a way of avowing that there can be thinking without models just as there can be no specialist models of thought except as interpellations of worldliness. In that fertile and contingent "between" that lies between the complexity of the "word" and the protean versatility of the "world" theoretical thinking takes roots.

Chapter 1, "The Changing Subject: The Politics of Theory," has for its focus epistemology and the theoretical production of knowledge. The two questions that get mutually inter-braided are: What is the subject of theory, and Who is the subject undertaking the production of theory as the subject of epistemological discourse? The all important question that underlies these two investigations is the following: What is the relationship between the "subject" taking shape as the object of theory, and the human subject, in its capacity as the *Cogito*, that is committed to such a project? What is the nature of the dynamic between the two subjects? If there is change, and sure enough there is, which of the two changes is primary, and which epiphenomenal? Drawing on formulations in phenomenological thought, the self-reflexive subtleties of Heideggerian hermeneutics, the measure of the human and the simulacrum in structuralism, and finally, the rigorous ways in which poststructuralism hoists structuralism on its own petard, this chapter seeks to understand the ways in which the human subject remains caught and caught up in its own constitutedness by itself. In making paradigmatic use of moments from Roland Barthes, Louis Althusser, Jacques Derrida, and Michel Foucault, this essay critically traces the movement of theory from the grammar of representation with its fidelity to the original as "presence," to the production model that inaugurates a political as well an epistemological break from the pieties of representational thought, and finally towards Derridean deconstruction that makes a crucial distinction between a "centered play" and a "decentered" play of the human subject in the social sciences, and the Foucauldian insistence, *a la* Nietzsche, that the human subject should be allowed to dissolve itself in the processes of its own "knowing." This chapter ends with the understanding that theory is by no means "always already" political, and that the onus is on theory to understand and evaluate its own autonomous temporality within an ongoing dialectical relationship to the world without.

How reliable and empirical is the famous pronouncement that "representation no longer exists?" Is the death of representation real, or is it the seductive effect of a "theoretical" gimmick? These questions constitute the agenda of the essay, "Towards an effective intellectual: Foucault or Gramsci?" I must confess that thinking my way through this piece helped me elaborate my own position with respect to the politics of "the post-." How far would I follow Foucault's lead, and where and for what specific reasons would I break with Foucault? Enormously persuasive as Gramsci is as a deep macro-political theorist of change and transformation, where, why, and how does the Gramscian model break down in response to the micro-postal imperatives and demands of contemporary cultural realities and temporalities? What in particular happens to the figure of the intellectual, once we accept the thesis of the superannuation of representation by theory? Whereas to Foucault and Deleuze it seems axiomatic that regimes of representation are part of politics as a problem, Gramsci as a partisan "organic intellectual" holds on to the representational paradigm even as he seeks to transform it from within. Is it the case, as Gayatri Chakravorty Spivak argues powerfully in her classic essay, "Can the Subaltern Speak?," that Foucault and Deleuze have been guilty of an unconscious Eurocentric universalism when they make representative and representational truth claims on behalf of their diagnosis that representation no longer exists? Following up on Spivak's lead, this chapter critically examines the relationship between the temporality of theory/epistemology and that of political change. In the ongoing negotiations between the post- in poststructuralism and the post- in postcoloniality, not to mention the many ambivalences that constitute a variety of post-Marxisms, is it possible to re-think and re-theorize the political as such, keeping in mind the reality of an uneven world structured in dominance? By and large, this essay is hopeful that the lessons learned both from Foucault and from Gramsci can be re-territorialized in the name of an emerging political subject.

The two essays, "Ethnic Identity and Post-structuralist Differance," and "Culture as Common Ground," (in particular, the former) were among my first attempts to use theory in the form of an application to a specific context. Is there really an experiential and historical relationship between ethnic identity and Derridean differance, or is this relationship willed into existence by the unilateralism of theory forever trying to instantiate its avant-gardism in domains that it barely understands? Broadly speaking, there were three responses to my essay. There were those who praised the essay lavishly and told me with great generosity that it was a major intervention both in theory and in ethnic studies. A second group consisting mainly of "pure theorists" found my piece to be crudely reductive of theory, and reprimanded me for having politicized and instrumentalized theory in a more or less vulgar manner. To these folks I was guilty of having contaminated the radical post-al temporality of theory with the politics of post-ethnicity. The third response came from traditional scholars of ethnicity and they found my application of poststructuralist theory to ethnicity quite high-handed, pretentious, and even obscurantist. I had added nothing to the discourse except the gratuitous avant-gardism of theory that in their evaluation was only a fussy and discursively dense way of saying something that they had said already in their own clear and transparent way. The deep questions that subtend these disagreements are the following. When and under what conditions may theory be said to have added some new knowledge? Is theory a constituency in and by itself? If not, when and under what conditions does theory take on a constituency? How should the organicity of theory to any political project be evaluated? Should theory be native to a constituency, or, could it be borrowed from elsewhere, and then made one's own through an act of signification? In the context of ethnic double-consciousness, how effectively can theory empower itself as a form of minority insurgence and affirmation? Finally, is there a place for deconstruction, with its emphasis on deep structure and transformations of the second order, in subaltern or identity politics? To put it differently in the context of post-ethnicity and Derridean difference, what is wrong with deconstructive thinking that empowers "identity" while at the same time it relentlessly critiques and destabilized Identity, i.e., "identity" with a capital I? My confident claim here is that subaltern cultural politics and deconstructive thought do need to come together to create a coalitional subject beyond the poverty of identitarian and representational thinking.

The piece on Raymond Williams and "the politics of location," (Adrienne Rich) and the essay on "subject positions" (Michel Foucault) explore possibilities of engaging in a self-reflexive cultural politics that rejects both facile totalization and an unexamined universalism. I argue that the same human subject can and does often occupy at the same time a dominant and a subaltern location. Being Welsh, Raymond Williams is subaltern, but as English and cosmopolitan-western, he is dominant. The predicament of Rosa Burger in Nadine Gordimer's novel *Burger's Daughter*, as she straddles two incommensurable positionalities *vis a vis* the brutality of apartheid and patriarchal oppression, demonstrates the inadequacies of monovalent blueprints of revolution based exclusively on gender, or race, or class, or sexuality. It is precisely by problematizing the regime of representation and exacerbating the agony of ambivalence in a contradictory and overdetermined *realpolitik* that Nadine Gordimer enables Rosa Burger to re-invent her sense of political subjectivity and agency. Gordimer's fiction, while acknowledging the given-ness of objective reality, insists that each situated human subject has to "access" this very objective reality in his or her own way. Gordimer's narrative techniques are indeed difficult and theoretically fraught for the simple reason that any mode of narration less complex would only have resulted in gross and egregious mis-recognitions of the given-ness of objective reality. What makes Gordimer's fiction persuasive both ethically and politically is the fact that it does not accept formulaic or politically correct formulations of character or action. On the contrary, it creates a fiction that is prepared to transform itself through agonizing modes of self-reflexivity. The fiction and the theory are rendered mutually accountable.

Is "postcoloniality" a legitimate formation, and if so, who or what interests are represented by the term? Why postcolonial and not neo-colonial; or for that matter, what happened to "Third World," "Commonwealth," "Anglophone," and "Francophone?" Does the term "postcolonial" have greater explanatory power or analytic intensity than any of the others? Is it true that "postcoloniality" is unabashedly metropolitan, intended to confer special honor and prestige to those diasporan and double-conscious intellectuals of a third world provenance who live and teach and produce in the first world? What about the "post-" in the postcoloniality: does this seemingly innocuous pre-fix highjack what used to be the study and analysis of third world cultures and realities towards the heart of the metropole and its always already disseminated high Eurocentric theory? The chapter entitled, "Postcoloniality and the Boundaries of Identity" responds to these questions and concerns, and argues strongly that there is indeed a case for postcolonial double consciousness: a carefully cultivated partnership between postcoloniality and poststructuralism, the acknowledgement of diasporas both within and without the nation state, and a vigilantly ambivalent stance and attitude towards the regime of representation. Making strong differentiations between metropolitan and subaltern forms of hybridity, and between an elitist and a subaltern interrogation of "representation," I make the argument that there is much at stake for the third world out there and the third world within the first world in the ongoing elaborations of "the post-." I also suggest that the dialectical dialogues between nationalisms and diasporas need to be carried out in an attitude of reciprocal respect, without either constituency resorting to a "holier than thou" politics of ethico-political grandstanding.

Very much part of the same problematic of the postcolonial representation of the nation and the nation state, "Nationalism, Gender, and the Narrative of Identity," following up on Partha Chatterjee's brilliant essay on the relationship between the nation and the "woman question," enacts a constitutive tension between the pedagogical authority and the performative contingency of the nation state. Notions of material exteriority and spiritual interiority are deployed in the name of the nation and in the allegorical name of the woman who becomes the mute ground on which the postcolonial drama of the nation state gets played out. So, in what ways does a woman acknowledge the legitimacy of the postcolonial nation, and in what other ways does she declare, in potential allegiance with women across the world, that she knows no nation? Just as the rhetoric of decolonization instrumentalizes women in the service of the independent struggle, it also produces something called the "people." But who are the people and how are they to be known by national leaders? Who are the people during the period of decolonization, and who are they post-independence? Chatterjee points out that there is indeed a yawning ideological gap between Gandhi who was of the people, and Nehru whose "discovery of India" is framed by the gaze of colonial modernity. In Chatterjee's deft analysis, nationalism has already become a "derivative discourse" for the postcolonial subject, i.e., despite the fact that there was an intimate relationship between decolonization and nationalism. Can a derivative discourse be made one's own? If the blueprint of the postcolonial national state is already underwritten by Eurocentric reason and epistemology, is there any hope for the postcolonial subject to produce its own sense of agency? And finally, are postcolonial peoples condemned to fetishize the national form and the national state as the only guarantors of effective collective political being, or can feminist and other subaltern movements produce the nation against itself in search of broader and more inclusive solidarities?

The essay on poststructuralist pedagogy raises "authority," and "canonicity" as problems rather than solutions in the context of the institutional production of knowledge. Reading the Socratic dialogue and the consequent injunction "Know thyself" as instances of a non-democratic and unilateralist methodology that disavows its "Socratic ideology," I invoke other forms of dialogue, made possible by Freud, Lacan, Freire and others, where 1) pedagogy itself is recognized as part of the problem, 2) the teacher-student relationship, however salutary and reciprocal, is diagnosed as a specific instantiation of the deeper Self-Other problematic, and 3) forms of emancipatory pedagogical practice are read in the context of larger ideological struggles that demand an ongoing dialectical conversation between immediate remediation of problems through knowledge and an "analysis interminable" of the kind envisaged by Freud. How is a sensitive pedagogy to retain the passion as well as the progressive partisanship of "the oppressed," and at the same time deconstruct the canonical imperative that dwells in the very heart of all pedagogy? Unless pedagogy avows dialogics as its basic methodology, it is bound to degenerate into a form of sanctimonious unilateralism. Once we bring in dialogics, it is difficult not to invoke the disseminative valences of the diaspora: and it is to these nuances that the other three chapters in the book are addressed.

The essay, "Is the Ethnic "Authentic" in the Diaspora?" argues against the dangers of essentialism, strategic and otherwise, and of the mono-radical pursuit of roots in the diaspora. Espousing "the politics of representation" rather than identity politics, this piece warns against the limitations of insiderism and insiderist cultural politics. The ongoing relationship between nationalisms and diasporas has to be based on a secular and historical reciprocity where there is no room for primordial, nostalgic, transhistorical forms of authority. Diasporic identity formation takes place in response to multiple pressures, and this formation should not be reduced to paranoid invocations of authenticity: authenticity in fact is an ideology to be abjured in the name of multi-lateral historical flows and energies. The discontinuously continuous location of the diaspora offers exciting prospects, both intra- and inter-generational, for the elaboration of new connections between past history and the history of the present. It is precisely because diasporan subjectivity perceives home as location and location as home, it is in a position to re-imagine the relationship between knowledge and belonging. The diasporic citizen who is renamed and minoritized as an Asian-American has a double duty to perform between the regnant nationalisms of India and the USA. How to read one history in terms of another without succumbing to the seductions and ruses of either dominant historiography: that indeed is the subtle and complex challenge that faces the diasporic subject as it envisions an emerging sense of community.

"Conjunctural Constituencies, Academic Adjacencies" makes an explicit connection between diasporic subjectivity and the institutional-academic production of knowledge about this subjectivity. What happens when diasporas get constituted as departments of Diasporic Studies? Should these departments remain generic, or should they take on names such as Asian

American, and African-American, Chicano, and Latin-American, and Arab-American Studies? What about the epistemologies and the methodologies that should inform these academic departments? Is diaspora a perspective and a way of knowing, or is it a thematic content? What is the relationship between the rationale of Diasporic Studies and bodies of knowledge such as Structuralism, Poststructuralism, Postmodernism, Ethnic Studies, Feminism, Transnationalism, Global Studies, Cosmopolitanism, etc? What are the differences and the commonalities between statements like, "I am a postmodernist," and "I am an Asian-American?" How do living and thinking, ontology and epistemology intersect intellectually, affectively, and cognitively in the diasporan context? These questions and responses to these questions make up the agenda of this essay.

"Diaspora, Hybridity, Pedagogy" begins with a strategic reading of the silence of the teacher motif in the Dakshinamurthy story. What is the nature of the pedagogical relationship between the teacher and the taught, and how is this relationship actually performed? Who learns from whom in this process, and what forms of transference and cathexis are effected between teachers and pupils in the diasporan context? Who is the Self and who is the Other in the diaspora? How do generational differences and disjunctures affect the flow of pedagogy? Making a thematic as well as a formal connection between teachers and students, and between parents and progeny, this essay makes the case that the diasporan situation is an eloquent context that warrants a meta-pedagogical critique of the very meaning of pedagogy. How to valorize hybridity, and how to differentiate between erudite and historically rich hybridities and those that are purely cosmetic and skin deep is a major concern here. If there is an unavoidable connection between diasporic location and hybridity, such connections exist both as performances and as potentialities to be submitted to pedagogical analysis and appreciation. The chapter ends with an invocation of the pedagogical moment in all its intransitivity: a staged moment that dissolves the authority of pedagogy into the contingencies of the history of the present: a history where the truth of pedagogy dangles between the will of the teacher and the desire of the student, and *vice versa*.

I am truly grateful to Orient Longman, to R. Sivapriya and Hemlata Shankar in particular, for their generous and genuine interest in my work and to the University of Minnesota Press for allowing a reprint in India. Finally, in acknowledgement of my reader: "Dear reader, I hope that the distance that opens up between us as you flip through these pages is one of rigorous intimacy where there is all sorts of room for critical solidarity."

1 / The Changing Subject and the Politics of Theory

How does one change the subject?[1] Is the "one" the subject that changes itself? What are the limits of such a recursive, autotransformational project? To play a little on the very phrase, "changing the subject," are we involved here in a facetious *detour* or digression, a form of inattention or irresponsibility whereby we are changing the subject? Or, are we talking about an epistemological "break" that simultaneously changes the subject and the very discourse in which change is being theorized? Is "change" the main theme of which the "subject" is the fleeting instance, or are we talking about the "subject" seeking control over processes of change? It is quite clear that we are dealing with a problem that provokes critical and metacritical analysis, for any talk about the "subject" in a poststructuralist context implicates the "subject" in protocols of deconstruction. Not only is the "subject" the constituting agent, but it is also the "constituted" that can have no privileged self-knowledge.[2] There is further ambivalence about the status of the "subject": when a particular "subject" is said to have been changed, what is the magnitude as well as the order of the change? Has a particular axiology been replaced by another (for example, God by Nature, or Nature by the State, or Man by Woman) without any peril to the language of axiology itself, or is it a second-order change at the level of deep structure of which any ostensible content is but one mediated instance? What is the relationship between "subject as structure" and "subject as content"? At what level is change valorized: at the level of content or at the level of structure? What is the ideological or transideological telos that underwrites any theory of change and how is such a telos dialectically mediated by the history of subject-structures?

My purpose in this essay is to elaborate the structure-subject-ideology conjuncture and explore within that relationship some of the profound contradictions that underlie the attempt to theorize radical change. As I unpack this agenda, I shall be anticipating a poststructuralist denouement, if I may so call it, for the entire essay. For indeed, I would like to conclude the essay with a number of crises, asymmetries, and "interruptions" that are almost mandated of the poststructuralist subject.

As the subject moves from phenomenological plenitude and freedom into poststructuralism by way of the desubjectification processes inaugurated by structuralism, it begins to trace a contradictory history. The contradiction lies in the fact that the more the "subject" produces knowledge about itself, the less it is able to assume political agency on behalf of that very knowledge. Whereas knowledge proliferates into an infinite series of microprocesses and elaborations, the legitimating basis of knowledge loses its a priori status. Radical poststructuralist epistemology produces the deconstructive knowledge that the very basis on which the subject acts is putative, not real; constructed, not natural. Thus, epistemology loses the sanction, as it were, to ground ethicopolitical legitimacy. The radical poststructuralist subject of epistemology, with its commitment to a nameless and open-ended process, finds itself at odds with the exigencies of political subjectivity, for the latter is not easily served by a deconstructive epistemology of perennial disaccomodation. The political subject requires the determinate authority of names, identities, and constituencies.[3]

Is it really the case then that poststructuralism has opened up an unbridgeable chasm between politics and epistemology? Is this gap to be mediated by other practices, or is it an irreducible condition? If poststructuralist epistemology cannot, by definition, be yoked to a political will, does it mean then that political projects will be imagined and carried out in the old-fashioned way, as though the poststructuralist revolution had not even occurred? Obversely, is poststructuralism to be validated purely as an epistemic temporality that is doomed to be perennially out of sync with the ethical and sociopolitical realm? Or is it possible for the poststructuralist subject to take on both political and epistemological tasks and highlight, in the process, the profoundly asymmetrical and "interrupted" relationship of the epistemological to the "ethicopolitical"? I shall be contending that these ambiguities are not to be foreclosed in the name of a positivistically oriented ethicopolitical correctness. Rather, these ambiguities need to be posed as problems: problems that poststructuralism creates as it complicates and problematizes the very category of the "ethicopolitical."[4]

I begin, then, with a general definition of "structure" as offered by Roland Barthes in his programmatic essay "The Structuralist Activity":

> The goal of all structuralist activity, whether reflexive or poetic, is to reconstruct an "object" in such a way as to manifest thereby the rules of functioning ("the functions") of this object. Structure is therefore actually a *simulacrum* of the object, but a directed *interested* simulacrum, since the imitated object makes something appear which remains invisible, or if one prefers, unintelligible in the natural object. Structural man takes the real, decomposes it, then recomposes it; this appears to be little enough (which makes some say that the structuralist enterprise is "meaningless," "uninteresting," "useless," etc.). Yet, from another point of view this "little enough" is decisive: for between the two objects, or the two senses, of structuralist activity, there occurs something new, and what is new is nothing less than the generally intelligible: the simulacrum is intelligence added to object, and this addition has an anthropological value, in that it is man himself, his history, his situation, his freedom and the very resistance which nature offers to his mind. ("Structuralist," 1196–97)

A word perhaps is in order here about the passage from Barthes that I have chosen for my purpose. It is not my intention to nail Barthes down to what after all was an early essay. I am quite aware that Barthes's own thinking evolved rapidly, and in many ways, away from his earlier "strong" structuralist modes. Nor am I using Barthes as an easily available straw person for polemical hits. Rather, much of what Barthes has to say in this early essay is quintessential of the structuralist intervention: the insistence on "activity," the emphasis on the "natural-intelligible" nexus, and the anthropological addition of "structure as meaning" to a given raw material. As for the themes taken on by Barthes later on in his career, in response to the works of Foucault, Derrida, Lacan, Althusser, Cixous, and Irigaray, it is my position that whatever Barthes had to say about these issues had already been articulated more comprehensively and rigorously by these other theorists. What I find most valuable in Barthes is his rhetoric: the essayistic and the "nonprofessional" generic nature of his writings. But that is a different issue and as such is not my concern in my present project.

To go back to the Barthes quotation, Barthes's claim on behalf of the structuralist activity is that it is productive of *intelligibility as such* and of human historicity in general. This production is mediated by the concept of structure, which, according to Barthes, is a simulacrum that inheres invisibly and unintelligibly in the original/natural object. It is then the task of the structuralist activity to identify, extract, and abstract this simulacrum and produce it autonomously outside the primordial context of the original object. It is this production of the simulacrum qua simulacrum that renders the "original" intelligible. Although Barthes does not use the term "reading" in this passage, it is evident (especially in light of some of his later work on "textuality" and the "pleasures of reading," where he galvanizes and empowers the activity of "reading" to break open the ideologically finite "work" and step into the realm of open-ended textuality)[5] that the structuralist activity is both a "production" and a "reading." It is in fact the interchangeability of "reading" and "production" as historically situated activities that complicates the structuralist scenario. I wish to claim that the reading-production relationship is hierarchical in nature and not so felicitously egalitarian as Barthes would have us believe. The relationship between "production" and "reading" is quite contestatory. In other words, it matters a great deal if "production" is valorized as "reading," or the other way around.

A few words may be in order here about what I mean by the reading model and the production model. There are both similarities and differences between the two models. Insofar as both are models, both acknowledge their artificial or secondary nature. The reading does not coincide with the selfsame original natural script of things, and the produced object is in a state of epistemological rupture from the original raw material.[6] And yet, in a certain way, both "reading" and "production" are accountable to an anterior reality: the reading is a reading of a preexisting script, and the produced object is a defamiliarization of an original raw material. As models, both are a form of epistemological intervention: the act of reading constitutes the prior script of the real as an intelligible text, while the act of production, with its own secondary history of ideology and intentionality, launches the raw material into a knowable history.[7] And here comes the tricky part. Having acknowledged its heteronomy, how does any reading valorize itself? Is the reading valorized in the name of its own historicity, or does it naturalize its interpretive truth claim in the name of an originary Truth?[8] Analogously, does an ideologically produced structure lay claim to an original nature, or does it testify to its own second nature without any semblance of ontological nostalgia?[9]

Barthes is quite successful in making a connection between the reading model and the production model. And yet—and this is in anticipation of my discussion of Althusser's structuralist Marxism—Barthes's invocation of the simulacrum (despite his claim that it is an "interested" simulacrum) makes him captive to a representational/mimetic epistemology.[10] The model that adds intelligibility to reality remains representative of that very reality. It turns out that this very simulacrum was somehow precontained as a code within the body of the real. It is quite appropriate that Barthes should use the phenomenology of vision while describing the relationship of the simulacrum to the real/natural. The meaning of the real was always "there": only it had to be made visible. An originary phenomenology of signification subsumes and subtends the structural production of meaning, and the addition of "something new" is only the elaboration of a primary plenitude. Committed to the primacy of such a phenomenology, Barthes's reading does not go beyond the status of the commentary, the murmur, the echo. This is precisely the criticism that Pierre Macherey has to offer of the "structural man" of Barthes:

> Analysis is a repetition, another way of saying what has already been said; reading complements writing. This repetition ensures a certain fidelity: structural criticism will not say anything that has not already been said in the work itself. We are told that this repetition is not entirely futile because it produces a new meaning: this is obviously a contradiction: meanings can only be elucidated ("revealing that which was inevitable") because they are already there. (*Theory*, 143)

The question that Macherey is headed toward is the following: "Can there be a criticism which would not be commentary, which would be a scientific analysis adding an authentic knowledge to the speech of the work without, meanwhile, denying its presence?" Macherey's science "is not an interpretation of its objects; it is a transformation, an attribution of significations which the objects themselves did not initially possess" (*Theory*, 149).

Macherey's literary analysis is an application of Althusserian structuralist Marxism, and it is to Althusser I turn next. The production model as developed by Althusser is more challenging and persuasive than Barthes's structuralist analysis. To Althusser, epistemology consists in the "cognitive appropriation" of the object of thought, and as such, it has a history of its own. It is not to be collapsed harmoniously within the jurisdiction of an original "signified." Althusser develops a theory of reading that is "authentically productive" and not merely reflexive or mimetic. Briefly stated, whereas the Barthesian model textualizes and thus dehistoricizes the activity of production, Althusser's theory inaugurates a structuralist politics of reading within a transformed Marxist horizon. It is only natural that to Althusser "ideology" is a crucial part of the politics of reading and meaning-production, whereas, to Barthes, the term "ideology" has a vague adjectival significance. Furthermore, we will find Althusser using the concept "structure" to raise questions that are virtually unthinkable within the Barthesian framework. These questions are directed by a critical theory that, in reading "structure" diagnostically and symptomatically, transcends Barthes's readings, which are all too innocent of the incompleteness of structure and of the "gaps" and the "not-saids" that are constitutive of any structure.

The structuralist Marxists, however, found a different way to articulate the importance of the structure-production and the text-reading conjuncture. Louis Althusser, Etienne Balibar, and Pierre Macherey have different reasons from those of Barthes for their investment in structural readings. Althusser's critical theory (my focus here will be exclusively on Althusser) seeks to theorize changes, breaks, ruptures, epistemological discontinuities, the complex and unevenly mediated relationship between the "contents" and the "structures" of history, and the tensions between "descriptive" theory and "scientific" theory. In the chapter entitled "From 'Capital' to Marx's Philosophy," in *Reading Capital*, Althusser delineates his epistemological-theoretical position quite rigorously, a position that he attributes to Marxist theory, but only by actively producing it through a "differential" reading.

> But we have gone far enough in this work for a return to the difference between the order of the object of knowledge and that of the real object to enable us to approach the problem whose *index* this difference is: the problem of the relationship between these two objects (the object of knowledge and the real object), a relation which constitutes the very existence of *knowledge*. I must warn the reader that we are entering here a domain which is *very difficult* to approach for two reasons. First, because we have very few Marxist reference points with which to stake out its space and orient ourselves within: in fact we are confronted by a problem which we not only have to solve but also to *pose*, for it has not yet *really* been posed, i.e., uttered on the basis of the required problematic and in the rigorous concepts required by this problematic. Second—and paradoxically this is the most serious difficulty—because we are literally swamped by the abundance of solutions offered to this as yet not rigorously posed problem, swamped by the solutions and blinded by their "obviousness." (*Reading*, 51–52)

To paraphrase briefly: first Althusser emphasizes not just the difference between the order of the object of knowledge and that of the real object, but the differential relationship between the two orders. "By what mechanism," asks Althusser, "does the process of knowledge which takes place entirely in thought, produce the cognitive appropriation of its real object, which exists outside thought in the real world?" (*Reading*, 56). Second, and this is my focal point, the unprecedented and even preposterous difficulty that Althusser recognizes is nothing but the epistemological gap between orthodox Marxism and the challenges posed to Marxism by structuralism. The relative lack of reference points within the body of Marxism is an indication of its finitude and, hence, of the need to open up a new terrain where certain problems may be posed for the first time. The problematic that Althusser mentions is one lodged within the body of Marxist thought: a dormant problematic that can now be articulated through structuralist protocols of reading. The problematic is identified as "Marxist," but only if we think of the very identity of Marxism as the expression of a "difference" from "itself." The diagnostically structuralist reading of Marxist theory brings into philosophical awareness what the theory itself is unconscious of. The macrological primacy of the Marxist semantic horizon is materialized as "structure," that is, as both what "it is" and what "it is not," and is thus submitted to the micrological open-endedness of the reading process. The singularity of Althusser lies in his attempt to express the semantic truths of Marxism by way of the antiessentialist and antihumanist protocols of structuralism. In "textualizing" Marx, Althusser goes a step beyond Marx to "appropriate cognitively" the real Marx. From an Althusserian standpoint, structuralism is a newly opened up field or topos to be inhabited and enriched by Marxist theoretical insights. To put it the other way around, structuralism becomes that radical "science" of reading that awaits the breakthroughs of the Marxist text.

Why and how does Althusser read Marx? He reads Marx not merely because he is a committed Marxist ordained to a precritical solidarity with a dogma, but rather because he is interested in the process of *reading as such*. He is interested in exploring how the theory of *reading as such* can be produced from the Marxist text as a movement of difference from itself. What Althusser does is (1) to destabilize the "identical" authority of an orthodox and unrigorous Marxism, (2) to locate and valorize within Marxist theory an epistemological break, and (3) to provide, in reading *Capital* as a text, a reading of "reading" itself:

> Hence a philosophical reading of *Capital* is quite the opposite of an innocent reading. It is a guilty reading, but not one that absolves its crime on confessing it. On the contrary, it takes the responsibility for its crime as a "justified crime" and defends it by providing the necessity. It is therefore a special reading which exculpates itself as a reading by posing every guilty reading the very question that unmasks its innocence: what is it to read? (*Reading*, 28)

Althusser goes on to demonstrate how Marx "reads" Adam Smith. My emphasis here will not be on the "contents" in Althusser's reading of Marx as reader, but rather, on the formal, second-order question of *reading as such*. In raising the activity of reading to full philosophic status, Althusser also raises other questions, such as, What is a reading and what does it do? How does one reading secede epistemologically from earlier readings? How is the structure of history as text constituted, dissolved, and reconstituted by and through readings? We can clearly see how these concerns that are central to the task of envisioning a revisionist historiography are entirely absent in Barthes. And this is how

Althusser finds Marx, demonstrating as it were, the theoretical and polemical practice of reading vis-à-vis Adam Smith's text.

> Marx can see what escaped Smith's gaze because he has already occupied this new terrain which, in what new answers it had produced, had nevertheless been produced, though unwittingly, by the old problematic.
>
> Such is Marx's second reading: a reading which might well be called symptomatic (*symptomale*), insofar as it divulges the undivulged event in the text it reads, and in the same movement relates it to a different text, present as a necessary absence in the first. (*Reading*, 28)

We thus have a reading-on-reading effect without any guarantee of a final and definitive arrival of the text at its meaning. The text-reading conjuncture, formalized thus, goes beyond questions like, "Which came first: the text or the reading?" There is no privileged first text; what we get instead is the ongoing critical momentum of the reading process that constitutes texts only to deconstruct them through further acts of reading. The Marxist-structuralist conjuncture becomes a macro-micro conjuncture where Marxism provides certain "fundamental" categories that are both addressed and transformed by reading practices toward a utopian and hence differential resolution. Surely, there is something unmistakably Marxian about the scenario just described, for are we not talking about a revolutionary "subject" that proceeds autocritically through discrete phases toward a utopian indeterminacy, the Marxian name for which is the stateless society? Are we also not talking about two kinds of theory, one descriptive, and the other transformative, the former inane without the latter and the latter quite unreal and unhistorical without the former? If the purpose of a Marxist epistemology is to change the world through a knowledge of it, structuralist Marxism seeks to deliver Marxism from its own closure by way of autocritical readings. So, then, how does one change the "subject" even as one describes and understands it? Given the "omnihistorical" reality of ideology, how are we to theorize change as simultaneously historical and revolutionary?

The ongoing or perennial symptomatic reading raises a number of questions. What are the limits of critical transformation and how are these derived? In the name of what principle or telos are these transformations undertaken? Who or what is the protagonistic agency that is in control of these operations? Is such an agency extrinsic to the transformative operations, or is it itself subject to the contingencies of these operations? Where and from what specific perspective does the revolutionary subject-as-agency act from? Is the revolutionary subject totally rid of its obligations to its prehistory? As a subject that is produced ahead of its own proper history, by what means does it achieve its own legitimation? Is this nascent subject capable of generating ex nihilo critical practices that are autochthonous in their purity, or is a strategic bricolage the only way available to such a subject?

All these questions and anxieties point to one demand: the demand for an outside space, a viable *hors-texte*, a tactical location that is discontinuous with the status quo. What we seem to be demanding of the revolutionary agency and its potential subject is that they be heterogeneous with the object of their critique and yet not be so radically removed from the object of their critique as to lose their oppositional impact on their object.[11] The agency of radical change is caught up within the figurality of the inside-outside double bind. The disturbing realization that the revolutionary subject runs up against is that its capacity to launch a differential and countermnemonic future is an expression of its capacity to understand itself as a structure constituted by its prehistory.[12] Is there a contradiction in being both "subject" and "subjected," that is, in being subject only to the extent to which one is subjected? In acknowledging the subject to be constituted, are we abdicating the possibilities for a willed, free, and agential change? How does the human subject get hold of structure and master it intentionally? How should the "subject" entrust its agenda with the secondary history of structure?[13] The double bind here is that structure both enables and delimits possibilities for change. Moreover, there is no clear-cut, qualitative distinction or opposition between the subject's free will and intentionality and the instrumental materiality of structure, for we know now that the subject itself is structural through and through. The prestructuralist episteme gave us the comforting illusion that the self or subject of history was in authorial and unilateral command over the processes that shape history, but the structuralist and the poststructuralist subject finds itself more constituted than ever before. As Michel Foucault would have it, "Expressing their thoughts in words of which they are not the masters, enclosing them in verbal forms whose historical dimensions they are unaware of, men believe that their speech is their servant and do not realize that they are submitting to its demands" (*Order*, 297). The result of the epistemological doubling into "subject" that Foucault theorizes so brilliantly in *The Order of Things* applies in general to all critical programs of change. To intend change does not any more mean the ability to bend structures (in their merely instrumental materiality) to our human subjectivity that is historically and ontologically transcendent of these structures, but rather to realize the very historicity of our human intentionality as the expression of structural differentia. Human history is unavoidably caught up in the history of its forms and structures; there is no other primordially self-evident or apodictic history.

I hope my invocation of Foucault in this context makes it clear that I am reading structuralism against the grain. The much-vaunted "death of the subject" is indeed quite problematic. A number of clarifications need to be made here. It is indubitably true that structuralist epistemology de-realizes a fundamentalist or foundational ontology: we thus have subject effects in the place of the natural subject, the author function in place of the godlike author. But this displacement does not get rid of the all-too-worldly nature of "effects" and "functions." It is in fact the failure of structuralism that it will not and cannot account dialectically for the "constituting-constituted" nature of the subject. Having, quite appropriately, deconstructed the univocity of the humanist subject, structuralism would like to believe that the subject as such is dead. But this is the result of a misreading, a misreading that often persists within poststructuralism. This misreading, as Gayatri Spivak argues trenchantly in a different context,[14] conflates politics with epistemology. The different "representation" offered of the "subject" by structuralism is essentially epistemological and not political. Questions of agency, the ideological and the perspectival production of meaning, the naturalization of the subject by ideology: these precisely are the significant issues that structuralism has the potential to raise but will not raise, all because the humanist subject is dead. But as we shall see, in different ways, Foucault and Althusser find a way back to these central issues. Neither Foucault nor Althusser would concede that the historical subject is defunct, just because it is severed from its putative, self-evident history.

For lack of such self-evident history, the subject of radical change is constrained to problematize itself even as it empowers itself. The movement forward is thus compelled to route itself through a movement of recursion. The positivity of the subject of change that acts in forgetfulness of its "constitutedness" is interrupted by the critical negativity of the autocritique that transgresses and calls into question the "original" solidarity of the positive and spontaneous subject. The subject in action is held in abeyance by the subject as construct. The production of theoretical knowledge about the subject discloses it as an effect in profound structural complicity with ideology. This seemingly correct and "obvious" subject, Althusser tells us, is a structural effect interpellated by ideology. The task of working out the coordinates of a position "outside" becomes triply difficult, for that position now has to escape the triangulated trap of "structure," "subject," and "ideology." The subject, after all, turns out to be the problem and not the answer. And it is to this subject-ideology connection that I turn next, and my reference again will be Althusser. First I will consider his "notorious" assertion that ideology has no history and then deal with his thesis of the "interpellation of the Subject."

Althusser adopts the terms of Marx's *The German Ideology*, but develops his thesis of ideology as "radically different" from the positivist and historicist thesis of Marx:

> For on the one hand, I think it is possible to hold that ideologies have a history of their own (although it is determined in the last instance by the class struggle); and on the other, I think it is possible to hold that ideology in general has no history, not in a negative sense (its history is external to it), but in an absolutely positive sense. This sense is a positive one if it is true that the particularity of ideology is that it is endowed with a structure and functioning such as to make it a nonhistorical reality, i.e., as an omni-historical reality, in the sense in which that structure and functioning are immutable, present in the same form throughout what we can call history, in the sense in which the Communist Manifesto defines history as the history of class struggles, i.e., the history of class societies. (*Essays*, 34–35)

To work a little more on this thesis, particular ideologies are all characterized by different historical determinations and subject positions, and yet each particular ideology, in addition to being a particular structure or formation, is also an instantiation of the "structure as such" of an omnihistorical ideology. In other words, these particular ideologies are different and diachronic, and at the same time they are all underwritten by the synchronic regime of the "ideological in general," which is not reducible to any one of its instances. Within each particular ideological structure, there are two temporal or historical markings: an active and particular marking and what I term a "null" or zero marking, which is that of the *ideological as such*. This latter marking is of the second order and is unavailable as history to those determinate instances that it underlies. Within the *longue durée* of Ideology, each of these ideologies, such as bourgeois, proletarian, and so forth, are both "different" and "identical." All these ideological structures produce "subjects," mandate certain forms of imaginary identification, reproduce the very modes of production that brought them into existence, and finally naturalize themselves. It is up to Althusserian Marxism to produce a scientific critique of ideology by taking into account the reality of "ideologies" and "Ideology." This entire dimension of ideology critique in Althusser becomes possible only because, to Althusser, "to conceive Marx's philosophy in its specificity is therefore to conceive the essence of the very movement with which the knowledge of it is produced, or to conceive knowledge as production" (*Reading*, 34).

In his discussion of the category of "ideology in general," Althusser is heavily influenced by Freud, and Althusser acknowledges this debt quite explicitly:

> To give a theoretical reference-point here, I might say that, to return to our example of the dream, in its Freudian conception this time, our proposition:

> ideology has no history, can and must (and in a way which has absolutely nothing arbitrary about it, but, quite the reverse, is theoretically necessary, for there is an organic link between the two propositions) be related directly to Freud's proposition that the unconscious is eternal, i.e., that it has no history.
>
> If eternal means not transcendent to all (temporal) history, but omnipresent, trans-historical and therefore immutable in form throughout the extent of history, I shall adopt Freud's expression word for word, and write ideology is eternal, exactly like the unconscious. And I add that I find this comparison theoretically justified by the fact that the eternity of the unconscious is not unrelated to the eternity of ideology in general. (*Essays*, 35)

Taking my cue from Althusser, in my analysis I shall be using the "unconscious" and "ideology" interchangeably. In what sense does the unconscious have no history? In the sense that the unconscious is coeval with history itself; and insofar as every history has its "unconscious," the determinate forms of the unconscious are all subtended by the "unconscious in general." Freud's great theoretical contribution is his thematization of the unconscious in general. The function of psychoanalysis, by way of analysis "terminable" and "interminable," is both a determinate remediation and the elucidation of the undisclosable, that is, fully undisclosable, nature of the Unconscious. In other words, it is not within the competence of "analysis terminable" to exhaust the structure of the unconscious in general. On the contrary, very much like the manner in which the Heideggerian principle of *Gelassenheit* "lets the [earth] be" in all its radical unknowability despite the particular instances of "worlding" that take place in history,[15] "analysis interminable" has a commitment to the concealment of the unconscious in general. Although this is not directly true of the critique-ideology relationship, the effect is very similar. For the critique, by virtue of not being its own substance, is invested in the structure of ideology for its own scientific operation. No more ideology, no more demystification; no more demystification, no more production of knowledge. And a plenary thematization of the unconscious can only result in the falsification of psychoanalysis, just as any final critical demystification of ideological history can only be a denial of history: that "final balancing of the ledger" of life that Nietzsche so passionately resisted.[16] In terms of this line of thinking, ideology and the unconscious cannot be dispensed with. The category of "the general" abides absolutely in both cases. Althusser's theorization of ideology spells this out unequivocally.

> Ideology Interpellates Individuals as Subjects. This thesis is simply a matter of making my last proposition explicit: there is no ideology except by the subject and for subjects. Meaning, there is no ideology except for concrete subjects, and

this destination for ideology is only made possible by the subject: meaning, by the category of the subject and its function.

By this I mean that, even if it only appears under this name (the subject) with the rise of bourgeois ideology, above all with the rise of legal ideology, the category of the subject (which may function under other names: e.g., as the soul in Plato, as God, etc.), is the constitutive category of all ideology, whatever its determinate (regional or class) and whatever its historical date—since ideology has no history.

I say: the category of the subject is constitutive of all ideology, but at the same time and immediately I add that the category of the subject is only constitutive of all ideology insofar as all ideology has the function (which defines it) of "constituting" concrete individuals as subjects. In the interaction of this double constitution exists the functioning of all ideology, ideology being nothing but its functioning in the material forms of existence of that functioning. (*Essays*, 44–45)

The binding mutuality and complicity of this double constitution functions at both the general and the particular levels, and the general underwrites the particular irrefragably. It is the fundamental relationship of mutual constitution between ideology and the subject that validates the interaction between any particular ideology and its subject. If a particular subject carries the sovereignty of a name, it is only because this particular name carries the imprimatur of the name of the name, the subject. As Althusser summarizes it:

The duplicate mirror-structure of ideology ensures simultaneously:
1. the interpellation of "individuals" as subjects;
2. their subjection to the Subject;
3. the mutual recognition of subjects and Subject, the subjects' recognition of each other, and finally the subject's recognition of himself;
4. the absolute guarantee that everything really is so, and that on condition that the subjects recognize what they are and behave accordingly, everything will be all right: *Amen–So be it.* (*Essays*, 54–55)

The critique of ideology has to shatter the adequacy of the mirror structure and the "imaginary" pattern of recognition that it reproduces.[17] But to be able to do this, the critique must first of all acquire a detailed and scientific awareness of how the duplicating structure works. After having exposed the comforting "obviousness" of the subject as an ideological effect, the critique should proceed toward a different kind of knowledge, the scientific knowledge of a "process without Subject or Goal(s)." What could be the locus of such a knowledge, and in what modality would it express itself? Althusser's recommendation is as follows: "Now it is this knowledge that we have to reach, if you will, while speaking in ideology, and from within ideology we have the beginning of a scientific (i.e., subject-less) discourse on ideology" (*Essays*, 47).

Althusser dramatically associates subjectlessness with the rigor of scientific discourse; in my view, that is an unfortunate lapse into positivism. He leaves us with two parallel discourses, the ideological and the scientific, and the impact of the scientific on the ideological is merely posited and not dialectically mediated by the processes of history. Given the omnihistorical nature of ideology and therefore the omnihistorical nature of the ideology critique as scientific discourse, we are left in a suspensive situation where "history" is bracketed from the process of the critique. But why "scientific," and how does any discourse become scientific? What are the criteria and the thresholds of scientificity, and who achieves this universal consensus concerning the binding validity of scientific discourse? Althusser is quite satisfied to function both as the universal subject of Marxism and as the professional theorist who believes unproblematically in the right to speak for the subject. It will not occur to Althusser to ask the following questions that Foucault raises so eloquently in profound skepticism both of the universality of Marxism and of the rectitude of professional discourses, such as science:

> What types of knowledge do you want to disqualify in the very instant of your demand: "Is it a science"? Which speaking, discoursing subjects—which subjects of experience and knowledge—do you then want to "diminish" when you say: "I who conduct this discourse am conducting a scientific discourse, and I am a scientist"? Which theoretical-political *avant garde* do you want to enthrone in order to isolate it from all the discontinuous forms of knowledge that circulate about it? When I see you straining to establish the scientificity of Marxism I do not really think that you are demonstrating once and for all that Marxism has a rational structure and that therefore its propositions are the outcome of verifiable procedures; for me you are doing something altogether different, you are investing Marxist discourses and those who uphold them with the effects of a power which the West since Medieval times has attributed to science and has reserved for those engaged in scientific discourse. (*Power*, 85)

The themes that are resonant in Foucault are entirely missing in Althusser: sensitivity to subaltern and "subjugated knowledges" that find no place in official histories and theories; the critique of the avant-gardism of theory as it seeks to represent heterogeneous, multiple, and nonsynchronous experiences and histories; the false consciousness of theory with regard to its own ideological and historical specificity; the critique of a professionalist-expert methodology and its near-divine hubris. In assuming scientific infallibility, Althusser's discourse removes itself from the sphere of hermeneutics and perspectival politics; the subjectless methodology of scientific discourse perpetrates a false universalism. True, Althusser steers us away from the false representational claims of historicism and empiricism in the realm of epistemology, and yet his theory continues to represent, that is, speak for, a whole range of subject positions, histories, and knowledges that are outside the pale of official theory. It is not surprising that Althusser does not raise the questions of "oppression by theory/scientificity"; nor does he problematize the elitist claims of theory, its putative forwardness. Althusser's epistemological cleansing of method has virtually deprived it of a sense of constituency. Scientific knowledge is accountable only to itself. It is ironic that the very same Althusser who opened up possibilities of "symptomatic reading" exempts the text of scientific theory from the rigors of a symptomatic reading. To him, scientific knowledge would seem to have transcended problems of historical and hermeneutic situatedness. The scientific investigator refuses to place himself or herself within his or her questions, and scientific theory becomes a privileged discourse. Scientific theory becomes a pure answer to the impure questions of history. The daring insistence on the epistemological *coupure* from ideology turns into a purely formal "break."

Finally, in response to the question, "Where does the critique come from?,"[18] a question concerning the positionality of the critique, Althusser resorts to a "strong" theory that idealizes a relationship of pure externality to structures of history and ideology. This preference has dire consequences. Given already the omnihistorical nature of ideology, the scientific production of knowledge is doubly removed from its object of explanation, namely, history. It becomes a pure metalevel operation. Also, as strong theory, Althusser's discourse completely disregards the highly nuanced pressures of dialectical thinking with its emphasis on contradiction and on the shifting interplay between "identity" and "difference." Here again, Althusser, who had contributed so much to our understanding of "contradiction" and "overdetermination" at the level of the diagnostic critique, chooses to purify his positive/scientific knowledge of these very anomalies and ambiguities. It was as though science were to enter the scene as a total answer to these problems. My tentative explanation is that in an unwitting manner, Althusser continues the scientific imperative in structuralism that lives and dies by binary oppositions. Unlike dialectical thinking where content and form, history and structure, projects and formations, theory and practice are caught up in a reciprocal and historically mediated movement, Althusser's discourse merely reproduces binary ideology. The fact that Althusser bypasses the dialectic does not mean he has transcended it. In contrast, poststructuralist thinkers such as Derrida and Foucault, in their many projects on behalf of "difference," have addressed the ideological limits of the dialectic in explicit terms. In the final analysis, Althusser's scientific discourse falls well short of the deconstructive turn of the poststructuralist subject.

However unsatisfactory Althusser's scientific resolution of the problem may be, we cannot deny him the depth as well as the acuity of his diagnosis. His is a kind of Pyrrhic triumph, since his diagnosis is so profound and fundamental that it challenges the very possibility of remediation and hence the escape to science. Since Althusser's thinking as a diagnostic theoretician owes a lot to Lacanian psychoanalysis, I would like to digress a little into just those aspects of Lacan that have influenced Althusser's thought.

The Lacanian interrogation of history, despite Lacan's statements to the contrary, carries forward the Heideggerian project of the de-struction of metaphysics and ontotheology. And like Heidegger's project, the Lacanian project questions not "history," but History. As I have already observed, the interrogation of History is done in the name of the unconscious in general. In declaring the unsutured nature of reality and the languagelike structure of the Unconscious, Lacan enables readings that focus on the gaps, the fissures, and the lacks in the text. Clearly, this shift in emphasis has tremendous consequences for revisionist historiography. History can now be "rubbed against the grain" in the name of all that has been unconscious and repressed within the text. And here lies the problem.

The "unconscious" has both a determinate content and an abiding underlying structure that is the unconscious in general. In telling us that the determinate is in fact the fleeting expression of an underlying structure, Lacan rids us of our epistemological naïvete. But that is not all that happens. Paradoxically, in deepening the quality of our self-understanding and diagnosis, Lacan has rendered impossible the very possibility of transformation. In understanding the reality of our subjection we come to acquiesce in it. At this point Lacanian theory turns descriptive, that is, it loses its power to be interventionary and transformative. If we indeed are subjected to a second-order subjection to capitalized concepts, namely, Lack and not "lack," Subject and not "subject," Other and not the "other," then there is very little we can do about it. In enriching our diagnostic awareness of our pathology we have also come to accept it as inevitable. The demystification of the mirror structure in the name of the realm of the Symbolic really does not take us far, since the Symbolic itself is conceived of as radical loss and alienation. Changes and transformations at the level of history are doomed not to have an effect on the Symbolic that transcends "history" absolutely.

I would argue that this ideological entrenchment of deep structure from the forces of history is reflected in Lacan's theory of language, too. As Lacan demonstrates brilliantly in his seminar on *The Purloined Letter*, the meaning of the letter is not some deep hermeneutic interiority. The meaning is nothing but the fact of the letter's literal transfer from place to place. Both Lacan and Dupin can solve the problem without.ever having to open the letter, or even showing the slightest curiosity about the contents of the letter. All that we need to know at the level of history/semantics/thematics is that the letter is "blackmail-worthy." There is no doubt that Lacan's reading is formally elegant and persuasive, but that precisely is the problem. Its elegance is based on a question begging innocence of history. Content with the tautological piece of information that the letter is "blackmail-worthy," this formal theory accounts for meaning as a literal/lateral transfer. But let us consider other narratives. What if the contents of the letter had to do with specific historical themes (for surely, the letter was *about* something): the queen's collusion with a foreign power, or some form of subaltern insurrection within the country, or the emergence of a pannational populist consciousness? Should this information not make any difference to the solution? Obviously not; for the Lacanian rejoinder would be that whatever the contents, the "structural" solution still holds good. The intellectual algebra works in total abeyance of the contents of the letter. It works by overlooking the specifics of history and by trivializing the tensions between history and metahistory. The answer to history is a formal second-order allegory that in attempting to explain history, explains history away. The deep-structure diagnosis of specific instances and the generous "letting be" of the unconscious are structural counterparts of each other. The former enables the latter by preempting particular histories of their power to question their implication in general and concealed structures. The structure of the symptom and the structure of the cure are fused within a common identity.[19]

The common problem concerning all critical discourses that seek to "change the subject" is that of distance. In other words, what is the paradigmatic distance between the critique and the object of the critique? From what sort of remove does the critique produce knowledge about the object under study? No one has taken on this question more persistently than Derrida, who in all his writings has played with notions of inside and outside as expressions of an underlying binarity. As he articulates the politics of location, he has always warned us that there are no easy ways of stepping out of the text of the *longue durée;* one can, however, turn the pages of that text in a certain way. But even in Derrida, this desire to situate local and historically determinate instances of oppression within the more basic histories of centrism, logocentrism, the History of the Name, and so on, results in huge, inconsequential generalizations. Thus, for example, his essay "Racism's Last Word," while not without its etymological subtleties, virtually dehistoricizes the reality of apartheid.[20] The problem is not so much with Derrida the individual person or agent, but with the kind of discourse that he chooses to privilege: a discourse that prefers a purely theoretical consciousness to a historically situated critical consciousness.

The relationship, in poststructuralism, of the theoretical or epistemological subject to the political subject has been particularly problematic. The ability of theory to abstract away its own spatiality from the "chronotope" of the times, as evidenced in the proliferation of "post-" terms such as "postfeminist," "postethnic," "postpolitical," "posthistorical," and so on, raises serious concerns. What gives theory the legitimacy to open up formal spaces that have no basis in history, and how are these spaces to be evaluated? Even more seriously, what is one to make of a situation where epistemology refuses to sanction the "ethicopolitical?" This incommensurability surfaced strongly in a European television show where Noam Chomsky and Michel Foucault addressed one another on ethicopolitical issues.[21] While they agree with each other about what is to be done (there is never any doubt that they are on the same side, politically), their epistemological accounts of their ethicopolitical practice are so different as to be mutually exclusive. While Chomsky grounds his practice in a neo-Kantian epistemology, it is impossible for Foucault the genealogist to theoretically endorse the very principles (freedom, justice, equality, and so on) he would seem to be fighting for. His Nietzschean epistemology reads in these very truths the history of an error. To Chomsky, who is not a poststructuralist, the "subject" is a total subject, whereas to Foucault, the "ethicopolitical" and the "epistemological" come together only strategically. The two are not unified within a single consciousness.

This was the question that I started with: whether the radical development of epistemology has made it forever incommensurable with ethicopolitical modes of authority. As I conclude my essay, I will be looking at two poststructuralist models of change that take this "incommensurability" quite seriously: the early Derrida and Nietzsche as developed by Foucault.

In the famous and by now fetishized essay "Structure, Sign and Play in the Discourse of the Human Sciences," Derrida announces and explicates a certain "break" from structuralist closure. Derrida's critique of structuralism raises questions concerning the structurality of structure and, in doing so, invokes the notion of "play" as radical and "unthinkable" change. Here then is Derrida:

> Nevertheless, up to the event which I wish to mark out and define, structure—or rather the structurality of structure—although it has always been at work, has always been neutralized or reduced, and this by a process of giving it a center or referring it to a point of presence, a fixed origin. The function of this center was not only to orient, balance, and organize the structure—one cannot conceive of an unorganized structure—but above all to make sure that the organizing prin-

ciple of the structure would limit what we might call the play of structure. By orienting and organizing the coherence of the system, the center of a structure permits the play of its elements inside the total form. And even today the notion of a structure lacking any center represents the unthinkable itself. (278–79)

Derrida is pointing up an inevitable epistemological contradiction (a contradiction formalized in mathematical theory by Kurt Godel): the incompleteness of any so-called "finished" system or structure and the constitutive nonreferability of the axiomatics of any structure or system to its own descriptive paradigm. In many ways, the nuanced elaboration of this contradiction has been the mainstay of Derridean deconstruction. Derrida's strategies of and for change have consistently offered battle to notions of mastery and ideological consolidation. His deconstructive readings of texts have even gone so far as to suggest that the real enemy is a homely thinking that seeks to accommodate the thinking subject. His deconstructive protocols of vigilance have adroitly deferred any sort of authoritative and rightful arrival into a "home" or system. To Derrida, thinking that arrives and thus celebrates its own legitimacy is repressive thinking.[22] Disaccommodation and radical indeterminacy: these have been the preoccupations of Derrida. In opening up the "play" that is foreclosed by the ideology of official structure, Derrida is inaugurating a politics that is mindful of the oppression inherent in any structure. The Derridean politics of play takes the form of a decelebration of all strong and identitarian forms of thinking, for Derrida is well aware of Walter Benjamin's claim that "there is no document of civilization which is not at the same time a document of barbarism" (Benjamin, "Theses," 256). But this notion of play, despite its libertarian impulse, is fraught with problems. For here, too, one senses a disjuncture between a purely epistemological or theoretical revolution and a historically accountable revolution. The perennial opening up of structure to its own factitious structurality no doubt results in all manner of transgressive play. But politically speaking, the notion of limitless play is quite dangerous. Is the notion of play random in nature, aleatory in its potentiality? Who is the subject of play and what is being played with? Is "play" its own subject, or do we look for a responsible agent who will operate play according to certain rules? Can one invoke the notion of rules in the context of a free play that laughs at all rules? Is play a seductive name for anomie? From what or whose point of view is this play to be engaged in, and will there be any room at all for the "ethicopolitical" within such play? Isn't the notion of play a pure fabrication of theory that rejoices in the act of leaving history and the world behind? Isn't such play the ultimate abdication of all forms of responsibility?

The perilous limits that the poststructuralist subject finds itself playing with are the limits of legitimacy as such. Not content with rebelling against particular forms of interpellation, this subject revolts against the very notion of interpellation. The rebellion is not against the tyranny of any particular ideological system or name, for example, God, the Father, or the State, but against the authority of the Name in all its omnihistorical generality. And epistemology becomes the site for this subjectless revolution.[23]

Foucault, in his reading of Nietzsche in "Nietzsche, Genealogy, History," envisions a similar scenario where the will to truth "loses all sense of limitations and all claim to truth in its unavoidable sacrifice of the subject of knowledge" (*Language*, 164). As he formulates the theme of the destruction of "truth" by the "will to truth," Foucault quotes the following passage from Nietzsche:

> It may be that there remains one prodigious idea which might be made to prevail over every other aspiration, which might overcome the most victorious: the idea of humanity sacrificing itself. It seems indisputable that if this new constellation appeared on the horizon, only the desire for truth, with its enormous prerogatives, could direct and sustain such a sacrifice. For to knowledge, no sacrifice is too great. Of course, this problem has never been posed. (*The Dawn*, 45; qtd. in Foucault, *Language*, 164)

The an-archic and a-nomic free play that Foucault is hinting at here is a movement "beyond good and evil," beyond any semantic horizon. It is also an epistemic assertion about truth within a horizon where there can be no truth. The genealogist in Nietzsche, as brought out by Foucault, problematizes and renders un-innocent our every attempt to reconcile knowledge with goodness and justice. I do not for a moment endorse this vision in toto, but I believe that this version of the poststructuralist subject does tell us something quite valuable. In our attempts to change the subject on the basis of what we hold to be good and desirable, and moral and politically correct, we cannot afford to forget how this very blueprint or telos that we are acting upon could be potentially wrong and repressive, even barbaric. For example, did humanity always know that racism is wrong and sexism abhorrent, that colonialism and imperialism are illegitimate and unconscionable bodies of knowledge, that homophobia and normative heterosexuality are unacceptable? Briefly, did we always know that our norms have a flip side that is objectionable? Is not the very moment of the emancipatory critique the expression of a contradiction? Will not the very document of civilization that we are scripting now be found retroactively to be something quite other? How is the subject in its present moment of affirmation and positivity to come to terms with its own potential blindness and error? How is today's protagonistic subject to make room for the emergence of other subject positions that follow a different historical trajectory? The contradiction about knowledge is that it makes us pretend that we "always knew." In monumentalizing itself, the knowing subject removes itself from the processive, contingent, and often aleatory flows of "knowing." In polemical opposition to such a "knowing" subject, the poststructuralist subject discloses the reality that knowledge is a phenomenon that is always out of step with itself. The best guarantee that the will to knowledge offers us as we "change the subject" is our liability to radical error. This situation does not have to demoralize our political ethic (we must remember that Nietzsche himself was a value-laden and didactic thinker who had clear intentions of making history); it only challenges us to open up even our most righteous and "correct" positions to the possibilities of error, finitude, and contingency. It also encourages us to consider our moment of righteous affirmation as one that conceals its own system of exclusions and repressions.

We must keep in mind, however, that such a thesis of the poststructuralist subject is through and through polemical in nature. And, as is always the case with polemical articulations, there is a great deal of overkill and overcompensation in this case, too. In many ways, the poststructuralist subject represents the "return of the repressed": it stands for all those themes, possibilities, and emergences that have been repressed by a tradition that has been naturalized in the name of "identity," "continuity," "stability," and subject-oriented epistemologies. It is in radical and binary opposition to this hegemony that poststructuralist thinkers take up the cause of discontinuity, difference, processes and flows, and epistemologies that dissolve, in a Nietzschean mode, all forms of systemic authority. Identifying canonical modes of thinking with the denial of the vitality of "living" (yet another Nietzschean move, for does Nietzsche not arraign conventional philosophy for its life-denying "nihilism"?), the poststructuralist subject seeks to celebrate life through ceaseless anomie. But this of course is not the whole story, for there is a place for continuity and a place for discontinuity, a place for consolidation and a place for destabilization, a place for conserving the past and a place for deauthorizing it, a place for identity and a place for difference. In its attempts to valorize those realities that have been rendered "other" within the binary axiology, the poststructuralist subject goes to the other extreme of the binary opposition, thus refusing dialectic mediation. The language of this subject is the language of difference seeking total escape from the dialectic. No wonder that this difference is at best a "theoretical" difference: a difference in theory that has not yet been translated into a difference in history. In a theoretically real sense, this radical subject is indeed seeking escape from history itself. True, this wish of the subject may be construed as a death wish, as a form of anarchic antinomianism. Although bereft of its own affirmation, this "destitute" subject does have a lesson to offer. It enables a form of thinking that refuses to privilege answers and resolutions; in its place, it advances an interrogative and perilous epistemology that warns us that what we might "next know" may well be a threat to what we "now know."

Notes

1. For interesting variations on the theme of changing the subject, see Nancy K. Miller, "Changing the Subject." For a social psychological formulation of the subject, see Julian Henriques et al. *Changing the Subject.*

2. For a challenging discussion of the human subject as both "constituting" and "constituted," see Michel Foucault, *The Order of Things.*

3. The issue of grounding the "subject" for political purposes without necessarily essentializing the "subject" comes up repeatedly in poststructuralist feminist theory. Is essentialism desirable or not? Is it possible to have recourse to a "strategic essentialism" for purely political reasons? Gayatri Chakravorty Spivak and Teresa de Lauretis have been particularly successful in their attempts to politicize "difference." In both their works, the feminist subject remains historically specific even as it envisions ongoing change along poststructuralist trajectories. For an illuminating differentiation of the many meanings of essentialism, see Naomi Schor, "This Essentialism Which Is Not One." See also Nancy Fraser, *Unruly Practices,* for a powerful account of a nonessentialist feminist political project that nevertheless does not "cop out" at the level of theory.

4. Gayatri Chakravorty Spivak theorizes the notion of "interruption" throughout her book, *In Other Worlds.* See in particular "A Literary Representation of the Subaltern," 241–68, and "Subaltern Studies," 197–22.

5. Roland Barthes sets out some of the definitive distinctions between "the work" and "the text" in his two essays, "From Work to Text" and "Theory of the Text."

6. For an original and pathbreaking discussion of "secondarity," see Jacques Derrida's notion of the "dangerous supplement" in *Of Grammatology.* From a different but related perspective, Foucault discusses the noncoincident relationship between words and things in *The Order of Things.* See in particular the section entitled "The Prose of the World," 17–45.

7. I have in mind here the distinction that Marx makes between human labor and the home-building activity of animals that are driven by instinct. In Marx's view, human labor carries with it the notion of an ideal that precedes and validates the activity of labor.

8. The relationship of truth to method is thoroughly formulated by Hans-Georg Gadamer in his *Truth and Method* and other subsequent works. In my view, the early Gadamer is more radical than the Gadamer of the latter years, who all too easily genuflects to the "eminent text" in furtherance of the Tradition.

9. Jean-Paul Sartre's novel *Nausea* dramatizes the inevitable slippage between a primary ontology and discursivity. The very symptom of "nausea" expresses the unease felt

by the human being when confronted by the phenomenon of "chosisme" (thingness). But this anxiety can be posed in a significantly post-Sartrean way: Is it inevitable that human structures will turn into lifeless mechanisms? Is reification unavoidable? In producing its own history as an act of rupture from "the natural," does humanity lose touch with nature altogether? Is the production model based on epistemic violence? These questions form the basis of ecofeminism that rightly points out the unabashedly anthropocentric ethic of an exclusively production-oriented epistemology. For a coherent and well-coordinated Marxist-feminist critique of Marxist theory, see Seyla Benhabib and Drucilla Cornell, *Feminism as Critique*.

10. The concept of "mimesis" has had an interesting and discontinuous history, from Aristotle to Auerbach, from the Marxist theorists to contemporary theorists of postcoloniality. Depending upon how it has been deployed, "mimesis" has taken on both conservative and adversarial valences. For a parodic and oppositional elaboration of the doubleness of "mimesis," see Homi K. Bhabha, "Signs Taken for Wonders." For a similar "double" articulation on behalf of ethnicity, see chapter 3 in this volume.

11. Derrida develops this notion of the heterogeneity of the critique vis-à-vis its object in his essay "The Principle of Reason." Derrida's objective here is to politicize the location of the university by making it the site where protocols of radical self-reflexivity are to be elaborated perennially. Also see the interview with Derrida in Imre Salusinszky, *Criticism in Society*. The interview with Edward Said, in the same volume, demonstrates how different Said's model of a worldly critical consciousness is from Derrida's academically oriented critique.

12. For a superb articulation of the relationship of "remembering" to "forgetting" in the context of history making, see Friedrich Nietzsche, *The Use and Abuse of History*. The powerful Foucauldian notion of the "countermemory" is genealogically derived from Nietzsche.

13. Raymond Williams's contribution in this area is as formidable as it is brilliant. Unlike simulacral postmodernists and theorists of "panic" and "excremental culture," Williams insists on raising the question of agency despite its seeming evaporation through technologies of the so-called hyperreal. It is of the utmost importance to Williams that critical consciousness not be objectified by mere systems of thought and that "projects" undertaken in response to human needs and crises not turn into mere lifeless academic formations. In a similar manner, Said's notion of "worldliness" and his advocacy of a secular, oppositional consciousness call into question the validity of a theoretical mode of thinking that loses critical valence for lack of a "world." Both Said and Williams are in this sense Gramscian "organic" intellectuals. See Williams, *The Politics of Modernism*.

14. Spivak's essay "Can the Subaltern Speak?" argues for a critical position that is simultaneously and differentially both poststructuralist and postcolonial. Even as she avails herself of a number of poststructuralist insights and attitudes, Spivak rightly critiques Deleuze and Foucault for their unexamined Eurocentrism. For other conjunctural articulations of "postcoloniality," see Samir Amin, *Eurocentrism*, and the special issue of *Inscriptions* entitled "Traveling Theories/Traveling Theorists," in particular, the essays of Lata Mani and Vivek Dhareshwar. See also chapter 2 in this volume. This essay seeks to build a bridge between the organic politics of Gramsci and the post-representational political practices of Foucault.

15. My reference here is to Martin Heidegger's essay "The Origin of the Work of Art." Heidegger's intention here is to adumbrate a phenomenology of art as a form of "unveiling" that in the very process of revealing Being protects its transcendent inviolability.

16. See Nietzsche's *Use and Abuse of History*, the first part of which is an impassioned indictment of Hegelian historiography and its grand project of resolving life into the closure of an absolute history of the spirit.

17. The entire preoccupation in poststructuralism with the "imaginary" and with the "mirror stage" would not have been possible without Jacques Lacan's critique of imaginary identification as developed in his *Ecrits*.

18. The work of the Subaltern Studies Group of historians and theorists in situating the "critique" has been outstanding in its capacity and willingness to submit "theory" to historical interrogations. These theorists work in a mode that combines modes of highly nuanced self-reflexivity (some of it derived from poststructuralism) with the pressures of historical exigencies. Thus, in "speaking for" the subaltern subject, these historian-theorists come up with complex diagnoses of coloniality, postcoloniality, and bourgeois nationalism. My particular reference here is to Ranajit Guha's brilliant essay, "Dominance without Hegemony and Its Historiography." Equally relevant in this context are Partha Chatterjee, *Nationalist Thought and the Colonial World*, and Kumkum Sangari and Sudesh Vaid, *Recasting Women*.

19. Gilles Deleuze and Felix Guattari make this point quite convincingly in their *Anti-Oedipus*. Also see the special issue of *Critical Inquiry* entitled "The Trails of Psychoanalysis," in particular, the essay by Ernesto Laclau that maps out the disjuncture and the conjuncture of Marxism and psychoanalysis and the essay by Stephen Melville that raises the question, through close readings of Lacan, of the positionality of psychoanalysis vis-à-vis history.

20. Derrida's involvement in the Paul de Man controversy has been quite different. In this instance, Derrida's framework has been historically specific and circumstantial.

21. Edward Said discusses this exchange between Chomsky and Foucault (transcript to be found in Fons Elders, *Reflexive Water*) in his essay "Traveling Theory."

22. See Gayatri Chakravorty Spivak's "Translator's Introduction" to Derrida's *Grammatology* for a detailed analysis of deconstruction and its attitude to "homely thinking."

23. The spirited exchange between Hélène Cixous and Catherine Clément in *The Newly Born Woman* foregrounds the question of law and interpellation in all its generality. Should the newly born woman inaugurate a new form of law and mastery, or should she go beyond these categories altogether? In the same "Exchange," Cixous and Clement discuss possibilities of a psychoanalytic model of pedagogy that would transmit knowledge without authority.

References

Althusser, Louis. *Essays on Ideology*. Trans. Ben Brewster. London: Verso, 1984.
Althusser, Louis, and Etienne Balibar. *Reading Capital*. Trans. Ben Brewster. London: Verso, 1979.
Amin, Samir. *Eurocentrism*. New York: Monthly Review Press, 1989.

Barthes, Roland. "From Work to Text." In *Textual Strategies,* trans. and ed. Josue V. Harari, 73–81. Ithaca, N.Y.: Cornell University Press, 1979.

———. "The Structuralist Activity." In *Critical Theory since Plato,* ed. Hazard Adams, 1196–99. New York: Harcourt, 1971.

———. "Theory of the Text." In *Untying the Text,* ed. Robert Young, trans. Ian McLeod, 32–47. London: Routledge, 1981.

Benhabib, Seyla, and Drucilla Cornell, eds. *Feminism as Critique.* Minneapolis: University of Minnesota Press, 1987.

Benjamin, Walter. "Theses on the Philosophy of History." In *Illuminations,* trans. Harry Zohn, 253–64. New York: Schocken, 1968.

Bhabha, Homi K. "Signs Taken for Wonders: Questions of Ambivalence and Authority under a Tree outside Delhi, May 1817." *Critical Inquiry* 12, no. 1 (1985): 144–65.

Chatterjee, Partha. *Nationalist Thought and the Colonial World.* Delhi: Oxford University Press, 1986.

Clifford, James, and Vivek Dhareshwar, eds. "Traveling Theories/Traveling Theorists." *Inscriptions* 5 (1989).

Cixous, Hélène, and Catherine Clément. *The Newly Born Woman.* Trans. Betsy Wing. Minneapolis: University of Minnesota Press, 1986.

de Lauretis, Teresa, ed. *Feminist Studies/Critical Studies.* Bloomington: Indiana University Press, 1986.

Deleuze, Gilles, and Félix Guattari. *Anti-Oedipus: Capitalism and Schizophrenia.* Trans. Robert Hurley, Mark Seem, and Helen R. Lane. New York: Viking, 1977.

Derrida, Jacques. "Jacques Derrida." In *Criticism in Society,* ed. Imre Saluszinsky, 8–24. New York: Methuen, 1987.

———. *Of Grammatology.* Trans. and intro. Gayatri Chakravorty Spivak. Baltimore, Md.: Johns Hopkins University Press, 1974.

———. "The Principle of Reason: The University in the Eye of Its Pupils." *Diacritics* 13 (1983): 3–20.

———. "Racism's Last Word." *Critical Inquiry* 12, no. 1 (1985): 290–99.

———. "Structure, Sign and Play in the Discourse of the Human Sciences." In *Writing and Difference,* trans. Alan Bass, 278–93. Chicago: University of Chicago Press, 1978.

Dhareshwar, Vivek. "Toward a Narrative Epistemology of the Postcolonial Predicament." *Inscriptions* 5 (1989): 135–57.

Elders, Fons, ed. *Reflexive Water: The Basic Concerns of Mankind.* London: Souvenir, 1974.

Foucault, Michel. "Nietzsche, Genealogy, History." In *Language, Counter-Memory, Practice,* trans. Donald F. Bouchard and Sherry Simon, 139–64. Ithaca, N.Y.: Cornell University Press, 1977.

———. *The Order of Things: An Archaeology of the Human Sciences.* Trans. Alan Sheridan. New York: Vintage, 1973.

———. "Two Lectures." In *Power/Knowledge: Selected Interviews and Other Writings,* trans. Colin Gordon, Leo Marshall, John Mepham, and Kate Soper, ed. Colin Gordon, 78–108. New York: Pantheon, 1980.

Fraser, Nancy. *Unruly Practices: Power, Discourse, and Gender in Contemporary Theory.* Minneapolis: University of Minnesota Press, 1989.

Gadamer, Hans-Georg. *Truth and Method.* Trans. and ed. Garrett Barden and John Cumming. New York: Seabury, 1975.

Guha, Ranajit. "Dominance without Hegemony and Its Historiography." In *Subaltern Studies VI: Writings on South Asian History and Society,* 210–309. Delhi: Oxford University Press, 1989.

Heidegger, Martin. "The Origin of the Work of Art." In *Basic Writings,* ed. David Farrell Krell, 149–87. New York: Harper, 1977.

Henriques, Julian, et al., eds. *Changing the Subject.* London: Methuen, 1984.

Lacan, Jacques. *Ecrits.* Trans. Alan Sheridan. New York: Norton, 1977.

Laclau, Ernesto. "Psychoanalysis and Marxism." *Critical Inquiry* 13 (1987): 330–33.

Macherey, Pierre. *A Theory of Literary Production.* Trans. Geoffrey Wall. London: Routledge, 1978.

Mani, Lata. "Multiple Mediations: Feminist Scholarship in the Age of Multinational Reception." *Inscriptions* 5 (1989): 1–23.

Melville, Stephen. "Psychoanalysis and the Place of *Jouissance.*" *Critical Inquiry* 13 (1987): 349–70.

Miller, Nancy K. "Changing the Subject: Authorship, Writing, and the Reader." In *Feminist Studies/Critical Studies,* ed. Teresa de Lauretis, 102–20. Bloomington: Indiana University Press, 1986.

Nietzsche, Friedrich. *The Use and Abuse of History.* Trans. Adrian Collins. Indianapolis: Bobbs-Merrill, 1949.

Said, Edward W. "Edward Said." In *Criticism in Society,* ed. Imre Salusinsky, 123–48. New York; Methuen, 1987.

———. "Traveling Theory." In *The World, the Text, and the Critic,* 226–47. Cambridge: Harvard University Press.

Salusinszky, Imre, ed. *Criticism in Society.* New York: Methuen, 1987.

Sangari, Kumkum, and Sudesh Vaid, eds. *Recasting Women: Essays in Colonial History.* New Delhi: Kali, 1989.

Sartre, Jean-Paul. *Nausea.* Trans. Lloyd Alexander. New York: New Directions, 1969.

Schor, Naomi. "This Essentialism Which Is Not One: Coming to Grips with Irigaray." *Differences: A Journal of Feminist Cultural Studies* 1, no. 2 (1989): 38–58.

Spivak, Gayatri Chakravorty. "Can the Subaltern Speak?" In *Marxism and the Interpretation of Culture,* ed. Cary Nelson and Lawrence Grossberg, 271–313. Urbana: University of Illinois Press, 1988.

———. *In Other Worlds.* New York: Methuen, 1987.

———. "Translator's Preface." In Jacques Derrida, *Of Grammatology,* ix–xc. Baltimore, Md.: Johns Hopkins University Press, 1974.

Williams, Raymond. *The Politics of Modernism.* London: Verso, 1989.

2 / Toward an Effective Intellectual: Foucault or Gramsci?

Any attempt at theorizing politics in the poststructuralist context is immediately caught up in a contradiction. On the one hand we experience, more urgently than ever before, the need to posit a common and solidary humanity that faces global threats of unprecedented magnitude. On the other hand, our situation is characterized by an unbounded heterogeneity of subject positions, each of which is a world unto itself insofar as it is informed and semanticized by its own macropolitics. These subject positions are indeed so diverse and, as instances of a nonsynchronous global development, so hopelessly out of sync with one another as to resist the kind of collective totalization implicit in such formations as "our world" and "our problems." In the domain of critical theory, the very use of the word "we" has become profoundly problematic. Meanwhile, in the "real world," a number of coalitions of oppressed, marginal, and minority groups have developed under common and collective principles, with the objective of empowering themselves in a variety of political arenas. Yet another example of the theory-reality disjuncture is the fact that even as an avant-garde and postrepresentational theory rages against identity, the voice, and the self, myriad groups are voicing themselves with conviction into Self and Identity. It is quite an anomalous scenario in which the best of progressive theory seems bereft of objects of explanation, while emerging historical realities seem oblivious of high theory. Is this really the case?

I do not think so, and to elaborate my conviction I turn to the all too real phenomenon of the Rainbow Coalition, to its achievements in the 1984 and the 1988 campaigns, and in particular to some of the crucial pronouncements made by the Reverend Jesse Jackson. For it seems to me that the coalition is taking place at that very juncture where theory and reality are finding each other within a shared axis. After a selective discussion of some of the themes of the Rainbow Coalition, I will attempt to demonstrate how these very themes have exercised the political and critical intelligence of Antonio Gramsci and Michel Foucault, each of whom in different but related ways has sought to give new meaning to the agency of the political intellectual.

During the course of the 1988 campaign, Jackson made the point emphatically that it is imperative for individuals and constituencies to feel, think, and identify themselves beyond the irreducible immediacy of their own regional rationale. Stated in theoretical terms, Jackson's message has been that the contents and causes of disparate and seemingly unrelated regions are indeed subtended by a common structure and etiology, and that every position is characterized by both a regional and a global structure.[1] The political ethic, then, of the coalition is to honor and do justice to the specificity of subject positions such as black, Chicano, feminist, immigrant, ethnic, gay, and lesbian, and at the same time, to enable structurally homologous and isomorphic readings of one situation in terms of the other. This is the change in direction that Jackson explains in response to Stuart Hall's questions in the pages of *Marxism Today*:

> So it became patently clear to me that our drive for self-respect and self-determination would have to be led by us and that we had to change the direction. There's a broad body of people in this country across lines of race, religion, region and sex who desperately want that new direction within this country and new connections with other people and forms of government in the world.[2]

Jackson asserts that the "rainbow is not so much about race as a direction, because all colours are in the rainbow," and goes on to argue that within the overarching context of the coalition, "the black vote is not a selfish and isolated vote, it is the trigger vote, the catalytic vote, for the entire progressive coalition."[3] Jackson's claim here on behalf of the coalition is both representational and postrepresentational, just as the valence of the black vote within the rainbow spectrum is both "itself" and more/less than "itself." Jackson's model, in moving beyond the canonical mode of representation and its insistence on a one-to-one correspondence between "identity" and "representation," reaches out toward a postrepresentational politics, but in doing so enriches the meaning of political representation. In other words, each constituency within the spectrum goes beyond and outside itself (the postrepresentational move), but only to reclaim the significance of representation within a more inclusive and collective organicity. Each constituency is representative not of itself but of a constitutive relationality that can only be eccentric to the givenness of any one of the components of the coalition. The resemblance between this model and the notion of hegemonic articulation developed by Ernesto Laclau and Chantal Mouffe is indeed striking. In both cases, given identities are articulated within a relational field whose differential disposition brings identity and difference into relationships of mutual accountability.

Jackson's rhetoric at the 1988 Democratic convention pointed up the necessity of dealing with "identity in difference" and "difference in identity." For example, his statement that he and Michael Dukakis had come to the United States of America on different ships but were now "in the same boat" vivifies the reality of a common but unequally and asymmetrically shared history.[4] In the same spirit, Jackson insisted on the need for a new and different "equation." The term "equation" covers a lot of significant ground. With its connotations of equality, it carries the moral urgency of affirmative action and the need to redress existing imbalances and asymmetries. As an algebraic trope, it establishes the valence of any given variable within the equation as a function of a collectively negotiable reality. In other words, given the operational logic of the equation, no variable within it can remain aloof, isolated, and unaffected by the equational process. Even as he develops the idea of the coalition representing itself from within its own space, Jackson is vigilant about the dangers of being represented and exploited by the dominant ideology. To state this differently, the burden of the coalition is both specific and transcendent in its specificity. It articulates "universal" themes even as it commits this universality to the contingencies of specific perspectives. (I shall return to this theme later in this essay in the context of Foucault and Gramsci, where I will be discussing the nature of the relationship between "what" is being said and "who" is saying it.) Thus, in his conversation with Stuart Hall, Jackson comments that "differences have been exaggerated for the purposes of exploitation."[5] This critical capacity of Jackson to situate or coordinate the locus of the coalition both in terms of itself and in relation to the dominant ideology calls to mind a Gramscian hegemonic politics that makes rigorous distinctions between allies and opponents. Equally Gramscian is the emphasis on "interests" and "interestedness." For example, Jackson has this to say about some of his political positions: "I would call them the most moral as opposed to the most radical positions, because radical has the connotation that you are out of step with reality or out of step with our interests."[6] In preferring the "moral" to the "radical" (a term used by Stuart Hall in his question), Jackson seems to be (1) stressing the pragmatic and felt nature of the entire enterprise, (2) asserting very strongly that one cannot have a politics that is out of step with present-day interests, and (3) distancing himself from the elitist language of academic theory. As a matter of fact, at one point in the interview Jackson responds to Hall's question with the following disclaimer: "Well, I am not sophisticated enough to understand all the labels you made up. I just try to use the natural reasoning process."[7] I will not get into an analysis of what "natural reason" might mean in the context of Jackson's politics, but I will merely observe in passing that Jackson's category is not all that different from the notion of "common sense" in Gramsci's political theory. I shall reserve for a later section of the essay a more detailed analysis of the relationship of natural and commonsensical worldviews to professionally theoretical worldviews; there I will also take up the question of whether professional intellectuality denaturalizes and therefore steps beyond its organic solidarity with the commonsensical and the natural.

Having delineated some of the trajectories of the Rainbow Coalition, I would now like to connect these trajectories with a number of theoretical issues that constitute the space where Michel Foucault and Antonio Gramsci may be said to address each other in critical dialogue.

Who or what is an intellectual? Who or what is the intellectual accountable to? How does the topos of the intellectual remain true to its own relatively autonomous specificity while continuing to perform a more collective, organic, and representational function? Are we still within a world-historical conjuncture where there are the "leaders" and the "led"—a situation that necessitates the avant-gardism of the intellectual? Or, have we reached a stage where the very category of "the intellectual" has become historically obsolete? And indeed, when we talk about "our world-historical conjuncture," what particular world or worlds are we taking about: first, second, or third world, dominant subject positions or subaltern? If there are multiple worlds subtended unequally and asymmetrically within a more inclusive coeval history, is it even worthwhile to think of the intellectual as a global and/or universal figure? Will not each situation produce its kind of intellectual formation, in response to its own specific agendas and priorities? But conversely, since no place is an island, how does any given location carry simultaneously both a global and a regional valence, and moreover, by what authority does any location work out a satisfactory, effective, and progressive equilibrium of the regional with the global? Given the multiplicity of intellectual and political models, how do these models communicate with one another, and in the name of what global assumption is such communication carried out? What is the nature of the very category of the "political"? Is it still caught up within a representational episteme or has it gone beyond representation toward the phantasmal areas of a postrepresentational, heterogeneous, and differential politics? Are our theoretical representations of the world somehow out of sync with our political representations of the world? In other words, as Jackson's disapproval of the term "radical" points out, does theory all too easily leave the world behind to indulge in a contentless utopianism? How do critical negativity and the need for affirmation negotiate with each other under the aegis of the "political"? Is it still possible, or desirable, to think in global terms when so much recent history seems to warrant a critique of globalness? Do our times insist that "thick politics" be replaced by "thin politics" and the "macropolitical" by the "micropolitical"?[8] Has the necessity to practice an acutely subject-positional politics deferred and/or problematized the need for an alliance politics that intends to recover global connections along different lines and directions?

These themes and questions have occupied center stage in Michel Foucault's theater of thought. In a different though related way, Antonio Gramsci has elaborated these problems from within the prison walls of Mussolini's Italy. My purpose here is to highlight aspects of the models of resistance that these two theorists of praxis have to offer, to compare and contrast some of their crucial formulations, and eventually, through a process of mutual exposure and interrogation, to account for the specificity as well as the finitude of each model. It is to Foucault I turn first.

There is something constitutively contradictory about Foucault's location as a political intellectual. He has been a privileged, empowered, and "sane" thinker who has sought fraternal membership among the insane, the marginal, and the powerless. He has even become their theoretical representative, even as his very thought thematizes the duplicity of his location vis-à-vis that of the insane, the marginal, and the powerless. As a rigorous and honest thinker, Foucault has quite thoroughly foregrounded the irrelevance and the untenability of his own theoretical authority even as he has transformed the course of Western historiography by rendering it fundamentally vulnerable and accountable to what it has systematically repressed. In his own brilliant and probing ways he has tried to think the "unthinkable," but from a subject position that has been assigned by the dominant ideologies of Western thought. The valence of his critical thought is then by definition "always already" homeless and marginal: on the one hand it lies "outside" the contours of official Eurocentric thought, but on the other hand, it cannot and will not be part of an emerging order interested in establishing its own hegemonic articulations. In short, his is a highly attenuated but diagnostic politics that will not affirm a new axiology: a politics that paradoxically achieves its interventionary effects within a macrological vacuum. It is an orphaned politics that cannot be "in the name of" any principle or cause. His appreciation and endorsement of what he calls "subjugated knowledges" are held in position within a genealogical practice that is constrained to posit the dominant knowledge as the primary point of departure. Ergo, we have Foucault identifying subjugated knowledges as "those blocs of historical knowledge which were present but disguised within the body of functionalist and systematising theory and which criticism—which obviously draws upon scholarship—has been able to reveal."[9]

It is by enacting an oppositional relationship between "historical contents" and a certain kind of theory that Foucault opens up a space where subjugated knowledges can announce and pursue their insurrection. He is pointing to two kinds of narrative: that of historical contents characterized by ruptures and struggles, and that of a totalizing and systematizing theory that defuses and reconciles ruptures and discontinuities in the name of a theoretical and systemic unity. In this respect Foucault's critique is not unlike Gramsci's, which makes a similar distinction between a traditional intellectuality that seeks to be timeless and unitary and an organic intellectuality that posits historical contingency and conflictuality. Foucault's critique is also aimed more generally and fundamentally at the very algorithm of representation that, in "speaking for" historically discontinuous and different events, deregionalizes these events and denies them their legitimacy as local and autochthonous articulations. Grand theory may be said to represent "historical contents" through an act of epistemic violence. How can these events and contents be enabled to speak "for and from within" themselves as subjugated knowledges? *How* does one—and *who* should be the one to—speak on behalf of the authentic location of these knowledges?

This raises a profound question concerning the historical reality of subjugated realities and knowledges. These blocs are characterized by a contradictory formation: they have always existed in history, but in the domain of theory they have been written out of effective existence. Within the auspices of the dominant theory their very historical and material reality has been dehistoricized and rendered nonexistent. Situated as absences within a theoretical historiography not their own, these knowledges are faced with a problem at the moment of their insurrection. Where will they speak from: rupturally from within the hegemonic body or from a position "without" that is not complicitous with the mandates of the official body of knowledge? Foucault's reading is that these blocs "were present but disguised" *within* the body of the dominant or master theoretical discourse. And it is here, I believe, that, notwithstanding his theoretical rigor and political sensitivity, Foucault's "subject position" vis-à-vis the locus of these subjugated knowledges falters and acknowledges its own limits. For the positional status of Foucault's own discourse *about* these knowledges is not clear. Does it speak from within the legality of these emergent spaces, is it the voice of the official discourse critically deconstructing itself and thus speaking as *its own other,* or is it the expression of a tertiary and disinterested space that functions at a "panoptic" remove from its object of criticism?[10] Stated in world-historical terms, who or what is speaking here? What "subject" is making these attributions about subjugated knowledges and from what perspective? My argument is that the choice of the "in/out" figurality is not merely rhetorical, nor is it coincidental. Contemporary theorists of subjugated subject positions (feminists, ethnic theorists, critics of colonialism and imperialism) have contested the necessity to conceive of their positions as "lacks" and "absences" within the dominant structure. Why not "think" these spaces as separate and disjuncted from the official body and therefore capable of engendering their own theories? The choice to locate these insurrectionary spaces within the hegemonic totality forecloses possibilities of "separatist" and "alternative" historiographies that may have nothing to do with the lacks and insufficiencies of the hegemonic model. Besides, this way of looking at these events exclusively as "insurrections" foists on them an eternally "transgressive" and "reactive" identity that is forced to feed parasitically on what it should effectively forget and "prehistoricize." The ability of these constituencies to historicize themselves remains the obverse of the capacity of the "official lack" to identify itself. In psychoanalytic terms, the realities of "others" are essentialized into a grand alterity (the capitalized Other), which in itself is nothing "other" than the ruling ideology in an antithetical or "reverse narcissistic" contemplation of itself.

In spite of these shortcomings or blind spots, Foucault's critical articulation retains its diagnostic acuity. Foucault is eminently successful in turning the tables on established "regimes of thought" and in securing possibilities for "local criticism" and a "noncentralized kind of theoretical production." In the name of what, then, does he position himself alongside these local criticisms, and how does he valorize the impulses that shape and inform local criticism? Foucault is very clear in his appreciation of the polemical trajectories of local criticism:

> It is here that we touch upon another feature of these events that has become manifest for some time now: it seems to me that this local criticism has proceeded by means of what one might term "a return to knowledge." What I mean by that phrase is this: it is a fact that we have repeatedly encountered, at least at a superficial level, in the course of the most recent times, an entire thematic to the

effect that it is not theory but life that matters, not knowledge but reality, not books but money etc.; but it also seems to me that over and above, and arising out of this thematic, there is something else to which we are witness, and which we might describe as an *insurrection of subjugated knowledges*. (Emphasis in original)[11]

The keynote here is the "return to knowledge," life, and, eventually, life knowledge. Here again the theme is the occlusion of reality and knowledge by theory. If theory suffocates differences, discontinuities, and the heterogeneities and polyvalences of reality (what Bakhtin has termed the "dialectic of real life"), then it is clear that an effective articulation of real knowledge has to look elsewhere for fulfillment. And it is here that Foucault introduces the notion of people, of populism, and of singular lived realities that are their own meaning-events. He gives the name "genealogy" to "the union of erudite knowledge and local memories which allows us to establish a historical knowledge of struggles and to make use of this knowledge tactically today." Genealogical researches, he says, are also "anti-sciences" that seek to eliminate "the tyranny of globalizing discourses with their hierarchy and all the privileging of a theoretical *avant-garde*."[12] (It is interesting to note that Foucault cites Marxism and psychoanalysis as examples of global theories and therefore parts company with them, but only after acknowledging that they have indeed provided and "continue to provide in a fairly consistent fashion useful tools for local research"; there will be more on this in my discussion of Gramsci's Marxism.) Theory-political knowledge (the people as a collective) and the intellectual as a residual avant-garde—that is the nexus I turn to next, for the question of the status of subjugated knowledges cannot be sufficiently probed unless we also simultaneously raise the question of the intellectual/masses relationship and the underlying ideology of the individual/society paradigm. The challenge that Foucauldian thought has to take up is that of postrepresentational politics and of accounting for the politics of intellectuality in a different way. And sure enough, Foucault has a lot to say about this.

In a conversation with each other, subsequently published in English as "Intellectuals and Power," Foucault and Gilles Deleuze announce the death of representation and the total obsolescence of the cadre known as the "intellectual." Both Foucault and Deleuze are interested in "lateral connections" and "networks of relays" that go beyond the representational paradigm and its dyadic (the spokesperson and his or her constituency) structure. In the words of Deleuze, "A theorising intellectual, for us, is no longer a subject, a representing or representative consciousness," and "those who act and struggle are no longer represented, either by a group or a union that appropriates the right to stand as their conscience." The upshot of it all is that "representation no longer exists."[13] This is an insight with which Foucault is in enthusiastic agreement.

How do we understand the claim that representation no longer exists? Are we to understand that in our contemporary world there are no more representational models to be found, no more leaders and constituencies, no more delegated/parliamentarian/democratic forms of government, but only and exclusively "groupuscules" *being* and legitimizing themselves in total freedom? Clearly this is a bizarre scenario that has nothing to do with the way the world is running. We must then interpret the statement to mean that although the world is rife with forms of representation, theory has proved that "representation is defunct; that is, in the avant-garde and futuristic world of theory, "representation is no more." But would not such an interpretation revalorize that very forwardness of theory that Foucault finds so irrelevant and indefensible? The difficulty here is that of "routing" and historicizing the progressive temporality of theory through the actualities of the given situation. It is clearly not evident (if anything, it is quite the contrary), given France's current national and international politics, either that representation is dead or that intellectuals like Foucault and Deleuze and their several regional and nomadic projects (however laudable their regional efficacy, and here I am thinking of Foucault's groundbreaking work on the prison system) are even remotely influential in shaping France's domestic and foreign policy. What we have instead is an intellectual fringe, both marginal and marginalizing of itself, that has debilitated itself for lack of "pure" means and a fear of complicity in existing forms of political struggle. As a result, the adumbration of a daring and different future finds itself completely severed from the world "as it is." The question of how to get "there" from "here" is bracketed indefinitely in favor of an aporetic thinking that monumentalizes the gap between forms of current history and practices that are utopian. As a result, the "unthinkable" is removed from its dialectical implication with the determinacy of historical thinking. We are left with an anarchist version of a permanent revolution.

What is particularly significant in the conversation between Deleuze and Foucault is the necessary connection between the "end of representation" and the celebration of the knowledge that the masses produce without the help of the intellectual. Clearly the events of May 1968 in Paris provide the underlying logic of this connection. Those events have taught intellectuals like Foucault and Deleuze the disquieting lesson that there exists a profound asymmetry, within society, between the perspectivity of the intellectual and that of the masses. The May events become that transformed space where the masses *are* their own protagonists fully capable of empowering themselves and speaking for themselves without the mediation of the intellectual. Is there then a role in this unfolding drama for intellectuals like Foucault? The answer seems to be no. Foucault's symptomatological reading of the intellectual in this context is quite unsparing in its honesty. For not only does he celebrate the masses who "no longer need him to gain knowledge," but he also fiercely decelebrates the intellectuals who "are themselves agents" of a repressive system of power that "blocks, prohibits, and invalidates" the discourse of the masses. The intellectual's role, Foucault declares, "is no longer to place himself somewhat ahead and to the side" in order to express the stifled truth of the collectivity;[14] rather, it is to struggle against the forms of power that transform him into its object and instrument in the sphere of "knowledge," "truth," "consciousness," and "discourse."

This self-critical and deconstructive rhetoric certainly sounds correct and politically wholesome except for one little problem: it is not clear "who" is speaking here, and "why" and "about whom" and from what point of view. If it is really the case that the movement of the masses has definitively superannuated the agency of intellectuals like Foucault and Deleuze, surely the question then arises: why are Foucault and Deleuze even saying anything at all about the movement? If it is true that the people have found their voice, and furthermore, that Foucault and Deleuze are "in the way" of the people's movement, how then do we understand and interpret the "representations" that Foucault and Deleuze are compulsively producing about the nature of the movement? Do these representations have any validity at all? Are these representations capable of making any cognitive truth claims at all, that is, given the poverty and irrelevance of their perspective in relation to whatever is really happening out there? How are we to receive and valorize a point of view that persists in articulating itself on the assumption that it has nothing worthwhile to say? How are we to read these pronouncements of a totally contentless critical negativity against the emergence of an affirmation by the masses? Are intellectuals like Foucault and Deleuze, on the one hand, and the masses, on the other, citizens of the same world, or is it the case that in spite of their best intentions, Foucault and Deleuze are guilty of creating an Us-Them divide?

The problem here is that Foucault's (and Deleuze's) protocols of self-problematization do not go far enough, a point Edward W. Said makes in his appreciative critique of Foucault's political imagination:

> We may finally believe with Foucault and Lyotard that the great narratives of emancipation and enlightenment are over, but I think *we must remember more seriously what Foucault himself teaches,* that in this case, as in many others, it is sometimes of paramount importance not so much what is said, but who speaks.

So that it can hardly pass muster that having declared the "assujetissement du discours," the same source that does so erases any opportunity for adversarial responses to this process of subjugation, *declaring it accomplished and done with at the start.* (Emphasis added)[15]

Said's quarrel in this passage is not with Foucault's intentions but with the reality of Foucault's practices: they do not go far enough. In spite of Foucault's intentions, his discourse ends up privileging "what is said" without raising the question of "who is speaking." In other words, in active transgression of his wonted exhortations on behalf of specificity and contingency, Foucault does end up making a number of representational truth claims. No one has made this criticism with more force and rigor than Gayatri Chakravorty Spivak, whose critical epistemology, I must add, is in many ways quite Foucauldian, but whose politics are quite different. Commenting on the conversation between Deleuze and Foucault, Spivak acknowledges "the most important contributions of French poststructuralist theory: first, that the networks of power/desire/interest are so heterogeneous that their reduction to a coherent narrative is counterproductive—a persistent critique is needed: and second, that intellectuals must attempt to disclose and know the discourse of society's Other."[16] But at the same time, she criticizes Deleuze and Foucault because they "systematically ignore the question of ideology and their own implication in intellectual and economic history." She goes on to say that "neither Deleuze nor Foucault seems aware that the intellectual within socialized capital, brandishing concrete experience, can help consolidate the international division of labor."[17]

I have already made the claim that Foucault's critical-intellectual practice does not go far enough. I would now like to elaborate the specific ways in which it does not go far enough. It is quite astonishing that Foucault, the thinker of specificity, does not identify himself problematically as a European and Eurocentric intellectual who has gone on to make sweeping generalizations about power, discourse, subjectivity, disciplinary societies, and micropolitics, on the basis of limited and exiguous French realities. Of course Foucault's criticism of all that has been harmful and oppressive in global emancipatory programs has to be lauded for its honesty and polemical specificity. But my point is that Foucault's critique of global strategies does not in itself invalidate the global dimension or the historical fact that all "differences" and "local subject positions" are part of a given global reality. By merely expunging the term "global" from his world of reference the mighty philosopher cannot be said to have gotten rid of the world itself. It is one thing to opt for a strategy (for whatever reasons) that is local rather than global and quite another to maintain or believe that in the choice of the "local" one has somehow abolished the "global." I would rather argue that the "global" controls and articulates Foucault in ways that he is not aware of. In a super-Nietzschean move on behalf of a local and discontinuous perspectivity, Foucault forgets that even the most disjunct perspective is globally subtended and that the very local perspectivity he champions against the claims of universality envisions its "own world" and thereby sneaks in through the back door the authoritarianism of global thinking into the terrain of the local. In other words, the local perspective itself is symptomatic of a certain choice on behalf of a certain world. Moreover, the will to power that resides within even the most local perspective shores up certain priorities and agendas, thus providing for that location the authority of a "world." It is also ironic that Foucault, the theorist of constituted subjectivities and assigned subject positions, suddenly "chooses" freely and joyously to be a specific, deglobalized, local, and countermnemonic intellectual. What gives him the right to make that choice, that is, given his historical proximity to the regimes and narratives of colonialism and imperialism? By what mandate, global or regional, does Foucault assume a statute of limitation on the long *durée* of colonialism and imperialism so as to inaugurate his local and countermnemonic discourses?

To understand this contradiction in Foucault's politics, a word is in order here about the absolute and axiomatic prominence given to the events of May 1968 by French poststructuralist thought. Without at all questioning the significance of those events, I would like to suggest that their idealization confers on them a kind of pure and autotelic significance. It is as though May 1968 had occurred as a singular event in defiance of all preexisting histories and historiographies. The impassioned valorization of May 1968 as a "break" results in a willed loss of memory: a forgetfulness of the generation of Sartre, Camus, Merleau-Ponty, and de Beauvoir, who had all been embroiled in the "macro" discourses of French colonialism, international communism, and Stalinism. We cannot, for example, forget the strong Algerian connection in the philosophical-political fiction of Sartre and Camus, the moral-political-existential enervation of a Roquentin and a Meursault, whose "world" and "center" fell apart as a microcosmic symptom of the bankruptcy of Western/French colonialism. We also need to remember that the highly individualistic philosophy of the absurd, as propounded by Camus, was at the expense of an Arab who had to be bumped off meaninglessly so as to provide the European individual with the negative ontology of "an indifferent universe." Nor can we forget the resurgence of racism and xenophobia in France today. My point is that the West has had and continues to have global investments, and it is not up to anyone's intentional choice to declare a sudden and dramatic deglobalization. If anything, such historically "innocent" moves only serve to conceal the connectedness of the world's problems. Whereas in the macropolitics of the Marxists one perceives a sense of accountability to the past, we see in the countermnemonic Foucault an all too felicitous willingness to "forget" his genealogical determinations. Yes, indeed, it is a strength of Foucault's genealogy effectively to combat and break with the past, but no break can ever be "pure." Impressive as the achievements of French poststructuralism may be, it would be quite erroneous and harmful to assume that the "present" juncture is radically different. To put it slightly differently, the Foucauldian task of writing the history of the present in all its willed discontinuity has to renegotiate with the received past and its many ramifications.

A pure European countermemory is suspect and disingenuous, for it would seem to exonerate Europe's past all too easily and thereby forfeit the lessons to be learned from the past. A contemporary Europe that will not negotiate with the moral authority of its erstwhile "Other," Africa and Asia, is a Europe that will not pay a price or atone for its colonialism. More generally, any dominant subject position that is in the process of deconstructing or calling itself into question cannot do so in solipsistic isolation, but must do so rather in a participatory dialogue with the subaltern positions.

We can detect a clear difference between Foucault's local and specific politics (a politics that will resist possibilities of coalitional articulation) and Jackson's call for "common ground," or for that matter, Edward Said's emphasis on the need for a cooperative thinking across and beyond existing asymmetries. Foucault's practices remain incapable of generating a positive politics, for he has foreclosed those possibilities; as one of the European "Us" haunted by Stalinism, the failure of Western Marxism, and the nightmare of the Gulag, he cannot have a macropolitics, and by virtue of his assigned subject position he cannot be one of "Them": the masses, and a whole range of subaltern positions. There is something wrong with this way of positing the choices, for it does away with the very possibility of influence and dialogism. I will now try to demonstrate how Foucault's (and Deleuze's) reading of the revolution of the masses reinstates the Us-Them divide.

The basic thesis that Foucault and Deleuze propose in their conversation is that the masses are "at one" with their reality and that they have no need for theories of mediation. Reality just happens in factories, asylums, and prison houses, and the expressions that emanate from these sites are not "about" (as in the false panoptic mode of representation) experiences: they *are* those unmediated meaning-events that are expressive in their very intransigent concreteness. The assumption here is that the collective purity of the people's movement in the very moment of its praxis translates itself into its own theory, and therefore, every member of the collective is already a living demonstration of a freedom that theory can only distort or destroy. Here is a reality that has transcended the need for theory: "they" do not need theory, for "they" are theory in practice. Such a characterization is incredibly romantic, for now the masses have been reified as a pure form of alterity. Here again we can see that what underlies this romanticism is a lack of specificity. In the guise of retiring the "universal intellectual," Foucault retires the entire cadre of the intellectual and the many typologies that comprise that cadre. Of course we are left with the specific intellectual, but this intellectual is "always already" dispossessed of macropolitical intentions. We need only contrast Foucault's strong denial (ironically, on behalf of the people) of the masses' need for an intellectual with the very different historical emergences of recent movements to see how mutually exclusive the two models are. Ethnic, feminist, anticolonialist, and independence movements assume an authentic organicity of constituency where leaders are delegated to lead and the people accept and empower the leaders as *theirs*. Martin Luther King, Mohandas Gandhi, Jesse Jackson, W. E. B. Du Bois, and many others were not coercive leaders, nor did they usurp the sovereignty of the people they spoke (and speak) for. Between the leaders and the people there can be a sense of active political community that makes the act of representation genuine and historically real. These leaders seek confirmation with the people and proceed to elaborate programs of action that take into account questions and details of organization. Within the movement, there are many different mediations and many different layers of structure and organization. The people and the leaders together discuss ways and means of historicizing the revolution through political, institutional, and administrative processes. These movements create their own leaders and intellectuals who are interested in making sure that the revolution does not peter out into an "eternally displaced present" or into the intransitivity of *jouissance* as an anarchist nirvana. Here, as in other areas, Foucault fails to make crucial distinctions between forms of representation that are legitimate and those that are coercive, between leaders and intellectuals who are organic with the movement and those that are traitors, between forms of power that are repressive and those that are libertarian, ameliorative, and emancipatory.

The troubling aspect in all of these pronouncements is that the masses continue being "spoken for" by Foucault. What are the masses themselves saying? Have they designated their leaders? Will the masses, for example, claim that an ideal reality has already occurred and that there is no need for further elaborations and representations? Is the revolution beyond all ideology, and if not, is it not important for the masses to find ways of expressing and historicizing the revolution in terms of its own ideology? How can this ideology be embodied if not through a whole range of carefully orchestrated mediations and political, intellectual, and institutional thresholds? The phenomenological privileging of concrete experience, argues Spivak, forecloses "the necessity of the difficult task of counterhegemonic ideological production." What follows is a telling diagnosis: "It has helped positivist empiricism—the justifying foundation of advanced capitalist neocolonialism—to define its own arena as 'concrete experience,' as 'what actually happens.' Indeed, the concrete experience that is the guarantor of the political appeal of prisoners, soldiers, and schoolchildren is disclosed through the concrete experience of the intellectual, *the one who diagnoses the episteme*" (emphasis added).[18] Spivak's analysis forces Foucauldian thought out into a global space: a space that it is unwilling to acknowledge. The point to be made here is that the discovery of "concrete reality" in a particular region is in itself symptomatic of a larger and more inclusive location, that of advanced capitalist neocolonialism. I read Spivak as saying that local regions in France (or Europe) cannot be treated as disjunct epiphanies that are rid of a "global before and after." Speaking of them as "concrete reality" confers on them an unquestionable transparency that radiates "with the historical sun of theory, the Subject of Europe." Spivak's reading also stresses that the concrete intellectual continues to be the custodian and interpreter of the truth of the episteme. The specific intellectual may be less absolutely oriented than the universal intellectual, but he is still the mouthpiece through which the episteme declares itself.

To sum up this part of my argument, Foucault's ambivalent rhetoric vis-à-vis the masses lands him in a dilemma he will resolutely not resolve. Having begun to "speak about them," he cannot but employ the categories of his own intellectual formation. Once he mobilizes these categories and protocols of analysis, he is paralyzed by the insight that these procedures do not apply to "them," and so, for fear of doing epistemic violence to "them," he forecloses his own analysis, thus denying "them" the historical materiality of "representation." His predicament is rather similar to that of Samuel Beckett, who "cannot go on, but must go on." Having disarmed "representation" universally, Foucault denies "them" the perspectivity of their particular form of representation. This universal and unsituated delegitimation of "representation" does away with distinctions between "who" is saying and "what" is being said, and also between forms of representation that are organic and coercive—in other words, insider/outsider differentiations are entirely dismantled. Since "representation as such" is "speaking for," and since "speaking for" is an act of violence, all representations are inauthentic and/or culpable. At a rarefied structural level, a feminist speaking on behalf of women, the African National Congress representing black South Africans, and Foucault speaking on behalf of the masses are all one and the same, notwithstanding the historical and macrological density of each of these situations within its own "organic space." To put it perhaps a little too harshly, European intellectuals, having lost their sense of "organicity," ordain that "organicity as such" is dead. The reason for this slippage, as Spivak demonstrates, is that "two senses of representation are being run together: representation as 'speaking for,' as in politics, and representation as 're-presentation,' as in art or philosophy."[19]

Unfortunately, from my point of view, Foucault's not going far enough has the following results. He will not allow his agenda to be interrogated, transformed, and recontextualized by the agenda of the "masses." I will argue that such a macropolitical change is indeed possible, that it is possible for Foucault to be one of "them," provided he makes room for a certain kind of "self-consciencization" in the context of the emerging subaltern realities. It is possible for the specific intellectual of a certain formation to declare solidarity with a revolutionary politics, but on the condition that this intellectual allow himself to be represented and reparsed within the syntax of the emerging subaltern politics. I am not suggesting that the revolutionary politics of the oppressed does away with the extreme differences in subject positions, but rather that self-reflexivity concerning one's own subject position does not have to deny the possibility that different subject positions negotiate with one another in the name of a certain globalness. But any declaration of solidarity becomes impossible to Foucauldian epistemology, for, with its insistence on "difference," this epistemology completely undermines the collectivist assumptions that underlie the notion of solidarity. To Foucault (after the gulags, after Stalinism, and so on), collectivity connotes organization and organization connotes totalization, and totalization spells tyranny and oppression. Hence, the reference to the masses remains undifferentiated. There is the individual and there are the masses, and there is the additional understanding that each individual is a "groupuscule" that cannot be represented. So with what or whom can solidarity be declared? Unless of course it be with "difference." But what would a solidarity in "difference" mean except a contradiction?

For lack of a clear theory of ideology (whether it be that of class, gender, sexuality, nationality, or a heterogeneously crosshatched interpellation), "the freeing of difference" is at best redolent of an idealist thinking devoted to the bohemianization of all that is singular and exceptional and a near-solipsistic aestheticization of the political. The presiding principle of a difference that "requires thought without contradiction, without dialectics, without negation," a difference that expresses itself through the "thought of the multiple— of nomadic and dispersed multiplicity that is not limited or confined by constraints of similarity,"[20] is the ideology of a privatized self in search of rarer and rarer thresholds of uniqueness in transgression of social limits and commonalities. Such an insurrection of difference is in many ways a throwback to the Sartre of *Being and Nothingness* and to the artist in Camus in *Exile and the Kingdom*, in search of the solitary/solidary. The quarrel with the individual and the unified self eventuates not in a more complex understanding of the dialectically mediated relationship between individuality and collectivity but rather in the apotheosis of multiplicities or "groupuscules" that are intra-individual. The shattering of the unity of the individual Self takes the form of an *implosion*, that is, a fallout "within." It is still a world where "liberation" is a banner that the "individual as multiple" waves against society.

I am well aware that Foucauldian enthusiasts might find me guilty of locating Foucault in an altogether erroneous context and thereby of misreading him. The historical and historiographic question concerning Foucault's location could be stated quite simply: does Foucault still operate within the Marxist *durée*, or is his thought post-Marxist? Foucault himself never, except in passing and in polemical asides, deals with this question seriously. But even these minimal confrontations tell us something. So, let us hear Foucault on Marxism.

As the advocate of difference and the singular "meaning-event,"[21] Foucault cannot (and rightly so) allow any one model of opposition officially to install itself as the set of all oppositional subsets and thus naturalize its right to vanguardism. As a result, his approval of proletarian and class-specific politics has at best been provisional. The reality of each individual and local resistance, in Foucault's view, is in danger of being betrayed by the univocity of the proletarian revolution. His apprehension is that "as soon as we struggle against exploitation, the proletariat not only leads the struggle but also defines its targets, its methods, and the places and instruments for confrontation; and to ally oneself with the proletariat is to accept its positions, ideology, and its motives for combat." He argues against such a total identification and suggests instead that "if the fight were directed against power, then all those on whom power is exercised to their detriment, all who find it intolerable, can begin the struggle on their own terrain and on the basis of their proper activity (or passivity)."[22] This is vintage Foucault. It is difficult to argue with Foucault here, for in our own times the danger of one oppositional perspective becoming *the* perspective is all too real. Given the multiple determinations of gender, class, race, sexuality, nationality, and so forth, Foucault is absolutely right to warn us against monolithic, monological, and monothetic opposition. Each group has to enter the revolutionary process in its "ownmost" way. We must also remind ourselves that Foucault does acknowledge that "these movements are linked to the revolutionary movement of the proletariat to the extent that they fight against the controls and constraints which serve the same system of power." His interest in "the fight directed against power" leads him, understandably and significantly, to the problem of understanding power in general—its omnihistorical ontology and its omnipresent microphysics. Foucault asks, "Isn't this difficulty of finding adequate forms of struggle a result of the fact that we continue to ignore the problem of power?" He then goes on to speculate that "it may be that Marx and Freud cannot satisfy our desire for understanding this enigmatic thing which we call power, which is at once visible and invisible, present and hidden, ubiquitous."[23]

Equally important is Foucault's critique of Marxian scientificity. Having declared that the theoretical and methodological task is to effect "the union of erudite knowledges and local memories which allows us to establish a historical knowledge of struggles and to make use of this knowledge tactically today," Foucault asks "what types of knowledge" might be disqualified when something becomes a science. He is fearful that in the name of science a number of speaking, discoursing subjects will get discounted. Arguing against a certain kind of theoretical professionalism, Foucault accuses the theoretical avant-garde of isolating itself "from all the discontinuous forms of knowledge that circulate about it." But even here, we must take heed that as he takes theoretical avant-gardism to task, he does so in the name of popular knowledges that are *discontinuous*. In Foucault's scheme of things, "discontinuity" is the empowering principle, that is, the articulation and empowerment of discontinuity qua discontinuity.

A number of interesting and contradictory themes are at play here. First, there is the critique of Marxist universality and the attempt to empower each resistance in "its difference." There is then the interest in "power" as something both transitive and intransitive—power in determinate forms that are subservient to particular ideologies, and Power as an "in-itself" that is transcendent of particular instantiations of itself. Finally, there is the investigation into knowledge as practice, tactic, and intervention. In each of these inquiries there is a persistent tension between the "historical" and the "utopian." The historical need to unpack and pluralize a monolithic Marxism correctly and crucially identifies the heterogeneity of subject positions, but, having done so, rather than attempt to articulate these multiple positions within a relational field, Foucault's rhetoric leaps away into the realm of pure difference. Analogously, having identified the realities and effects of both power (lowercase) and Power (capitalized), Foucault's thought is attracted more toward the transideological and transhistorical phenomenology of power. Finally, and in a similar manner, having empowered local knowledges against theoretical professional theory, Foucault's agenda privileges the local and discontinuous knowledges as *discontinuity*, rather than pressuring these knowledges to form new and different alliances among themselves. In every instance, the utopian impulse to deterritorialize turns into a ceaseless anarchism for lack of mediation with determinate history. Foucault's project turns out to be very different from Jackson's "common ground" coalition or Laclau and Mouffe's "hegemonically articulatory practices."[24] Laclau and Mouffe are as much aware and solicitous of differences and discontinuities as Foucault is, but their plan of action, from within Marxism, is radically different. Their interpretation of the situation is that "the problem of Marxism has been to think these discontinuities and, at the same time, to find forms reconstituting the unity of scattered and heterogeneous elements." Their concern is with "the relational moment" (among the elements), "whose importance increases to the extent that its nature becomes less evident."[25]

As I move toward my discussion of Gramsci, I would like, by way of Barry Smart, to reask the question concerning Foucault's post-Marxian politics. For clearly there are a number of similarities between Foucault's notions of intellectuality and Gramsci's, and yet the terrains on which they operate are vitally different. Of course there is also the more specific question of whether or not a number of Gramscian elaborations anticipate a number of Foucauldian practices. Here, too, there is the question of the "before" and the "after." Furthermore, there is a certain amount of undecidability about the status of the "after": does the "post-" do away with the regime of the "before," or does it unpack the "before" within its own macrology?

Focusing on the categories of "the intellectual" and "hegemony," Smart claims that a case can be made for reading Foucault's work "as providing a radically different approach and a new set of concepts through which to develop analysis and understanding of the exercise of power and the associated effects of hegemony in modern societies."[26] Foucault is also said to have critically stepped away from the Gramscian and Marxist problematic of ideology so as to discover how "truth" and "power" constitute hegemony. Eschewing global analysis, Foucault's genealogical approach "is directed towards the multiple processes through which events are constituted, in particular to the study of technologies of power, their strategic deployment, and effect(s) respectively." Smart also advances the thesis that "Foucault's work can be considered to provide a reconceptualization of the problem of hegemony, shifting it away from the essentially humanist philosophy of action to be found in Gramsci's work to an examination of the production, transformation, and effects of the true/false distinction which has been at the centre of processes of government in modern Western societies."[27] Lastly (to limit my agenda to just a few of the interesting intersections between Foucault's and Gramsci's theories), there is the Foucauldian "specific intellectual" (in opposition to the universal intellectual), who works "within specific sectors at the precise points where [the specific intellectual's] own conditions of life or work situate" him or her. The specific intellectual is intended in demystification of the universal intellectual just as the Gramscian organic intellectual exposes the ideological underpinnings of the traditional intellectual. But there the similarity ends, for the agencies of the two intellectuals have very different orientations.

The putative post-Marxist articulations are, first, an attempt to account for hegemony not in terms of "interest" or "ideology," but in terms of the truth-power network; second, a move away from discourses of interiority and temporality to those of spatiality and externality whereby technologies and bodies constitute themselves as meanings rather than relate in a symptomatic way to "meaning"; third, the emphasis on processes that postpone or render untenable the very notion of "intentional meaning" and the consequent denaturalization of "human agency" (whatever the ontological nature of the "human"); and fourth, the casting of the intellectual in a thin or micrological matrix whereby he or she (*a*) is neither a representative nor a revolutionary consciousness and (*b*) is merely a nodal point within an elaborately specialized system that cannot be available to any consciousness in its plenitude—furthermore, the specificity of each node commits it to purely local imaginings and operations. Which is to say, there is no Subject, nor are there subjects—only operations, practices, and deployments. If these practices of truth power are constitutive of human subjectivity (that is, are not merely epiphenomenal), how is this subjectivity to seek control over and direct these processes? How is "history" to be thought of except in technological forms? As we discuss the question of whether these problems are post-Marxist or not, let us turn to Antonio Gramsci and see to what extent his political theory of praxis is aware of these issues as autonomous issues. Perhaps, in his context, these are not all that autonomous after all.

From Foucault to Gramsci is both a predictable and a farfetched connection. The themes and the anxieties that concern the two are very similar, and yet their intellectual formations are very different. They did not live and theorize in the same world: Gramsci precedes Foucault and, unlike the latter, works on Marxist terrain even as he fundamentally transforms it. Between Gramsci's Italy and Foucault's France, a number of crucial and decisive events, both regional and global, have taken place. The meanings of terms such as "Marxism," "international communism," "nationalism," "internationalism," and "class" have undergone great changes. And finally, if Gramsci seems to represent a historical conjuncture that is hopefully expectant of the triumph of international communism, Foucault represents a moment that has been disillusioned of the very dreams that animated Gramsci's world. One could even say that poststructuralist pessimism is the expression of what was unconsciously inherent in Marxist thought: its potential to failure. In spite of all these differences, some questions seem to have survived from Gramsci to Foucault.

I begin with Gramsci's essay "What Is Man?" with the intention of opening up a significant area of disagreement between Foucault and Gramsci. In this essay, Gramsci contends passionately that "it is essential to conceive of man as a series of active relationships (a process) in which individuality, while of the greatest importance, is not the sole element to be considered." According to Gramsci, "The individual does not enter into relations with other men in opposition to them but through an organic unity with them, because he becomes part of social organisms of all kinds from the simplest to the most complex." These relationships that man enters into "are not mechanical" but "active and conscious," so much so indeed that man changes or modifies himself "to the same extent that he changes and modifies the whole complex of relationships of which he is the nexus." Gramsci concludes resoundingly that "if individuality is the whole mass of these relationships, the acquiring of a personality means the acquiring of consciousness of these relationships, and changing the personality means changing the whole mass of these relationships."[28]

It must be quite clear by now how different Gramsci's enterprise is from Foucault's. First of all, well before the agency of the intellectual comes under discussion, Gramsci's critical anthropology takes on an even more fundamental obsession of Western thought: the binary opposition between individuality and collectivity. The intellectual/masses opposition is but the exacerbation of a more basic binary antagonism: group versus individual. Given this basic valorization in Western thought of "individuality," the figure of the intellectual is also drawn up in the image of the preeminent individual who will resist homogenization (by the masses) and thus be in control of "quality" (as against quantity and numbers) in cultural intellectual life. Even Foucault, who is brilliant in his deconstruction of the "identical and self-same subject," remains trapped within the ideology of Western individualism: hence his valorization of "difference" as discrete and singular. Foucault's destabilization of the univocal subject remains philosophical; that is, it does not become political. More generally, a philosophically subversive move does not automatically and simultaneously translate into a politically subversive strategy simply because, given the relative autonomy of the philosophical and the political, the two realms are often (even within the episteme) out of sync with each other. The way out of this contradiction (a way Foucault does not take) is to make philosophical thought accountable to political practice. And this is what Gramsci does ceaselessly: the "superstructural" shoring up of individuality is perennially dialogized within a constitutive organicity.

To unpack Gramsci's position further, the individual is seen as a function of the collective that in itself is perceived as the expression of a mobile and ever-changing system of relationships. Nowhere in Gramsci's thought is "collectivity" imposed as an apriorism; the collective dimension itself is historically produced in response to changing situations and crises. In arguing for a "change in the conception of man," Gramsci historicizes "man" through and through by declaring the "human" to be a process. Is Gramsci guilty of "humanism" here just because he privileges the term "man"? Has not poststructuralist and structuralist thought thoroughly and radically denaturalized and desubjectified the "human," and has not Foucault's discourse on archaeology banned forever not merely forms of essentialism but also notions of unilateral human agency? Yes, all this is certainly true, but what seems even truer is that Gramsci is well aware of these so-called post-Marxist wrinkles. I would even claim that not only is Gramsci not a humanist, he is well ahead of his time, a structuralist thinker who anticipates Althusserian Marxism. But there is a difference. Even as Gramsci *commits* (a term I use very deliberately in thematic opposition to that Nietzschean-Foucauldian word "sacrifice"; I have in mind the thesis of the "sacrifice of the subject" to the processes of knowledge) "man" to a field of relationships (and to what after Hayden White we might call the "history of forms," and the "forms of historical contents"), he insists that these relationships are not "mechanical." In other words, to Gramsci the issue of agency is a valid and live one. There might not be "agency" except in terms of these relationships that are "external and exterior" to "agency," but this does not result in the complete collapse or immanentization of agency. Gramsci keeps this question alive: how, why, and *in the name of what* do these relationships change? In denying the purely mechanical model, Gramsci revives the issue of historical human intentionality and its corollary, the issue of the instrumentality of "process." On the one hand, process may be considered "subjectless," but this long view of process has to be dialectically instantiated in and through specific histories of affirmation and consolidation. In other words, the road to utopia is not a fortuitous or aleatory path, but rather a determinate path with determinate signposts that can tell us whether we are really on our way to utopia or merely on a trip to an eternally anarchist "anomie." (As a matter of fact, in the works of such post-Marxists as Baudrillard and his many postmodern and postpolitical and postsocial epigones, not only do we find that "anomie" is accepted on the basis of its immanence, but we also realize that we are not going anywhere at all: we are already "there.") Hence, the insistence in Gramsci on the interplay between "man as structure" and "man as intentionality." It is of paramount importance to Gramsci that even as these relationships historicize the "human," they continue to "be" and bear the signature of the "human." Gramsci would have no difficulty with a systemic or Foucauldian interpretation of the "nodal" situatedness of the "human," but he would go on to say that the human being, by entering the relationships, constitutes a nexus agentially and intentionally. The "constituted" nature of "man as node" does not preempt the possibility of man functioning as an agent in relatively and historically constituted freedom. The "relationships" are a means to an end; they are not the end in themselves. It is no wonder then that the emphasis in Gramsci's discourse is on "change." Change is to be produced through a critical consciousness and a critical knowledge of these relationships. There is a relationship of transitivity between the "relationships" and the "human" whereby when the complex of relationships is modified, man is modified, too. The point to make here is that "man" is not passively identical or synonymous with the complex of relationships, for Gramsci is not interested in generating a tautologous identity that is timelessly true and therefore invulnerable to historical criteria. To Gramsci, "man" is what man does, and what man does is the active realization of changing complexes of relationships. The "is" and the "does" are not transfixed within a mutual identity; they indicate a relational noncoincidence that is essential to the intentional production of the future from and by the present based on its knowledge of itself and its past.

Superficially, it would seem that Gramsci's conception of individuality as "the whole mass of these relationships" is a forerunner of the individual as "groupuscule" (in Foucault and Deleuze), but a closer analysis reveals irreconcilable differences. In Gramsci's context, there is always an emphasis on "relationships," relationships that can be thematized, understood, problematized, and modified. To be located within a relationship does not mean the same thing as being condemned to that complex of relationships in a spirit of passive acceptance. Through a synthetic consciousness of these relations, knowledge can be produced as change and as a theory of change. Unlike the Foucauldian scenario, (1) questions concerning totality and organicity can be raised from the specificity of one's position because one's position is always already both *specific and specific relationally* to the whole complex of relationships; and (2) the internally dialogized and heterogeneous individuality is mediated by the heterogeneity of the entire field. There is therefore no need to protect the "individual as groupuscule" from the so-called violence of a collective representation. Gramsci's questions have to do with generating a programmatic agenda for change based on theoretical knowledge. How to organize, persuade, and represent were concerns that were always uppermost in Gramsci's theory. And it is in response to these concerns that Gramsci raises the question of the "organic intellectual" and his or her capacity to elaborate "hegemony."

In elaborating his notion of the "organic intellectual," Gramsci "established a particular framework," explains Anne Showstack Sassoon, "for the discussion of the intellectuals in order to highlight the mystification of their role by such thinkers as Croce, who, he [Gramsci] argued, contained a tradition going back to Plato and culminating in Hegel."[29] "Every social group, coming into existence on the original terrain of an essential function," writes Gramsci, "creates together with itself, organically, one or more strata of intellectuals which give it homogeneity and an awareness of its own function not only in the economic but also in the social and political fields."[30] As Sassoon observes, Gramsci's concept of the intellectual fulfills a number of tasks. It critiques the idealist view that intellectuals "exist above and outside the relations of production." It determines intellectual activity as "a very real but also a very mediated relationship," while it is also "aimed against the lack of comprehension in the socialist movement, based on an economistic interpretation of reality, of the social and political role of intellectuals." Sassoon concludes convincingly that on the one hand "Gramsci attempts to demystify intellectual activity *per se* and on the other he assigns it a specific place and importance within the complex of social relations, thus arguing both against an idealist tradition and an economistic one." Gramsci's theory of the intellectual is coextensive with his theory of mediations, and since there are multiple mediations within any given society, there are multiple modes of intellectual activity, each of which is mediated in its very organicity. In Gramsci's theory, mediations enhance, unpack, and elaborate organicity into a multidimensional reality, whereas to Foucault, "mediations" as "specificities" are not "mediations of" an organic and inclusive reality. In Gramsci's world picture, the relationship between intellectuals and the world of production is "'mediated' by the whole fabric of society and by the complex of superstructures, of which the intellectuals are, precisely, the 'functionaries.'"[31]

The telling insight in the last passage is that intellectuals are functionaries of *the whole complex and the social fabric*. In other words, they are not intransitive Kafkaesque functionaries cut off from their representative and, if you will, synecdochic relationship to the totality. Of course, we must acknowledge, against Gramsci's theoretical lucidity, that in our own times the autonomous logic as well as material circumstantiality of mediations (as technologies, apparatuses, practices, local applications, bureaucratic and governmental protocols, institutional and disciplinary codes, and so on) has become so dauntingly autonomous that we are tempted to conclude that this realm signifies nothing but itself. We experience great difficulty in moving from these formal significations to that ideological reality *of which* they are the signications. We are tempted, in our enervation, to call the search off and be contented with *mediations as such* that are no longer *mediations* of, and with a simulacral reality that frustrates and mocks our every attempt to achieve what Edward Said (after Gramsci) calls *"worldliness."* But here again, as Said has memorably and persistently contended, the fact that we as intellectuals are having great difficulty deciphering our *"worldliness"* does not mean that we are *"not had"* by the world. Whether intellectuals are aware of it or not, they are functionaries of an inclusive macropolitical logic, whether it be that of the state or capital or nationality or whatever. Said's complaint is not that people in contemporary Western societies do not have a politics, but that these very people seem not to know what it is to be political as *intellectuals*. Meritocracies, professional tags, membership in esoteric discourses and practices, and in general, various forms of professional specialization deracinate the intellectual from a total and "primitive" sense of constituency.

It is within this sense of organic constituency that Gramsci asserts that although "all men are intellectuals, all men do not have the function of intellectuals in society." For, to Gramsci, "the 'organic' intellectuals which every new class creates alongside itself and elaborates in the course of its development, are for the most part 'specialisations' of partial aspects of the primitive activity of the new social type which the new class has brought into prominence."[32] As Sassoon points out, "Organic intellectuals are specialists who fulfill technical, directive, organisational needs."[33] The specialist and superstructural autonomy of the intellectual is always relative to a "primary" organicity, ergo its commitment to organizational tasks is valorized, not in the name of the specialist activity, but in the name of a primary organicity. It is interesting to note that Gramsci's "new intellectual," from the point of view of poststructuralist thought, is guilty of avant-gardism, but this avant-gardism, in Gramsci, is not bereft of a sense of constituency; if anything its forwardness is undertaken in the name of the entire constituency. A representational politics underwrites the whole program. And this is how Gramsci describes the new intellectual, in terms that are purposeful, agential, and organizational.

The mode of being of the new intellectual can no longer consist

> in eloquence, which is an exterior and momentary power of feelings and passions, but in active participation in practical life, as constructor, organiser, "permanent persuader" and not just a simple orator (but superior at the same time to the abstract mathematical spirit); from technique-as-work one proceeds to technique-as-science and to the humanistic conception of history, without which one remains "specialised" and does not become "directive" (specialised and political).[34]

We can see Gramsci attempting here to effect, through processes and history, a number of transformations, transformations Foucault would seem to take for granted as part of an "always already" revolution. First, there is the move from the mere tropological or rhetorical "exteriority" of "pure eloquence" to the "internalized" solidarity of "persuasion." As persuader, the intellectual cannot afford to be idealist, nor can he or she remain bereft of a sense of constituency. As "persuader," the intellectual is inserted into historical participation whereby his or her eloquence is given terms of purpose. Someone is being persuaded by somebody toward some determinate purpose: the persuader is thus made accountable historically and politically. Second, the activity of persuasion as construction and organization allows for the analytic discreteness of the superstructure and infrastructure while at the same time it binds the two as one historical bloc. Third, the task of persuasion is "permanent," which is to say that it is terminable (as in the achievement of specific historical objectives), but it is also interminable as process (that is, as the expression of a long revolution). Fourth, the intellectual activity is neither merely visceral and impassioned nor purely abstract and formal but a judicious and successful synthesis of thought and feelings. Fifth, *technique-as-work* and *technique-as-science* are related by a progressive movement; they are not two isolated activities. Gramsci makes room for the autonomization of specialist and professional spheres of activity, but insists that the autonomization has a prior and more inclusive placement within the totality.

In doing this, he also moves decisively away from the ironclad determinism of the base/superstructure model. To Gramsci, superstructural activities are a form of praxis that are in effective mediation with the total structure. And finally, in Gramsci's humanism (and we must remember that his humanism has nothing to do with the humanism that has been so ably trashed by thinkers beginning with Martin Heidegger up to the contemporary poststructuralists), the category of the "directive" is an inalienable constituent of the "political." What is at stake here, in the difference between Gramsci and Foucault, is the very meaning of the term "political." Gramsci will not entertain a politics without direction: not for him the "politics of abandon or abandonment" or the "politics of the specific" without relation to the general. Not having lost the vision of a total (and not totalized) historical bloc collective, it is still meaningful for Gramsci to take into account the imbalances and inequalities within the same society; hence his didactic and pedagogical anxiety on behalf of the entire constituency. His aim is to cure and rectify these imbalances through the critical-theoretical practice of a dialectical relationship between the masses and "its" intellectuals. As he puts it with characteristic rigor:

> The process of development is bound by an intellectuals-mass dialectic; the stratum of intellectuals develops quantitatively and qualitatively, but every leap towards a new "fullness" and complexity on the part of the intellectuals is tied to an analogous movement of the mass of simple people, who raise themselves to higher levels of culture and at the same time broaden their circle of influence with thrusts forward by more or less important individuals or groups toward the level of specialised intellectuals. But in the process, times continually occur when a separation takes place between the mass and the intellectuals (either certain individuals or a group of them), a loss of contact, and hence the impression [or theory] as a complementary, subordinate "accessory."[35]

First of all, unlike Foucault, Gramsci is interested in telling a story, in producing a developmental narrative. The production of narrative is also the production of unevenness and contradictions, and one such contradiction is the mass/intellectual contradiction. Unlike much poststructuralist thought that shies away from contradiction in the name of "difference" or an acategorical thought or the singular event or an all-enveloping and undifferentiated heterogeneity, Gramsci's theory takes on contradictions substantively even as it anticipates, in utopian fashion, the disappearance, in and by and through history, of contradiction. (The disappearance of "contradiction," we know, would signify the end of the "political" itself.) Also, in the preceding passage, the loss of contact between the mass and the intellectuals is perceived as a problem. The seeming separateness of theory is diagnosed and demystified, not celebrated or merely recorded as an event in its own right. Surely it is obvious from all this that Gramsci does take for granted the "leader-led, the rulers and the ruled" division. But it must be noted that his belief in this division is based on historical reality; it does not mean that he wishes for the perpetuation of this division. He does raise the question whether one wishes "there always to be rulers and ruled, or does one wish to create the conditions where the necessity for the existence of this division disappears." And yet, he asserts that "it needs to be understood that the division of the rulers and the ruled, though in the last analysis it does go back to divisions between social groups, does in fact exist, *given things as they are, even inside the bosom of each separate group, even a socially homogeneous one* [emphasis added]."[36] Unlike Foucault and Deleuze, who speak about subaltern reality from without, Gramsci voices this reality from within. These are very different forms of representation, and their messages are very different, too. By conflating the two meanings of representation (a criticism made persuasively by Spivak), Foucault and Deleuze romanticize the subaltern and arrive at the conclusion that "theory is practice," whereas Gramsci states that "a human mass does not 'distinguish' itself and does not become independent 'by itself'" without organization by intellectuals. It is extremely significant that poststructuralist admirers of subaltern reality glibly do away with the theory-practice distinction, whereas Gramsci, the subaltern practitioner of subaltern reality, asserts that "there is no organisation without intellectuals, that is, without organisers and leaders, *without the theoretical aspect* of the theory-practice nexus distinguishing itself concretely as a stratum of people who 'specialise' in its conceptual and philosophical elaboration."[37] In terms of my polemical interest, the "who" that speaks here is of critical importance.

Our situation now is not post-Gramscian. The problem faced by an entire range of emerging groups is indeed one of organization. Decolonized independent nations are looking for nationally organic leaders and an intelligentsia that is of the people as against the metropolitan intelligentsia that is all too easily drained away into a deracinated international continuum. Within feminism, there are active concerns regarding the political valence of the more academic and university-based elaborations of feminism. Minority intellectuals and minority activists worry constantly about the problem of depoliticization by institutionalization and superstructural validation. A point in question is the relationship of the black intellectual to black schools, black ghettos, black modes of pedagogy, culture, and so on. In the context of the civil rights movement and the battle against racism, questions of leadership, delegation, representation, the creation of broad and democratic bases, and the articulation of a common identity characterized by multiple mediations were active during the days of Martin Luther King Jr. and they are active now as the Rainbow Coalition seeks to politicize itself over increasingly broader and crosshatched constituencies. But all these programmatic and organizational commitments, from Foucault's point of view, would seem erroneous or unwarranted. Who is right, Foucault or Gramsci? This is surely a vulgar and reductive way of posing options, and I am doing so only to drive home the point that on a certain level there is a mutually exclusive relationship here that has to do with the location of each politics: on the one hand, the "outsider" politics of Foucault that, in spite of its best intentions of "letting the masses be," ends up in a prescriptive mode telling the masses what they should know and, on the other, the solidarity politics of the insider Gramsci, who has no difficulty giving his politics a name from "within."

I have been suggesting all along that what makes Gramsci's politics more real and worldly than Foucault's is that it carries with it a strong sense of hegemonic agency. Now let us look at the concept of hegemony in Gramsci and examine how and in the name of what positivity (economic, social, political, or moral) hegemony is exercised. It would seem that a poststructuralist politics of heterogeneous subject positions (and the poststructuralist deconstructions of a univocal, positive, full, and representable social reality) would escape easy marking by the notion of hegemony. Hegemony as the expression of a collective will and poststructuralism with its emphasis on pure difference would seem to escape mutual influence.

What does Gramsci have to say on hegemony? Here again, typically, he gives us not a definition but the growth of a process. Hegemony has a history and a developmental process. "The first and most primitive moment," in Sassoon's reading, "the economic corporative one, is when members of the same category feel a certain solidarity toward each other but not with other categories of the same class."[38] "A second moment," in Gramsci's words, "is that in which consciousness is reached of the solidarity of interests among all the members of a social class—but still purely in the economic field."[39] The third moment, which Gramsci calls "the most purely political phase," marks the transcendence of the "corporate limits of the purely economic class" and the inauguration of broader, coalitional sympathies that reach out to "the interests of other subordinate groups too." This moment is also the passage from a union "of political and economic aims" to possibilities of "intellectual and moral unity."[40] (It is not coincidental that Jesse Jackson's rhetoric also strongly rings the moral bell even as it does full justice to themes of economic and political enfranchisement.) According to Laclau and Mouffe, it is in the movement from the "political" to the intellectual and moral plane "that the decisive transition takes place toward a concept of hegemony beyond 'class alliances.'"[41] Since I find Laclau and Mouffe particularly convincing on this point, I will quote from them extensively:

> For, whereas political leadership can be grounded upon a conjunctural coincidence of interests in which the participating sectors retain their separate identity,

moral and intellectual leadership requires that an ensemble of "ideas" and "values" be shared by a number of sectors—or, to use our own terminology, that certain subject positions traverse a number of class sectors. Intellectual and moral leadership constitutes, according to Gramsci, a higher synthesis, a "collective will," which, through ideology, becomes the organic cement unifying a "historical bloc." All these are new concepts having an effect of displacement with regard to the Leninist perspective: the relational specificity of the hegemonic link is no longer concealed, but on the contrary becomes entirely visible and theorized.[42]

I am aware that there is a problem with this reading: is this a Gramscian reading of Gramsci, or is it a poststructuralist extension or adaptation of Gramsci? For my purposes, this is a convincingly strategic reading, and as for its fidelity to Gramsci, I would say that there is no tendency in his elaboration of alliances that resists this reading. The manner in which Laclau and Mouffe import their terminology of "subject positions" into Gramsci's discourse is highly suggestive. It raises the question of whether or not "class specificity" is adequate to the task of orchestrating and organizing the hegemonic link. If class is not, as Spivak has argued deconstructively, an "inalienable aspect of reality," but a useful and powerful category that cannot escape the contingency of its own historicity, what is its relational position within the hegemonic link? Is it one among many determinants, or is it, as a construct, primus inter pares, first among a number of equal determinants, such as gender, race, and sexuality? What is its hierarchical space within the arrangement of the historical bloc? While unpacking hegemony into a differential link, Laclau and Mouffe still hold on to the "collective will" in Gramsci. In other words, the explicit thematization of the relational specificity of the hegemonic link does not, as it does for Foucault, retire the notion of collective will. On the contrary, a politics of collective and relational difference, to Laclau and Mouffe, is predicated on the fact that "hegemony" alludes to "an absent totality." If "hegemony" is an allusion to an absent totality, and if furthermore there is no effective way of arbitrating among the elements that comprise the historical bloc, how will the bloc speak on its own behalf? Are we back to Foucault's apprehension that one element within the bloc will set the pace for all others and for the entire formation?

The concept of the historical bloc works quite complexly in Gramsci, and it is important not to simplify it. The bloc is the political expression of what I have called, in the context of the Rainbow Coalition, "difference in identity" and "identity in difference." The bloc functions both as a descriptive category and as a didactic/interventionary/organizational principle. As a descriptive category, it makes sure that our description of the social political field is adequate to the complexity of the field. It looks for multiple positionings and multiple determinations and multiple alliances rather than for a single unifying principle or essence, say, class in the context of orthodox Marxism. As Laclau and Mouffe have demonstrated, "hegemony" and the "historical bloc" have been responses to a crisis, namely, the fracture of the social sphere and the irruption of contingency within the category of "historical necessity."[43] In other words, any description of the world, after the failure of orthodox Marxism, has to thematize, within its own descriptive space, the contingency of its own categories. If we keep in mind that political (and in particular, Marxist) descriptions are not merely descriptions but are also predictive, interpretive statements that set the stage for a certain kind of transformation of society, then it turns out that political descriptions are accountable to history in very specific ways. The Marxian category of class thus predicts a certain kind of narrative and a certain kind of unpacking of world history; and if, in reality, this narrative does not work or is superseded by other forms of narrative (each with its own axiology), then it is time to let this particular narrative be historicized by its own failure and inadequacy. An honest Marxist then will not hold on to "class" as the only key to the essence of the historical process, but will rather look for alliances among other emerging categories such as gender, race, and sexuality. The failure to relativize class in light of multiple subject positions and determinations can only result in poor and inaccurate descriptions of the world. In other words, the "identity of the world" and the "identity of our model of the world" will have lost contact with each other.

The "bloc" as a concept is the description of a space and not of a thing or an essence. The bloc can only be made up of heterogeneous elements, but elements that seek common cause. In this sense, the formation of the bloc is the expression of a contradiction: on the one hand it announces the death of classical notions of identity, and on the other, it forges together a strategic identity effect that is the result or function of a constitutive relationality among the elements that comprise the bloc. The hegemonic articulation of the bloc (and here I am paraphrasing Laclau and Mouffe's theory as it covers and goes beyond Gramsci's praxis) is the possibility of a perennially political displacement. The emphasis, I must add, is both on "political" and "displacement": "political," insofar as the question of change and agency has to be posed strongly and programmatically, and "displacement," because in "our times," the political in itself is constituted by the shifting nature of subject positions in relation to one another. Given the "built-in-ness" of displacement, the hegemonic bloc is capable of responding to Foucault's valid critique. Yes, it is certainly possible that at any given world-historical conjuncture or its locally inflected conjuncture, a particular constituent of the bloc will play the dominant role or cast the trigger vote. But there is nothing to be alarmed about since (1) the trigger vote will be cast on behalf of the bloc with the consent of the bloc and (2) the structuration of the bloc is not a constant through history: the positions within the bloc will be in a state of constant change. Thus at a certain time, the black vote will be the trigger vote, while at another, this function may be performed by the feminist vote. The superiority of the hegemonic articulation lies in the fact that the dominant constituent (or constituents or even a subrelational alliance within the bloc) is made to be both itself and more (or less) than itself. In being the trigger vote, the dominant element is made to sacrifice some of its specificity (a sacrifice it can afford historically, that is, relative to a number of "even more minority" elements within the bloc) in the name of a wider and more inclusive commonality. In poststructuralist terms, the "other" is being perennially acknowledged "within" and "without." Extending Gramsci in a Bakhtinian direction, I would say that this constitutive exotopy of the field makes for a practice that is always undertaken in the name of the weakest (the most oppressed) element within the formation.

What Gramsci achieved with the conceptualization of hegemony may be likened to Althusser's formalization of structuralist Marxism. Both theorists returned to Marx and, in the very process of speaking for Marxism, articulated it as radical difference from itself. In developing, with the help of structuralism, a critical reading of *reading as such,* Althusser radicalized the orthodox macrology of Marxism toward relatively autonomous micrological processes without forfeiting the Marxist horizon. Gramsci, in his theory of hegemony, employs class specificity but only to discover that the nature of alliances transcends the category of class. "Class" is thus both preserved within the Marxist terrain and generalized beyond an exclusively Marxist determination. In a sense it is not all surprising that "class" becomes the basis for the political expression of *identity in difference and difference in identity.* For do we not have Marx describing "class" in the following way? "In so far as millions of families live under economic conditions of existence that cut off their mode of life, their interest, and their formation from those of the other classes and place them in inimical confrontation, they form a class," and insofar as "the identity of their interests fails to produce a feeling of communiy . . . they do not form a class."[44] The Gramscian themes of alliance and opposition are both adumbrated here. The emphasis on economic-corporative interests marks class in a certain specific way, but at the same time the motif of finding commonality across forced separation paves the way from economic and political alliances to moral-intellectual alliances. The insistence on transforming separateness into connectedness is both class specific and transcendent of class specificity.

The awareness that it is only by creating "common ground" from a seemingly "disparate" scenario that human beings effect their own hegemony is not the sole prerogative of class specificity. It is only by progressively deconstructing itself in the name of whatever has been suppressed within it that any specific model achieves hegemonic politicization. Thus, paradoxically, the generalization of an insight that is specific to a particular model (in this instance, class) results in the depriveleging of that very model. In other words, how can "class" (and analogously, Marxism) disallow to "gender" and to "sexuality" the sense of political agency that it had discovered for itself? Is "class" the trendsetter, or should "race" or "gender" take that place? These are indeed questions that need to be asked. But it seems to me that the more productive question is, How can we read each history or category in terms of the other? (Merely bemoaning the fact that Marxism has been the most recent global theory seems pointless and counterproductive. For one thing, we cannot change that fact, and second, there is much to be learned from Marxian revolutions—lessons that can be modified and questioned as they "travel" from one context to another.) My anticipation is toward a hegemonic future where "class" will be genderized, "race" discussed in terms of class, and so forth. While this would be taking place within the hegemonic formation, it is to be hoped that the hegemonic ensemble as the articulation of subaltern realities will be achieving a related but discontinuous effect on the "enemy," that is, the dominant formations. I am persuaded that this effect "without" should be one of the progressive subalternization of the dominant discourses. Is this a Gramscian vision? Yes and no: yes, insofar as Gramsci is always interested in critically generating a utopian future from present history; and no, insofar as Gramsci's historical need for a certain kind of affirmation and consolidation would not allow him to take on questions of the "post-" in their own right. My critical position is that there is great need to mix Gramsci in with Foucault: to cultivate and elaborate "postpolitical" practices but with reference to the reality of particular histories, and to thematize with increasing complexity the asymmetry of what it means to be global in these "our regional times."

Notes

1. For a significant discussion of regional and global structures, see Louis Althusser and Etienne Balibar, *Reading Capital*, trans. Ben Brewster (London: New Left Books, 1970).

2. "Jesse Jackson: Stuart Hall Interviews America's Leading Black Politician," *Marxism Today*, March 1986, 6.

3. Ibid., 7, 8.

4. Edward W. Said articulates this asymmetry between the colonizer and the colonized in his essay "Intellectuals in the Postcolonial World," *Salmagundi* 70–71 (Spring–Summer 1986): 44–81.

5. "Jesse Jackson," 8.

6. Ibid., 11.

7. Ibid.

8. See "Interview with Cornel West," in *Universal Abandon? The Politics of Postmodernism*, ed. Andrew Ross (Minneapolis: University of Minnesota Press, 1988), 268–86.

9. Michel Foucault, "Two Lectures," in *Power/Knowledge: Selected Interviews and Other Writings, 1972–77*, ed. Colin Gordon, trans. Colin Gordon, Leo Marshall, John Mepham, and Kate Soper (New York: Pantheon Random House, 1980), 81–82.

10. My use of the term "panoptic" is derived from Foucault's powerful critique of Bentham's Panopticon. I have also been influenced by the inclusively critical manner in which William V. Spanos uses this term to interrogate the "overlooking" capacities of dominant discourses.

11. Foucault, "Two Lectures," 81.

12. Ibid., 83, 85.

13. See "Intellectuals and Power," in Michel Foucault, *Language, Counter-Memory, Practice: Selected Essays and Interviews* (Ithaca, N.Y.: Cornell University Press, 1980), 206.

14. Ibid., 207–8.

15. Edward W. Said, "Foucault and the Imagination of Power," in *Foucault: A Critical Reader*, ed. David Couzens Hoy (Oxford: Blackwell, 1986), 153.

16. Gayatri Chakravorty Spivak, "Can the Subaltern Speak?" in *Marxism and the Interpretation of Culture*, ed. Cary Nelson and Lawrence Grossberg (Urbana: University of Illinois Press, 1988), 272.

17. Ibid., 275.

18. Ibid.

19. Ibid.

20. Foucault, "Theatrum Philosophicum," in *Language, Counter-Memory, Practice*, 185.

21. Ibid., 174–76.

22. Foucault, "Intellectuals and Power," 216.

23. Ibid., 212, 213.

24. See Ernesto Laclau and Chantal Mouffe, *Hegemony and Socialist Strategy: Towards a Radical Democratic Politics*, trans. Winston Moore and Paul Canmack (London: Verso, 1985), 105–44.

25. Ibid., 18, 19.

26. Barry Smart, "The Politics of Truth and the Problem of Hegemony," in *Foucault*, ed. Hoy, 158–59.

27. Ibid., 164.

28. Antonio Gramsci, "What Is Man?" in *The Modern Prince and Other Writings*, trans. Louis Marks (New York: International, 1959), 77.

29. Anne Showstack Sassoon, *Gramsci's Politics* (Minneapolis: University of Minnesota Press, 1988), 135.

30. Antonio Gramsci, "The Formation of Intellectuals," in *The Modern Prince and Other Writings*, 118.

31. Sassoon, *Gramsci's Politics*, 135, 136, 138.

32. Gramsci, "The Formation of Intellectuals," 121; Gramsci, *Selections from the Prison Notebooks*, trans. Quintin Hoare and Geoffrey Nowell Smith (New York: International, 1971), 6.

33. Sassoon, *Gramsci's Politics*, 139.

34. Ibid., 122.

35. Antonio Gramsci, "The Study of Philosophy," in *The Modern Prince and Other Writings*, 68.

36. Gramsci, "The Modern Prince," in *The Modern Prince and Other Writings*, 143.

37. Gramsci, "The Study of Philosophy," 67.

38. Sassoon, *Gramsci's Politics*, 117.

39. Gramsci, *Selections from the Prison Notebooks*, 81.

40. Ibid.

41. Laclau and Mouffe, *Hegemony*, 66.

42. Ibid., 66–67.

43. Ibid., 7–8.

44. Karl Marx, *Surveys from Exile*, trans. David Fernbach (New York: Vintage Books, 1974), 239.

3 / Ethnic Identity and Poststructuralist Differance

Ethnic "identity" and "differance": surely an untenable conjunction. Well, the purpose of this chapter is to suggest that such a conjunction is not only tenable, but also desirable and, in a sense, ineluctable. I also articulate the intersection of "ethnicity" with "difference" or "differance" and suggest ways in which this reciprocal "identification" can, on the one hand, historicize and situate the radical politics of "indeterminancy" while, on the other, situating the politics of empowerment as a transgression of the algorithm of "identity."

The constituency of "the ethnic" occupies quite literally a "pre-post"-erous space where it has to actualize, enfranchize, and empower its own "identity" and coextensively engage in the deconstruction of the very logic of "identity" and its binary and exclusionary politics. Failure to achieve this doubleness can only result in the formation of ethnicity as yet another "identical" and hegemonic structure. The difficult task is to achieve an axial connection between the historical-semantic specificity of "ethnicity" and the "posthistorical" politics of radical indeterminacy. A merely short-term affirmation of ethnicity certainly leads to a substitution of the "contents" of history but leaves untouched the very forms and structures in and through which historical and empirical contents are legitimated. On the other hand, an avant-gardist advocacy of "difference as such" overlooks the very possibilities of realizing, through a provisionally historical semantics, this "difference" as a worldly and consequential mode. I posit the notion of the "radical" or the "postethnic" as the moment that materializes the temporality of the "post-" as a double moment that is as

Ethnic Identity and Differance / 63

disruptive as it is inaugural. My elaboration of the "post-" also works itself through such historically determinate issues as Jesse Jackson's Rainbow Coalition in the context of binary (two-party) politics and the nature of the "intellectual-constituency" relationship. I conclude with the claim that poststructuralist politics will not allow us any kind of return to naive empiricism or historicism. What it does, instead, is to transform the very meaning of the term "political."

My title then represents my choice to conceptualize "ethnicity" through poststructuralism. Why such a choice? My reasons are that I believe it is possible to do the following: to generate through poststructuralism a "radical ethnicity" even as we legitimate "programmatic and short-term ethnicity"; to prevent the discussion of ethnicity from relapsing into such precritical modes as naive empiricism, naive historicism, and unselfreflexive praxis; and to disallow, in the process, the notion of theory as mastery and, instead, to enable an articulation of historically determinate and intentional, but nonauthoritarian, attitudes to "reality" and "knowledge." I hope this prefatory statement of intention makes it clear that my essay does not seek to effect the hierarchic subsumption of ethnicity under poststructuralism.

In a recent article on the situation of the black intellectual, Cornel West offers the following diagnosis:

> In addition to the general anti-intellectual tenor of American society, there is a deep distrust and suspicion of the black community toward black intellectuals. This distrust and suspicion stem not simply from the usually arrogant and haughty disposition of intellectuals toward ordinary folk, but, more importantly, from the widespread refusal of black intellectuals to remain, in some visible way, organically linked with Afro-American cultural life. The relatively high rates of exogamous marriage, the abandonment of black institutions, and the preoccupation with Euro-American intellectual products are often perceived by the black community as intentional efforts to escape the negative stigma of blackness or viewed as symptoms of self-hatred. And the minimal immediate impact of black intellectual activity on the black community and American society reinforces common perceptions of the impotence, even uselessness, of black intellectuals. In good American fashion, the black community lauds those black intellectuals who excel as *political Activists* and cultural artists; the life of the mind is viewed as neither possessing intrinsic virtues nor harboring emancipatory possibilities—solely short term political gain and social status.[1]

West goes on to draw some conclusions:

> And, to put it crudely, most black intellectuals tend to fall within the two camps created by this predicament: "successful" ones, distant from (and usually condescending toward) the black community, and "unsuccessful" ones, disdainful of the white intellectual world. But both camps remain marginal to the black com-

munity—dangling between two worlds with little or no black infrastructural bases. Therefore, the "successful" black intellectual capitulates, often uncritically, to the prevailing paradigms and research programmes of the white bourgeois academy, and the "unsuccessful" black intellectual remains encapsulated within the parochial discourses of Afro-American intellectual life. The alternatives of meretricious pseudo-cosmopolitanism and tendentious, cathartic provincialism loom large in the lives of black intellectuals. And the black community views both alternatives with distrust and disdain–and with good reason.[2]

The critical and theoretical unpacking of the many issues that West raises so brilliantly and perspectively in his piece will provide the momentum for my own reflections. Here, then, are the questions that I wish to generate and in some sense resolve during the course of my essay. What is the nature of "constituency" and how does it coimplicate the intellectual and the community? What are the connections between "representational" politics and the "organicity" of the intellectual/theoretical enterprise? Is the relationship of the ethnic intellectual to the ethnic community an isomorphic reproduction of the relationship that holds between the so-called "nonethnic" intellectual and her community? That is, does "organicity" have the same incidence in both cases? How generalized a category is or should ethnicity be in light of the demystified understanding that even the so-called "white" constituency has always been "ethnic?" What is the nature of the topos occupied by the intellectual and how is this space structurally coordinated, on the one hand, and determined, on the other, by semantic/historical specificity? And finally, what is the status of a specific "ethnic" intellectual, for example, the "black" intellectual within the "rainbow" of the "ethnic-in-general?" Is it exemplary? representative? of heuristic value? In other words, what bearing does the mode of self-empowerment of one ethnic constituency have on ethnicity as constituency, ethnicity as heterogeneity, that is, ethnicity as such?

Even if we grant the intellectual as theorist (for my purposes here, I am making an equational connection between the role of the intellectual and that of the theorist, an identification that might well need differentiation in another context) the credentials of being well-intentioned, the paradox still remains that whereas the intellectual perceives theory to be an effective intervention on behalf of ethnicity, the people, or masses, that are the constituency are deeply skeptical and even hostile to the agency of the theorist. The circumstantial reality of this problem forces open the occluded connection between theory and history and between theory and experience; that is, it argues for the "medial" function (as against the "autonomous function") of theory. Does theory then by definition operate preemptively both of history and of experience? If her commitment to theory is what renders the intellectual suspect and duplicitous in the perception of her constituency and if, furthermore, popular consciousness detects in theory an intrinsic drive toward mastery, dominance, and rarefaction that renders it amoral and apolitical, on the one hand, and disinterested and meritocratic, on the other, then surely the very historicity of theory needs to be examined and perhaps called into question. It is even conceivable that the very meaning of theory is to be transformed, revolutionized in the context of "ethnicity as emergence." The theory we are looking for may have to fulfill all of the following requirements: it must divest itself from economies of mastery and yet empower the "ethnic" contingently and historically; it must generate critical statements even as ethnicity is affirmed, endorsed, and legitimated; and it must be able to conceptualize the "postethnic" as a radical and necessary extension of the "ethnic."

How should theory express ethnicity, especially when its own history is at organic variance with the phenomenon of the "ethnic"? Does theory have a place in the ethnic program? One possible option is to assume that the historical experience of the ethnic as such is its own unmediated theory. Another option is to discredit the very notion of ethnicity as unmediated, as an experiential given, and, consequently, to accord theory the task of reading ethnicity as a sociopolitical-cultural construct caught up in the connectedness of its own history to prehistories and other histories. Or theory could engender itself as a metacritical mode with an avant-gardist momentum all its own that founds its own autonomous and autotelic discourse and, in the process, abdicates its referential commitment to history and experience. It is this last tendency in some versions of poststructuralist theory that is rightly perceived by political activists as self-serving and in the ultimate analysis as status quo politics. What is at stake here is the representative and representational connection between theory and constituency. Should the ethnic theorist be empowered to speak on behalf of the collectivity? To put it crudely, do the interests of the ethnic theorist, who teaches, publishes, and disseminates theory culturally and institutionally and academically, coincide with the interests of the collectivity? Does not the academic or institutional affiliation of the theorist always already dispose her toward a transethnic network? Is the theorist a friend or foe, a mercenary, an opportunist, or a supercilious patron?

I feel that even before we can begin to ask any of these questions, we need to come to grips with the very representational algorithm, historicize it, and make distinctions between modes of representation. Broadly speaking, there are two possible attitudes to representation: the axiomatic and the problematic. In the first instance, representation is reliable, and in the other it is suspect, organic, or poststructuralist. Here I wish to bring in two of the most consequential, adversarial theorists in recent history and pit them against each other—Antonio Gramsci and Michel Foucault. Right away we can see drastic differences: Gramsci wrote so much of his powerful theory while incarcerated, and he suffered and died in an Italian Fascist prison, whereas Foucault was one of the most privileged and overdetermined thinkers of his time, dominating the French scene along with such others as Jacques Lacan, Jacques Derrida, and Roland Barthes. I am not suggesting that Gramsci's life in itself authenticates his revolutionary theory, whereas Foucault as theorist stands to lose because of his academic and institutional legitimation. But I am saying that between the two models lies a world of difference: differences in historicity, nationalistic situation, and differences in what was at stake. Given these differences, Gramsci advocates the model of the organic intellectual, while Foucault rejects the very framework of representation.

For Foucault, nothing is more ignominious than being spoken for. He sees representation as disciplinary, panoptic, and coercively theoretical and, therefore, argues for struggles that can only be regional, singular, and nomadic. The best that an intellectual can do is to thematize her own marginality and not presume to speak for the other. And yet the fact is that, more than any other poststructuralist thinker, it was Foucault who tried to voice the "other" in project after project. How then does one valorize such works? Are these attempts progressive or are they merely symptomatic of the deficiencies of the empowered point of view from which they are undertaken? (We cannot but recall in passing here Derrida's critique of Foucault's representation of madness). If it is the case that the ethnic intellectual straddles two temporalities, the organically representational and the postrepresentational, then what can be expected from such a position? Let us now juxtapose two passages, one from Foucault and the other from Gramsci. First we will look at Foucault in the context of a published conversation with the French philosopher, Gilles Deleuze:

> In the most recent upheaval, the intellectual discovered that the masses no longer need him to gain knowledge: they *know* perfectly well, without illusion; they know far better than he and they are certainly capable of expressing themselves. But there exists a system of power which blocks, prohibits, and invalidates this discourse and this knowledge, a power not only found in the manifest authority of censorship, but one that profoundly and subtly penetrates an entire societal network. Intellectuals are themselves agents of this system of power—the idea of their responsibility for "consciousness" and discourse forms part of the system.[3]

Gramsci in his elaboration of the organic intellectual dispels the mythic status of the "traditional intellectual" and deconstructs the categorical distinction between the intellectual and the "nonintellectual":

All men are intellectuals, one could therefore say; but all men do not have the function of intellectuals in society. When we distinguish intellectuals and non-intellectuals we are in fact referring only to the immediate social function of the category of professional intellectuals, that is to say, we are taking account of the direction in which the greater part of the specific professional activity, whether in intellectual elaboration or in muscular-nervous effort, throws its weight. This means that, if we can speak of intellectuals, we cannot speak of non-intellectuals, because non-intellectuals do not exist.[4]

Earlier on in the same essay, "The Formation of Intellectuals," Gramsci demystifies the notion of the "true," ideal, and transcendent intellectuals who speak a nonspecific, nonperspectival truth. Such traditional intellectuals deny history and the many breaks in history, and they also naturalize their ideological investment in their own class, constituency, and so forth.

Gramsci is arguing for a situation where all human beings are intellectuals, a situation that provides a structural and ideological continuity between what I call the "general" intellectual and the "professional" or specific intellectual. What we are seeking here is a conjuncture where there is not only the availability of a sociopoliticocultural infrastructure but the continuous and homogeneous expression of this infrastructure in the professional superstructure, as well. It is significant that Cornel West, in his analysis of the contemporary black situation in the United States, identifies the increasing nonavailability of such a consistent infrastructure as one of the determining causes of the alienation of the black intellectual from the black constituency.

To paraphrase Gramsci further, the traditional intellectual inheres in a "timeless" and therefore prerevolutionary episteme and is inimical to revolutionary emergence. As the agent of a true and timeless order that claims to be culturally autonomous from specific modes of production, exchange, and elaboration, the traditional intellectual is a leveler, that is, she homogenizes, neutralizes, and defuses the circumstantial reality of oppositions and contestations for dominance and hegemony. The reality of the organic intellectual, on the contrary, is coeval and coextensive with the reality of the class to which she belongs. The locus of the intellectual is but a specific elaboration of the general intellectuality of the entire class or constituency. The professionalization of a few intellectuals does not result in the betrayal of their representative function.

However attractive and emancipatory Gramsci's analysis, two questions need to be raised: first, does "professionalization" in our contemporary context have the same meaning as it did for Gramsci? One of our problems in the postindustrialist information society is "professionalism" itself and with it the problem of "institutionality." (I am aware that here I am guilty of a totalization, for the third world represents a very different temporality where the reification of the "institutional" has not yet taken place. We could then say, following Gramsci's line of thought, that institutionality itself is specific to a certain society.) But in spite of this reservation, the value-free, self-serving logic of the institution, we must admit, has been one of the chief agents of depoliticization—to such an extent, indeed, that to say that someone or some philosophy has been "institutionalized" has come to mean an academic and not a political legitimation. What Gramsci could not have foreseen, then, is the extent to which the institution, the academy, the university, the government, and multinational corporate structures function across semantic and ideological territories, thus reducing the intellectual to a predetermined structural space within the microspace of the "institutional." The confidence that Gramsci exudes as he talks about the capacity of the intellectual to control intentionally the elaborations of her program sounds to me quite naive in its optimism when applied to the present context. My point here is that the present context has to include, but also go beyond, the Gramscian paradigm. The disciplinary apparatuses and the "microphysical" inscriptions of power, about which Foucault cautions the intellectuals, need to be taken seriously.

The second question that should be raised concerns the relationship of the organic intellectual to her own traditional prehistory and, analogously, the manner in which the "ethnic" intellectual is implicated in the "colorless" and, to many, the "colored" or preethnic past. The question of genealogy remains to be answered. Is there a pure and radical "break" between the two regimes? If the "ethnic" is the emergent mode, where is it emerging from? How does the "emergent" mode emerge countermnemonically (to use Foucault's telling concept) from the dominant and the hegemonic models? And crucially, how does the "ethnic" name itself? What kind of identity is asserted through this name? The problem here is as ethnic as it is theoretical and epistemological. "Naming," "identity," and the "self" already have a sedimented history of their own, and, therefore, it becomes crucial to ask how this present historical instance of "naming" repeats or recuperates the general economy of the "name." Is it possible or even politically feasible to isolate the protocol or the morphology of the present instance from the algorithmic logic of the general? It is true that the present historical context is anything but the semantic repetition of an earlier content, and yet it remains complicitous with the exclusionary logic of the "self." In an essay entitled, "I Yam What I Am: The Topos of Un(naming) in Afro-American Literature," Kimberly Benston emphasizes this very problematic of the "name" and the active interplay within the "name" of the negative and the affirmative:

Social and economic freedom—a truly new self—was incomplete if not authenticated by self-designation. The unnaming of the immediate past ("Hatcher's John," etc.) was reinforced by the insertion of a mysterious illness, a symbol of the long-unacknowledged, nascent selfhood that had survived and transcended slavery. On the other hand, the association with tropes of American heroism ("Lincoln," "Sherman," etc.) was also an act of naming, a staging of self in relation to a specific context of revolutionary affirmation.[5]

Having situated the sociopolitical and historicoeconomic specificity of the occasion of "naming" and "unnaming," Kimberly Benston "remembers" the theological and metaphysical origins of the impulse to "unname," that is, to be nameless, ineffable, and sublime:

> The refusal to be named invokes the power of the Sublime, a transcendent impulse to undo all categories, all metonymies, and reifications, and thrust the self beyond received patterns and relationships into a stance of unchallenged authority. In short, in its earliest manifestations the act of unnaming is a means of passing from one mode of representation to another, of breaking the rhetoric and "plot" of influence, of distinguishing the self from all else—including Eros, nature and community.[6]

But isn't this precisely the kind of ahistorical fundamentalism about which poststructuralist thought warns us? The program of naming and unnaming takes the following historically determinate steps (different phases of a developmental sequence): ethnic reality realizes that it has a "name," but this name is forced on it by the oppressor, that is, it is the victim of representation; it achieves a revolution against both the oppressor and the discourse of the oppressor and proceeds to unname itself through a process of inverse displacement; it gives itself a name, that is, represents itself from within its own point of view; and it ponders how best to legitimate and empower this new name. The last phase brings up a complex problem: the problem of the "second or 'meta-' order." I call it the problem of "in the name of." In whose name is this new name being authorized, authenticated, empowered? This appeal to an authority that "enables" but is extrinsic to the immediate or historical name betrays the desire for the absolute and the irrefragable self. The assumption that there exists an essence (African, Indian, feminine, natural, and so on) ironically perpetuates the same ahistoricism that was identified as the enemy during the negative and critical or "deconstructive" phase of the ethnic revolution. Doesn't all this sound somehow familiar: the defeat and overthrow of one sovereignty, the emergence and consolidation of an antithetical sovereignty, and the creation of a different, yet the same, repression? What the appeal to the "nameless" forgets is, first, that any emancipatory, emerging movement of the "self" carries with it a set of repressive mandates that are the obverse of the emancipatory directives, which is to say that the legitimate affirmation of any identity cannot but constitute in the long run another determinate alterity unless this very problematic is critically thematized in the very act of affirmation; and second, that the very immediacy of felt, lived, historical, and existential reality does not obviate the need for an analysis of the forms in which this reality is packaged, comprehended, accounted for, and judged. In other words, there is a place, and a necessary one at that, for a critical analysis of the morphology of historical content in conjunction with its real effects. Disregard of the mediated nature of these historical realities (and the consequent neglect of what Foucault calls the historical a priori that enables and conditions discursive possibilities, in other words, an a priori that in its very epistemic constitution of historicity denies history its primordiality as well as its plenitude) can only result in mystified assumptions about "freedom" and the propriety of the "revolutionary self."

But there is yet another problem: the attempt to shore up authority for the revolutionary self "namelessly" perpetrates a monologic ideologization, that is, the valorization of a "unitary" or "monothetic" revolutionary identity that is insensitive to what I term the "axial" or heterogeneous momentum of the revolutionary emergence—a point that is tellingly made by Medvedev and Bakhtin in *The Formal Method in Literary Scholarship*:

> For in the ideological horizon of any epoch and any social group there is not one, but several mutually contradictory truths, not one but several diverging ideological paths. When one chooses one of these truths as indisputable, when one chooses one of these paths as self-evident, he then writes a scholarly thesis, joins some movement, registers in some party. But even within the limits of a thesis, party, or belief, one is not able to "rest on his laurels." The course of ideological generation will present him with two new paths, two truths, and so on. The ideological horizon is constantly developing—as long as one does not get bogged down in some swamp. Such is the dialectic of real life.[7]

The error in monologic ideology is not just formal or theoretical. The fault lies in that it betrays and falsifies "the dialectic of real life." (I will not get into the problem of whether or not the dialectic inheres in reality.) The ideologization, in the name of an affirmative programmatic, of heterological, heteroglossic, and heterogeneous realities into a single, identical blueprint is just not in touch with lived reality. But this does not mean that lived realities can be expressed without formal mediation; such an assumption can only lead to mysticism or an immanent phenomenology. Realities are always mediated, but what needs radical transformation is the mode of mediation: from the "mono-" to the hetero-." I will be dealing with the problem of the politics of the "hetero-" a little later in my essay in the context of "axial temporality," a category that I claim has the capacity both to express the "heterogeneous" and at the same time to move toward legitimation and contingent empowerment.

The concern expressed by Medvedev and Bakhtin is not just academic, for some of our poststructuralist political and cultural anxieties fall within the problematic raised by them. A recent essay by Deborah E. McDowell on black feminist criticism makes a very similar diagnosis:

> Not only have Black women writers been "disenfranchised" from critical works by white women scholars on the "female tradition," but they have also been frequently excised from those on the Afro-American literary tradition by Black scholars, most of whom are males. For example, Robert Stepto's *From Behind the Veil: A Study of Afro-American Narrative* purports to be "a history . . . of the historical consciousness of an Afro-American art form—namely, the Afro-American written narrative." Yet, Black women writers are conspicuously absent from the table of contents.[8]

It is clear that the model of "identity" and its corollary, the representational algorithm, are inadequate when the realities, exclusions, and jeopardies that we are experiencing are, at the very least, multiple. To speak, then, unproblematically of a single black, feminist, or third world model of revolution is as repressive as it is naive. These emergences are pressing for a different language, a different politics and temporality, and an infinitely complex program of action that has to fulfill the following objectives: empowerment and enfranchisement of contingent "identities," the overthrow of the general hegemony of identity, and the prevention of the essentialization, hypostasis, and fetishization of "difference."

How then do we reconcile "short-term ethnicity" with "radical ethnicity," that is, "present ethnicity" with "postethnicity"? The two programs, while not antithetical ideologically, do seem discontinuous; they occupy different planes of resistance. What I recommend, then, is a critical interaction between poststructuralism, in particular the politicized practice of "difference" and the strategy of "countermnemonic" practice, and short-term ethnic activism. Such interaction, I believe, can point the way not merely to the achievement of imminent objectives but to the coordination and creation of a different historico-epistemic topos where heterogeneous realities (all of which have one structural similarity, that is, they have all been victims of "identical" representation) may be lived, expressed, and "legitimated" heterogeneously. This articulation cannot but be "double" (that is, in the sense in which Derrida talks about the "double session," which when politicized is not all that different from the

"Manichaean" episteme as invoked by Abdul JanMohamed),[9] insofar as it has to invoke two temporalities: that of oppression, memory, and enforced identity, and that of emergence after the "break," the countermemory, and heterogeneous difference. Emerging movements, then, straddle two historicities: that of the oppressor and that which is "their own," and besides, within their own "territory," these movements experience the structural synchronicity imposed by their common etiology and a "heterochrony" that is expressive of different historical densities and circumstantialities. Thus, feminism, postcolonialism, ethnicity, homosexuality, and lesbianism, to name just a few constituencies, are both singular and isomorphically irreducible multiple expressions. Both along a horizontal and a vertical axis, the identity of these movements is marked by "difference."[10] What is necessary, then, is a critical tactic that will call into question both the economy of identity and the axiology of binarity that underwrites the nomology of identity. To demonstrate this point, I choose two seemingly unconnected examples that on deeper reading turn out to be obverse expressions of the same intention: first, Jacques Derrida and second, Jesse Jackson's Rainbow Coalition politics.

When Derrida keeps insisting that the critic-activist has to make a "deep-structure" diagnosis and detect the logocentric (and its other versions, the phallogocentric, the photo- and the phonocentric, and in short the "centric" itself) imperative that undergirds even the most local oppression, he definitely steps beyond Gramscian notions of resistance. But precisely because he transcends the Gramscian problematic, he also overlooks what is significant within the Gramscian framework. Let me explain with the help of an ad hoc mock allegory. Imagine this scenario: vast crowds of people protesting apartheid with placards and slogans that read "Abolish apartheid" and "Down with Racism,"[11] and imagine also a "canonical" Derridean in the midst of this large group with a placard in her hand that reads, "Death to Binarity, End Logocentrism." It would be quite appropriate if everyone else looked at this person and the placard quizzically, even suspiciously, as if to ask, "Friend or Foe?" The politics of the placard is as unclear as it is indeterminate. The slogan rarefies the protest into a structural shibboleth. First I will raise the political objections to this slogan, and then I will construct the Derridean objection to these objections.

Even if it is the case that apartheid is, in the ultimate analysis, the expression of a more generalized malaise, that is, logocentrism and binarity, the slogan makes its point at a level of abstraction and generalization that is of no significance whatsoever. It is generalized to the point of tautologous emptiness; in other words, to say that apartheid is logocentrism is to say "nothing" at all, and besides, the very choice to represent and semanticize the significance of apartheid at a certain syntactic/structural remove that preempts the semantic/historical specificity of apartheid posits its own politics of a distantiated and Olympian wisdom that in turn becomes one with status quo politics exactly because it resists local, circumstantial, and historical identification. The Derridean would retort (and it is as amusing as it is frustrating that the anti-Derridean will find the Derridean apolitical on precisely those grounds on which the Derridean rests her case of political radicality) by saying that it is myopic to separate the politics of apartheid from the politics of logocentrism and that unless the mode of production known as "binarity" is confronted as such (for Derrida binarity and, in general, the structures of the past cannot be "stepped beyond"; they can only be turned against themselves for purposes of "revolution," in other words, there can be no pure "breaks" or ex nihilo formations that are organic with themselves),[12] we will be "always already" co-opted into the very regime that we are opposing (a fear that Gramsci, armed as he is with the notion of "organicity," does not take seriously—if anything, he might suggest quite the opposite competence, that is, competence of the "organic" to convert and transform the "traditional"). What is at stake here is the correctness of strategy locked within binarity: a syntactic strategy[13] as against a semantic strategy. But does it have to be one or the other? Can we not define the very topos of political struggle as the determinate tension between the syntactic and the semantic, the critical and the affirmative, the radically indeterminate and the intentionally determinate?

Now to my second example. My focus is on three aspects of Jackson's campaign for the Democratic nomination to run for president: "the Rainbow Coalition," the radicality of the slogan "our time has come," and the positionality of Jackson's politics within the binary space of the two-party system. I shall begin, then, with the last of the three areas, since that is immediately relevant to my critique of binarity. A critical point that Jesse Jackson kept making throughout the campaign was that his politics and his constituency would work with and work through the logic of the Democratic Party and its binarily constituted opposition to the Republican Party. This approach set Jackson's candidacy apart from that of Walter Mondale and Gary Hart, both of whom, in spite of many adventitious differences, were exemplary of the Democratic Party rhetoric. The singularities of their positions could be ideologically and hierarchically subsumed under the Democratic Party logic, which in its turn is determined by its binary relationship to the rationale of the Republican Party. Jackson's reality, in many ways, is not expressible within this binary space. He could only work with and within the more progressive of the two parties while at the same time interrogating and *not* fetishizing the identity of the Democratic

Party. The sociopolitical and historical reality of the cry "our time has come" and the strategy of the Rainbow Coalition can at best, by way of an opportune bricolage, make use of the institutionality known as the two-party system, but it cannot afford to be "identified" within the binary grid. Jackson's purpose was to transform the very nature of the Democratic Party from within, destabilize it from within so as to make it more sensitive to "interests" that lie outside its framework. One could say that Jackson's strategy vis-à-vis the party was that of the Derridean "double session." For after all, even within the Democratic Party, whose loyal and card-carrying member Jesse Jackson is, he was identified and found not genuinely representative because he was the spokesperson of "special interests," a term that is of "special interest" to the poststructuralist intellectual. If Jackson's interests are "special interests," the implication is that certain interests are "natural," "general," "representative," and ideologically neutral and value free. Corporate, military, business, male "white," nonethnic interests are general and representative to the point of being nonideological, objective, axiomatic, and even "disinterested," whereas the axis of constituencies represented by Jackson are distortions of political reality. Should we be surprised, then, that the Rainbow Coalition is in an eccentric and differential relationship to the authority of the Democratic Party and also to the space of binary politics? If "our time is to come" in its own way, then, the "rainbow-coalition" will have to situate itself subversively within the exigencies of binary politics.

All of this brings us to that continuum that collocates the theoretical with the political task, that of living, expressing, formalizing, and legitimating heterogeneity in a heterogeneous way. Another way of saying it would be to transform "our time has come" into "the time of 'our times have come'" or, better still, "our times have come." The two real dangers here are the cognitive and theoretical homogenization of the heterogeneous, and the celebration of heterogeneity as deliquescence, as nonpurposive and indeterminate. Again, we have to look for the answer in the determinate-indeterminate, in a historically contextualized application of the "double session." Before that, we need to make a thematic connection between the "ethnic" and the "heterogeneous," that is, if we are to take radical ethnicity seriously.

What the ethnic self, the nonself, has to contend with is the reality of its entrapment in multiple temporalities and histories. It has to empower itself as "identity" and, at the same time, realize its potential to be a site, the topos of a revolution that is also its own metarevolution. What do I mean by different histories and temporalities?

First, we have the history of the self, which is also obversely the history of the silence of the nonself. These two histories are synchronic and simultaneous,

Ethnic Identity and Differance / 75

and yet semantically they occupy different temporalities. But they are identical in a way since they are coimplicated, periodized, and historicized within the logic of binarity that founds both the self and the other. The relationship of the "self" to the "identity of binarity" and that of the "other" to this same "identity of binarity" opens up yet another threshold. Furthermore, there is the rarefied and "nomologized" identity of the very binary structure and its putative temporality that has a juridical hold over all the historical deployments of the "self" and the "other." In other words, we cannot but come to terms with the canonicity of the binary mode. The task for radical ethnicity is to thematize and subsequently problematize its entrapment within these binary elaborations with the intention of "stepping beyond" to find its own adequate language. My point here is that the emancipation of the "ethnic" from the "preethnic" is both semantically specific and an instance of the differential emergence of "difference" from the hegemonic grid of "identity." The politics of the ethnic becomes radical only when it is situated within the emergence of "difference." To suggest how crucial this is, I would like to quote from Foucault:

> Difference is transformed into that which must be specified within a concept, without overstepping its bounds. And yet above the species, we encounter the swarming of individualities. What is this boundless diversity, which eludes specification and remains outside the concept, if not the resurgence of repetition?[14]

Foucault's concern in this essay is not overtly political, but the consequences of his articulation are indeed deeply political. The attempt to enfranchise difference "differentially" is but another name for the politics of heterogeneity.

We must, of course, make clear distinctions between heterogeneity as bohemianism, anarchism, and political indifference and heterogeneity as political destiny. We must also distinguish between a categorical heterogeneity, that is, a heterogeneity construed by the homogeneous logic of the "category" and an acategorical heterogeneity that finds its "self-expression" through the breakdown of the "categorical." In its efforts to inaugurate its own kind of language, heterogeneity is bound to face two types of dangers, one from without and the other from within. First, the danger from without would take the form of heterogeneity considered as a lapsarian version of homogeneity (the danger that Foucault anticipates in the passage quoted earlier). Second, the danger from within would actualize itself in the ascendancy of one of the "heterogeneous" elements into a position of hegemonic dominance. This would result in acute contestations among different versions of heterogeneity, a total violation of the decentered and nonauthoritarian spirit of heterogeneity. To schematize this situation a little, we seem to have the following options: heterogeneity or difference as an expressive or phenomenological reality with no clearly articulated political strategy for survival; heterogeneity as a limited secession from the rhetoric of the "homogeneous"—that is, heterogeneity as expressively and experientially and historically disjunct from the norm of the homogeneous, but with its "official" reality to be constituted within the framework of centrist and representational articulation; or the celebration of heterogeneity as the pluralization of effective identities within the normativity of identity so that we will have as many offficial and empowered versions of heterogeneity as there are heterogeneous elements, for example, Jewish, black, feminist, and postcolonialist heterogeneities. My recommendation is that none of the above are adequate and that what we are in need of is the practice of "axial temporality."

There is nothing new about the idea of the axis; it is as old as political struggle. What is new, however, is the conceptualization of axial reality in opposition to identical reality. The valorization of the "axial" as an interrogation of the integrity of the "identical" initiates a countermnemonic break from the regime of a certain identical history. The dynamics of poststructuralist thought and the trajectory of radical ethnicity can be seen in the convergence at the point where "axis" replaces identity. Both radical ethnicity and poststructuralist reality warrant the space opened by the conceptualization of the "post-": the space after the "break" where radical ethnicity and poststructural discourse can come into their own, now that "representation" and "identity" have been prehistoricized. The politics of the "post-" may now enable the generous production of nonauthoritarian and nonterritorial·realities/knowledges whereby boundaries would be recognized and transcended and limitations accepted and transformed.

The strategy of "postpolitics" is double, that is, it conjoins in a relationship of complementarity the twin tasks of semanticizing the indeterminacy of the temporality of the "post-" and radicalizing the ethnic momentum beyond authoritarian closure. Having done this, my essay too will have come full circle, for we began with a brief reflection on the appropriateness of my title, and I will end with the reiteration that "theory" and "ethnicity" cannot and should not be conceived as antithetical modes.

The term "post-" has assumed substantive and autonomous significance in the poststructuralist context. I say "substantive" and "autonomous" since poststructuralist thought in many ways has liberated the prefix "post-" from its position of semantic heteronomy and enabled it as the "substance" of "difference" and "differance."[15] When we think of such coinages as postfeminism, postrepresentation, post-Marxism, postethnic, and so on, and think about them seriously, we realize that what is being proposed is a new and differential temporality: the deferred temporality of the "after." In the traditional understanding, the prefix "post-" is a relational and nonnominal term that occupies the nonspace between an anterior knowledge that has a "name" and a future knowledge that has as yet no name. The "post-" is the nondescription of an anomie that in the fullness of time, it is hoped, will acquire a proper name and with it a proper temporality, history, and periodic identity. The tacit philosophic assumption here is that periods, histories, phenomena, and names are characterized intrinsically by the potential for an ideal and identical development marked sequentially by a before and an after. With the advent of poststructuralist thought, the term "post-" has taken on an adversarial and phantasmal meaning,[16] whereby one always occupies a position of radical contingency in the wake of identity formation. In its very relational and differential disposition, the "time of the post-" makes perennial prehistories of grounded, authoritative time. The flow of the "post-" is hence the transformational and critical momentum of a certain way of knowing that is incompatible with knowledge as conservation.

The rhetoric of the "post-" indicates a kind of mercurial, theoretical progression that is constantly marking out new thresholds, frontiers, and boundaries, and in this very marking keeps crossing, traversing, and transcending these frontiers through a momentum that is irrepressibly indeterminate, nameless, and anomic. But it also represents the discovery of a temporality that deconstructs the authority of such structures as "genre," "period," "epoch," "episteme," "canonicity," and so on. Here again, there is the need to proceed with caution. The easy option is to submit to avant-gardism and remain indifferent to the pressures and urgencies of "fleshing out" the structures opened up by critical thought. The more difficult and the more meaningful choice is to mix this critical energy with the convictions and intentional commitments of affirmation. To restate this in the context of my entire presentation, if the "ethnic" were to remain purely ethnic it would still be trapped within the many larger and general economies of repression that I have been problematizing so far. The "postethnic," on the contrary, is the moment or the topos that dramatizes, I could almost say allegorizes, its own doubleness. As the radically ethnic, it is the last in an entire series of identity that, by virtue of choosing to be terminal in that series, inflicts fatality to the entire series and, in that very breath, inaugurates the time of the "after." The "ethnic" that is exemplary of "that which comes after" decelerates the logic of priority, primogeniture, primordiality, and so forth, and founds the timeless time of the "after" divorced from the temporality of the "before." In Derridean terms, "radical ethnicity" is that "dangerous supplement" that demonstrates that "it," namely "identity" (and the identity of authority as in "in the name of"), is pre-post-erous. The momentous undertaking that radical ethnicity is entrusted with is the creation of a future where oppression will not just be immoral or unconscionable, but virtually "unthinkable." The "time after," I hope, will be such a future.

Notes

1. Cornel West, "The Dilemma of the Black Intellectual," *Cultural Critique* 1 (Fall 1985): 112–13.

2. Ibid., 113.

3. Michel Foucault, "Intellectuals and Power," in *Language, Counter-Memory, Practice: Selected Essays and Interviews* (Ithaca, N.Y.: Cornell University Press, 1980), 205–17.

4. Antonio Gramsci, "The Formation of Intellectuals," in *The Modern Prince and Other Writings*, trans. Louis Marks (New York: International, 1957), 121.

5. Kimberly Benston, "I Yam What I Am: The Topos of Un(naming) in Afro-American Literature," *Black Literature and Literary Theory*, ed. Henry Louis Gates Jr. (New York: Methuen, 1984), 151–72.

6. Ibid., 153.

7. P. N. Medvedev and M. M. Bakhtin, *The Formal Method in Literary Scholarship*, trans. Albert J. Wehrle (Baltimore, Md.: Johns Hopkins University Press, 1978), 19–20.

8. Deborah E. McDowell, "New Directions for Black Feminist Criticism," in *The New Feminist Criticism*, ed. Elaine Showalter (New York: Pantheon Books, 1985), 187.

9. I am referring here to Abdul JanMohamed's groundbreaking work, *Manichean Aesthetics: The Politics of Literature in Colonial Africa* (Amherst, Mass.: University of Massachusetts Press, 1983), and his more recent piece, "The Economy of Manichean Allegory: The Function of Racial Difference in Colonialist Literature," Critical Inquiry 12, no. 1 (Autumn 1985): 59–87. I am not claiming that the Derridean "double session" and the category of the "Manichean" as developed by JanMohamed are identical or synonymous. But I am suggesting that the "doubleness" or the ambivalence that characterizes both structures can be used strategically in the context of the postcolonialist emergence and its attitude to its own prehistory.

10. I am thinking here of the many serious problems confronting the theoretical and practical formulation of the feminist programmatic. Third world feminists, for example, have been raising questions that they believe cannot be adequately dealt with if the feminist movement is privileged in the name of the white woman. The reality that identity is constituted along multiple axes (race, gender, nationality, sexual preference, and so on) makes any univocal or representative solution unacceptable.

11. Jacques Derrida, "Racism's Last Word," *Critical Inquiry* 12, no. 1 (Autumn 1985): 290–99, is a good example of the kind of strategy I am discussing here. While Derrida's discussion of racism in this essay is neither irrelevant nor lacking in political perspectivity, it is pitched at a level of theory and formalization that comes close to overlooking the historical specificity of apartheid. One gets the feeling that here was another pretext for Jacques Derrida to "instantiate" his gestural radicality, which is never inopportune but, by the same token, is never, so to speak, "right on." A much earlier piece of Derrida's, "The Ends of Man" (in *Margins of Philosophy*, trans. Alan Bass

[Chicago: University of Chicago Press, 1982], 109–36), displays the same rhetorical orientation. While being, in my evaluation, one of his brilliant deconstructive essays, "The Ends of Man" does only token justice to its occasionality, the U.S. involvement in Vietnam. Derrida makes it a point to refer to his critical attitude toward U.S. foreign policy, but does not develop it any further. This "gestural" or "citational" mode of invoking sociopolitical and historical reality and refusing to take it seriously, I maintain, itself needs to be historicized. I would also submit that in the context of apartheid, the Derridean gesture is at best effete, at worst seriously objectionable.

12. The term "organic," which to Gramsci represents a sociopolitical vitality, has come to mean, in the poststructuralist discourse, conservatism of the worst kind. Insofar as the term "organic" is complicitous with the logic of the "natural" and the primordial," it is construed by poststructuralists as ahistorical, but it may well have other connotations and cognate implications that are missed by the poststructuralist critique. The "organic" as *construct* may well represent the kind of collectivity and the consequent decenterings that are so central to the poststructuralist enterprise. The refusal to historicize the very genealogy of words that turn authoritative, I submit, often results in imprecise differentiations. Another concept in question is "theory" itself, for this word used totalizingly covers up the presence of different temporalities. Therefore, to be "for theory" or "against theory" does not really reveal much unless we also specify *what kind of theory*. Both Ronald Reagan and Michel Foucault are opponents of "theory," but surely they do not have the same kind of theory in mind.

13. Jacques Lacan's "allegory of the signifier," based on this reading of Edgar Allan Poe's "The Purloined Letter," proves its point by dealing with the letter syntactically, that is, without ever having to ascertain what the "semantics" or the "contents" of the letter might have been. I am in full support of this revolutionary way of accounting for meaning production insofar as it calls into question the metaphysical conspiracy of "meaning" as pure interiority. My critique of the Lacanian model, however, is that it entirely does away with "semantic" or "historical" significance. The insight that meaning is produced through a structural relay does not have to negate the possibility that these very structural or algebraic slots can be differentiated on the basis of the "contents" therein. Both the privileging of algebra and the detective imagination indicate a certain "disinterest" in historical and existential specificity. The detective, we know, is "interested" in crime in its capacity as "case"; for the detective imagination, the rarefaction of a story into the algebra of analysis is all that matters. Such an ascesis of interest in a very real sense prevents the production of a new knowledge. I believe I would not be too wrong in calling this state of affairs "the narcissism of the signifier."

14. Michel Foucault, "Theatrum Philosophicum", in *Language, Counter-Memory, Practice*, 182.

15. My reference here is to Jacques Derrida's virtuoso essay, "Differance," in *Speech and Phenomena*, trans. David B. Allison (Evanston: Northwestern University Press, 1973), where he coins the formation "differance" to suggest the radical, "unheard" (for the *a* in "diffe*r*ance" can only be seen and not heard), and nonconceptualizable play of "difference."

16. The term "phantasmal," initially for Deleuze and derivatively for Foucault, is symptomatic of an acategorical thinking that reproposes, in opposition to philosophic thought in its various guises, an entirely different orientation to time and thinking. Also relevant is the concept of the "meaning event" in Foucault.

4 / Culture as Common Ground: Ethnicity and Beyond

My purpose here is to consider the textual structure of race in the contemporary American context and the implication of this structure in the larger cultural field. When I say "textual structure," I wish to raise the following questions: What history is embodied in this structure? Who is the "subject/object" of such a text and what are the formal conventions that generate this text? Who reads and interprets this text and from what point of view? Given the ideology of race and its resurgence lately, what common interests and visions are being denied their sense of history, constituency, and self-representation? What are some of the ironies, inequities, and asymmetries that characterize the representation of race, and how does the mainstream ideology prolong a politico-cultural scenario where race is "willed" as a divisive and irreducible reality?

In isolating race as a determinant, I am not denying the reality that at any instance culture is multiply and heterogeneously determined. My perception is that in the American context, race, among the many determinants, plays a preeminent role. Race has indeed been coextensive with the very birth and consolidation of this country. Walter Benjamin's thesis that every document of civilization is equally a document of barbarism is particularly relevant to this new and revolutionary world,[1] whose very genesis and growth into international power has also been the narrative of racism and the willed production of a hierarchized "difference."

My examples for analysis will be both from the contemporary political scene (the Jackson campaign and the race to the White House) and from the academic formation known as critical or literary theory, which in its own way has been made to receive the ugly heritage of race. Following the lead provided by Jesse Jackson in the political field, I will be suggesting that the notion of "common ground" is of the utmost importance to cultural theory of ethnicity and postethnicity. A close reading of the Jackson campaign and the polemical rhetoric that constitutes the discourse on race (as seen in the 1986 special issue of *Critical Inquiry*, "Race, Writing, and Difference") warrants the conclusion that no common ground can be coordinated unless and until the ideology of difference (in this instance, hypostatized as race) is unmasked in all its historical specificity.

No sooner do we mention "race" than we are caught in a treacherous bind. To say "race" seems to imply that "race" is real; but it also means that differentiation by race is racist and unjustifiable on scientific, theoretical, moral, and political grounds. We find ourselves in a classic Nietzschean double bind: "race" has been the history of an untruth, of an untruth that unfortunately is our history. The truth of racism as a lie: that is what we need to unpack before we successfully put behind us the ugly and brutal regime of race. We are not yet in a historical situation where we can afford to say that race is not and has not been a determinant of culture, for racism is still too much with us, abiding in many forms. The challenge here is to generate, from such a past and a present, a future where race will have been put to rest forever. But meanwhile, we are trapped in a present where the color bar is still active. We are still committed to the task of demystifying and indicting the ideology of race and its brutality. The irony of the situation is that we have to deal with the reality of a world history that did not and could not preknow the enormity of racism. Indeed, the subject of history had to go through the story of racism in order to condemn that history. And indeed it is only appropriate that we should remember the barbarism of that history by way of forgetting it effectively. This commitment to the past is both mnemonic and countermnemonic.[2] And this is not all; there is a further complication, and a very important one at that. This history of racism is not a unified or unifiable history, for it has already established the reality of the color line. Just as in history in general there is the narrative of the victors and that of the vanquished, so, too, in the history of racism there is the subject position of the perpetrators and that of the victims of racism. Although a common temporality structurally subtends both histories, there is an irreducible asymmetry in the positionality of the two subjects. This continues to be true even after more than two decades of civil rights activism that has enlisted both white and black. We are still too close to racism and apartheid to be able to generalize the specific charge of the fight against racism. To put it simply, affirmative action is and should be valid.

The status of the discourse on "race" in the United States today has a double base: (1) the generalizable and universal authority of antiracism that finds a home in every individual and (2) the political and polemically specific authority of the same cause as it applies, at this particular historical juncture, exclusively to those populations that have been the objects and victims of racism. The recent campaign by the Reverend Jesse Jackson and the treatment meted out to him by the media and by some of his fellow Democratic candidates offer important insights into the subliminal mechanism of "race" and its hold over the American psyche. The fundamental difficulty the "other" candidates had (some more than others) was in identifying Jackson. What were they supposed to do with his "blackness"? Did his "blackness" make him different? What was that "difference" all about? Could they name that "difference" without running the risk of being called racists? Could they speak for him? Should they take him on as just a fellow American seeking office? On the one hand, there was the fallacy of treating him as no "different" from themselves, and on the other, there was the folly of treating him so separately as to preclude all ideological contact with him. One could not but notice that there was a deep-seated paranoia about the way the white hegemonic formation (and this has nothing to do with individuals and their choices) was dealing with Jackson's "difference" and "alterity." It was "white fright." To deal with Jackson in real-historical terms would amount to accepting and legitimating his agenda as both specific and general. Unable to take this historic step, the white hegemonic formation ghettoized Jackson's candidacy and made sure that the so-called "mainstream" could continue "business as usual."

Was "race" an issue, and who made it an issue? The press for its part was utterly paralyzed by its own duplicitous and circular logic. By posing the question "What does Jesse want?" it reconfirmed its racism; for this question was not asked of any of the other candidates. Somehow, what *they* wanted was natural, wantable, and quite self-evident. At the initial stages, the question was intended to confer unreality on Jackson's candidacy. But unfortunately for the press, the candidacy gained ground and the Rainbow Coalition won a number of substantive victories. The numbers swelled and the momentum was unmistakable. But the question persisted, only this time around, the press had learned to propagate the myth and the charisma of Jackson. The press, in acknowledging and reporting the surge of the Jackson campaign, had literally made it "incredible." This was not real: there was too much passion, too much committed and poignant rhetoric, excessive idealism, and an unrelenting focus on issues, ideas, and principles. It was all getting more and more "unreal." The press was talking about the spectacular Jackson phenomenon as though one were talking about a comet or a meteor streaking through the sky, leaving us in shock, disbelief, even wonder. Crippled and framed by its own self-fulfilling prophecy, the press was doomed to misread the campaign. All it did was to deny Jackson's campaign a sense of history and duration, while it reported circumstantially the nonevents and nonstatements made by the other candidates.

The irony in the case of the candidates themselves was even more amusing, as amusing as it was illuminating. As far as Jackson was concerned, race was not and could not be an issue, that is, from where he stood in relation to the color line. But "white fright" was trapped in the reality of its own making, namely, the illusion of race. Thus, time and again, one could see the candidates having difficulty in thinking of Jackson as American and black within the same thought. It had to be one or the other: if American, the race question became an untenable and unpalatable special interest issue; if black, then there was difficulty in factoring that into the "mainstream." As a result, many of the candidates went out of their way to handle Jackson with kid gloves or chose not to deal with him. The point that they missed was that the coalition was "different" and that this "difference" was not taking place elsewhere, that is, where the mainstream did not flow. The reality of the coalition was in fact "the difference within identity," "the other within the Self." If anything, it was Jackson's claim that his coalition was more broad-based and representative than the putative mainstream. What was particularly revealing was that while Jackson was not foregrounding the race issue, the mainstream candidates were obsessed with race. In all this, the fact that Jackson was seeking "common ground" went virtually unnoticed. It was unthinkable that Jackson could want anything real or that the Rainbow Coalition could have a very different but real political vision.

The heart of the matter is that the white hegemonic formation is so used to naturalizing and universalizing its own perspective as the mainstream that it cannot conceive of other ways of achieving common ground. The hegemonic mainstream cannot but consider itself the only center of all activity. It also assumes that any kind of politicization has to take place in its terms. Therefore, when confronted with the Jackson coalition, the hegemonic mindset either insisted that the coalition was too far off center to be politically viable or it demanded that the politicization of the coalition take the form of incorporation by the mainstream. One of the more arrogant mainstream analyses was that the coalition needed the Democratic Party mainstream, the implication being that the party did not need the support of the coalition. This vehement and insolent denial of reciprocity is but the surface expression of a deep-structure phobia of oppressed subject positions. That a coalition made up of blacks, Hispanics,

Chicanos, immigrants of various color, feminists, civil rights activists, left-wing intellectuals, lesbians, gays, and several others who have experienced the pain and the hurt could be politically viable was a nightmarish thought to the dominant mainstream. In short, the mainstream found the coalition quite unintelligible.

The broad thesis that I am trying to outline is that race has been essentialized as a basic form of alterity. By this strategy, the white hegemonic formation contains the intelligibility of "colored culture." To quote from Henry Louis Gates Jr.:

> Race has become a trope of ultimate, irreducible difference between cultures, linguistic groups, or adherents of specific belief systems which more often than not also have fundamentally opposed economic interests. Race is the ultimate trope of difference because it is so very arbitrary in its application. The biological criteria used to determine "difference" in sex simply do not hold when applied to "race." Yet we carelessly use language in such a way as to will this sense of natural difference into our formulations. To do so is to engage in a pernicious act of language, one which exacerbates the complex problem of cultural or ethnic difference, rather than to assuage it or redress it. This is especially the case at a time when, once again, racism has become fashionable.[3]

Gates's point is well taken. Patterns of identity and difference, selfhood and alterity are always historically produced in a world where different histories respond to and acknowledge the reality of one another. And any acknowledgment of another's reality necessarily involves the acknowledgment of "the self in the other" and "the other in the self." Neither identity nor difference, neither self nor other is an immutable state of being: the two are necessarily inmixed. This was a point that Jackson made quite memorably in his speech at the Democratic convention when he declared that although Dukakis and he had reached the United States on "different" boats, they were now in the "same" boat. With telling rhetoric he pointed out that although the two are bearers of different histories, they are now faced with the task of envisioning the same and common history. Jackson's political wisdom lay in the fact that he stressed "difference" and "identity" within the same field so that they may deal with and influence each other He did not privatize either (there was no separatism here), and he did not resort to a binary language of opposition. Instead, he was seeking common ground on the basis of "difference in identity" and "identity in difference." For there is nothing to be gained in essentializing either or in establishing a hierarchic order whereby one is made more natural than the other.

The anomalies and ironies that surround the discourse of "race" have to do with the issue of "representation." As I have stated already, by way of Gates, "race" has been essentialized as a fundamental form of Otherness. The direct and pernicious effect is that questions of history remain unasked. The pathological preoccupation with "race" precludes a critical appreciation of the histories of different cultures and ethnicities. As Edward Said has pointed out over and over again, in formulating real differences in history as an essentialized Other, the dominant ideology denies those different subject positions their histories and their perspectival productions of their own agendas.[4] In the case of the Jackson campaign, the dominant ideology vigorously denied the basic reality that what any group envisions depends on "where it comes from." The reality that the Rainbow Coalition had achieved something truly revolutionary—that is, for the first time in American history it had put together a constituency that was truly heterogeneous and deserving of this "nation of nations," this "immigrant melting pot"—went unacknowledged by the dominant ideology. The coalition was being denied "representation" in both senses of the term—*Vertreten* and *Darstellen* (and here I draw on the brilliant critique of Deleuze and Foucault by Gayatri Spivak in her essay, "Can the Subaltern Speak?").[5] First, the coalition was being denied its "representation" of the world, that is, its cognitive-epistemological view of the world, and second, it was being denied its ability and its right to "represent" or speak for itself (the political denial).

The paranoid structure of the dominant ideology kept consistently missing the point that the Jackson coalition had indeed succeeded in bringing the two senses of "representation" together. The coalition was re-presenting (*Darstellen*) to itself its own coherent vision of the world, and it was also effectively taking responsibility to represent (*Vertreten*) itself politically. A certain worldview and a sense of agency appropriate and "organic" to that worldview had fused together momentously.[6] To put this in overtly Marxist terms, millions of people who "live under economic conditions of existence that cut off their mode of life, their interest, and their formation from those of the other classes and place them in inimical confrontation"[7] had succeeded in preserving and canceling their mutual differences in the name of a common goal. While all of this transformative experience was going on, it was both galling and amusing to watch the other candidates wrestling with utterly trivial notions of "representation." We had both Dukakis and Bentsen flaunting their polyglot abilities, as though the ability to speak Spanish or Greek in itself confers on the candidate an authentic ethnicity. The tacit assumption here seemed to be that "ethnicity" is a role or a costume that could be put on as a matter of theatrical performance, that is, that a sense of constituency could be proxied from the outside by a person whose "interests" do not actually coincide with those of the constituency. It was painfully ironic that the mainstream did not pause to think that the victory of the coalition would have resulted in the formation of a government where every color of the rainbow would be representing itself both in relative autonomy and in response to the pulls and tugs of the other colors within the spectrum.

There are a number of examples from contemporary America that testify to the resurgence of racism, and I will limit myself to just two. A recent report from the Boston Police Department says that a number of applicants to the department had faked their racial or ethnic backgrounds so that they could get jobs. This seems to suggest that histories and ethnicities can be easily assumed and that somehow being a member of the oppressed groups is a source of tremendous advantage. We can sense right away that the thesis lurking behind this perception is the outrageously nonsensical thesis of "reverse discrimination," which, in isolating individual instances from their historical background and conditioning, would have us believe that blacks and women and minorities in general are somehow hogging the pie. (The film *Tootsie,* for example, misrepresents women vis-à-vis the employment crisis and goes on to argue that men are the victims.) My second example is from the field of sports, where blacks have long been abused, misrepresented, and dehistoricized by the use of stereotypes. A recent controversy concerning the Detroit Pistons basketball superstar Isiah Thomas, who had said that if Larry Bird, the Boston Celtics superstar, had been black he would have been considered an ordinary player, received racist coverage in television. Here, too, a whole history of oppression, discrimination, and stereotyping in which, time and again, sportscasters could talk with impunity about the "physical, instinctual athleticism" of black athletes was completely forgotten so that a single incident could be covered in isolation. Even this single incident was not placed within a narrative; had even this local narrative been provided the entire sequence of events would have revealed a different truth. The result of it all was that Thomas the black athlete was close to being publicly arraigned on national television as racist, and the television interviewer held an inquisition on him. The denouement contrived by the TV scenario was that Thomas in the end (his charming personality was factored into this, as was his friendship with Bird) had exonerated himself, and Larry Bird with great magnanimity had forgiven and forgotten the incident. It certainly looks as if there can be no end or limit to the extent to which the ideology of race can mystify itself.

It is not surprising at all that this "accusation of reverse racism" also found a place in the pages of the learned journal *Critical Inquiry*.[8] I refer here to Todorov's reading of Gates and Gates's response to it. Todorov's contention is that Gates's belief that "we must turn to the black tradition to develop theories of criticism indigenous to our literatures" is "reverse-racialist" in its exclusivity. This attack, as Gates demonstrates correctly in his response, is disingenuous, for "Todorov attempts nothing less than a neocolonial recuperation of the sense of difference upon which a truly new criticism of world literature must be granted."[9] Not only does Todorov get rid of the historically necessary distinction between "representations from within" and violent representations that are applied from "the outside"—that is, Todorov all too easily allegorizes history—but he also glibly exonerates the universalist ideology of race that has for so long served the interests of white perspectivity. As we read that special issue of *Critical Inquiry* critically, we find ourselves wondering if all the contributors are on the same wavelength at all. Are they all citizens of the same world, and are they all mutually intelligible? Again, it is revealing that the theorists who seek "common ground" are the "oppressed theorists," whereas the deconstructing theorists from the dominant formation tend to fetishize and reify "difference."

As I switch now to the epistemological meaning of "re-presentation" (*Darstellen*) and apply it to the debates and discussions that occurred in two or more issues of *Critical Inquiry*, I find that what is at stake is the very "intelligibility" of the world and of culture. Although different cultures may be different expressions and instantiations of "intelligibility," can and should we not make the hypothesis that the "condition of intelligibility" subtends all reality?[10] Is it not possible to "inmix" (in a Bakhtinian sense, whereby even in a milieu of heterology and heteroglossia each "subject" respects and "acknowledges" the "subject" in the "other" and in the process "others" itself from "its-self") this commonality or universality or worldliness with the respect for "otherness," "heterogeneity," and "difference"?[11] From the point of view of cultural studies, an important lesson is to be learned here (especially when we consider how cultural studies does and should lead into cross-, multi-, and intercultural studies): there is nothing to be gained by freezing or exoticizing "alterity" and "difference" into a mystique. It has become the obsession of the dominant cultural paradigm to insist that "difference" somehow remain "different," transcendent in its alienness. And here lies the asymmetry: whereas the victims of otherness are creating and producing diverse and heterogeneous subjectivities eager to assume "common ground," the dominant structure, or formation, comes up with a grand and totalized theory of alterity, or difference. Alterity thus becomes a source of transcendent and ineffable wisdom, and "pockets of difference and otherness" are constrained to prolong their difference and marginality. As Hélène Cixous puts it, the master paradigm is adept at "building monuments to lack" and mandating that this "ontologized lack" function as a remedy or anodyne for the painful neurosis that ails the master paradigm.[12] In other words, in the very project of producing "otherness," the dominant paradigm (or the master code) dehistoricizes it within the "sameness" of the dominant identity. These pockets of difference are maintained as the untouched health resorts where the ailing dominant identity may revive itself endlessly. This attitude is "neurotic" because it refuses to deal with the historical reality of those different alterior constituencies. Business goes on as usual, and the dominant ideology succeeds in protecting itself from the repercussions of whatever is happening elsewhere. Todorov can assume that his framework will not have to negotiate with some of the important consequences of Gates's delving into his tradition; that is, we can continue to read Conrad as though Soyinka and Achebe do not exist and have not commented on Conrad. But I think the joke is on the dominant ideology, for the chances are that readers of Soyinka and Achebe will have read Conrad, but the converse does not hold true.

A corollary and a variation of this neurosis is the tendency of the dominant ideology to expect that the marginal constituencies make mysterious sense within their respective ghettos. This, as I have pointed out already, is a ruthless denial of world-historical possibilities of intelligibility. It is also an excuse not to read, not to take seriously, not to want to understand, and not to face the change represented by these alien texts. Deep down, the hegemonic consciousness is aware that taking these other texts seriously constitutes a threat to its own continued dominance. The defense mechanism is to say, "That is not my business or constituency." Of course, it is quite typical of the dominant ideology to demonstrate elaborate sophistication in its abnegation of its responsibility. I will just mention one particular instance of the speciously generous behavior of the dominant ideology. It always asks the marginal formation to produce a complete and universal theory of its own—a demand that provokes an understandably indignant response from Barbara Christian. I will quote here from Barbara Christian's essay "The Race for Theory," which historicizes the fad for theory, and it is not coincidental that Christian makes use of "race" in its double sense. Says Christian, as a black feminist critic:

> Some of us are continually harassed to invent whole-sale theories regardless of the complexity of the literature we study. I, for one, am tired of being asked to produce a black feminist literary theory as if I were a mechanical man. For I believe such a theory is prescriptive—it ought to have some relationship to practice. Since I can count on one hand the number of people attempting to be black feminist literary critics in the world today, I consider it presumptuous of me to invent a theory of how we ought to read.[13]

Christian's response identifies the paranoia of the dominant ideology, which thinks it has the right to demand of the marginal groups that they produce, reactively, a totalized theory that will in fact dehistoricize their complex and heterogeneous sense of history or histories.

In stark contrast to such a neurotic-paranoid view of the world, we have the transformative generosity of a Jackson who seeks "common ground" and common enfranchisement: not a fixed or static common ground but an ever-changing and critically self-reflexive common ground where the different patches within the quilt will have the ability and the opportunity to historicize and dignify one another. And, to add what I think is implicit in Jackson's rhetoric, there is also the need to look into what is "not common." This relationship of the "common" to the "not common" has to be constantly negotiated and renegotiated and not allowed to degenerate into a transcendent form of antagonism. And finally, there is also the imperative, in a world flawed by unequal development and unequal enjoyment of resources, that certain issues had better be "common" (or else we won't survive). The appeal to "common ground" is both an invitation and a commitment to responsibility whereby we might all "as subjects" honor and fight "for the other in us."

Self-other, identity-difference, majority-minority, mainstream-special interests, us-them, integration-separatism: these are some of the issues that we are talking about here. As I have already argued, while the emerging and hitherto oppressed constituencies are envisioning a "common world," the dominant structure is deeply invested in the preservation of binary oppositions. It is in this context that the term "ethnicity" takes on great political and epistemological significance. I would like to consider two uses of the term "ethnic" as designated from the point of view of the dominant culture before I proceed to a substantive unpacking of "ethnicity."

One of the unvarying features of the American supermarket is an aisle labeled "Ethnic Foods." This taxonomy establishes an island of singular difference within an overarching and self-same identity. A number of questions arise immediately: What *isn't* ethnic food? What, by definition, is nonethnic? What is the ideology or point of view that finds it convenient to use "ethnic" as a category of description and evaluation? The definitive and taxonomic use of the term "ethnic" suggests that certain foods are so mainstream as to be natural, transparent, and invisible—that is, these foods are in no need of being "marked"—whereas certain other foods are marginal, partial, exotic, and in need of being "marked" as different. These "ethnic items" bear as a mark of their identity the label of difference that is foisted on them by the dominant culture. To state it simply, no Chinese or Mexican-American would describe her food as "ethnic."

My second example is overtly political, and I am referring to the almost automatic use of the phrase "ethnic violence." This phrase implies that there is a built-in connection between ethnicity and violence. It is as though the term "ethnic violence" were a lexical constant within a universal dictionary. Given the national identity at the present time (a potentially multicolored, multi-ethnic rainbow identity that has been violently ideologized into a normative male, white, heterosexual identity), the term "ethnic" as articulated from the dominant perspective designates an absolute form of racial otherness. In other words, "ethnicity" that is multiple and historically produced is dehistoricized and posited as something alien, dangerous, criminal, violent, and spontaneously and instinctually terroristic. In effecting this rhetorical connection, the mainstream ideology conceals the reality that the "mainstream" itself is constituted ethnically but has been nationalized and generalized now to the point of absolute ideological dominance. The so-called mainstream thus disallows to other ethnicities the very same political and representational rights and privileges that made "the mainstream" possible in the first place. Also, in its totalized use of the term "ethnic," the dominant point of view lumps together different histories and constituencies, each of which has a history of its own. "Ethnicity" thus operates for the dominant ideology as a way of not dealing with a whole range of "minority" groups and discourses.

We also notice that the "ethnic" is ensnared within a circular logic that condemns it to "irrationality" and "violence." From the mainstream perspective, the "ethnic" by definition is that category that has not been successfully factored into the national equation and is therefore alien or eccentric to it. It is a threat to national identity but, since it is a threat, it has to be quelled as a form of violence or criminality. At any rate, it is not to be read as a political expression of genuine interests. Thus, "ethnicity" is maintained by the paranoia of the dominant culture as eternally illicit, transgressive, and lawless. It is sufficient to point out that no "white violence" is ever easily characterized as "ethnic," for "white" has achieved the status of a "noncolor" and a generality that is transcendent of special interests. Yet another connotation of the phrase "ethnic violence" is that it is a special kind of violence, with a singular and different phenomenology of its own, somehow removed from common and universal patterns of intelligibility—a point that I have made earlier, in the context of Jackson's campaign. Certain ethnicities are precluded from contributing to and transforming the existent national equation. It is not coincidental that Jesse Jackson has suggested that blacks in the United States identify themselves as "African-Americans." Jackson's recommendation acknowledges the multiple nature of identity and the negotiated nature of all collective identities. The purpose of ethnic identity is to be recognized and valorized as ethnic and at the same time to be empowered and legitimated as a national identity. The term "African-American" indicates a triple empowerment: (1) It is an empowerment of ethnicity and rootedness insofar as the blacks trace their roots back to Africa; (2) it empowers blacks as Americans within the national context; and (3) it enables their American identity as African-American, that is, in being Americans, their specific ethnicity will not be falsely represented, spoken for, or proxied, especially in a situation where white ethnicities (given the ideology of racism) are in the privileged position of being able to naturalize national identity in their terms. Here again, Jackson's message has been the celebration of identity in difference and difference in identity: an identity that will not be foreclosed ideologically and a difference that refuses to be disempowered.

It is interesting to see that a number of "white ethnic" and "white pride" movements have emerged of late; these movements are all informed by a deep-seated racism, the most notably racist of these being the Skinheads. Whereas the discourse of ethnicity developed by the minority groups embraces a common human vision, the neo-Nazi and the neo-KKK expressions of ethnicity express a deep-seated paranoia. These movements project a fear of "white vulnerability" that has no objective correlative in actual history. White pride of this sort is at odds with other ethnicities, and it demands that white be back at the center or that the very identity of the United States be seen to correspond with "being white."

It seems to me then that the historical expression of ethnicity can take one of two paths: that of an extreme individualism and separatism that pits one ethnicity against another, or that of a post- and transethnic collectivism whose objective is an ever-expanding coalition that insists on the need to honor both the irreducible specificity of the ethnic and a connectedness that goes beyond the absolutism of purely local ethnicities. In my terms, coalitional politics operates in the space between ethnicity and postethnicity, between a representational and a postrepresentational epistemology.

No sooner do we say "postethnic" than legitimate fears creep in about the kind of theory that we should employ in historicizing ethnicity. The term "post-" carries with it connotations of a glib and theoretical avant-gardism that thinks nothing of the dangers of deracination. How could any theory be "post-anything" and still serve a specific constituency? Aren't theories of the "post-" incapable of engaging in identity politics? Aren't these modes of thought examples of a hovering and unsituated intellectualism that uses theory to unify, generalize, and ultimately get rid of historical differentiations, markers, and thresholds? Does not the theory of the "post-" (with its strong European formation) eventually operate as a mercenary mode that overlooks the value as well as the necessity of historical commitments? Don't we all too often come across "theorists" who in teaching "pure theory" (whatever that may mean) disaffiliate themselves from the actualities of particular literatures and cultural formations and thereby perpetuate the universalism that has been practiced by the dominant ideology, whether it be white, Western European, male, or heterosexual? Aren't such theorists traitors, in Julien Benda's sense of the term,[14] or traditional intellectuals, in Gramsci's sense of the term?[15] I think that these apprehensions are both timely and relevant. In pointing up the crisis between theory and ethnicity or, for that matter, any sense of constituency, these fears in fact thematize some of our very basic anxieties about the modality called "theory." What I offer in conclusion is an articulation of a certain kind of theory with the historical density of experiences such as ethnicity. It seems to me that a certain kind of theorizing is inimical to history, but that does not invalidate all theory. It all depends on what theory is.

The purpose of theory is "to make us see" connections, homologies, similarities, and isomorphisms among disconnected and disparate realities. It helps us realize often that the local as an instance of the global can be changed by realignments at the regional level. In this sense then, the capacity of theory to generalize and travel[16] among constituencies can have a positive and progressive impact on the constituencies themselves, each of which is enabled to look beyond its immediate area or zone. The problem then seems to be not with globality per se (for we are all globally connected, and no one political agenda can be evaluated without reference to other agendas that are simultaneous with it), but rather with the manner in which theory produces a reading of globality, that is, of a common ground or world. The kind of theory that is rightfully and rightly attacked by ethnic scholars is one that universalizes and generalizes in bad faith—it accepts, receives, and repeats the "given" version of the world picture. Such a picture is falsely universal since it is the exclusive expression of the dominant point of view that, in speaking for all humanity, denies its own ideological perspectivity and ends up with an oppressive and repressive totality that does not reflect the interests of all the components that make up that totality. For too long a time, theory has been the executor of such a colonialist and imperialist will.

But theory can work very differently. It can demystify the claims of the status quo and work toward a very different organization of the many regional spaces that constitute the "total picture." It is this kind of theory that I advocate: a theory that inmixes the politics of particular formations or subject positions with the global connectedness of each position to every other position. Such a theory is particularly appropriate in the context of ethnicity, which, on the one hand, is universal—insofar as there is no cultural reality that is not subtended by ethnicity (there is nothing called the "nonethnic")—and is, on the other hand, the phenomenological and historical expression of a particular group experience from within its locus. Thus, ethnicity as such is common to all realities—African-American, Chicano, Ojibway, Jewish, Swedish-American, Japanese-American, and so forth—yet each "named" ethnicity bears the right to call itself into history in its own terms. The theory that we require is nonobjectifying and connecting theory that in honoring "subjectivity" will honor the "subject" in each group or constituency.

In this connection I wish to make a distinction between a postrepresentational cultural politics that breaks completely away from representational modes and one that recapitulates and builds on the representational mode; it is the latter that I advocate. Such a politics, while building on the gains of a representational or identity politics, progresses toward a more inclusive and general politicization that does not make a fetish of inside/outside and us/them distinctions. It is only natural that the ethnic anticipate the trans- and the postethnic, for, if we follow Bakhtin, is it not true that any identity such as ethnicity is already "internally dialogized"?[17] This built-in "internal dialogism" within any given constituency or identity (and the active acknowledgment of this dialogism) opens up a different worldly space where the "purity" of a particular group's sense of home does not exile another.

The historical bonding between such a theory and ethnicity is to make possible a generous but critical articulation between a purely local sense of ethnicity and a common and global heritage within a shared and simultaneous history.

Notes

1. Walter Benjamin, "Theses on the Philosophy of History," in *Illuminations*.

2. I am referring here to the terms "memory" and "counter-memory" as developed by Michel Foucault in *Language, Counter-Memory, Practice*.

3. Henry Louis Gates Jr., "Editor's Introduction: Writing 'Race' and the Difference It Makes," 5. See also Anthony Appiah's essay, "The Uncompleted Argument: Du Bois and the Illusion of Race," in the same issue of *Critical Inquiry*.

4. See Edward Said's *Orientalism* and "Orientalism Reconsidered" for original and powerful articulations on this issue. Beginning with the publication of *Orientalism*, Said has succeeded in bringing together an extremely subtle and self-reflexive theory with the historical acuity of constituency politics.

5. See Gayatri Chakravorty Spivak, "Can the Subaltern Speak?" In this essay, Spivak critiques Michel Foucault and Gilles Deleuze for conflating the two meanings of the term "representation." Also see "Intellectuals and Power," in *Language, Counter-Memory, Practice*.

6. I am using the term "organic" as developed by Antonio Gramsci, that is, in opposition to the "traditional," which remains insensitive to changes in history.

7. Karl Marx, *Surveys from Exile*, 239.

8. I refer here to the follow-up issue of *Critical Inquiry* (Autumn 1986), edited in response to the Autumn 1985 special issue, "Race, Writing, and Difference."

9. Henry Louis Gates Jr., "Talkin' That Talk," 205–6.

10. See chapter 2 in this volume, "Toward an Effective Intellectual: Foucault or Gramsci?"

11. For an applied use of Bakhtin in the context of "ethnicity" and coalitional politics, see my "Post-Structuralist Politics: Towards a Theory of Coalition" and chapter 3 in this volume, "Ethnic Identity and Poststructuralist Différance."

12. See Hélène Cixous and Catherine Clément, *The Newly Born Woman*.

13. Barbara Christian, "The Race for Theory," 53.

14. See Julien Benda, *The Treason of the Intellectuals*.

15. See note 6. Gramsci's significance lies in the fact that he elaborates for the intellectual a position that is part of a constituency, party, and platform politics.

16. See Edward Said, "Traveling Theory," in *The World, the Text, the Critic*.

17. The notion of "internal dialogism" as developed by Bakhtin enables a complex sense of collectivity informed, on the one hand, by contestation and, on the other, by an ongoing heteroglossia that resists hegemonic and official foreclosures of lived realities.

References

Appiah, Anthony. "The Uncompleted Argument: Du Bois and the Illusion of Race." *Critical Inquiry*, 12, no. 1 (Autumn 1985): 21–37.

Bakhtin, M. M. *The Dialogic Imagination*. Ed. Michael Holquist. Trans. Carol Emerson and Michael Holquist. Austin: University of Texas Press, 1981.

Benda, Julien. *The Treason of the Intellectuals*. Trans. Richard Aldington. 1928; reprint, New York: Norton, 1969.

Benjamin, Walter. *Illuminations*. Trans. Harry Zohn. New York: Schocken, 1969.

Christian, Barbara. "The Race for Theory." *Cultural Critique* 6 (Spring 1987): 51–63.

Cixous, Hélène and Catherine Clément. *The Newly Born Woman*. Trans. Betsy Wing. Minneapolis: University of Minnesota Press, 1986.

Foucault, Michel. *Language, Counter-Memory, Practice*. Trans. Donald F. Bouchard and Sherry Simon. Ithaca, N.Y.: Cornell University Press, 1977.

Gates, Henry Louis, Jr.. "Editor's Introduction: Writing 'Race' and the Difference It Makes." *Critical Inquiry* 12, no. 1 (Autumn 1985): 1-20.

———. "Talkin' That Talk." *Critical Inquiry* 13, no. 1 (Autumn 1986): 203–10.

Gramsci, Antonio. *The Modern Prince and Other Writings*. Trans. Louis Marks. New York: International, 1959.

Marx, Karl. *Surveys from Exile*. Trans. David Fernbach. New York: Vintage, 1974.

R. Radhakrishnan. "Post-Structuralist Politics: Towards a Theory of Coalition." In *Jameson/Postmodernism/Critique,* ed. Douglas Kellner. Washington, D.C.: Maisonneuve Press, 1989.

Said, Edward W. *Orientalism.* New York: Pantheon, 1978.

———. "Orientalism Reconsidered." *Cultural Critique* 1 (1985): 89–107.

———. *The World, the Text, the Critic.* Cambridge, Harvard University Press, 1983.

Spivak, Gayatri Chakravorty. "Can the Subaltern Speak?" In *Marxism and the Interpretation of Culture,* ed. Cary Nelson and Lawrence Grossberg, 271–313. Urbana and Chicago: University of Illinois Press, 1988.

5 / Canonicity and Theory: Toward a Poststructuralist Pedagogy

An essay on pedagogy should, I believe, begin in the classroom, so here are two situations as they occur in the classroom. After narrating these two scenarios, I will analyze them from a poststructuralist perspective, setting up the framework of the entire chapter in the process.

The first situation is almost comical in its typicality. The teacher hands back papers, the student looks at the grade, reads through the comments scribbled by the teacher on the margins and between the lines, shakes her head in shock and astonishment, and finally gathers enough courage to go up to the teacher to contest the grade. She opens her dissent with the statement, "But I didn't know that was what you wanted." The teacher now is in quite a perilous position, for the student's understanding of the pedagogical process has opened up a veritable abyss. Assuming that the teacher is not despotic enough to foreclose further discussion, we can say that she has two broad choices: demonstrate to the student that the "value" of the paper has nothing to do with what the teacher wants, but is measurable objectively and intrinsically, or concede that the "value" of the paper is entirely dependent on its capacity to anticipate, invoke, and satisfy a particular set of pedagogical expectations in themselves conventional and not natural, arbitrary and not absolute. What will perhaps help the teacher make up her mind is her attitude toward her own pedagogical authority and the extent to which she believes in the centrality of this authority in the educational process. The teacher could either legitimate her evaluation in the name of some transcendent truth or value and thereby teach with authority, or she could foreground or thematize the very conventionality of pedagogy and thus open up a dialogue with the student, a dialogue in which pedagogical authority is called into question even as it exercises its magisterial and juridical function. The objective of such a dialogue would be not merely a "change in the grade" (although it might well achieve that effect in the process), but a deep-down transformation of the pedagogical model itself. In other words, the model of pedagogy as the transparent vehicle of truth and knowledge would be succeeded by pedagogy caught up recursively in its own ponderous, uncertain, and opaque materiality.

My second narrative has to do with the realities of deconstructive pedagogy; it is also autobiographical. After a month and a half of a graduate seminar on poststructuralism and deconstruction, one of my students made the following comments by way of summing up the significance of the postpedagogical intentions of deconstructive thought. (1) He had never before experienced anything as profound, as complex, and as radical as deconstruction; yet (2) it was all in a sense a waste, or perhaps a Pyrrhic triumph, for (3) the very notion of a nonauthoritarian mode of knowledge production (and its corollary, the nonauthoritarian teacher) is at best romantic and utopian, but really quite disingenuous. He did not deny the significance of deconstruction as such, for he did claim with enthusiasm and intensity that he had learned a great deal, more than ever before. But he did resent the fact that radical deconstruction seemed to force him to unlearn or problematize the very things he had learned. At this point, he said, he began to suspect deconstruction of bad faith and unethicality. As theory, it did not provide him with the certitude of an axiology, much less the comfort of a "home." He also observed that deconstruction could certainly be useful and valuable if only it could be taught "nondeconstructively." He was troubled by the fact that deconstruction does not take itself seriously, that it refuses to identify or semanticize itself. I was struck by his distinction between "deconstruction as method" and "deconstruction as philosophy." When taught deconstructively, deconstruction differs from itself and never arrives at philosophic identity or plenitude. The radical deconstructive method deauthorizes itself as domain and its practitioner as a responsible and authoritative teacher. To sum up, a philosophy that undermines itself through its own operations and a pedagogue who melts away in his own pedagogy are, in the ultimate analysis, not worthy of "value." These were the reasons why my student was disenchanted after having been initially attracted, even galvanized, by deconstructive pedagogy.

Both of these examples introduce problems and issues concerning pedagogy and authority, pedagogy and transformation, the structural dynamics of the "teacher-student" bind as a specific version of the "self-other" nexus, and finally, the very nature of pedagogy as a special kind of epistemic space and its topology within the context of larger cultural and social practices. Since pedagogy itself is an ancient tradition—moreover, since the very best poststructuralist thought enjoins on us a certain countermnemonic responsibility—I begin my reading of pedagogy by going all the way back to that prototypical teacher-intellectual-critic and theorist, Socrates (by way of Plato). I "remember" that primal and foundational pedagogical occasion in a certain way.

In his "dialogue" with Ian the rhapsode, Socrates formalizes and constitutes divinely inspired poetic frenzy into "valuable" meaning. While doing so, Socrates empowers himself in a threefold way: (1) as a theorist who both demonstrates and prescribes a method or heuristic for the correct investigation into "meaning," (2) as an intellectual who has the moral and the epistemological sanction both to represent an entire culture and to represent for that culture the true meaning of phenomena, and (3) as a teacher who founds, by way of the universality as well the objectivity of his method, the pedagogical transmissibility of knowledge and truth. While doing this, Socrates carves out or territorializes for himself a space of authority, a space from which the philosopher-teacher can effectively denaturalize the notion of an unmediated truth and simultaneously naturalize the right of the philosopher-teacher to make everlasting truth claims in the name of his own agency, which is none other than the agency of Truth itself.

In that dialogue Socrates does not entirely do away with the poet's utterance or the naive and precritical agency of the rhapsode. While retaining the "primordiality" of the poetic word, Socrates succeeds in rectifying the rhapsode and in committing truth value to the agency of the Socratic interpretive method. This is a crucial achievement: it recognizes on the one hand that "truth" can only be the result of interpretation and theoretical formalization, but on the other hand it maintains, by way of an autoaffective self-naturalization, a privileged connection with the "divine," or the original word or utterance itself. The role of the theorist as critic-interpreter is doubly enabled: the interpreter has the "autonomous" right to displace the original text into its meaning and to recuperate this very correction/displacement/representation as ontologically natural and as originally sanctioned. The Socratic juncture thus inaugurates the history of truth as precisely that regime that will naturalize the historically dispersed artificiality of interpretation in the name of a suprahistorical and self-evident truth. The purpose of teaching, then, is to celebrate the self-evidence of an original truth. Pedagogy is thus a secondary occupation, but in that very way it performs a venerable and apostolic function: it synchronizes its own temporality with the transcendent temporality of the "original." In other words, pedagogy constitutes itself as a totally reliable and transparent vehicle of Truth. In a poststructuralist-Nietzschean sense, the Socratic conjuncture represents the ideologization of a certain will to knowledge and interpretation into the normativity of truth itself, just as, in an analogous way, it represents the ontological recuperation of the historicity of truth within the natural law of transcendence and the accommodation of the rhetoricity of truth within the logic of a categorial truth.

The emergence of the Socratic model is the emergence of *modality as such*, that is, within the Western philosophic tradition. It marks the awareness that the inauguration of knowledge is coeval and consubstantial with the inauguration of method. Hence the power of the philosopher-teacher. The founder of philosophic methodology operates both in the name of Truth and in the name of that particular system that she founds. Her love for truth is also her passion for the rectitude of Truth, which in turn is identical with the rectitude of her system. What effects this synonymy or identity is the powerful principle of "in the name of." The preposition "of" that commits interpretation to the legality of an antecedent and natural truth also makes possible the systemic internalization of this very referential function. The axiological imperative that is tacit in the structure of "in the name of" effects an identical relationship between Truth and System. It now becomes possible for the philosopher to assert and legitimate the truth of interpretation as the "truth" of Truth/Reality itself. The philosophic system claims universality and objectivity, even as it remains constitutively insensitive to its own contingency and figurality.

The Socratic episteme is sustained by two axioms: value and correctness, or rectitude. The Socratic method depends for its success on its capacity to demystify and correct the un- or prephilosophic consciousness. Thus, in his encounter with the rhapsode, Socrates generates and valorizes his truth claims at the expense of the rhapsode's. Lacking a critical or second-order consciousness, the rhapsode is unaware that he, too, is making a certain kind of truth claim. The rhapsode's mode of understanding, Socrates claims, is repetitively identical with the poetic frenzy itself and is thus not critically differentiated from what it speaks of. This mode, Socrates demonstrates, cannot be productive of truth; furthermore, it cannot be taught. The rhapsode is not cognitively aware of the poetry that he so vulgarly, affectively, and credulously theatricalizes. Significantly, Socrates claims that the gods who inspire the poets into utterance have also made them blind, that is, cognitively incompetent. Poets "express" but know not what they express; the rhapsode, insofar as he merely repeats affectively the articulation of the poets, is equally devoid of cognitive skills. In attributing blindness to the poets, Socrates is in fact creating and legitimating his own role as teacher and interpreter. A contradictory situation develops here: the poets who, in their unselfconsciousness, express the divine become promulgators of doxology and apocryphal knowledge, whereas the philosopher, in his secondary capacity as knower-theorist-interpreter, founds epistemic truth. What is at stake here is the nature of the relationship between the poets (and indirectly, the very gods who inspire the poets) and the rhapsode, on the one hand, and the poets (and the gods) and the philosopher, on the other. One of the two relationships is incorrect, and the "incorrect" is necessary for purposes of correction, reformed representation, and disciplinary constitution. Hence the centrality in the Socratic method of the notion of truth as demystification, as also the importance of the interrogative rhetoric that finally elicits the right structure from the erroneous one. The production of knowledge is simultaneously creative and corrective.

The Socratic philosopher is best equipped to teach, since he identifies and corrects erroneous models of investigation, knows cognitively what the correct answer is, and demonstrates through the universality and objectivity of his method that truth is both knowable and teachable. (Pedagogy renders truth knowable; that is, the "true" is identical with the "teachable.") This demonstration takes place through the figurality of the Socratic dialogue within whose dynamic the "self" of the teacher centered in the "true" wins over to proper epistemic citizenship the "other" of the erring student. To this end, the interlocutor in all the dialogues is nominated by the philosophic self as its own "other," to be reclaimed within the domain of the "true" and the "identical." For nowhere in the dialogues does the "other" challenge the Socratic axiology itself; thus the Socratic claim that the gods have rendered the poets blind in their furious eloquence remains uncontested by the rhapsode. The apriorism of the Socratic givens is beyond critique and transgression. It is not coincidental that Socrates' primary intention in invalidating the rhapsode is both civic and political. As a teacher committed to the inculcation of value and identity, he cannot allow for the possibility that the rhapsode's dramatization of the poets is in fact a reading in itself, a reading that reveals that the gods speak in many, often contradictory, voices. As teacher, Socrates makes a certain investment in "value" and valorizes "value" through a certain categorical apriorism, the apriorism of identity. Socrates cannot and does not deny that the gods seem full of contradictions, or that the poetic text is characterized by heterogeneity, but he will not allow contradiction and heterogeneity the privilege of value and identity. The heterogeneous and contradictory text is refined into a monothetic and identical text, and it is by the elimination of heterogeneity and contradiction that true value is constituted. This true value is embodied by the identity of the text as established by the pedagogical will. Socrates the teacher decides what can and should be transmitted as education to the student. If the purpose of education is to create obedient and docile students, how, Socrates asks, can the teacher make it known to the student that the original text itself is characterized by a nontotalizable recalcitrance? The two telling insights on which the Socratic school is based are that teaching can take place only with the help of a canonical text, not just any text, and that an essential and nonnegotiable distance must be maintained between the school that students attend and the school that teaches "teaching." Only by withholding from the student the awareness that canonical texts are not natural can the teacher deal authoritatively with the student. Only on the basis of such a nondialogic and absolute pedagogical authority can the teacher demonstrate to the student that Truth is both the macrology of the telos and the micrology of the pedagogical process that arrives at the telos unerringly. It is quite clear that this unerring pedagogical process or method is productive of education; in each dialogue the interlocutor not only is edified but is "made" to acquiesce in the correctness and legitimacy of the very process by means of which this edification is realized. The effect of the Socratic method is the creation of an atmosphere where the student or the "other" is made to "know herself" by internalizing and appropriating the authority of the teacher. The "know thyself" principle is both apodictic and the product of the pedagogical encounter. Socratic authority is well earned; even the student will certify so.

To provide a certain inculcation of the "self" and to demonstrate and exemplify the citizenship of such a "self" in the domain of the "true": this indeed has been the pedagogical mission through history, and it has not changed all that much right down to our own time. The fact that the Socratic model is advertised even today as open-ended, democratic, and dialogic is clear proof that the educational model of "Catch 'em young and make docile citizens of them" is still dominant. Poststructuralist pedagogy finds itself heir to the Socratic tradition, a bequest that it can neither completely forget nor completely remember. How to dissipate such a tradition in the very act of inheriting it—that is the countermnemonic project that poststructuralist pedagogy sets for itself.

Before I turn to the detailed complexity of such a project, there is still some unfinished business with the Socratic scheme of value. Within his pedagogical space, Socrates posits the "self" both as a given and as something knowable. When Socrates axiomatizes the "know thyself" dictum, he achieves the following theoretical-epistemological results: (1) He makes the givenness of the "self" available for philosophic cogitation whose purpose is to produce the certitude of knowledge. (2) Even as he calls for the philosophic formalization of the self, he recuperates the process of formalization within the aprioristic logic of the "given self," such that the formalization itself can do nothing other than execute the mandate assigned to it, that is, find the "self" and institute it epistemologically as the principle of "identity" and "self-coincidence." (3) He thus founds a philosophic system that guarantees against all recalcitrant models by proposing this identity that is complicitous with the Socratic pedagogical authority. In other words, the moment that philosophical thinking is constituted as an acquiescent response to the mandate "Know thyself," it is committed, in the act of knowing the "self," to asserting the reality of the self. (Such thinking cannot come up with the finding that "there is no self.") (4) Consequently, Socrates legitimates the principle of the "identical self" as an *Ur*-concept that, in naturalizing the "knowable," imposes on the theoretical-pedagogical process a *micrological* identity that is ineluctably complicitous with the *macrological* identity of the "self to be known." (5) Pedagogy, and with it the authority of Truth, is realized as profoundly conservative, noncritical, and nontransformative. Finally—and this, from a poststructuralist perspective, is what is astonishing about the Socratic model—Socrates does allow a limited play of irony whereby he can seemingly disparage himself without forfeiting any of his authority. Actually, this pedagogical irony operates at a level of intelligibility that is not open to the "other"/the student/the interlocutor. In insisting that his dialogic comrade be critically aware of his own "blindness" as a precondition for the production of epistemic truth,[1] Socrates conceals from his student the historicity of Socrates' own rhetorical and prejudicial stance.[2] Whereas in demystifying his interlocutor's truth claims Socrates is prepared to radicalize the notion of "error," he is not prepared, in his own autocritique, to reveal how his own truth is the rhetoricization of a primary error.[3] Only from a position of absolute correctness can Socrates rectify or correct the position held by his "other" and thereby pave the way for true knowledge. The authority of teaching is sustained, on the one hand, by the nonpositional mystique of the teacher and, on the other hand, by the willingness of the student to internalize the logic of the teacher. What Socrates achieves, from a poststructuralist point of view, is a kind of pedagogy management: he constructs a specific model of teaching and learning, makes it work, demonstrates its operationality, and thereby ordains the Socratic school as the exclusive domain where Truth is incarnated.

It might be objected that in the *Dialogues* there are ironic, metapedagogic, second-order passages that testify to the open nature of the Socratic method. But it turns out on a closer analysis that Socratic irony is the irony of the master who has the capacity to invoke and at the same time contain oppositional possibilities. Here is an interesting example of a carefully cultivated Socratic innocence from *Meno*, and it is not coincidental that Shoshana Felman's searching essay, "Psychoanalysis and Education: Teaching Terminable and Interminable,"⁴ cites this passage as part of its epigraph:

> MENO: Yes, Socrates, but how do you mean that we do not learn, but that what we call learning is recollection? Can you teach me how this is so?
> SOCRATES: . . . Meno, you are a rascal. Here you are asking me to give you my "teaching," who claim there is no such thing as teaching, only recollection.⁵

Felman begins her essay with the following paraphrase of Socratic self-awareness: "Socrates, that extraordinary teacher who taught humanity what pedagogy is, and whose name personifies the birth of pedagogics as a science, inaugurates his teaching practice, paradoxically enough, by asserting not just his own ignorance, but the radical impossibility of teaching."⁶

While I am profoundly persuaded and enabled by Felman's essay, this is my one area of disagreement with her interpretation. I believe Felman all too readily deconstructs the omniscience of the Socratic strategy. Her argument then quickly makes sympathetic connections among Socratic self-doubt, Freudian self-interrogation, and the Lacanian thesis of alterity and radical ignorance. My reading, on the contrary, is that unlike Freud and Lacan, Socrates remains the strong teacher whose pedagogical techniques foreclose possibilities of "transference." In the *Meno* passage quoted above, Socrates will not participate in a second-order discussion with Meno, for such a metapedagogical dialogue can only result in a loss of pedagogic authority. Unlike the Freudian and the Lacanian models, the Socratic model is teleological and hence cannot displace the method from the answer that is already there. Whereas Freud and Lacan leave room within their teaching for the irruption of alterity, Socrates stage-manages and prescribes the very questions that scandalize his pedagogical persona. In terms of *Meno*, the thematization of *pedagogy as such* that Meno is asking for never takes place in the dialogue. What we get instead is a charming disclaimer that there indeed is no system; the anamnestic basics of teaching are left untheorized.

To return now to the two episodes with which I started: the student who had a problem with the grade meted out is in some sense the Socratic interlocutor who has dared to demur, and the student who felt abandoned by deconstructive pedagogy is in fact lamenting the loss of Socratic authority. And a deconstructive/poststructuralist teacher who finds herself in the classroom is identified and evaluated within a Socratic framework: either an inoperative Socrates or a Socrates manqué. In the first instance, the teacher must turn

Socratic and make the grade stick or else lose credibility; in the latter instance, the teacher must come up with a Socratic thematization of deconstructive pedagogy.

A contemporary literature professor's pedagogical situation is still inherently Socratic: she has a responsibility to the student and a responsibility to the canon that she elaborates assertively and correctly. She is doubly representative: she represents the text that she teaches and makes available to her students, and she represents a cultural-intellectual meritocracy whose purpose is to educate and "bring up" uninitiated youth. She is the teacher both of the text and of the method of reading. She is the medium through whom the wisdom of the tradition is passed on to the student generation. However original and iconoclastic, she works through the authority of received categories: genre, period, the masterpiece, literary criticism, the canon, the reading list. The official and institutional capacity that she assumes as teacher already confers on her a legitimate selfhood and an authoritative and authoritarian subject position. She is in an institutional situation that valorizes binary thinking: the teacher and the taught, the self and the other, literature and the nonliterary, the canonical and the noncanonical, core curricula and peripheral courses and requirements, majors and minors, to name just a few regulative categories. My purpose is to explore how and why a radical poststructuralist theory can and does make a difference in the classroom. In using the term "radical" I will not be subscribing to some ex nihilo theory of a pure epistemological "break" from the past; I would, rather, be interested in articulating possibilities for a perspective that takes history so seriously that it refuses to be co-opted by it. It seems to me that some of the most substantive contributions of poststructuralist theory have been in the area of didacticism. My purpose would be to examine to what extent radical theory enables revisionist-historiographic projects that, in proposing a second-order transformation of *teaching itself,* seem to envision alternatives for a heterogeneous and noncoercive production of knowledge. I am aware of a certain lack of precision in my use of the term "poststructuralist theory," but that is quite intentional. I am here attempting the articulation of a provisional and strategic solidarity among the many discourses that comprise the "poststructuralist episteme." For my purposes here, the salient poststructuralist trajectories are deconstruction, the Foucauldian countermemory, feminist theory, and psychoanalytic accounts of the self-other nexus. And why is Socrates crucial in all this? "Socrates" is both the name of a particular teacher-philosopher and the generic name for a kind of hegemonic and authoritative teaching that is still the dominant model. Even some of the most adversarial pedagogy is constrained to recuperate problematically that very Socratic model it calls into question.

I begin this part of my chapter with a generalized conceptual definition of that decidedly Socratic theme, the canon. The canon is an official body of texts, and as an official body it makes exemplary and prescriptive statements about history, time, identity, and pedagogy. By existing as an ideal and representative order, the canon naturalizes a continuous, monolithic, and nonproblematic relationship between the past and the present. It establishes and valorizes a transcendent and universal "identity" of texts, culture, and civilization: an identity that persists inviolably despite historical breaks and ruptures. It also legitimates the notion that history is a mode of conservation to be incarnated by a narrative that has the assurance of a privileged beginning and the guaranteed sanctity of a telos. Having structured identity and historicity in an axiomatically complicitous relationship that is as natural as it is ideal, the canon mandates a determinate role for pedagogy: that of celebration, acquiescent and apologistic exegesis, and ultimately genuflection, and the chastened acceptance of its own secondary status. In other words, the immaculate *macrology* of the canon enjoins and enjoys the subservience of the pedagogical *micrology*, so the question of "value" is settled long before the canon itself is "unpacked" pedagogically. A canonical text both *is* and *knows* itself, and therefore it can dictate to the pedagogical discourse the correct protocols of explication and interpretation. The teacher-interpreter infers the "value" of the canonical text from the text itself through a set of procedures again prescribed by the text itself; hence the labor of interpretation is truly unproductive and redundant. The canonical mode declares that "value" is synonymous with the "canonical" and that the "canonical" is a representative and universal category. Whose canon? How was "canonicity" historically produced in the first place, and in the service of what ideological interests? Such questions are disallowed.

We thus have a pedagogical occasion that inherits a "truth" (the truth of the canon) that is in fact the history of an error,[7] but an error with demonstrable truth effects. The task of a deconstructive pedagogy is to demystify the canon (and, with it, the very algorithm of canonicity) by acknowledging the historical reality of the canon without capitulating to the regime of the canonical. What is called for is an ambivalent "double" strategy of reading that, in actualizing the contingent historicity of the "canonical," will transgress the temporality of the "canon." Here, then, are the tasks that face deconstructive pedagogy: (1) To deal with the canon oppositionally, expose its ideological underpinnings, and proclaim the fact that the canon itself is the result of a reading and not a transcendent order that inaugurates the order of reading and interpretation. (2) Having demystified the putative status of the canon conceptually and theoretically, to deal intransigently with the reality that the "canon as a lie" has perpetrated truth and reality effects that demand oppositional confrontation at the level of history, and not just at the level of metahistorical theorization. In other words, the epistemological overthrow of canonicity does not automatically result in the annulment of the many privileges, exploitations, repressions, and exclusions engendered by the canonical mode during periods of its undisputed truth. (3) To locate its own historicity as an anterior reading. The deconstructive operation on the canon is an improper reading that is neither entirely secessional (reading as such that is totally forgetful of that which it is a reading) nor commemorative. It is a double reading that complicates memory and promise in a reciprocally incommensurable mode.[8] (4) To discredit the notion of a one-to-one correspondence between truth and method, offering as an alternative its own "methodic truth" without at the same time authorizing its own method in the name of an aprioristic axiology. (5) Finally, to embody and historicize its own perspectivity without the guarantee of absolute political epistemic morality. This last task would involve a kind of double thinking and double teaching that would have to establish its own pedagogical-theoretical authority contingently, as an expression of a deeper and fundamental dispute with *authority as such*. This, in turn, would entail the necessity for a vigilant autocritique. The postpedagogical enterprise that deconstruction underwrites does not perceive its own operations, by virtue of their polemical and intentional investment, as being ideologically and structurally free of the "will to canonicity."

Is deconstructive pedagogy alienated from all truth? Or, to state it in terms of the skeptical student of deconstruction, is the deconstructive method so impoverished and eviscerated of all interiority that in asserting its Nietzschean "truth" that "there is no truth," it is stranded in the ascetic mode of pure negativity? No one has dealt with this aporetic aspect of deconstructive theory more rigorously than Paul de Man, whose entire career has manifested a metacritical awareness caught up in its own nonauthorizable liminality. His influential and meticulously argued essay "The Resistance to Theory" begins powerfully, but only by disabling itself in a certain way. This essay, de Man tells us, was commissioned and eventually rejected by the Committee on the Research Activities of the Modern Language Association, since it did not fulfill its programmatic purpose of synthesis and clarification. Instead, the essay tries to explain "as concisely as possible, why the main theoretical interest of literary theory consists in the impossibility of its definition."[9] De Man then goes on to account for the reasons for such concerted resistance to this theory that unmasters both itself and the pure identity of that which it addresses—in this case, "literature, as such." Says de Man:

As a controlled reflection on the formation of method, theory rightly proves to be entirely compatible with teaching, and one can think of numerous important theoreticians who are or were also prominent scholars. A question arises only if a tension develops between methods of understanding and the knowledge which those methods allow one to teach. If there is indeed something about literature, as such, which allows for a discrepancy between truth and method, between *Wahrheit* and *Methode,* then scholarship and theory are no longer necessarily compatible; as a first casualty of this complication, the notion of "literature as such" as well as the clear distinction between history and interpretation can no longer be taken for granted. For a method that cannot be made to suit the "truth" of its object can only teach delusion. Various developments, not only in the contemporary scene but in the long and complicated history of literary and linguistic instruction, reveal symptoms that suggest such a difficulty is an inherent focus of the discourse about literature. These uncertainties are manifest in the hostility directed at theory in the name of ethical and aesthetic values, as well as in the recuperative attempts of theoreticians to reassert their own subservience to these values. The most effective of these attacks will denounce theory as an obstacle to scholarship and, consequently, to teaching. It is worth examining whether, and why, this is the case. For if this is indeed so, then it is better to fail in teaching what should not be taught than to succeed in teaching what is not true.[10]

De Man rightly concludes that traditional literary critics, ethical or aesthetic, resist theory precisely because theory does not submit to the logic of instrumentality; the logic of formal theory as method cannot be made to suit the "truth" of its object. Theory comes into its own (as against, for example, the logic of practical criticism and its easy referential adherence to the truth of its object) when it expresses and formalizes the noncoincidence of method with truth. But this does not mean, as de Man has warned critics over and over again, that the activity itself is nonpurposive or predictable. It may be considered futile only if the ethic or the rationale of theoretical discourse is deemed subaltern to the truth itself of "literature, as such." But this is precisely the assumption that de Man's theory critiques. If traditional literary critics argue that theory is not teachable because it does not terminate (and, of course, originate) in the literary text and that, furthermore, it makes a pre-text of the literary text, de Man counters with the argument that only by repressing the rhetoricity of theoretical cognition itself can these practically, aesthetically, or ethically oriented critics lay claim to cognitive transparency. The anti-Socratic thrust of de Man's thesis is quite evident. In coming down on the side of rhetoric, de Man calls the bluff of the cognitive Socratic philosopher. Not that de Man denies cognition its truth claims (if anything, he insists on the cognitive nature of all scholarship), but he points out that all cognitive models are "always already" rhetorical and figural. Later in the same essay de Man shrewdly makes the diagnosis that the resistance to theory is nothing but the resistance to the constitutive agency of language. That referentiality itself is a linguistic function is an insight that totally destroys the certitude of a literary tradition deeply invested in prelinguistic and intuitive mysteries. De Man's notion of theory as rhetoricity compels the teacher to teach "teaching" to her student, but without the support of the ideology of anamnesis that underlies the truth of Socratic pedagogy. De Man thus forces the pedagogical tradition to thematize its own contradictory and paradoxical situation. No wonder a tradition developed to categorize "contradiction" and "paradox," as the definitive threshold of *error itself* is incapable of theorizing the aporetic context opened up by the concept of radical rhetoricity.

What promise does the rhetoricity of literature hold out for the project of decanonization? If the task of decanonization is to take place through the agency of pedagogy and if, furthermore, the history of canonicity is complicitous with an authoritative and masterful pedagogy, then it follows that decanonization and a self-deconstructive pedagogy are obverse aspects of the same endeavor. In the name of what emerging authority is the canon to be decanonized? Analogously, what is the new pedagogical imperative that sustains the activity of teaching? Can we even use the term "imperative" in the context of a pedagogy that rhetoricizes its claims to authority? De Man's thesis, in spite of its very real adversarial and counterhegemonic potential, ultimately domesticates itself for lack of a specific constituency. Sure enough, in liberating rhetoricity from the cognitive straitjacket and in enabling the secession of theory from the sovereignty of truth, de Man's discourse makes it impossible for any system of thought to rest on principles of nostalgia or a natural innocence; yet it fetishizes rhetoricity itself into an unassailable and undifferentiable first principle. The first principle as characterized by de Man still remains capable of producing certain reality effects. In other words, de Man's radical rhetoricization of ontology cannot and does not prevent "rhetoric" from participating in hegemonic and ideological practices. Having opted out of the worldly effects of rhetoric, de Man's strategy does not enable particular rhetorical commitments.

To use a concrete example, what valence can we attribute to the feminist decanonization of the phallogocentric tradition? The process of decanonization takes the form of a denaturalization that reveals the ideological underpinnings of the phallogocentric tradition. Its ideologically loaded rhetoric exposed, phallogocentrism is effectively deconstructed and delegitimated. But the question that remains unanswered is "Deconstructed from what point of view, and for what revisionist/adversarial/revolutionary purpose?" If one answers, "From a feminist point of view," then the deconstructive critique has already taken on, if not an identity, at least the imprimatur of a specific constituency whose own truth is in active hegemonic contestation with the truth of its oppressor. Unlike Paulo Freire's *Pedagogy of the Oppressed*, de Man's pedagogy remains a rebel without a cause. If the condition of rhetoricity were the sole criterion for the unreliability of any pattern of knowledge or truth, then all patterns would stand equally indicted and guilty or equally innocent and value free.

Salient questions that face poststructuralist pedagogy are: (1) How should it identify itself: as a comprehensively negative-critical operation with decanonization as its main task? Or should it also envision a pattern of affirmation after and beyond decanonization? (2) Should it seek out an emerging "truth" and pledge its own expertise in the service of this new "truth"? (3) Should it remain indifferent to the "nature" and "truth" of what is being taught, on the assurance that the postpedagogical revolution will produce its own progressive effects, irrespective of the texts that constitute the syllabus/canon/reading list/core curriculum?

I shall try to answer these both discretely and in a synthetic way, since, different as these questions are, they are all part of a larger question. Let me use an example again. At a seminar devoted to psychoanalysis, feminist theory, and the question of the other, a question repeated with great relevance and urgency was "Why should feminist theory even have to deal with the male ideology of psychoanalytic thought?" The argument was that, in positioning its own radical politics and theory in the context of a male-centered psychoanalytic discourse, the feminist revolution will be constrained to "identify" itself as a parasitic and negatively critical model of the second order, rather than to assert its "own difference" and independence in its "own positive" terms. The particular example we were discussing was that of Luce Irigaray, the French feminist psychoanalyst and theorist. The very fact that Irigaray was engaging in dialogues, however adversarial and critical, with such male masters as Plato, Nietzsche, and Freud was being perceived as inimical to authentic feminist interests.[11] The questions that emerged were the following: (1) Why should feminist emergence be experienced and valorized as an antithetical reaction-formation to the male thesis? (2) Isn't the "difference" of feminism a radical difference, and not just a "difference from" or a "difference within" or a "difference against" the identity of phallogocentric thought?[12] (3) If feminism is the signification of *difference itself*,[13] then isn't there the need to think of difference "differentially" and not merely to codify it as a "lack" or a "gap" within the text of Identity?[14] Before addressing these questions, I will set up yet another situation that brings up a similar problem from the point of view of pedagogy; I will then conflate the two examples so as to investigate the theory-pedagogy dyad.

Let us think of a revisionist, feminist, poststructuralist teacher conducting a course in American Romanticism. To what extent should she engage in decanonizing the male trinity that constitutes the canonical category known as American Romanticism: Emerson, Hawthorne, and Thoreau? (Melville, Poe, and Whitman have some difficulty fitting in.) Is such an engagement meaningful? Would her interests be better served if she were to spend her time teaching Emily Dickinson, Margaret Fuller, Harriet Beecher Stowe, and Rebecca Harding and discovering and valorizing the many journals, diaries, and other "private" writings maintained by American women in the nineteenth century? Are these two projects related obversely or not at all? Would the decanonization of the patriarchs automatically result in the enablement of the suppressed female voices? If so, would this empowerment originate from the negativity of the defeated male model or would such a power be coincident with the "feminine"? The question concerning the status of feminist psychoanalysis as a theoretical question is inseparable from the pedagogical question that confronts the feminist teacher of American Romanticism. In either case, there is the problem of the past and the reality of history that intrudes into our most contemporary and oppositional projects. How should we prehistoricize the oppressive and unjust past: by problematizing it and deauthorizing it, or by tactically ignoring it altogether?

A Derridean approach would suggest that the mere fact that Emerson or Thoreau becomes the "subject" of feminist discourse does not invalidate the critical-revisionist perspectivity of the discourse. On the contrary, Derrida would insist that revisionist and counterhegemonic discourses cannot afford to consider their constituencies and historiographies as completely disjunct from their prehistories. In other words, canonical texts ought to be read adversarially, deconstructively, and against their grain. The Derridean model does not valorize the binary opposition of deconstruction and affirmation, of positivity and negativity. Rather, it proposes an intentional "double valence" as the precondition for effective historicity: neither negativity nor positivity, neither a pure deconstruction nor a pure affirmation, but thinking as an impure liminality, or as an orphaned mode that must be ambivalent.[15] Following a Nietzschean line, Derrida refuses to sever trajectories of promise from structures of memory.[16] From a Derridean perspective, the separatist radical project is inadmissible for the following reasons: (1) The emerging constituency can find its "identity" only as a form of difference from that which precedes it. (2) The strength of this "difference" consists in its capacity for critical vigilance, not in its desire to escape history altogether. (3) The deconstructive critique as the countermnemonic invocation of the past is neither a primary nor a secondary mode,[17] but the interrogation of that very binary economy that begets the "primary" and the "secondary." (4) To be radical, the present must function as a "poisoned present,"[18] that is, as a poison within the system it seeks to destroy. (5) The historicity as well as the polemical perspectivity of the present cannot be simultaneous with itself, for its self is "always already" implicated in other histories. Analogously, the insurrection of the present cannot be characterized by an identical purity construed as cause, name, or revolutionary apparatus. The very weapons with which one wages revolution can only be the apparatus of the enemy, now turned against itself. (6) Consequently, there can be no definitive distinction between an affirmative pedagogy that valorizes feminist texts and a deconstructive pedagogy that destabilizes patriarchal texts. If the canonization of the "male" is but a local expression of the ideology of binarity, any attempt to overthrow the "male" must be wary of resorting innocently to binary methods of transformation. To affirm "femininity" in opposition to the "masculine" would merely amount to replaying binary historicity, whereas to abstract away the structure of affirmation from its binary opposite, "negation," would amount to dehistoricizing the reality of those very binary modes of organization that account for who, what, and how we are. The tactic that Derridean deconstruction advocates is neither a total overthrow of binarity nor a capitulation to it, but a perennial displacement and subversion of binarity from within. If canonical binarity ordains the male and the female and hierarchizes this relationship by naturalizing and empowering the male and marking the female as inferior and "lacking," the Derridean subversion of binarity mixes modes, draining binarity of its hierarchic status.[19] But such a pedagogy does not see itself escaping the logic of binarity; it can at best pervert it, displace it, and use it against itself. Derridean logic would contend that if history has been the history of binarity, it follows that a denial of the reality of binarity is a denial of history itself. Hence a radical historiography can only take the form of a critically vigilant recursiveness, what Derrida terms "protocols of vigilance."

The Derridean formulation has a tremendous impact on pedagogy. If the history of pedagogy is inseparable from the "truth of its object" and if, furthermore, this truth itself is an "error," then it follows inevitably that pedagogy, too, is the practice of self-delusion. The pedagogical tradition that the poststructuralist/deconstructive teacher inherits is the simultaneity of a double error, the error of a certain truth and the error of binary pedagogy that has promulgated such an erroneous truth. But by the same token, she is also the recipient of the history of such an erroneous truth, a history that she must assume, but only to dissipate. Her "subject position" in history precludes the possibility of generating ex nihilo a pedagogical method identical with her desire. In the context of the separatist feminist, no pure affirmative pedagogical strategies will be equal to her task or, for that matter, to the affirmative dimension of those feminine texts lost or quelled by a phallocratic tradition. The activity of reading and valorizing Virginia Woolf, Kate Chopin, or Mary Austin does not place the feminist critic in direct and putative contact with a feminine positivity that survives separate from the male canonical ambience. Nor does it generate from the feminist texts a pure space unmediated and untrammeled by male representation. What the feminist reading achieves, however, from a deconstructive standpoint, is the shaking up of a certain order, a repressive order that genderizes a Clarissa Dalloway and a Septimus Warren Smith within mutually exclusive spaces. And if Woolf's emancipating vision can realize a feminist (and, beyond that, an androgynous) horizon, it is only by confounding the hegemony of the existing binary order. To confound that order, her fiction must take into account the circumstantial reality of that very order. A separatist venture, on the other hand, remains trapped by inner contradiction. If the separation is absolute, it loses valence for not making visible that very prehistory from which the separation occurs.

The ideology of a separatist theory of pedagogy brings to the forefront a vital issue: that of authority and the willed production of knowledge. What can a nonauthoritarian pedagogy achieve? If the revolution in pedagogy consists in the loss of pedagogical certitude, in what cause can one teach such a pedagogy? The transformation of *pedagogy as such* seems to have rendered the notion of a terminable pedagogy quite untenable.[20] Radical pedagogy is bereft of subject matter and a proper domain; besides, it seems to lack a mission. The anomaly of the poststructuralist occasion is that, on the one hand, it stands committed to the truth of certain repressed constituencies that pedagogy should find and endorse, while on the other it repudiates the idea of a pedagogy that suits the truth of its object.

To alienate and denaturalize the pedagogy of the privileged is one thing; alienating and denaturalizing the pedagogy of the oppressed quite another.[21] If these two projects are neither covalent nor synchronous, then surely the postpedagogical advocacy of alterity and nonauthoritarian modes of producing knowledge is itself a poorly theorized ideological false consciousness. The question I am posing here is structurally similar to my earlier query about the nature of affirmation and negation in the context of critical thinking. Are the two modes separate? Mixed? Or are they characterized by an ideological solidarity in the context of a particular historical project that combines complementary activities of critique and of postcritical valorization? By way of example, the pedagogy of the oppressed could be perceived as demystifying colonialist and imperialist structures, or it could be seen as reading and valorizing the postcolonialist emergence positively in its own terms. A poststructuralist pedagogy could read E. M. Forster on India or Joseph Conrad on Africa deconstructively; it could read Salman Rushdie on India or Chinua Achebe or Buchi Emecheta on Africa constructively and affirmatively. Or should poststructuralist pedagogy, in the name of an "always already alterity," submit the latter literature to deconstructive scrutiny as well? The dilemma facing poststructuralist pedagogy here is that of purpose, historicity, and constituency. If pedagogy itself—the very structures of pedagogy, not merely its instrumentality—has been transformed intransitively by the poststructuralist revolution, can pedagogy situate and commit itself to a univocal model of partisanship? Is it not the tactical responsibility of a critical pedagogy to lodge itself subversively, even within the body of progressive, radically self-righteous texts? Is it also responsible for opening up, within the positivity of an emerging constituency, an active space for autocritique in the name of a namelessly utopian future? The postcolonialist or the feminist will to meaning and justice may be free from the brutalities of a particular prehistory, but not from certain patterns of exclusion and coercive representation that are coextensive with its own act of affirmation. The birth into identity of a particular constituency may in itself be morally and politically correct and righteous, but this determinate morality is itself powerless to separate this specific moment of identity formation from the general history of identity, a history that has also been the document of barbarism.

The underlying problem is the problem of authority. Should a radical pedagogy take up a perennially oppositional role to all forms of authority formation? Or should it discriminate among different historical situations and thereby redefine its role contextually? To locate this controversy in the context of literature and criticism, should critical pedagogy respect the authority of literature, since the authority of literature is in some ways the authority of experience itself? And is experience not truth itself? Again, making historically specific determinations, the advocates of experience would say that there are and can be no racist, sexist, ethnocentric, homophobic truths, but surely there are feminist, postcolonialist, antiracist truths. The reality as well as the authenticity of these truths is self-evident in their very historicity and expressivity. The literature that is the living embodiment of these liberated truths is already its own deconstruction and hence can (and should) do away with the agency of a deconstructive pedagogy. A feminist literature knows its own truth, a third world literature knows its own truth, and so on; for deconstructive theory and pedagogy to denaturalize these truths is as irrelevant as it is unethical. The "truths" in these formations are already there, experientially and historically.

To this a deconstructive pedagogue would respond that it is precisely in the name of such ideological purity that all revolutions have turned oppressive during their affirmative or legitimating phases, their truths now falsified by the will to absolute power. A case in question would be the predicament of contemporary white feminism, which is unified in its oppositional role but has difficulty securing its truths in its affirmative phase. The feminist truth, if conceived of as natural and identical, can do violence to the multiple constituencies within feminism: lesbian, heterosexual, white, black; first, second, and third world. This affirmative violence can be guarded against only if we keep alive those very protocols of vigilance that delivered us from the oppressor in the first place. The conviction that one has found a home in one's own truth does not render this truth natural, nor does it establish the truth of historicity above and beyond the conflictual politics of interpretation. The moment of affirmation may not be isolated from the time of critical reflection, and no subject position, not even that of the oppressed, can be blind to the will to hegemony that has been intrinsic to the history of identity.

Critical pedagogy should integrate a radical awareness of its own historical and institutional subject position within its affirmative agenda, and this awareness is incompatible with the theory of the self. Whereas the language of the self celebrates the moment of certitude and authority, the language of critical reflexivity postpones and problematizes such a moment. The former authorizes the self as natural and given; the latter realizes it as a position, the position of being subject.

Now to relate the philosophy and theory of teaching with the institutional base or position from which we as teachers teach, write, do research, and publish. In a sense I have come full circle, for in our own context within the university we can rethink the age-old questions concerning canonicity and the correctness of what we teach. As teachers we are inscribed in an academic situation that has strongly valorized the coincidence of pedagogical efficacy with the truth of what it teaches. So we find ourselves teaching the canon, or (since our training as teachers is profoundly complicitous with the canonical mode) we tend to canonize whatever we teach. We speak for the text; we also negotiate with the text on behalf of the student who expects edification from the way we mediate ourselves with the texts. Yet we are trapped in the hermeneutic circle. We are practitioners of diverse critical methodologies (Marxist, feminist, Lacanian, and so on), and we are trapped within the hubris of those methodologies; or we are seduced by the text, to the detriment of our own interventionary historicity. Some of us are concerned that our model of interpretation alienates literature from the literary experience, while others of us regard the very category "literary experience" with grave suspicion. Some of us are interdisciplinary by persuasion but would want literature to retain its own integral position; others (I include myself in this category) would argue that "literature as such" does not exist. Whatever our biases and agendas, we partake in the logic of our departments and the logic of hierarchy, reading lists, core curricula, and canonicity. Even as oppositional teachers, we operate within a departmental logic that ghettoizes certain modes of scholarship. We teach minority literatures, feminist theory, postcolonial formations, and all manner of radical theory, but as professionals we remain powerless to transform the very space within which we operate. The hiring of a feminist does not feminize the department, nor does the inclusion of an "Oriental" (of course I am using the term ironically) result in the problematization of such staple courses as "Masterpieces of the Western Tradition."

Does this indicate that the counterhegemonic fringes should unite and canonize themselves in the name of a new repressive hegemony? Emphatically not. Such unabashed acts of authority are entirely hostile to the kind of affirmation that poststructuralist thought at its very best teaches. The rich and complex controversy among feminists about the significance of Gilbert and Gubar's Norton anthology convincingly demonstrates the dangers of representational politics. A countercanon or even several countercanons is not the answer, for the problem is canonicity itself. We cannot "not deal" with the canon and the other forms of academic authority, for we ourselves are wielders of such authority. Nor can we envision a new authority that will be acceptable and persuasive in its self-evident moral and political rectitude.

The mere act of "forgetting" the canon does not make the canon mortal or vulnerable. And more significantly, not negotiating with the canon can have the disastrous consequence of dehistoricizing the entire revolutionary-pedagogical undertaking. Reading the canon subversively is an effective way to retrieve the past in all its determinate indeterminacy, and to condemn it at the same time. Critical attention to the past need not preclude the affirmation and enfranchisement of hitherto neglected forms of writing and culture.

Decanonization can be effective only if conceived of as a Derridean double session: the deconstructive and the affirmative in an impure, tactical, and nonsynchronous coalition. The postpedagogical teacher should be interested not just in the repudiation of any one canon, but in the general overthrow of the canonical episteme. The target should be canonicity as algorithm, not just a particular canon as symptom. I am calling for the deconstruction of the pedagogical space where identity, the self, and knowledge have been triangulated in chronic complicity. As for Socrates, we cannot forget him, but we must perennially do away with him. At best we can lay a ruse for him and turn on him the reality of what he repressed:[22] the radical ignorance that his teaching "made a nothing of,"[23] and the "other" and "heterogeneous" time of critical self-reflexivity that his authority foreclosed.[24]

Notes

1. The classic text that deals with the epistemological status of "blindness" and the vital role played by blindness in the production of truth is Paul de Man's *Blindness and Insight* (Minneapolis: University of Minnesota Press, 1983). See also Jacques Lacan, *Ecrits*, trans. Alan Sheridan (New York: Norton, 1977), and Hélène Cixous and Catherine Clément, *The Newly Born Woman*, trans. Betsy Wing (Minneapolis: University of Minnesota Press, 1986), for significant discussions of "scotomization" within any given visual field.

2. The relationship of prejudice to truth has to be the primary area of Hans-Georg Gadamer's philosophical investigations. See, in particular, his *Truth and Method* (London, 1975) and *Philosophical Hermeneutics* (Berkeley: University of California Press, 1976). Gadamer's work itself would not have been possible without Martin Heidegger's monumental achievements. It was Heidegger who initially posited the circular nature of all hermeneutic activity and insisted that any honest system of thinking should include "the questioner within the question."

3. Both the notion of "error" and that of "the primary" have received extensive treatment in poststructuralist thought. Following the Nietzschean lead, poststructuralist thought finds it untenable to posit a clear line of demarcation between truth and error. On the contrary, it is committed to the epistemology of "errancy" that has been repressed within the history of a monothetic and authoritarian truth. Much of poststructuralist thought is dedicated to the task of disinheriting and divesting itself from the history of a "primary error" variously known as logo-, phallo-, ethno-, and phonocentrism. For some of the most polemically spirited exchanges about the nature of error and truth in the field of human interpretation, refer to the debate between Michel Foucault and Jacques Derrida about the nature of the Cartesian cogito; in particular, see Jacques Derrida, "Cogito and the History of Madness," in *Writing and Difference*, trans. Alan Bass (Chicago: University of Chicago Press, 1978).

4. Shoshana Felman, "Psychoanalysis and Education: Teaching Terminable and Interminable," *Yale French Studies* 63 (1982): 21–44.

5. Passage from Plato's *Meno*, quoted as epigraph in ibid., 21.

6. Ibid.

7. See Paul de Man's *Allegories of Reading* (New Haven, Conn.: Yale University Press, 1979), in particular the chapters on Nietzsche, for a brilliant and thorough interpretation of the rhetoricity of truth and error in Nietzsche.

8. See Friedrich Nietzsche's *The Use and Abuse of History*, trans. Adrian Collins

(Indianapolis: Bobbs-Merrill, 1949), for a polemical perspective on the nature of the past-present-future nexus.

9. Paul de Man, "Resistance to Theory," in *The Resistance to Theory* (Minneapolis: University of Minnesota Press, 1986), 3–20. For a thoughtful discussion of de Man's essay, see S. P. Mohanty, "Radical Teaching, Radical Theory: The Ambiguous Politics of Meaning," in *Theory in the Classroom*, ed. Cary Nelson (Urbana: University of Illinois Press, 1986).

10. De Man, "Resistance to Theory."

11. I am referring here, by way of Luce Irigaray, to the ongoing debate among feminist theories about the relevance of male discourse in the context of feminist projects and interests. For example, can and should psychoanalytic theory be part of a feminist historiography? Refer to the works of Julia Kristeva, Hélène Cixous, and Catherine Clément, among others, for a general sense of the positionality of a deconstructive male discourse vis-à-vis feminist theory. For a profound and politically engaged sense of poststructuralist feminism, see Gayatri Chakravorty Spivak, "Feminism and Deconstruction, Again: Negotiating with Unacknowledged Masculinism," in *Between Feminism and Psychoanalysis*, ed. Teresa Brennan (London: Routledge, 1989).

12. See Gilles Deleuze's *Logique du Sens* (Paris: Minuit, 1969) and *Différence et Répétition* (Paris: Presses Universitaires de France, 1969), and also Michel Foucault's essay, "Theatrum Philosophicum," in *Language, Counter-Memory, Practice*, ed. Donald Bouchard (Ithaca, N.Y.: Cornell University Press, 1977), for a provocative discussion of the status of "difference" within the history of identity.

13. See Jacques Derrida's essay "Differance," in *Margins of Philosophy*, trans. Alan Bass (Chicago: University of Chicago Press, 1982). See also Alice Jardine's *Gynesis* (Ithaca, N.Y.: Cornell University Press, 1985) for a critical overview of French poststructuralism and its bearing on feminist theory, and *The Future of Difference*, ed. Alice Jardine and Hester Eisenstein (New Brunswick, N.J.: Rutgers University Press, 1985). My essay "Feminist Historiography and Post-Structuralist Thought: Intersections and Departures," in *The Difference Within: Feminism and Critical Theory*, ed. Elizabeth Meese and Alice Parker (Philadelphia: Benjamins, 1988), deals with some of the limitations of "differential politics," especially when conceived of as part of a "male-deconstructive" agenda.

14. The question of identity has often been the vexing issue between French feminists and their Anglo-American counterparts. By and large, the French feminists consider *identity as such* as a repressive structure that is to be deconstructed, whereas the Anglo-American feminists conceive of "identity" as a political necessity. See *The New Feminist Criticism*, ed. Elaine Showalter (New York: Pantheon, 1985). On identity, see my essay entitled "Ethnic Identity and Post-Structuralist Differance," *Cultural Critique* 6 (Spring 1987), and George Yudice, "Marginality and the Ethics of Survival," in *Universal Abandon: The Politics of Postmodernism*, ed. Andrew Ross (Minneapolis: University of Minnesota Press, 1988).

15. I am referring to Jacques Derrida's brilliant rendition of the "orphaned present" in his *Dissemination*, trans. Barbara Johnson (Chicago: University of Chicago Press, 1981).

16. See Jacques Derrida, "Racism's Last Word," *Critical Inquiry* 12, no. 1 (Autumn, 1985): 290–99, and the essays by Anne McClintock and Rob Nixon, as well as

Derrida's response to their essays, in *Critical Inquiry* 13, no. 1 (Autumn 1986). This series of responses on the nature of apartheid points up the highly ramified nature of the past-future relationship.

17. Michel Foucault, "Nietzsche, Genealogy, History," in *Language, Counter-Memory, Practice,* addresses the question of the countermemory in Nietzsche's terms.

18. See Derrida's *Dissemination.*

19. See Derrida's *Positions,* trans. Alan Bass (Chicago: University of Chicago Press, 1981). In a set of interviews, Derrida explains and accounts for the nature of his adversarial engagement with binarity as such. See Gayatri Chakravorty Spivak, *In Other Worlds* (London: Methuen, 1987), for a powerful version of Derridean affirmative deconstruction.

20. I refer to the fundamental tension in psychoanalysis between remedial analysis and a long-term radical analysis that has no ending. Whereas the ego psychologists have chosen to valorize short-term remediation, Lacan makes it a point to ridicule ego psychology for its egregious misrepresentation of Freud.

21. The reference is to Paulo Freire's *Pedagogy of the Oppressed* (New York: Continuum, 1985). See also Henry A. Giroux, *Theory and Resistance in Education* (South Hadley, Mass.: Bergin and Garvey, 1983).

22. The "return of the repressed" is both a Freudian and a Nietzschean theme. My focus here is on the extent to which such a "return" can destabilize dominant structures. My point is that projects of destabilization of master discourses need to be aligned with projects of affirmation.

23. It was Heidegger who made the statement that, in making a "nothing" of "the nothing," positivistic science conceals its own contingency.

24. In "The Principle of Reason: The University in the Eye of Its Pupils," *Diacritics* 13 (Fall 1983): 3–20, Derrida advances the claim that the university as institutional space should be developed as that "other" space.

6 / Negotiating Subject Positions in an Uneven World

Among the politically progressive aspects of poststructuralist thought has been its capacity to enable a dialogic and often contestatory articulation between "history as representation" and "history as production." The pressure has been particularly severe on the form known as "narrative," for now it has to tell a story or represent a reality as though it were a transcendental signified, and at the same time foreground this very activity of representation as an unnatural mode of production. The authority of the narrative is thus schizophrenically divided between a commitment to a truth value that is anterior to the narrative intervention and a formal allegiance that is internal to the narrative itself. In other words, having lost its instrumental transparency, narrative is forced into a metanarrative speculation and reflexivity, thus calling into question the once putative bonding between "narrative as meaning" and "narrative as technique or form." Our contemporary fictional and narrative scenario affords enough examples, on the one hand, of storytellers who dismiss metafictional reflexivity as precious and ultimately inane and life-denying and, on the other hand, of second-order fabricators who find narrative outmoded. The difficulty, in general, has been the lack of a space where the two modes could meet, negotiate, and generate through their mutual asymmetry an effective but a progressively complex and mediated sense of "history" and "reality." In many ways, the contemporary political novel could well be that space, for what is "political" demands a clear and unequivocal reference to reality and history, and contemporaneity insists that such a reference itself be subjected to autocritique and protocols of "self-enactment." This already complicated situation is problematized further when we consider the heterogeneous, nontotalizable, and postrepresentational nature of contemporary reality that rejects the authority of a univocal narrative that emanates from a universal Subject of history.

The story we need to tell is of a world characterized by a nonsynchronous and multitemporal development: a world animated by plural subject positions that are simultaneous but not synchronic. On the one hand, those in dominant subject positions, like whites who are against apartheid in South Africa, are in the process of deauthorizing themselves and seeking affiliation with emerging revolutionary subjects. On the other hand, those in emerging revolutionary positions, like blacks in South Africa, are striving to affirm and legitimate themselves by creating their own "insider space." Whereas the dominant position requires acts of self-deconstruction, the subordinate position entails collective self-construction.

It is in this context that Nadine Gordimer's fictions are to be read and evaluated. We have the individual subject position of a white woman whose dedication to the abolition of apartheid has to route itself via an interrogation of its own positionality, for such a subject position, however supportive it may be of black consciousness, is still not a historical and existential inhabitant of that consciousness. The "personal" and individual valence that Gordimer wishes to generate on behalf of herself and her fictions are out of sync with her given and filiative political valence as a "white."[1] Consequently, it is incumbent upon such a subject that it perennially divest itself of its own "assigned" position[2] before it can legitimately ask the question, What role should I play in the revolutionary black consciousness? Gordimer's *Burger's Daughter* takes on this question in all its ramified complexity. "The excellence of *Burger's Daughter*," as Abdul JanMohamed puts it, "is due to a judicious combination of the relative simplicity of its plot, the elegance and appropriateness of its style, and the integrity, acuteness, and courage of Rosa Burger's attempt to define her 'self.'[3] The attempts that Rosa Burger makes to thematize her own problematic and contradictory subject positionality are characterized by a certain psychological autonomy, but an autonomy that can only be relative to and ultimately determined by the larger political reality.

Elizabeth Meese's essay, "The Political Is the Personal: The Construction of a Revolutionary "Subject" in Nadine Gordimer's *Burger's Daughter*," reenacts, at a critical-interpretive but empathic distance, the agonies of a "self" in search of an authentic position. Through an interpretive strategy that combines rigorous and highly nuanced textual readings with the capacity to move speculatively and critically out of the text into "the world," Meese activates a readerly space where the reader is challenged to undertake the uneven and perilous task of "self-consciencization." As she asks in her conclusion to the essay: "How, in us as readers, the ultimate 'place' of Gordimer's South African narrative, will Rosa's story be 'concocted,' many more times in many more versions? How are we as readers finally to discover our places among its revolutionary 'subjects'?" (273). I am particularly grateful to Meese for the way in which she "identifies" and foregrounds her own position as reader as a necessary prolegomenon to the act of critical intervention. To quote Meese again: "Because her culture is inseparable from mine, it is my own position, the position of feminism, as much as Gordimer"s, I wish to interrogate" (255). I say I am grateful, since it is rare in the context of academic critical discourse for a professional critic to make constitutive reference to her own "person" and explicitly implicate the "noninnocence" of her own position in the act of producing a critical reading. Meese's sense of self-implication also enables me, I would even say that it enjoins me, to disclose the ideological and intellectual underpinnings of my position as a male feminist, third world, postcolonialist Indian subject deeply invested in poststructuralist practices. I will begin therefore with a brief critical analysis of three paradigmatic situations: one from my "personal" life, one from literature, and one from history, all by way of denaturalizing my own position and of opening up a significant area where I may join the already inaugurated dialogue between Meese and Gordimer.

The first situation has to do with my critical reaction to the movie *Out of Africa*. Simply stated, I walked out of the theater after the first twenty minutes or so, in great anger and indignation. I just could not bear to see the history of an entire culture being frozen and fetishized into a spectacle so as to better serve as a backdrop for the emerging psychodrama of a white woman's sense of identity. It seemed to me that the effective historicization of the white woman's consciousness was unfolding into narrative within a privileged and privatized space, or, if you will, a chronotope, that preempted the narrative of black African consciousness. (The fact that Dinesen's Africa is not the same as Gordimer's is a valid point, but it does not in any fundamental way alter my argument here.) Given the macropolitical situation of Africa, an individual's psychodrama seemed to me particularly lacking in valence, all the more so since the individual concerned was "white." But I must confess to feeling very angry and confused with my own "self" for having walked out with such an uncomplicated and righteous sense of my own "purity." What exactly did my reaction signify? Certainly, a bias, but how did this bias rule out my potential sympathy for the white woman's subject position, especially when I call myself a "male feminist"? Wasn"t there enough space within the area known as my "self" to accommodate both biases? Or perhaps it was all right to be unconcerned about the "scotoma" in my visual field, given the world-historical conjunction between my own identity as a postcolonial Indian watching a film about a white woman's conquest of Africa. What I found difficult to justify (although I didn't feel all that guilty about it) was the ease with which I chose not to listen to a particular narrative. If my real complaint was that the film did not have room for multiple conflicting and contradictory narratives, was I not guilty of a similar insensitivity?

The second situation in its own way points up the impossibility of constructing a narrative that is heterogeneous, multiple, and differential enough to offer fair representation to multiple subject positions. I have in mind E. M. Forster's *Passage to India* and the built-in antagonism between Adela Quested's sense of "subjecthood" and Aziz's sense of constituency. Given the asymmetry between the two predicaments, what can we demand of narrative and its commitment to a certain world and worldview? What or which world are we talking about? Here again is a text that places the reader in an anxious space where decisions and choices are not easy. There are two different subject positions, each imbued with its own historicity and each a potentially adversarial and revolutionary agency relative to the dominant mode that holds it in captivity. On the one hand, the text deals with feminine sexuality in opposition to phallocentric normativity, and on the other, with an emerging national consciousness in battle against the forces of colonialism. In each case, the personal element is part of a long *durée* that is not to be exhausted by any of its particular instances.[4] How is narrative to arbitrate between two macropolitical discourses and assign priorities? This is a problem that faces Nadine Gordimer, too, as she moves among black consciousness, feminism, and communism. First, there is the question concerning the transcendence of the "personal" into the "political," and second (and this is even more complicated), there is the problem of determining how different personal "selves," such as black, white, male, female, and so on, interact differently in their respective constituencies. For example, during the moments of the revolutionary emergence of a group consciousness, there is a solidarity of the personal with the political within the psyche of each "self" that makes up that group (that is, in such historical junctures, the "representative" nature and the "individual" nature of the self become virtually the same), a solidarity that is communicable but not easily sharable or generalizable beyond that group.

This brings me to my last example, which is a scene from the film *Gandhi*. Gandhi is in prison, and his white Scottish comrade, the priest Charles F. Andrews, visits him. The two of them have been intimate fellow travelers seeking paths to India's independence from British rule. And yet, in this scene from the movie, Gandhi, from behind bars, tells Charlie that the time has come for them to part, for from now on it is only Indians who can and should carry on the struggle. Charlie agrees and leaves after Gandhi assures him that in an ideal sense the two never are and never will be parted. This scene demonstrates both the historical finitude of subject positions and the extent to which "given" subject positions can be critically transcended in search of new and different affiliations. To play a little on the polysemy of the word "bar," Gandhi is behind "bars" whereas Andrews is not. As Meese puts it in the context of the apartheid color bar, "The 'essential gesture' for black and white writers alike in South Africa 'is a revolutionary gesture,' the nature of which for each, however, is marked by their different positions relative to the 'bar' (as line, law, institution and mark of subjectivity)" (255).

The epigraph to *Burger's Daughter,* a quotation from Claude Lévi-Strauss, "I am the place in which something has occurred," provides the reader with a historical-structuralist orientation to Rosa Burger's sense of identity and place. Meese's essay argues that

> Rosa Burger is one such place; South Africa, Gordimer's text (the discursive space of which begins by marking itself off there), the author herself, and ultimately the reader are other "places," sites for/of production and performance. Who this subject is, where the place and what the thing that has "taken place," the reader is to discover by reading between the lines of this textual complex of interlocking relationships. (256)

A point well taken, for it seems to me that the tension between "place" and "what takes place in it" is essential to an understanding of historicity. I wish to argue that the structuralist rhetoric of "positionality" does not have to result in empty allegorical readings of history, but instead can be used to sensitize our awareness of historical process as chronotopic, to use Bakhtin's influential terminology.[5] If one's sense of identity in "one's own time" endows the "self" with a sense of personal authenticity, a spatialized perception of one's own personal identity leads to the realm of the "political," which necessarily relativizes and/or sublates the *personal as such.*

As the very title of Meese's essay suggests, the personal-political nexus is of the utmost importance both to Gordimer and to Meese. Meese notes at the very beginning of her reading that the maxim "the personal is the political" has been a caveat of the contemporary feminist movement, authorizing the private, subjective experiences of the individual woman to be read in terms of or for its significance with respect to larger issues, or to stand as or for "the issues" of contemporary society. The microstructure of experience and the macrostructure of political forces are made synonymous and the former is dignified, given the significance and readability presumed to belong to the political space of "public" life; yet Meese is concerned that if the valorization of the personal as a gesture were "elevated to law-in-itself, [it] may become an exclusionary principle inhibiting other political actions—outside the private sphere, in the rest of or in other parts of the world" (253). Quoting Terry Eagleton, who reminds us that "political struggle cannot be reduced to the personal, or vice versa," Meese goes on to ask the all-important question: "What then is the excess, the 'more than' the personal which constitutes The Political (not as reduction) or the-political-taken-personally? And what is the 'more than' or 'other than' the political which constitutes The Personal in this non-identification which Eagleton suggests?" What she suggests then is "the critical elaboration of this complex relationship, the site of struggle in/between the self and the world—the working out of which might help us live in the tension" (254). The truly difficult task, it seems to me, is "to live in the tension," even live as tension without letting the "living" simplify tension or allowing the tension to render the "living" nonviable. I would like now to attempt a brief critical articulation of the kind that Meese is calling for.

The entire question of the conjunction of the personal and political partakes, to borrow from Althusser's structuralist Marxism, both of a general and omnihistorical reality and a particular reality. In other words, one may posit that human social reality is always such that the personal and the political are coimplicated within a dialectically oriented symbiosis. But one could also state that the particular forms that this coimplication takes in different sociopolitical, economic, and cultural conjunctures have specific histories of their own. For example, given the political age of a group, that is, the duration of its history as an independent and autonomous group, the persons who constitute that group may feel differently about the ontological status of their individuation and the extent to which they feel their "selves" to be explicitly politicized. Their conscious awareness of the manner in which they are "ideologically interpellated" varies. The protocols that determine the relative weight of the political over the personal also varies, depending upon how well established the group is. Generally speaking, the perception of one's individual "self" is hierarchically subsumed without any accompanying sense of personal impoverishment when the group is just becoming established, whereas the sense of individual autonomy is intensified when the group is firmly established as a dominant or hegemonic collectivity. To state this in the context of Rosa Burger, her sense of secure selfhood and subjectivity as a white is being made to respond sympathetically to a differently emerging historic self. Rosa's sense of her "white self" is made aware of the untenability of the very collective identity of which she has been a part, and hence her self is in double jeopardy: it is in an adversarial relationship with the hegemonic constituency that is her "base," so to speak, while it cannot entirely claim the revolutionary black consciousness as its new base. Whereas, for Baasie, her black "brother," his subjectivity and personal identity have already been parsed, as it were, within the developing revolutionary language, Rosa's displaced self is in search of an authentic constituency. The question that Rosa's self asks—"Where do whites fit in?"—can only be answered as an asymmetrical response to the black revolution. Indeed, the question "Where do whites fit in?" is politically meaningless in the context of a black majority consciousness historicizing itself into effective political existence. The tricky task facing the "white subject" engaged in "self-consciencization" is one of articulation: a transformed articulation that has to divest itself of authority and privilege. There is the black insurrectionary subject position, there is the subject position of the "white" "rethinking all its values," and there is a common political space that subtends both these positions. In his essay "Intellectuals in the Post-Colonial World," Edward Said makes a brilliant analysis of this unevenness: "The tragedy of this experience, and indeed of all post-colonial questions, lies in the constitutive limitation imposed on any attempt to deal with relationships that are polarized, radically uneven, remembered differently. The spheres, the sites of intensity, the agendas, the constituencies in the metropolitan and formerly colonized worlds overlap only partially. The small area that is common does not, at this point, provide for more than what I'd like to call a *politics of blame*.[6]

I am aware that the regimes of colonialism and apartheid are not the same. I am also aware that whereas Said's comments pertain to realities of the formerly colonized, the South African reality is of a related but different order, and yet Said's central point still holds. From a world-historical perspective, the white question "Can we stay on in South Africa?" is not and, in a sense, cannot be part of the progressive agenda at this particular point. And the irony is that this question intrinsically is an askable question that emanates from an existing perspective, albeit a perspective deracinated from its hegemonic history. The really meaningful question, a question that can eventually lead to a postapartheid cooperation across "the bar," is, What forms of "self-consciencization" should white consciousness practice in order to earn the merit to stay: ascesis, self de- and re-identification, a deracinated consciousness?

Gordimer does not spare her protagonist the intense agony of these questions. The problem confronting Rosa Burger, given her profoundly political upbringing, is that of choice. What sort of strategy and what kind of "ontological anchorage" would be most honest and appropriate for the conscientious white consciousness in apartheid South Africa? How best can Rosa as topos coordinate the political with the personal? Gordimer's own personal realization has been that the personal approach is "inadequate to combat an unyielding white supremacist regime." The personal developed as such is in great danger of easy trivialization or privatization. The dictum "the personal is the political" could atrophy into a form of inaction or into an all-too-easy acceptance of every form of the personal as the political. The personal as a result gets shielded from its responsibility to actualize itself in progressively political formations; instead, it is valorized in its very status quo as "always already" political. The other problem with this formulation is that in letting the personal be its own dispensation, it forecloses the insight that the personal itself can only be part of an overall pattern of socialization where each self exists in a state of exotopy (Bakhtin again) toward other selves within a mobile sociopolitical field where there is neither pure identity nor pure alterity. The fetishization of both "living for one's self" and "living for others" is the mediated expression of contradictions and overdeterminations within a structural totality where often the different regional logics are out of sync with one another.

But the irony in Rosa's case is the fact that she has indeed been brought up under Marxist-Leninist principles to valorize the political and the social over the personal. And this precisely is the problem: the doctrinaire internalization of communist tenets results in a curious blindness and insensitivity. As Meese observes shrewdly: "Part of what Rosa fails to see is that, because the tenets of white communism have been 'naturalized' in the family, they are as inseparable for her in the effort to 'identify' herself as they were for her father or mother. Likewise, the natural becomes the unnatural, or is it the other way around?" (259). Her analysis also makes the point that "Lionel Burger's household, with its pool, black servants, black 'son' 'Baasie,' and steak barbecues, embodies the domestication of white revolutionary South African politics in the 1950s" (258). We now see that Rosa as "place" is multiply coordinated and there are no easy ways to name or identify such a place. Rosa as "place" is also a topographic detail within the utopic communist map, a map whose algebraic and programmatic sense of space has led to the loss, within the space, of an existential and phenomenological density. And besides, communism itself, in having naturalized itself, has lost touch with its own contingency. In other words, it has hardened into a master discourse of a Eurocentric radicality that does not sit well on the South African scene, which is so strongly determined by race, not class.

The important issue that Meese raises here but does not elaborate is that of the formation of the revolutionary subject position. What is the modality of such a subject position and within what intellectual, cultural, and sociopolitical tradition of opposition is such a position being generated? What are the formal characteristics of the model and what are its master concepts and categories: Marxist, feminist, African Nationalist, ethnic? What if a given subject position like Rosa's straddles multiple realities and modes: feminist, communist, antiracist? Will a single model suffice or should the revolutionary subject resort to improper bricolage? In my response so far, in situating Rosa in an exclusively race-specific context, I have overlooked the feminist valence in her position. Is it conceivable then that the inordinate search for a personal "self," which seems so solipsistic and retrogressive in the context of the politics of the revolutionary black consciousness, might well be the appropriate demand of a legitimate "insider" if we situate Rosa within the feminist model? Meese, as a feminist critic, is quick to perceive this dimension in *Burger's Daughter*:

> In a sense Gordimer's question of what is the place of whites in South Africa . . . is conflated with what is "woman's place." That is, in *Burger's Daughter* we can read these as correlative questions. Rosa is offered an identity—as comrade-daughter (the communist family), South African white (state), cultural product (language and history), corporeal subject (menstruating girl turned woman). Her problem is how to be Burger's daughter and more, other—how to be white but not the master, colonizer—*finding a representation which permits a non-hierarchical play of difference.* (261; emphasis added)

How does this correlation of "woman's space" with the "white's place" work? And, as a result of this correlation, what new critical "place" is produced where the two agendas may be said to meet, interrupt, and throw each other into crisis? It is a particularly vexing question to answer since one of the two agendas, "woman's," world-historically speaking, is a progressive one, whereas the other, "white's," is, politically and world-historically speaking, part of a dying order. Whereas "woman's place" carries with it an irrefragable moral and political authority that is affirmative and future oriented, the "white's place" brings with it an autocritical, deconstructive, and an ascetic ethic. And of course, both these "places" are "subplaces" within the "place" known as Rosa. If the rationale of the revolutionary subject is the production of knowledge as change and not as adequation, on what terrain or axis should such a production take place, that is, given the overdeterminations and contradictions inherent in Rosa as structural topos? A sensitive topographical rendering of Rosa's positionality, it seems to me, should map her (and Gordimer, too) multiply so that the different factors that determine Rosa are correlated but not rendered mutually identical, interchangeable, or structurally isomorphic. For example, it is obvious that the woman's question in South Africa at this particular time does not have the same urgent priority as the color and race question, but this assignment of priorities is not immutable or transcendent. There are clear indications in *Burger's Daughter* that the woman's question is both part of and in excess of the race and color question. The difficulty comes in when a single monothetic revolutionary blueprint presumes to speak for an entire range of subconstituencies that make up the constituency of the oppressed.[7] After all, given a general history where "there is no document of civilization which is not at the same time a document of barbarism,"[8] should not the different groups that make up, however unevenly, the world of the oppressed seek an axial-coalitional expression of themselves rather than look for fiercely regional and autochthonous islands of self-fulfillment? One cannot but refer in this context to the eloquent critique elaborated during the early days of academic feminism in this country by Shulamith Firestone, who found that during the many revolutions in history (ethnic, Marxist, and Freudian revolutions), the "woman's question" had always been subsumed within a larger agenda, but never articulated in and for itself. To go back then to the question I posed earlier: how is the correlation to be achieved? But first let us look at "woman's place" as coordinated in Gordimer's text and Meese's sensitive interpretation of it.

I quote, for reasons of economy, from Meese's text as it interacts critically with the opening of *Burger's Daughter*:

> Rosa sees herself "in place, outside the prison," but her attention is not focused on the public spectacle that she is and of which she is apart. She stands in front of the prison and menstruates for the first time, becoming a woman, who, as JanMohamed puts it, is more/other than a daughter: "Thus her simultaneous yet unconnected existence as an object of public scrutiny and as a locus of private experience reflects her predicament as a bifurcated social being." In her version of the story, Rosa focuses on her bio-sexual identity, the biological fact of her womanhood, turning her private, internal experience into a public one where "the internal landscape of my mysterious body turns me inside out, so that in that public place on that public occasion . . . I am within that monthly crisis of destruction, the purging, tearing, draining of my own structure. I am my womb." She tells us in retrospect that it matters little whose identity story we read—theirs or hers—as "both would seem equally concocted." (257)

And my question is, Who is to decide or who can arrogate to herself the univocal authority to decide whose version has the maximum significance, that is, given the fact that they are all versions that are conscious and perspectival productions of meaning? Does or can one have the right to arbitrate against

Rosa's "focus on her bio-sexual identity" just because the macropolitical situation in South Africa has to do with race and color and not with "becoming woman"? But, even given the incontrovertible race-color specificity of the political situation in South Africa, how can any specific, particular subject position within that reality be expected *not to involve its own specific structure* in the act of hermeneutically understanding the macrosituation? To put it concretely in the context both of Rosa Burger and of Gordimer: Indeed it is true that the larger South African oppression has to do with race, but how can Gordimer and Rosa Burger interpret this reality except as *women?* Would their readings not be suspect and disingenuous from any other positional base?[9] Would it make a difference if they were black women? But then, what about the position "women" within the designation "black women"? Are there then exemplary norms of blackness that preclude other determinations? And whose black norms are these—black men's? While poststructuralism teaches us that "common reality" can only be understood through multiple and contradictory narratives, the politically aware reader has to choose positions that are either "inside" or "outside," despite her awareness that the very terms "inside" and "outside" can be deconstructed. Otherwise, Gordimer's and Rosa's narratives end up resembling Botha's.

Meese's critical study focuses on this "disjunction" quite appropriately. It is clear that Meese finds Gordimer's placing of feminism in the South African context quite unsatisfactory, but at the same time she is sensitive to the contradictory valences of Gordimer's own position as a white woman in that society. Writes Meese: "Obviously Gordimer believes in feminism; but feminism is not her highest priority." And again: "She shares the view of many women of color who are multiply oppressed. Theirs is a compelling position, *although Gordimer repeatedly represents feminism through trivializing examples*" (261–62; emphasis added). And further on: "Gordimer's critique of white privilege requires her to place the black woman first, limited though her understanding may be concerning who the 'black woman' is and what she wants and what that 'first place' might be. *It is the gesture* [my emphasis] that saves her in the endless struggle against her subject position, her racial privilege—what she as a white woman in South Africa *has* but does not necessarily want" (262). I particularly appreciate Meese's highly nuanced use of the word "gesture," for in many ways what we are talking about here are some of the differences between substantive politics and gestural politics and between representational politics and a postrepresentational sense of constituency. Gordimer cannot represent the black consciousness (this would be false representation), nor can she, in elucidating her subject position, *not talk* about it (such omission would be unconscionable).

In a global situation where "I cannot be you" and yet I have the moral and the political need to join coalitional forces with you, it seems more urgent than ever to articulate theories of critical-political solidarity that would "inmix" the substantive with the gestural, and the representational with the postrepresentational. Moreover, feminism, ethnicity, the third world, and many other constituencies share common enemies: racism, sexism, normative heterosexism, and ethnophallogocentrism. All the more reason to invest in coalitional processes and *not* to dissipate energy in precious insider fighting. There is a time to emphasize difference and a time to stress not identity but similarity and coaxiality.[10]

In conclusion, I revisit the scene where Rosa's "becoming woman" is turned inside out. That scene in many ways is paradigmatic of what a poststructuralist feminism (or feminisms) can bring to the politicization of theory: an awareness of reality and history as liminal and the need for liminal thinking. The figural-political representation of the inside/outside, as well as the private/public opposition, goes to the very source of the problem, which is binarity itself and not merely some of the particular forms that this binarity takes on.[11] That scene, in my reading, demonstrates with surpassing intensity and eloquence (1) that subject positions and the narratives that they produce about themselves are productions of reality that are in themselves historical; (2) that the second-order story of the subject position qua subject position and the story that it tells need to be understood together and in light of the reality of other subject positions and their narratives; (3) that the spatial nature of positions in general should allow for mobility among and across positions; and, finally, (4) that the binary historiography that we have "received" needs to be problematized and in a sense transcended so that critical thinking may respond to both the present and the permanent revolution in the present moment.

As for my subject position, it is cathected and politicized on the one hand by the desire for a worldliness that is "between Culture and System" (Edward Said) and on the other by an imperative to dwell within a tension as well as a "contradiction without recourse," where different and heterogeneous agencies within the same "subject" are perennially calling each other's absolutism into question.[12]

Notes

1. My reference is to Edward Said"s notions of "filiation" and "affiliation," where "filiation" represents given and received subject positions and "affiliation" signifies the capacity of the subject to displace and reaffiliate itself through the practice of secular and oppositional criticism. See Said 1983.

2. That subject positions are "assigned" is an important aspect of Michel Foucault's genealogical archaeology, which insists that "subjects" are both "constituting" and "constituted," both agential and determined. See Foucault 1966 and 1972.

3. JanMohamed 1983:126.

4. This is a conflated reference to Braudel's notion of the *longue durée*, as well as to the Althusserian thesis that particular histories and structures are interpellated in response to the authority of general structures. See Braudel 1980 and 1976. Also see Althusser 1969 and 1971, and Althusser and Balibar 1970.

5. Unlike most forms of Western European critical theory that are invested in bipolar and binary modes of thinking, Bakhtin's critical philosophical anthropology consistently works for a dialectical nexus where "opposites" negotiate with each other. The "chronotope," for example, does away with the highly overdetermined space-time/structure-history opposition in order to inaugurate a study of the morphology of historical forms. See Bakhtin 1981.

6. Said 1986: 45.

7. Radhakrishnan 1987:199-200.

8. Benjamin 1969:256.

9. This is as much a political probelm as it is a hermeneutric problem. How is the political to be actualized if not through interpretation, and how can interpretation (after Martin Heidegger and Hans-Georg Gadamer) not implicate its own positionality and historicity in the act of producing knowledge and truth?

10. See chapter 2 in this volume.

11. No one has taken on this task of thematizing and displacing *binarity as such* as brilliantly and relentlessly as Jacques Derrida, but it is still interesting to see that these formal, second-order critiques do not sometimes sit well politically. I am referring in particular to Derrida's essay, "Racism's Last Word" (Derrida 1985).

12. Gayatri Chakrovarty Spivak's subject position, as well as her choice of critical methodology as Marxist-feminist-deconstructivist-postcolonialist-Indian-subaltern, is exemplary of such a creative crisis. See Spivak 1987. See also Said 1983.

References

Althusser, Louis. 1969. *For Marx*. Harmondsworth: Penguin.

———. 1971. *Lenin and Philosophy and Other Essays*. Trans. Ben Brewster. London: New Left Books.

Althusser, Louis, and Balibar, Etienne. 1970. *Reading Capital*. London: New Left Books.

Bakhtin, Mikhail. 1981. *The Dialogic Imagination: Four Essays*. Trans. Michael Holquist and Caryl Emerson. Austin: University of Texas Press.

Benjamin, Walter. 1969. "Theses on the Philosophy of History." In *Illuminations*, ed. Hannah Arendt. New York: Schocken Books.

Braudel, Fernand. 1976. *Afterthoughts on Material Civilization and Capitalism*. Baltimore, Md.: Johns Hopkins University Press.

———. 1980. *On History*. Chicago and London: University of Chicago Press.

Clingman, Stephen. 1986. *The Novels of Nadine Gordimer: History from the Inside*. Amherst: University of Massachusetts Press.

Derrida, Jacques. 1974. *Of Grammatology.* Trans. Gayatri Chakravorty Spivak. London and Baltimore: Johns Hopkins University Press.

———. 1981. *Dissemination.* Trans. Barbara Johnson. Chicago: University of Chicago Press.

———. 1985. "Racism's Last Word." *Critical Inquiry* 12, no. 1(Autumn): 290–99.

Forster, E. M. 1952. *A Passage to India.* New York: Harcourt, Brace and World.

Foucault, Michel. 1966. *The Order of Things.* London: Tavistock.

———. 1972. *The Archaeology of Knowledge.* London: Tavistock.

Gordimer, Nadine. 1979. *Burger's Daughter.* New York: Viking Press.

JanMohamed, Abdul. 1983. *Manichean Aesthetics: The Politics of Literature in Colonial Africa.* Amherst: University of Massachusetts Press.

Said, Edward W. 1983. *The World, the Text, the Critic.* Cambridge, Mass.: Harvard University Press.

———. 1986. "Intellectuals in the Post-Colonial World." *Salmagundi* 70–71 (Spring–Summer): 44–81.

Spivak, Gayatri Chakravorty. 1987. *In Other Worlds: Essays in Cultural Politics.* New York and London: Methuen.

7 / Cultural Theory and the Politics of Location

It is unfortunate that we will not have the advantage of Raymond Williams's insights into the changing nature of the Left in the Eastern bloc countries. It would seem that the optimism and the sense of agency that Williams strove to keep alive during difficult and daunting times, with the poverty of ideology, on the one hand, and the sense of determinism produced by technology, on the other, have in a sense found concrete historical shape in the emancipatory subaltern movements throughout Eastern Europe. Of course, there is a relationship of both affinity and asymmetry between Williams's projects of hope and those emerging from the erstwhile Soviet Union, Czechoslovakia, Poland, and Hungary. Whereas Williams's oppositional courses of action are in search of a viable Left politics in the context of Thatcherite Britain, the people's movements in Eastern Europe find themselves deconstructing a repressive and dictatorial official Left politics: an originally emancipatory politics betrayed by the authority of the state, the Party, and their bureaucratic apparatus. But, despite the locational dissimilarity, there are a number of themes, issues, and anxieties that are common to both situations. My purpose here is to evaluate the "resources of hope" that Williams cherished and nurtured throughout his long and distinguished career as a committed public intellectual and to provide an appreciative critique of Williams from a point of view that is simultaneously postcolonial and poststructuralist. I will begin then with a selective analysis of the situation in Eastern Europe by way of framing my discussion of Williams.

The ongoing "tectonic" changes in Eastern Europe and the erstwhile Soviet

Union would seem to demonstrate (1) that a politics of change is possible and (2) that subaltern movements can succeed in toppling "dominant forms without hegemony"[1] and can initiate their own histories in opposition to all forms of top-down historiography. Clearly, these events have a global significance. The countries of the former Soviet Union are renegotiating their identity in response to long-suppressed ethnic and nationalist claims. Europe, too, is in the process of reconceptualizing its geopolitical identity both along national and pannational lines. Even the United States, whose custom it has been to remain ideologically insensitive to anything but its own interests, has been forced to open its eyes and restructure its foreign policy, which has long been entrenched in the Us-Them logic of the cold war.[2] Developing nations in the so-called third world are watching these happenings with great interest, wondering how best to contextualize the lessons learned from these transformations.

And yet, it is not quite clear what the lessons to be learned are. Ideologues of capitalism and free enterprise rejoice in the demise of Marxism and socialism. Defenders of individual rights are eager to announce the death of all forms of collective political endeavor and organization: we are now supposed to have discovered the only authentic bottom line—individual growth, desire, and profitability. Jeffersonian critics of "government" are busy glorifying governments that govern least. Poststructuralist theorists are only too happy to point out that all their critiques of "identity" and "totality" and their passionate advocacy of "difference" and "heterogeneity" have been right on all along, for haven't they, ever since May 1968, been arguing against a monolithic and monothetic Marxism? On the other hand, Marxist theorists who wish to remain Marxists, but with a difference, offer the interpretation that these huge changes are to be read as autocritical moments within the history of Marxism and not as total leaps out of the Marxist horizon into a nonideological human history.[3] Postcolonial readings in general would tend to notice with approval the subaltern nature of these changes: a characteristic that is so relevant in the context of postcolonial interrogations of elitist nationalisms.[4] At the same time, the postcolonial perspective would be wary of the Eurocentric character of these revolutions.[5] To put it briefly, these events do have undeniable potential for global meaning, but this meaning itself is by no means univocal. In fact, there are multiple contradictory and contested meanings that depend upon the regional or positional reception and interpretation of these processes or change. It is of the utmost importance that a theoretical understanding of these historic changes not simplify the many tensions, disjunctures, and asymmetries that underlie these vast structural realignments. On the one hand, there is the dire need to retrieve and salvage possibilities for global meaning; on the other, there is an equally urgent need to protect the differential play of regional and subject-positional politics from the dominance of a false globality or totality. And, of course, we cannot afford to be insensitive to the irony inherent in this entire scenario, that is, the fact that these emancipatory subaltern movements are pitted against an ideology (Marxism) whose intentions have always been to bring together and synchronize the regional and the global through a series of carefully coordinated revolutions.

There are many points of convergence between contemporary Eastern European politics and the agential and transformative cultural practices that Raymond Williams theorized and practiced throughout his long and brilliant career. I would now like to identify a few of these themes before I go on to a fuller analysis of Williams's contributions to the politics of cultural theory and cultural studies. First, there is the question of Raymond Williams's subject position and the politics that are available to such a position. Here is Williams operating as a revolutionary cultural critic, but from a position well within the international metropolitan axis. He speaks from within the English tradition even as he questions and problematizes it from his borderline position as a Welshman and a socialist activist. Such a position raises the same kind of issues that I have raised in the context of Eastern Europe. Williams's work also speaks with many voices and valences, and, furthermore, its significance is vulnerable to a range of regional and subject-positional receptions and appropriations. And yet, the singular appeal of Williams's theory is that it does push forward notions of a common humanity and visions of general solidarity that seek a way out of the impasse of local islands of resistance and political change. Attractive and welcome as these visions may be, they raise a few questions. For example, what are the limits of Williams's theory, and how and under what conditions can his theory be made to travel from the center to the periphery, from the first world to the far-removed postcolonial situations? Would the postcolonial situation be in any way enabled by Williams's analysis, and if not, what happens to his idea of solidarity and complementarity across national and other barriers? How self-reflexive is Williams about his own theories, and is his mode of self-reflexivity sufficient to prevent his well-meaning intervention from degenerating into yet another act of colonial violence from the center?

Second, what promise do Williams's projects hold out for the Left, now that the Left seems to have been thoroughly deglobalized? Deprived of the guarantee of a global Left, how are different pockets of Left politics to communicate with one another? How should the politics of any one location be articulated with that of another in a situation of "unsutured global reality"?[6] What is the nature of "location": is it autochthonous or movable? The state of location is informed by a rich and contradictory logic. On the one hand, it represents a poststructuralist demystification of a total politics of global coordination as well as a politics based on essentialism. By this logic, meanings and political possibilities are assumed as a mode of subjection to a particular location, and, as such, they are strongly determined. By definition, locations are perspectival and not global, limited and not infinite, produced and not free or natural.[7] On the other hand, by virtue of being positional and not intrinsic, identitarian, or essentialist, such a politics is nothing if not movable; its very meaning is the function of its travel and mobility.[8] To put it in Bakhtinian terms, locations are characterized by an internal "exotopy," and as such the logic of displacement becomes a corollary to the logic of position. Also, by virtue of its itinerant nature, any position is liable to take on charges that are simultaneous and contradictory. For example, deconstructive theories may be considered transgressive and radical within the European context, but these very theories, caught up within the ideology of Eurocentrism, cannot claim any radicality when placed, say, in an ethnic, feminist, or postcolonial context. The controversy over Salman Rushdie's *Satanic Verses* and the debate in France over the right of Muslim women to wear the veil thematize fully the difficulties of assuming a homogeneous norm in adjudicating claims that are contradictory and multidirectional. These issues also demonstrate the inability of any one macropolitical ethos such as nationalism, feminism, or Marxism to contain or represent one another: no single horizon is capable of subsuming or speaking for the other, nor do the different politics of ethnicity, sexuality, class, gender, and nationality add up into one unifiable political horizon. The problem then is this: how should theory help in translations among and across different and uneven political terrains?

Third, and this is as much a political issue as it is an epistemological one, in the wake of poststructuralism and the Eastern European movements, what meaning can we give to the term "representation"? The ability of the people's movements not just to be adversarial, but hegemonic in their own interests; the emergence of artists, intellectuals, writers, and "nonpolitical" leaders such as Vaclav Havel; the fundamental distrust of official rubrics and systemic mediations such as the "party": do these trends announce, in the manner of Foucault and Deleuze, the end of representation?[9] Are we witnessing a postrepresentational politics here? Are these intellectuals of the "organic" Gramscian variety, or has the people's movement succeeded in superannuating the very category of the "intellectual," for now theory has become praxis in action? Fourth, how will the nascent subaltern subject find unimpeded access to its own agency, and how and in what manner is this issue to be mediated?[10] What will be the ideological nature of these mediations, and what sort of institutional forms and structures are to bear the burden of this newly historicized agency? Has the purity of the people's movements entirely transcended the problem of institutional and other secondary structures, or is the problem, in the words of the subaltern historian and theorist Veena Das, "not whether we can completely obliterate the objectified character of social institutions, but rather whether it is at all possible to establish a relation of authenticity towards these institutions"?[11] And finally, what can we say about the space from which the intellectual acts? Is this space "between Culture and System," in Edward Said's sense of the term?[12] Should this space carry names such as socialist, leftist, Marxist, democratic, and the like, or should designations be avoided altogether (are these not ideological traps in the long run?) in a way that both Havel and Williams would approve? Analogously, how is the intellectual to carry his or her professional specificity in the context of a total constituency?

In a recent review of Raymond Williams entitled "Culture Heroes: Williams and Hall for the Opposition," in the *Voice Literary Supplement,* Rob Nixon sketches out a few significant characteristics of Williams that render him viable as an oppositional theorist of culture. First, there is Williams's "obsession with the practice of possibility [that] left him impatient with those critics of dominant culture who became grooved on an unimaginative cynicism empty of strategy or alternative ideals." Then, there is the Williams "who preferred the label 'revolutionary socialist' to 'Marxist' for similar reasons, believing that no tradition embracing millions of activists should be reduced to the name of any single figure, however grand." And finally, Williams was "a public intellectual, someone who spoke out in the conviction that knowledge was the shared property of cultures, in the most generous sense of that word, and could never be restricted to the little mounds of erudition kicked up by the archival moles tunneling beneath the lawns of his Cambridge surrounds."[13] The search for alternatives, a keen sense of the protean flows of experience that mock any single frame, a genuine populism that commits the intellectual to a general grassroots constituency, and a consistently critical attitude toward modes of intellectual labor that turn hermetic in the name of professionalization: such was the nature of Williams's motivation as a cultural theorist, a sense of motivation that stayed with him until the very end. In an essay written shortly before his death, we find Williams speculating strongly about the future of cultural studies and making a commitment to the future:

> Indeed, we should remind ourselves of that unpredictability, as a condition likely to apply also to any projections we might ourselves make, some of which will be

certainly as blind. Yet we need to be robust rather than hesitant about this question of the future because our own input into it, our own sense of the directions in which it should go, will constitute a significant part of whatever is made. And moreover the clearing of our minds which might lead to some definition of the considerations that would apply in deciding a direction is both hard and necessary to achieve, *precisely because of that uncertainty.* (Emphasis added)[14]

A number of themes emerge here. First, there is the confident assumption of an organic "we" as a collective agency. Second, there is the invocation of an intended future. In strong contrast to much poststructuralist thought that suspects collectivity from the point of view of "difference" and resists the project of willing an agential future for fear of repeating the history of the same, Williams takes a risk. In the face of unpredictability, not only does he make a choice, but he is also prepared to give that choice a name and an identity. Williams is aware that while progressive forces are absorbed in the task of infinite self-differentiation and protocols of pure self-reflexivity, right-wing forces, faced by no such identity crisis, march on, unmindful of their internal contradictions.[15] And third, Williams is warning us that if we choose not to will a certain kind of future, we will all "be had" by a future that will not be of our making or choice. Unlike poststructuralism that privileges the notion of errancy, Williams's focus is on possibility. While acknowledging the fact that political agency can never fully preknow its effect, Williams nevertheless insists that such an agency does make a difference. Here again, in opposition to the general trend of poststructuralism, Williams gives human intentionality an important, although not a unilateral, role in producing a directed and determinate history from uncertainty. The uncertainty (the indeterminacy, if you will) does not inhere structurally in the situation at some deep level that is impenetrable by human agency. To Williams, the historicity of uncertainty is the expression of a negotiable ratio of blindness to clarity; it is never a transcendent given. In a similar vein, Williams refuses to give in to the thesis of total objectification; his aim is to mobilize collective human intentionality by way of objective processes and formations. The theory of the collective subject is also a theory of intentional change. Very much in the tradition of Marxist cultural critics, Williams is interested in enabling historically specific changes; not for him those poststructuralist theories of subjectivity that provide explanations and rationalizations *après coup* or produce accounts of a second-order determinism that rule out possibilities of determinate change.[16]

The envisioning of the future, Williams reminds us, is equally a matter of accounting for the present and how we got there. It is only on the basis of such a historical self-understanding that the future may be delineated. Recalling the origins and the historical development of cultural studies, Williams makes the point that "one cannot understand an intellectual or artistic project without also understanding its formation; that the relation between a project and a formation is always decisive; and that the emphasis of Cultural Studies is precisely that it engages with both, rather than specializing itself to one or the other." Rejecting a reductionist model, Williams argues that project and formation are "different ways of materializing—different ways then, of describing—what is in fact a common disposition of energy and direction."[17]

The emphasis on commonality keeps alive a sense of constituency, and within this constituency, the history of the project and that of the formation are rendered mutually accountable. It is indeed true that the *formation as such* inaugurates a secondary or self-conscious form of history, but this history of the formation cannot be evaluated except in terms of its relationship to the project. In other words, the project functions both as a mandate and as an ethicopolitical horizon for the formation. The formation as a mediated expression of the project does enjoy relative autonomy, but it should not be allowed to move away from the project: the common ground between the two must be maintained and nurtured. Thus, when Williams exhorts cultural studies to question and rehistoricize itself as *formation,* he is in effect calling for a rehistoricizing and a reinvention, in light of contemporary realities, of the project itself. He is also reminding the cultural studies experts and professionals of the original ethic of the formation. Williams wishes to keep alive an experiential space that is external to the morphology of the formation. His concern is that this experiential project space not be structurally collapsed or made immanent within the secondary history of the formation. It is only in the name of the project that changes can be announced and initiated. The intentionality that drives the project requires the mediation of formations, but is not rigidly or deterministically constituted by them. In a sense, to Williams, human agency and intentionality are transcendent of the history of structures and formations; if they were not, then all changes would merely be structural or formational changes without a reference to the world outside. Thus, although analytically distinct, the project and the formation are part of a commonly experienced historical growth. Neither one is reduced to the other, although the project may be said to be the driving force with the formation as its instrument.

Leaning more toward Gramsci than Foucault, Williams's cultural theory is posited on the foundations of "constituency." The production of knowledge in response to general community needs, the role played by intellectuals in the organization as well as self-awareness of society, the legitimation of professional/intellectual/specialized knowledge by the felt needs and experiences of the people at large, and most significant, the self-representation achieved by any community by and through its "representative" intellectuals—these indeed are the Gramscian themes that provide fuel to Williams's activist energy as a public intellectual.[18] There is a certain tension in the very heart of Williams's enterprise. Here is a sophisticated cultural theorist who in many ways could be considered an example of the Foucauldian specific intellectual, who is dedicated to the professional and specialized production of knowledge and yet refuses to make this specificity an end in itself. For, to Williams, the term "representation" still retains a political meaning; the relationship between the intellectuals and the people is not done away with.

The institutionalization of cultural studies as an academic discipline represents the reification of what once was a project into a mere formation. Recalling the original intention of literary studies (and the argument holds in the case of cultural studies, too), Williams points out that "in every case the innovations in literary studies occurred outside the formal educational institutions." These innovations took place "in adult education, where people who had been deprived of any continuing educational opportunity were nevertheless readers, and wanted to discuss what they were reading," and "among women who, blocked from the process of higher education, educated themselves repeatedly through reading, and especially through the reading of 'Imaginative literature,' as the phrase usually has it."[19] It is in response to the demands of these powerless and disempowered groups that literary studies was able to fashion itself as a project of social change. It is precisely because these disenfranchised groups constituted a powerful "outside" or *hors-texte* to the system that the system was able to change. Thanks to the questions raised by these groups, each discipline within the university was made to realize its own lack of touch with "the world." These people in their very powerlessness were in a position to demand of their teacher, "Well, if you tell me that question goes outside your discipline, then bring me someone whose discipline will cover it, or bloody well get outside of the discipline and answer it yourself."[20] The open university and cultural studies, too, were formed in active response to such rebellious questioning from the outside.

Here perhaps is the space to articulate a poststructuralist critique of Williams's cultural politics. While it is quite appropriate that Williams is deeply solicitous of the need to maintain a sense of representative constituency (the kind of bloc sense that was important to Gramsci, too), it still does not explain why he has such an unproblematic notion of representative politics in general and of the pedagogical situation in particular. Historians will, of course, point out that Williams's participation in the adult education program was extrainstitutional and that there was a larger macropolitics underlying that effort. As Williams himself explains autobiographically, it was "distinctly as a vocation rather than as a profession that people went into adult education—Edward Thompson, Hoggart, myself and many others whose names are not known."[21] I am also aware that Williams's own class position at that time makes him organic and internal to the adult education program, yet I believe that my criticism is valid, for the poststructuralist problematization of representation is also an interrogation of organic political models.

Williams's analysis of the pedagogical situation would have us believe that there exists a relationship of organic solidarity between the dispossessed groups seeking answers and the teacher who is committed to finding the answers. The teacher, it is presumed, will come up with the answers that the groups "outside" are looking for. But I would argue that this situation is a lot more asymmetrical than Williams's explanation makes it out to be. First, we need to observe that more than one meaning of representation is involved here. In the exchange between the clamoring masses and the teacher, all moral and political authority rests with the masses, whereas epistemological authority resides with the teacher. It is indeed the questions that emerge from the dispossessed and the powerless that shake up and revolutionize the status quo, but the questioners at this stage are incapable of being the bearers of their own knowledge. They know enough to "ask" but not enough to produce their own answers in the form of an authentic and legitimate knowledge.

Let us examine this situation a little more diagnostically, perhaps. The people who initiate the representational transaction challenge the teacher to somehow answer their question. This is construed by the teacher as the bestowal of representational sanction. He or she becomes the representative of the people. But unfortunately, this representational model works in contradictory ways. To begin with, the people make a demand: that a certain knowledge or answer be made available to them by the teacher. Such knowledge seems either not to lie within the discipline practiced by the teacher (in which case, break out of the disciplinary ghetto and seek interdisciplinary assistance), or it does not exist within the institution (in which case, "bloody well get out" and find the answer). Let us take up the scenario of "bloody well getting out," for that is what interests Williams most, and I agree that it should. Does the mere act of "getting out" (whatever that may mean) ensure that the "getting out" is in the name of the people? If indeed it is true that the answer to the people's question is already "there in the world," then the people are already there with the answer, but do not recognize it as "knowledge"; whereas the theorist is "elsewhere" but his or her expertise is required in finding and formalizing the answer into knowledge and bringing it to the people. In bringing it to the people, quite paradoxically, the teacher also brings it to the pedagogical scene, which is within the university. In other words, the street scene as the site of knowledge has to be reproposed and transplanted as the pedagogical site before the answer to the question is apprehended as effective knowledge. This is a complicated and multileveled scenario. Is it a Gramscian scenario, where the historical reality that "all men are intellectuals" delegates the task of intellectuality to a select group of "professional intellectuals," or is it a Foucauldian scenario, which problematizes the very notion that representation is organic?

The contradiction deepens further. The people may be said to be the authentic holders of the knowledge, for it is their question asked from without that makes the production of the new knowledge. But whose knowledge is it? Although it would seem that the people are only demanding epistemological and theoretical representation of a knowledge that they do not have (except in the form of a perspectival question), what they are actually demanding is political representation. They are demanding that this knowledge be political, that is, that this epistemological representation be theirs. Not only does this knowledge represent a certain "material" or "content," it also represents the people within the knowledge and as agents of that knowledge. A merely theoretical or cognitive representation of knowledge would have us believe that knowledge can be "spoken for" by anybody for anybody, whereas the political model of representation, with its inalienably ideological sense of perspectivity, would insist on a distinction between "subject formation" and "agency formation."[22] To state this differently, the response to the people's question from outside the institutional walls may result in the formation of a new "subject," namely, cultural studies, but the emergence of this subject may not carry with it a different subjectivity and the agency appropriate to it. It is undeniable that cultural studies has made a difference, but to whom? It is also undeniable that in responding to the question from without, the teacher has stepped out into the world, but it is not clear if it is the same world as the one from which the question was posed. I will mention in passing that there is another poststructuralist nuance that Williams's narrative overlooks, namely, that the creation of a new subjectivity is not entirely emancipatory; it is equally a matter of subjection and ideological interpellation.

Such a poststructuralist critique does not in any way belittle the radical significance of Williams's undertaking; it is only an attempt to illuminate certain blind spots that are inevitable to any affirmative politics. What is interesting is that the blindnesses are the flip side of the insights. For example, one of the chief strengths of Williams is that he preaches and practices the "pedagogy of the oppressed,"[23] and yet forgets that "speaking for the other," in spite of the best possible intentions, is a problematic venture. Similarly, Williams is quite brilliant in his assertion that the criteria for change have to come from the outside and not be produced narcissistically within the internal dynamics of any system or mediation.[24] But in doing so, he unwittingly repeats the very binary in/out split that he would wish to avoid and ends up privileging the "outside" as the pure preserve of experience and reality. Again, he argues for the nonspecialist's experience (for example, adults and women always "read" books, although in an unprofessional way), but forgets that often the professionalization of common sense and experience may exceed or even falsify what seemed so self-evident in the experience.[25] Finally, his perennial questioning of the phenomenon of institutionalization, however necessary, oversimplifies the issue. For example, Williams is insensitive to the ambiguous and ambivalent politics of institutionality. I would contend that the institutionalization of any movement represents simultaneously a legitimation as well as a potential depoliticization. Thus, the setting up of womens' studies and African-American studies disciplines within the university is enabling on one level and problematic on another. Academic and disciplinary enfranchisement raises the problem of deracination from grassroots and constituency politics.[26] But Williams's perspective tends to be dismissive of subtleties that pertain to *institutionality as such;* in positing an absolute opposition between institutionality and politics, he denies the institution its own vital political dimension. This tendency in Williams makes him vulnerable to the charge that he is after all a romantic humanist who is still wedded to the idea of an authentic and universal human experience.

Williams's theoretical attitude to experience has a history too long to be discussed here. However, one notices a divide: the Williams of *The Long Revolution* still subscribes to the notion of unmediated experience,[27] but the later Williams admits to the inevitability of mediation. But even here, he has some misgivings about "mediation": "It is difficult to be sure how much is gained by substituting the metaphor of mediation for the metaphor of reflection. On the one hand it goes beyond the passivity of reflection theory; it indicates an active process, of some kind. On the other hand, in almost all cases, it perpetuates a dualism. Art does not reflect social reality, the superstructure does not reflect the base, directly; culture is a mediation of society."[28] The thrust of Williams's argument is twofold: avoid simple base-superstructure reductionism, and do not lose "experience" within the mere or sheer materiality of the mediation. A similar imperative may be seen at play in his formulation of "structures of feeling," where the emphasis is on the fusion between thought and feeling, between form and content. It is important to understand the polemical trajectory behind Williams's abiding advocacy of "experience" as something rich, resistant, and transformative. In response to the team of interviewers from the *New Left Review*, Williams comments that from "the industrial revolution onwards, there has developed a society which is less and less interpretable from experience," and the result is that we have become increasingly conscious of the positive powers of techniques of analysis, which at their maximum are capable of interpreting, let us say, the movements of an integrated world economy, and of the negative qualities of a naive observation which can never gain knowledge of realities like these. The privileging of such modes of analysis results in a corresponding undervaluation of areas where there is some everyday commerce between the available articulations and the general process that has been termed "experience."[29] Here Williams is attacking the hyperrealization of theory, and he is also implicitly critiquing high structuralism that in focusing on systemic generalities had lost touch with the historically specific and circumstantial aspects of experience, that is, the particular and the "concrete," which had become a predictable instantiation of the general systemic categories and laws. When asked by the *NLR* team if "the idea of an emergent experience beyond ideology" does not seem to "presuppose a kind of pristine contact between the subject and the reality," Williams makes it clear that his real quarrel is with a certain brand of formalists who "affect to doubt the very possibility of an 'external' referent." He declares that "we are in danger of reaching the opposite point in which the epistemological wholly absorbs the ontological: it is only in the ways of knowing that we exist at all."[30] The target of his criticism is a hypostatized theoretical consciousness that pretends to be its own material content. Williams, like Edward Said, is anxious that the "experiential" may get completely choked or denied by the formal densities of theoretical articulation. Experience to Williams is a powerful leverage to call into question the closure of systemic and theoretical orthodoxies. Williams's area of interest lies "between the articulated and the lived."[31]

The critical valence that Williams establishes for the phenomenon of experience is quite crucial. To Williams, "experience" functions as an independent principle of ethicopolitical legitimation, a principle that refuses to be reified or exhausted by the dogmatism of official systems and categories. It also works as a universal wavelength that cuts across situational and contextual barriers. This is particularly important when so much contemporary cultural theory, dedicated as it is to "difference," "heterogeneity," and "subject positionality," is unable to make global and general connections.[32] But this precisely is Williams's weakness: in his desire to give "experience" a strategically transcendent status, he fails to pay sufficient attention to its "constituted" nature, and, in his enthusiasm to envision a commonly shareable human experience,[33] he tends to oversimplify the disjunctures and asymmetries produced by the uneven histories of colonialism and imperialism. If in the earlier section I questioned Williams from a poststructuralist perspective (with its problematic attitude to the representational episteme), in this final part of my essay I shall be looking critically at Williams's theory from a postcolonial point of view. I will also try to demonstrate briefly that the poststructuralist project and the postcolonial project, despite basic differences in their geopolitical positioning, do enjoy great epistemological affinity. The articulation of poststructuralism with postcoloniality is both enabling and problematic.

In an impressive and moving conversation entitled "Media, Margins and Modernity," Raymond Williams and Edward Said discuss ways in which theories travel, and their basic consensus is that theories and models are capable of being applied successfully in areas far removed from their initial spaces of origination: the human condition, despite locational variations, is indeed shared and shareable. During this dialogue, Williams makes a number of interesting and far-reaching claims: that "the analysis of representation is not a subject separate for history but that the representations are part of the history" and that "people perceive situations, both from inside their own pressing realities and from outside them." Williams goes on to assert (1) that "a method of analysis, often initially of a strictly academic kind, can often find concrete embodiments which are more teachable and viewable and communicable beyond a narrow academic milieu," and (2) that "you can test the method of the analysis of representations historically, consciously, politically, in very different situations, and find that—subject always to argument about this detail and that—the method stands up."[34] To be fair to Williams, he does acknowledge that "there is an obvious distance between what is happening in the English countryside, or in the English inner cities, to the chaos of Lebanon," and yet, his basic faith in the method (and its ability to travel effectively) is unshakable. The two themes that Williams sounds here are very familiar to his admirers (myself included): the generalization of methods of analysis beyond their narrow disciplinary and academic provenance and the opening up of a global space characterized by complementarity rather than by radical differences. I endorse these themes heartily, so my criticism is not that Williams's claims are entirely wrong but rather that his approach is a little too felicitous and lacking in self-reflexivity. By way of offering a slightly different presentation of commonly shared experiences, I turn to Edward Said, who also cherishes the same possibilities as Williams, but with a difference. Said emphasizes a historical phenomenon that is dismissed to a mere epiphenomenal "detail" in Williams: the phenomenon of asymmetry that is so vitally constitutive of the postcolonial situation. (I am aware that my reading produces a difference between Said's and Williams's subject positions, whereas Said and Williams themselves, in their conversation, sound quite unaware of it.)

In an essay that has almost become a classic in the area of postcolonial studies, Said writes:

> The tragedy of this experience, and indeed of all post-colonial questions, lies in the constitutive limitation imposed on any attempt to deal with relationships that are polarized, *radically uneven, remembered differently* (my emphasis). The spheres, the sites of intensity, the agendas, the constituencies in the metropolitan and ex-colonized worlds overlap only partially. The small area that is common does not, at this point, provide for more than what I'd like to call a *politics of blame*.[35]

Unlike Williams, Said posits the asymmetry and the unevenness in their own terms before he begins to wish for something better than "a politics of blame." Surely, Said, too, would like theory to travel; we should not forget that it was Said who introduced this term to our critical vocabulary.

> Like people and schools of criticism, ideas and theories travel—from person to person, from situation to situation, from one period to another. Cultural and intellectual life are usually nourished and often sustained by this circulation of ideas, and whether it takes the form of acknowledged or unconscious influence, creative borrowing, or wholesale appropriation, the movement of ideas and theories from one place to another is both a fact of life and a usefully enabling condition of intellectual activity. Having said that, however, one should go on to specify the kinds of movement that are possible, *in order to ask whether by virtue of having moved from one place and time to another an idea or a theory gains or loses in strength, and whether a theory in one historical period and national culture becomes altogether different for another period or situation.* (Emphasis added)[36]

Said proceeds to periodize and spatialize the travel in terms of a "point of origin," "the distance traversed," the conditions of reception, and the final transformation of the original idea in its new habitus. Within Said's model, there is plenty of room for the travel to go wrong, or to be sabotaged, or to be found inapplicable or too aggressive in its new home. In contrast, Williams's confidence in traveling/comparatist method is entirely devoid of the kind of skepticism that comes out of serious self-reflexivity. This is particularly unfortunate since Williams's subject position is contradictory, for it is both oppositional-marginal and dominant-central. As a Welsh "border" voice expressing revolutionary socialism, it is indubitably oppositional in a Thatcherite context, but at the same time, as a Western voice invested in English studies, it is a demonstrably metropolitan voice. I am aware that in a work like *The Country and the City*, Williams produces such telling insights: "Yet when we look at the power and impetus of the metropolitan drives, often indeed accelerated by their own crises, we cannot be in any doubt that a different direction, if it is to be found, will necessarily change. The depth of the crisis, and the power of those who continue to dominate it, are too great for any easier or more congenial way."[37] But this insight, unaccompanied by a substantive awareness of unevenness and asymmetry, does not go far enough in deconstructing Eurocentrism or in raising the all-important question of "who is speaking" rather than merely "what is being said." As a result, the politics of the margins are too easily and prematurely adjusted and accommodated within what Williams calls "a connecting process, in what has to be seen ultimately as a common history."[38] Said, too, and other postcolonial theorists, are interested in the "connecting process," but are more capable of articulating marginality qua marginality before the connecting process begins. The significant difference in Williams's vision and the postcolonial vision is that the latter is aware (1) that often "traveling theory" hides within it the agency of the dominant structure; (2) that the travel is mostly in one direction: postcolonial models hardly travel to the center, much less transform it; and (3) the connecting process itself is undertaken on terms set at and by the center.

The idea of a successfully transplanted method in the name of an international commonality is strongly called into question in a number of postcolonial theoretical texts, most notably, Partha Chatterjee's *Nationalist Thought and the Colonial World*. In direct opposition to Williams's claims, Chatterjee proves that both the political project of nationalism and the epistemological project of the Enlightenment have been enacted in the postcolonial context to the detriment of indigenous subaltern possibilities. The postcolonial nationalist project, underwritten by the rational philosophy of the Enlightenment, perpetrates an indigenous form of elitism and consequently, the nationalist narrative fails to speak for the people. Moreover, there is all manner of disjuncture between the political and the epistemological practices of nationalsm. And besides, the transplantation of a Eurocentric nationalism in the postcolonial situation produces effects very different from those generated in Europe. The postcolonial people are often made to choose between being a nation and being themselves. Local and subaltern issues and themes do not figure in the nationalist equation precisely because the nationalist experiment is undertaken with a Western bias.[39] To Chatterjee and a host of other fellow subaltern theorists, such as Ranajit Guha, Kumkum Sangari, Sudesh Vaid, Veena Das,

Susie Tharu, and Dipesh Chakraborty, the notion of "location" plays a very special and complex role in the adjudication of postcolonial/subaltern identity. As postcolonial theorists, these writers exhibit and thematize a contradictory, fractal, and multivalent sense of "who they are": they are participants and citizens of multiple, uneven, overlapping, and cross-hatched worlds and discourses. On the one hand, they are committed to the "insider" task of theorizing a truly hegemonic national identity representative of the many "subidentities" that constitute it (an identity not based on essentialism), and on the other, to achieving an authentic transnational and global consciousness based not on the modernist imperative of deracination but on the concept of complex multiple rootedness. "Location," "position," and "travel" are so fundamental to postcolonial identity that we can perceive substantial variations among the postcolonial intellectuals: the resident theorist working through national and indigenous languages, the resident intellectual operating through Western discourses, and the diasporic, nonresident postcolonial intellectual who lives elsewhere but is abidingly committed to her or his nation. The differences among these types, although produced merely by varying subject-positional accents and inflections, often add up to a substantive disagreement about the nature of postcolonial politics and identity. There are debates about agendas and themes, about means and ends, about priorities, about insiders and outsiders, and about the conflict between what Gayatri Chakravorty Spivak calls "subaltern material and elitist methodology."[40] These contestations that are typical of the postcolonial-nationalist conjuncture find no place in Raymond Williams's scenario, simply because Williams's notion of a transcontextual method is incapable of dealing with the subtle nuances of the politics of location.

Strange as it may sound, the travel of Williams's theory to postcolonial spaces would have been more successful with the help of a few poststructuralist indirections and detours. For, although the postcolonial predicament and poststructuralist politics are unevenly related, this relationship is potentially enabling and healthy, provided it is cultivated strategically. In other words, the last thing I am calling for is an easy travel of poststructuralist theory to postcolonial contexts; but I am suggesting that a few poststructuralist attitudes, if not themes, have the potential to assist postcolonial ventures. Poststructuralist "weak thought" (in this expression I am conflating a number of poststructuralist trajectories: the questioning of representation, the perennial deconstruction of identity, the sensitivity to difference and heterogeneity, the insistence on ongoing autocritique, and a noncoercive attitude to the production of knowledge) finds congenial soil in postcoloniality. For, in the postcolonial situation, identity is shot through and through with difference, and yet identity is direly needed. Also, postcolonial reality demands multiple, nonsynchronous narratives, and not a single masterful story. The production of hegemonic subaltern historiographies requires the elaborate deconstruction of existing forms of dominant historiography. The attempt to forge a representative national identity is simultaneously an attempt to enfranchise many differences that comprise it. Like deconstruction, postcoloniality is involved in the contradiction of a "double writing":[41] on the one hand, it organizes itself as if nationalism were a desirable end, but on the other, it questions the very authority of the Eurocentrism inherent in nationalism. And like deconstruction it looks for other and different options, but without the guarantee of an absolute break with the past. In deconstruction, postcoloniality finds an ally across the asymmetrical divide, for poststructuralism (here I am using the two terms "poststructuralism" and "deconstruction" interchangeably in a limited sense) is an oppositional discourse within the metropolitan center. As opposition from "without," the semantics of postcolonial politics is bound to be different from that of poststructuralism, but syntactically, there is a complementary relationship between the two. The notion of a traveling or unfixed identity is yet another common feature, but the difference is that whereas poststructuralism (because it is of the first world) can afford to virtually "play" with identity, the postcolonial play with identity is much more serious: there is something at stake here. Gabriel García Márquez and Salman Rushdie are but two examples of serious fictional and narrative play. One might even say that the daring and the risk-taking that remain merely playful, ludic, epistemological (that is, disjuncted from real politics), and superstructural within poststructuralism take on a sense of constituency and therefore become political in the postcolonial juncture. The need to find alternative practices through an epistemological revolution and the desire to embody a historical significance for the language of the "post-" may be said to have found a concrete set of issues in postcoloniality that both uses and transforms poststructuralism.

I will conclude with a brief and selective look at a few postcolonial articulations that are perfectly compatible with Williams's cultural politics in a general sense, but are different because they have been touched by the poststructuralist attitude to "location." But in these articulations, the attitude takes on the temporality of concrete, historical struggle and contestation.

In a powerful essay entitled "Multiple Mediations," Lata Mani confronts some of the difficulties she has to face and theorize in her location as a third world feminist in the United States, who nevertheless presents her work in the United States, Britain, and India.[42] Drawing on Chandra Talpade Mohanty's definition of the politics of location as "the historical, geographic, cultural, psychic and imaginative boundaries for political definition and self definition," and enabled by Mohanty's description of location as a "temporality of struggle characterized by nonsynchronous flows and by "a paradoxical continuity of self,"[43] Mani presents the reader with the narrative of how her own work on Sati is assimilated varyingly in the United States, Britain, and India.[44] Mani is not suggesting for a moment that her project loses solidarity with itself because of these relativistic readings (she does not surrender intentional politics to the vagaries of a purely reception politics), but rather, she acknowledges and takes responsibility for the multiaccentual nature of her work. These different accents are constitutive of the work and are therefore not reducible to one dominant ideological valence. Nationalism, colonialism, first world feminism, third world feminism: all these macropolitical discourses are imbricated in Mani's subject position, and her account moves among these spaces with a finely tuned sensitivity to the underlying asymmetries, tensions, and contradictions. Not only does she tell us how differently her work is received (as part of contemporary feminism in the United States and Britain, and as part of the critique of nationalism in India), but also how much it matters how she is perceived: as insider or as outsider to the indigenous politics of postcoloniality. It is only after a thorough and painstaking rehearsal of her cross-hatched subject positionality that she makes the following recommendation: "The difficulties of straddling different temporalities of struggle cannot, however, always be resolved through listening for and talking about our specificities. There are political moments which pose limits to the possibility of conceiving of international feminist exchange as negotiated dialogues which, while they may alternately diverge and intersect, are ultimately benign and non-contradictory."[45] Unlike Williams's theoretical model, the politics of location sketched out by Lata Mani is laden with rich contradictions.

In a similar but differently inflected voice, Vivek Dhareshwar, in his essay "Toward a Narrative Epistemology of the Postcolonial Predicament," maps out some of the incommensurabilities faced by the postcolonial intellectual when he or she tries to find his or her narrative/political identity within the theoretical/epistemological framework provided by the metropolis. The thesis here, too, is that "traveling theory" is full of pitfalls and detours. Dhareshwar observes that "the traveling problems of contemporary theory have a special significance for postcolonial intellectuals who have traveled in the metropolis to see how their part of the world gets mapped."[46] Unlike Western or first world theorists who tend to "privilege their subject positions unreflectively," postcolonials cannot help noticing the condition of possibility of their theory." Dhareshwar is well aware that unreflective critical practice on the part of the postcolonial intellectual will only sell him or her to metropolitan interests. Emphasizing strongly the need for postcolonial intellectuals to be vigilant about their subject positionality (a theme inaugurated by Gayatri Chakravorty Spivak), Dhareshwar proposes that "instead of celebrating the pleasures of finding themselves in the tropics of metropolitan theory by theoreticlly recuperating the narratives of detour, postcolonial theorists must narrativize the dissonance of that detour, and out of that dissonance, outline a new theory, a new practice of theory that would initiate a poetics of return, which will undoubtedly be as complex and ambiguous as the poetics of detour that postcolonials have been living, narrating, and theorizing."[47]

It would seem that the travel thought up by these postcolonial intellectuals is less natural, more deliberate and self-reflexive, and less self-assured than the resources of hope that stem from a metropolitan assumption of universal experience.

Notes

1. For a thorough discussion of the problems faced by the subaltern project in its attempt to produce its own history, see Ranajit Guha, "Dominance without Hegemony and Its Historiography," in *Subaltern Studies* VI: *Writings on South Asian History and Society*, ed. Ranajit Guha (Delhi: Oxford University Press, 1989), 210–309.

2. For a clear, thought-provoking analysis of some of the political perils of a philosophical relativism, see Satya Mohanty, "Us and Them: On the Philosophical Basis of Political Criticism," *Yale Journal of Criticism* 2, no.2 (Spring 1989): 1–31.

3. For sustained analyses of the Eastern European situation in the context of Marxist history, see the following issues of the *Nation*: January 29, February 26, and March 19, 1990.

4. The thoroughly researched work done by the Subaltern Studies Group demonstrates with telling clarity the complicity of nationalism with elitist and dominant historiographies. See Ranajit Guha and Gayatri Chakravorty Spivak, eds., *Selected Subaltern Studies* (Oxford: Oxford University Press, 1988).

5. Samir Amin's *Eurocentrism* (New York: Monthly Review Press, 1989) is brilliant in its simultaneous and conjunctural critique of both capitalism and Eurocentrism.

6. Drawing on the works of Jacques Lacan, Chantal Mouffe and Ernesto Laclau posit their critique of a total reality, but nevertheless keep alive possibilities of articulating coalitional and democratic connections among different subject positions. See their *Hegemony and Socialist Strategy: Towards a Radical Democratic Politics*, trans. Winston Moore and Paul Cammack (London: Verso, 1985).

7. Michel Foucault develops this notion of the subject position as "assigned" in *The Archaeology of Knowledge*, trans. A. M. Sheridan (New York: Pantheon, 1972). For a politically specific application of the assigned subject position, see Gayatri Chakravorty Spivak, "A Literary Representation of the Subaltern: A Woman's Text from the Third

World," in her *In Other Worlds: Essays in Cultural Politics* (London and New York: Methuen, 1987), 241–68.

8. I am referring here to the theory of language developed by Jacques Lacan that has been so influential in the development of poststructuralist attitudes to cultural politics. Simply stated, to Lacan, meaning is constitutively implicated in the possibility of errancy. Also, meaning is represented through the network of signifiers where every word finds its semantic charge through a perennial process of syntactic transfer and displacement. See Jacques Lacan, *Ecrits: A Selection*, trans. Alan Sheridan (New York: Norton, 1977).

9. See Michel Foucault, "Intellectuals and Power," in *Language, Counter-Memory, Practice*, trans. Donald F. Bouchard and Sherry Simon (Ithaca, N.Y.: Cornell University Press, 1977), 205–17. For a substantive subaltern critique of the position held by Foucault and Deleuze, see Gayatri Chakravorty Spivak, "Can the Subaltern Speak?" in *Marxism and the Interpretation of Culture*, ed. Cary Nelson and Lawrence Grossberg (Urbana: University of Illinois Press, 1988), 271–311.

10. For a critical positioning of the postcolonial subject in the context of Foucault's and Gramsci's politics, see chapter 2 in this volume.

11. Veena Das, "Subaltern as Perspective," in *Subaltern Studies VI*, ed. Guha, 310–24, esp. 312.

12. Edward Said, "Criticism between Culture and System," in Said, *The World, the Text, the Critic* (Cambridge: Harvard University Press, 1983), 178–225.

13. Rob Nixon, "Culture Heroes: Williams and Hall for the Opposition", *Voice Literary Supplement* 79 (October 1989): 15.

14. Raymond Williams, "The Future of Cultural Studies," in *The Politics of Modernism* (London: Verso, 1989), 151–62, esp. 151.

15. I have in mind here passages in Marx's *Grundrisse* (Harmondsworth: Penguin, 1973), for example, 408–10 and 539–40, where Marx demonstrates the ability of capital to conceal its own internal contradictions and crises while continuing to perform its "universalizing function."

16. See R. Radhakrishnan, "The Changing Subject and the Politics of Theory," *Differences* 2 (Summer 1990): 126–52, for a detailed analysis of poststructuralist possibilities for the "changing subject."

17. Williams, "The Future of Cultural Studies," 151.

18. Antonio Gramsci's contribution to the cause of political pedagogy is of vital importance. See the pieces in "Part Two: Gramsci in Prison, 1926–1937," in Gramci, *The Modern Prince and Other Writings*, trans. Louis Marks (New York: International, 1957), 58–132. For a contemporary application of Gramsci's cultural politics, see Stuart Hall, "Gramsci and Us," in Hall, *The Hard Road to Renewal* (London: Verso, 1989), 161–73.

19. Williams, "The Future of Cultural Studies," 152.

20. Ibid., 157.

21. Ibid., 154.

22. Gayatri Chakravorty Spivak's essay, "Reading *The Satanic Verses*," *Public Culture* 2, no. 1 (Fall 1989): 79–99, deals with some of the differences between "subject formation" and "agency formation."

23. My reference here is to Paulo Freire, *Pedagogy of the Oppressed* (New York: Continuum, 1986).

24. See Tony Pinkney, "Editor's Introduction: Modernism and Cultural Theory," in Williams, *The Politics of Modernism*, 1-29, for a vigorous summary of Williams's attitude to the self-consciousness of high modernism. It is in the same spirit that Williams, in his review of Edward Said's *The World, the Text, the Critic* in the *Guardian*, praises Said as "someone who not only has studied and thought so carefully but is also beginning to substantiate, as distinct from announcing, a genuinely emergent way of thinking" (quoted on back cover). Here again, Williams valorizes "substance" over a self-conscious "form" that pretends to be its own substance.

25. There are two debates involved here. One concerns the issues of knowledge and experience. Is experience the raw material that is produced into knowledge, or does experience have its own direct epistemological status? For a discussion of this issue in terms of common sense versus professional knowledge, see Antonio Gramsci, *The Modern Prince and Selections from the Prison Notebooks,* trans. Louis Marks (New York: International, 1957). The second debate, within social psychology, pits the principle of ecological validity against the experimental validity achieved within the context of scientific study. For a provocative position paper on this issue, see Mahzarin R. Banaji and Robert G. Crowder, "The Bankruptcy of Everyday Memory," *American Psychologist* 44, no. 9 (September 1989): 1185-93.

26. For a significant discussion of the predicament of the black intellectual vis-à-vis her or his constituency, see Cornel West, "The Dilemma of the Black Intellectual," *Cultural Critique*, no. 1 (Fall 1985): 109-24.

27. Raymond Williams, *The Long Revolution* (London: Chatto and Windus, 1961), 63-65. See the question posed to Williams, *Politics and Letters* (London: Verso, 1979), 166-67.

28. Raymond Williams, *Marxism and Literature* (Oxford: Oxford University Press, 1977), 99.

29. Williams, *Politics and Letters*, 172.

30. Ibid., 167.

31. Ibid., 168.

32. For a coalitional application of poststructuralism to the theory of ethnicity, see chapter 3 in this volume.

33. See R. Radhakrishnan, "Culture as Common Ground: Ethnicity and Beyond," *MELUS* 14, no. 2 (Summer 1987): 5-19.

34. Williams, *The Politics of Modernism*, 179.

35. Edward Said, "Intellectuals in the Post-Colonial World," *Salmagundi* 70-71 (Spring-Summer 1986): 44-81, esp. 45.

36. Edward Said, "Traveling Theory," in Said, *The World, the Text, the Critic,* 226-47, esp. 226. For other and equally stimulating notions of geopolitical cultural travel, see the special issue of *Inscriptions* (vol. 5 [1989]) entitled "Traveling Theories, Traveling Theorists"; Arjun Appadurai, "Disjuncture and Difference in the Global Cultural Economy," *Public Culture* 2, no. 2 (Spring 1990): 1-24; and Adrienne Rich, "Notes Towards a Politics of Location," in *Blood, Bread and Poetry: Selected Prose, 1979-85* (New York: Norton, 1986), 210-31.

37. Raymond Williams, *The Country and the City* (Oxford: Oxford University Press, 1973), 288.

38. Ibid.

39. See Partha Chatterjee, *Nationalist Thought and the Colonial World* (Delhi: Oxford University Press, 1986), 1–53.

40. See Spivak, "A Literary Representation of the Subaltern: Deconstructing Historiography," in *In Other Worlds,* 197–221.

41. The reference here is to the Derridean notion of "double writing" as developed in Jacques Derrida, *Dissemination,* trans. Barbara Johnson (Chicago: University of Chicago Press, 1981).

42. Lata Mani, "Multiple Mediations: Feminist Scholarship in the Age of Multinational Reception," *Inscriptions* 5 (1989): 1–23.

43. Chandra Talpade Mohanty, "Feminist Encounters, Locating the Politics of Experience," *Copyright,* no. 1 (Fall 1987): 30–44, esp. 42.

44. The reference here is to Lata Mani, "Contentious Traditions: The Debate on Sati in Colonial India, 1780-1833" (Ph.D. diss., University of California, 1989).

45. Mani, "Multiple Mediations," 14.

46. Vivek Dhareshwar, "Toward a Narrative Epistemology of the Postcolonial Predicament," *Inscriptions* 5 (1989): 135–57, esp. 144.

47. Ibid., 156.

8 / Postcoloniality and the Boundaries of Identity

Why is it that the term "postcoloniality" has found such urgent currency in the first world but is in fact hardly ever used within the formerly colonized worlds of South Asia and Africa?[1] What is the secret behind the academic formation called "postcoloniality" and its complicity with certain forms of avant-garde Eurocentric cultural theory? Is the entire world "postcolonial," and if so, can every world citizen lay claim to an "equal postcoloniality," that is, without any historical reference to the asymmetries that govern the relationship between the worlds of the former colonizers and the colonized? Is "postcoloniality" (notice the ontological-nominalist form of the category) a general state of being, a powerful shorthand for an intense but traveling human condition, or is it a more discrete and circumstantial experience taking place within specific geopolitical boundaries? In general, how is postcoloniality as allegory a response to postcoloniality as a historical phenomenon? These are some of the questions that I wish to elaborate interconnectedly in this essay, and perhaps I might end up making certain suggestions, making certain preferences. But at any rate, "postcoloniality" is in need of a rigorous and situated unpacking before it gets canonized as a universal constant by the imperatives of metropolitan theory.

First of all, it is important to historicize the term with reference to its site of production, namely, the first world in general and, more specifically, the intellectual-theoretical-academic-cultural field within the first world. In other words, we need to contextualize the term both as "project" and as "formation," both macro- and micropolitically.[2] The first world conjuncture within which "postcoloniality" is taking shape is one of unmixed triumph and celebration. The first world or the West[3] is caught up in its own successful contemporaneity (experienced almost as epiphany), which more than ever before has a synchronic stranglehold over the rest of the world. Exhilarated by its many recent victories, the first world is in a state of countermnemonic innocence, freely and unilaterally choosing what to remember and what not to remember from the pages of history. We heard President Bush proudly declare that the memories of Vietnam have been effectively and legitimately buried in the sands of the Gulf War. There is the prevalent understanding that "we" somehow ended up winning the cold war and are therefore in a position of absolute ethico-political authority in relation to the rest of the world. "We" have earned the privilege of initiating a new world order on behalf of everybody else. If in the past, interventions in other spaces and histories had to be justified after the event, the current global situation lies in the form of a carte blanche for the ethico-political as well as epistemic signature of the first world. The entire world has been deterritorialized in anticipation of a democratic-capitalist takeover by the free world.[4] In short, the joyous countermemory of the first world has succeeded in putting to rest the troubling and ongoing histories of colonialism, neocolonialism, and imperialism.[5] Within the indeterminate spatiality of the "post-" the first world finds no problem or contradiction or experiences no sense of shame or guilt while it insists on a dominant role for itself in projects of identity reconstruction the world over. Unwilling to accept a nonleaderlike role, much less exclusion from third world projects, the first world mandates a seamless methodological universalism to legitimate its centrality the world over.[6] Clearly, this strategy is full of "betrayals within," in particular, the duplicitous take on nationalism and a protectionist attitude to American and/or Western identity.[7]

These very tensions, it turns out, occupy center stage when we consider "postcoloniality" in its theoretical-academic formation. The articulation of postcoloniality has gone hand in hand with the development of cultural theory and studies. If anything, postcoloniality is being invested in as the cutting edge of cultural studies. Now what can this mean? Is this a legitimation or a depoliticization of postcoloniality as constituency? The important thing to notice here is the overall *culturalist* mode of operation: in other words, we are not talking about postcolonial economies, histories, or politics. The obsessive focus is on postcoloniality as a cultural conjuncture. The implication is that whatever distances, differences, and boundaries cannot be transcended or broken down politically can in fact be deconstructed through the universalist agency of culture and cultural theory. Indians, Nigerians, Kenyans, Pakistanis, Somalians, Zimbabweans, Bangladeshis, and so on, however resistant they may be otherwise, are available to metropolitan theory in their cultural manifestations. Culture is set up as a nonorganic, free-floating ambience that frees intellectuals and theorists from their solidarities to their regional modes of being.[8] It is within this transcendent space that postcoloniality is actively cultivated as the cutting edge of cultural theory. This sacrifice of postcoloniality as potential politics or activism at the altar of postcoloniality as metropolitan epistemology is an effect inscribed in the very semantics of the term "post-," a point that Ella Shohat makes with telling effect in her essay, "Notes on the 'Post-Colonial'":

> Echoing "post-modernity," "postcoloniality" marks a contemporary state, situation, condition or epoch. The prefix "post," then aligns "postcolonialism" with a series of other "posts"—"post-structuralism," "post-modernism," "post-marxism," "post-feminism," "post-deconstructionism"—all sharing the notion of a movement beyond. Yet while these "posts" refer largely to the supercession of outmoded philosophical, aesthetic and political theories, the "post-colonial" implies both going beyond anti-colonial nationalist theory as well as a movement beyond a specific point in history, that of colonialism and Third World nationalist struggle. (101)

Shohat in this passage, as well as in the general trend of her essay, demonstrates how the theoretical metaphorics of the "post" conflates politics with epistemology, history with theory, and operates as the master code of *transcendence as such*. "Posthaste," states of historical being are left behind, and the seemingly nameless modality of the "post" shores up for itself an overarching second-order jurisdiction over a variety of heterogeneous and often unrelated constituencies. She also points out how the term "postcolonial" suggests a form of benign acquiescence as against the political activism and oppositionality available to the term "third world" (111). Although I agree with Shohat that the transcendence or "going beyond" implicit in the avant-garde use of the "post" is indeed in bad faith, I wish to argue that distinctions need to be made, based on historical and empirical criteria, between politically relevant and necessary acts of transcendence and mere gestures of transcendence.[9] Thus, a genuine and substantive transcendence of nationalism needs to be differentiated from an elitist transnationalist configuration, and a subaltern interrogation of the nationalist regime (an interrogation often premised on the notion of a "return")[10] must be read differently from a putative capitalist deterritorialization of the nation-state. Similarly, diasporic deconstructions of identity have to be understood differently from "indigenous" divestments from nationalist identity. But for us to be able to do this, the spatiality of the "post" has to be simultaneously critiqued and endorsed, that is, when the endorsement is in opposition to what Homi Bhabha calls "the pedagogical plenitude" of a unilinear historicism ("Dissemination," 291–322). I would like to add that in this instance the critique and the endorsement may not add up to a unified politics of constituency, for the critique of the "post" and the endorsement of the "post" are operating in two discontinuous but related spaces. Shohat's essay does not get into this problematic mainly because, given its immediate polemical concern, it overlooks the discourse of space altogether.[11] My point is that the chronotope of the "post" can be studied with reference to the "time-space" after colonialism without necessarily privileging the "post" as a free-floating signifier. For, in a real sense, aren't "we" all looking for a genuine "time-place"—that is, *after* colonialism, a chronotope that has made a break from the *longue durée* of colonialism? The challenging and complex question is how to enable a mutually accountable dialogue among the many locations that have something important to say about "the after" of postcoloniality.

The phrase "boundaries of identity" in this chapter's title suggests boundedness in a plural form. At the very outset the objection might be made that identities are monolithic and nonhyphenated by nature and therefore can have only single boundaries, each identity entrenched within its own single time. My point here is to multiply time by spaces to suggest (1) that the concept of identity is in fact a normative measure that totalizes heterogeneous "selves" and "subjectivities" and (2) that the normative citizenship of any identity within its own legitimate time or history is an ideological effect that secures the regime of a full and undivided identity. And in our own times, whether we like it or not, the dominant paradigm of identity has been "the imagined community" of nationalism. To backtrack a little, the theme of spaces times time is particularly appropriate in the context of peoples who have had colonialism forced on them. Before colonialism, these peoples lived in their own spaces with their own different senses of history. I am not suggesting that there were not other conquests or that there was pure undifferentiated indigeny before colonialism, but rather that colonialism is a very special and effective instance of intervention and takeover. In the case of India, for example, before the colonialist invasion, there were all kinds of battles, skirmishes, conquests for territories, and negotiations among the Moghul emperors and Hindu and Rajput kings and chieftains, and there was a different set of affairs among the peninsular kings of south India. But there was no real attempt at *unification* for purposes of effective administration. When the East India Company aggressively expanded its role into one of empire building, it also became a task of nation building on behalf of the "native" people.[12] Consequently, and in pursuit of this mandate, local times and spaces and modes of self-governance were dismantled and/or destroyed, and the British invented a tradition on behalf of the Indians and presented it to them so that, in their very act of self-understanding, they could acquiesce in the moral and epistemic legitimacy of British sovereignty.[13] This political gerrymandering of a heterogeneous people into nation-state identification for purposes of control and domination unfortunately creates long-term disturbances that last well into the postcolonialist/nationalist phase.

I am rehearsing this familiar thesis of the postcolonial predicament by way of arguing that heterogeneity or even hybridity is written into the postcolonial experience and that there is a relationship of historical continuity, however problematic, between colonialism and nationalism and between nationalism and its significant Other, the diaspora.

Let us consider the phenomenon of hybridity, a theme so dear to poststructuralist theories of deferral, difference (differance), and dissemination. The crucial difference that one discerns between metropolitan versions of hybridity and "postcolonial" versions is that, whereas the former are characterized by an intransitive and immanent sense of *jouissance*, the latter are expressions of extreme pain and agonizing dislocations. Again, whereas metropolitan hybridity is ensconced comfortably in the heartland of both national and transnational citizenship, postcolonial hybridity is in a frustrating search for constituency and a legitimate political identity. It is important to the postcolonial hybrid to compile a laborious "inventory of one's self"[14] and, on the basis of that complex genealogical process, to produce her own version of hybridity and find political legitimacy for that version. I say this in a Gramscian vein to insist on a fundamental difference between hybridity as a comfortably given state of being and hybridity as an excruciating act of self-production by and through multiple traces. When metropolitan hybridity begins to speak for postcolonial hybridity, it inevitably depoliticizes the latter and renders its rebellion virtually causeless. Let me explain further with reference to Salman Rushdie and *The Satanic Verses*. My general contention is that, although avant-garde theories of hybridity would have us believe that hybridity is "subjectless", that is, that it represents the decapitation of the subject and the permanent retirement of identitarian forms of thinking and belonging, in reality, hidden within the figurality of hybridity is the subject of the dominant West. All hybridities are not equal, and furthermore hybridity does carry with it an ideological tacit nominal qualifier, such as in *Western* or *European* hybridity. Although, theoretically speaking, it would seem that hybridity functions as the ultimate decentering of all identity regimes, in fact and in history, hybridity is valorized on the basis of a stable identity, such as European hybridity, French hybridity, American hybridity, and so on. So which hybridity are we talking about? It would be most disingenuous to use "hybridity" as a theoretical sleight of hand to exorcise the reality of unequal histories and identities.

In the case of Salman Rushdie, a book, intentionally a singing celebration of hybridity, got caught up in codes of identity, and the many scholars, writers, intellectuals, politicians, and religious leaders who responded polemically to the affair did so not from "hybridity's own point of view," but each from the point of view of a certain axiology, ideology, or "bottom line." And what is significant is that the putatively free and liberal Western scholars, with their First Amendment hang-ups, were no exception to this rule.[15] My simple point here is that every point of view on this issue was heavily and deeply identity-based, and the more each point of view encountered resistance from other perspectives, the more it receded into its own home of identity: Western secularism-freedom and the separation of church and state, or Islamic "fundamentalism" that seemed to deny to literature its own relative autonomy and mode of articulation. So, where was hybridity in all this, when the entire polemical pattern was a reminder of the Crusades? The integrity of the West was as much at stake as the rectitude of an authoritarian Islam. It would appear, then, that, in the act of responding to or evaluating a hybrid work, the critic/intellectual (secular or religious, that is, unless "the secular" as a Western norm is made to operate naturally and therefore namelessly) is compelled to step back from hybridity itself in the act of evaluating it. The problem has to do not with hybridity per se, but rather with specific *attitudes to hybridity*.

Next, the juridicolegal battle had to do with the following question: which of the many attitudes to hybridity got it right? But how could this question be adjudicated for lack of a common hermeneutic ground? The irony is that, once the text was internalized and reproposed by each interpretive code in its own way, the hybrid text as objective material was thoroughly derealized.[16] It really did not (and in a way, should not) matter that Western-trained aesthetes of literary detail and nuance went on and on about the "dream scenes" and about intrinsic textual problems concerning the locatability of the author's intention, and so on, for, from another and a different ideological perspective, no such distinction could be made between author and persona, between reality and figuration, or between performative and constative utterances. It then becomes a matter of brute interpretive authority: which authority is more powerful globally? Ironically, the *fatwa* (horrendous as it is) is in fact the protest symbol of the weak and much maligned-exploited-stereotyped-racialized-othered East trying to stand up to the unquestioned global jurisdiction of Western secular interpretive norms. Lest I be misunderstood, I am wholehearted in my condemnation of the *fatwa* and in my solidarity with Rushdie the individual, but that should not come in the way of a geopolitical (as against a merely individual) understanding of the entire affair. To code it all as exclusively individual versus society, or as the freedom of the artist versus political dictatorship, only simplifies, from a single point of view, the many valences of the issue.

To get back to the theme of hybridity, hybridity was exposed for its semantic insufficiency. In other words, Rushdie was being asked: In what identitarian mode or "as who" are you a hybrid? Obviously, the self-styling of hybridity from its own point of view left too much unexplained. Was Rushdie hybrid as a Muslim, or as an Indian, or as a Westerner, or as a Londoner, or as a metropolitan intellectual-artist? And even if one were to hyphenate all of these identities, one still has to face the question of unequal mediation. Among the many selves that constitute one's identity, there exists a relationship of unevenness and asymmetry, since each of these selves stems from a history that is transcendent of individual intentionality. And again, the canonization of individuality as a first principle is a Western and not a universal phenomenon. Let us also not forget the many vagaries and contradictions of Rushdie's own situation vis-à-vis a racist and ethnicity-busting contemporary England. There were real questions concerning whether or not his "internal politics" were worth defending; it was much easier to value his stand against the Islamic clerisy, but not so his many critiques of the racism and the ethnocentrism "within."

My argument here is that he was being protected as a Western individual with a prerogative to hybridity. When Rushdie got called upon to make "a critical inventory" of himself and furthermore make clear his representational stance, all hell broke loose. What had seemed a hybrid and postrepresentational expression of personal being was now being forced into the realms of representational cultural geopolitics. Who is Rushdie, and when his hybrid self speaks, who is being spoken for? How and in what direction does Rushdie's hybridity add up? And clearly, this is a question that any responsible reader of Rushdie does ask: one does not have to be an Islamic *ayatollah* to register some form of unease with the radical indeterminacies of Rushdie's *écriture* (Sangari, 216–45). There had been earlier contestations about *Shame* and *Midnight's Children*, and these arguments had to do with Rushdie's sense of perspectival location in relation to India, Pakistan, and South Asian nationalism. The hybrid articulation in all its hyphenated immanence was called upon to account for its representational truth claims. I am focusing strongly on the issue of representation so as to connect this discussion with issues concerning "constituency" and "transgression." For example, why is it more fashionable and/or acceptable to transgress Islam toward a secular constituency rather than the other way around? Why do Islamic forms of hybridity, such as women wearing veils and attending Western schools (here again I am not defending the veils, but I hope my readers will see that I am making a different point here) encounter resistance and ridicule? Why is it that the targets of "ethnic cleansing" are people who see their identities as coextensive with a religion? Why are Gypsies being persecuted the world over? I would argue that it is only in a philosophic-bohemian sense that Occidental hybridity is the victim, but historically speaking, the victims are those groups of people who are striving for any kind of collective identity other than the forms of sovereignty prescribed by Western secularism. In Rushdie's own case, victim though he is, undeniably and tragically, in another sense he is indeed a privileged figure whose perils have mobilized the entire West.

To sum up my argument, metropolitan hybridity is underwritten by the stable regime of Western secular identity and the authenticity that goes with it, whereas postcolonial hybridity has no such guarantees: neither identity nor authenticity. And strange and outrageous as it may sound to secular ears, secularism is one of the chief obstacles on the postcolonial way to self-identification and self-authentication (Chatterjee, *Nationalist Thought*). The question of authenticity has to do not just with identity but with a certain attitude to identity. In other words, authentic identity is a matter of choice, relevance, and a feeling of rightness. In other words, authentication also means ruling out certain options as incorrect or inappropriate. It needs to be stated here that the term "authenticity" deserves more sympathetic attention than it has been getting of late. I do agree that certain ways of theorizing authenticity have indeed verged dangerously toward blood-and-guts fundamentalism, mystical and primordial essentialism, or forms of divisive separatism. But what I mean by "authenticity" here is that critical search for a third space that is complicitous neither with the deracinating imperatives of Westernization nor with theories of a static, natural, and single-minded autochthony.[17] The authenticity I have in mind here is an invention with enough room for multiple rootedness; in other words, there need be no theoretical or epistemological opposition between authenticity and historical contingency, between authenticy and hybridity,[18] between authenticity and invention.

The postcolonial search for identity in the third world is beset primarily with the problem of location. Within what macropolitical parameters should such a narrative search take place? Given the reality of nonsynchronous histories within the so-called one nation, how are any blueprints to be drawn up towards authentic Indian identity? As Partha Chatterjee has shown us, the very project of nationalism, liberating though it may have been, has been proven to be flawed and ineffective after independence. Chatterjee goes on to demonstrate that, in the case of India, there had always been serious incompatibilities between the visions for the future thought up by Mohandas Gandhi and those championed by Jawaharlal Nehru (*Nationalist Thought,* 131–66). While Nehru was passionately persuaded by "the comity of nation-states" and the promise of a science-reason-technology-based internationalism (based on the unilinear chronology of developmental time), Gandhi's rural plans of decentralization and non-Western modes of organization had nothing whatever to do with nationalism or internationalism. It must be remembered that Gandhi was that early deconstructive thinker who proposed that the Indian Congress should dissolve itself after independence (and this never happened; if anything, the party got a stranglehold over electoral politics to the extent that the party virtually "became" the country), but he was totally marginalized by his own protégé, Nehru, after independence.

Nehru's insistence on heavy industries and progress as Westernization exacerbated the existing problem of nonsynchronous development. In philosophical terms, it was as if Nehru had conceded that India was indeed the third world and therefore should do everything it could to catch up with and be part of the first world. The flight of critical intelligentsia from India to lands overseas and the general problem of "brain drain" can be attributed to the uncritical haste with which Nehru yoked India's political destiny to a thoroughly Western epistemology.[19] It is not surprising that Nehru's career right now is being submitted to a rigorously harsh revisionism. The problem with the internationally oriented Nehru was that he did not make some all-important distinctions between Indian "subjecthood" and Indian "agency," whereas to Gandhi "agency" was of paramount importance. From Gandhi's point of view, an Indian subject who could not speak for India or a definition of India that brought about a serious rupture between "agency" and "subjectivity" was seriously flawed and actually not worth the effort. Whereas "subjectivity" represents a theoretical mode of self-consciousness that does not explicitly raise the issue of representation, "agency" is unthinkable except in terms of representation. "Subjectivity" all too often consents to remain an effect of an alien form of representation, whereas "agency" is an attempt to realize subjectivity as an effect of an authentic act of self-representation that one can call one's own.

Equally at stake is the category "constituency" and how it gets spoken for. If India is a constituency made up of other and smaller constituencies, how should it be represented: through unification or through decentralization? Where lies authenticity? Whereas to Nehru "constituency" meant the transgression of existing identifications toward Westernization, to Gandhi India already existed as a vibrant collection of constituencies. There was no need to abandon, disband, or rename these constituencies in the name of nation building. What comes to mind here is Gandhi's comparison of a free India to a house with open windows all around so that breezes may blow in from every possible side, but there is a constraint: that the house itself not be blown away by the force of the winds from without.[20] There are two important implications here. First, there is the need for a stable identity base for the assimilation of heterogeneous ideas. Second, the whole enterprise of international influence, global eclecticism, and the hybridization as well as the heterogenization of identity requires the specification of actual and historical parameters, alas, with all the inside/outside differentiations that parameters inevitably entail. To state it differently, the crosscurrents of international and eclectic exchange do not by themselves constitute a real-historical place. We need to have a prior sense of place, which then gets acted upon by the winds of change, for only then can we raise such significant questions as whether India is amenable to capitalism or computerization is good for the Nigerian economy. No place is a pure tabula rasa for inscriptions of arbitrary change, and it is important to build into the notion of change the possibility that certain forms of change may not be desirable for a particular people.[21] These resistances become virtually unthinkable (just as the Gandhian program by now has become "The Road Not Taken") once we accept the thesis of "pure subjectless change." And as we have already seen, the so-called pure change is nothing but the universal travel of Western modes of dominance.[22]

In a sense all that we have been talking about concerns the geopolitical coordination of postcolonial peoples. What are some of the better modes of postcolonial identification? What forms of collective organization as a people are authentic? What affiliations are real and which ones are merely virtual? In the context of postcoloniality, the significant signpost happens to be that of nationalism. Should postcoloniality be expressed through nationalism, or should it be antinationalistic? Is antinationalism the same thing as postnationalism? Are the "posts" in "postcoloniality" and "postnationalism" the same?[23] By and large, most of the options are premised upon the historical reality of nationalism. The significant alternatives are the following: (1) Historicize postcoloniality through nationalism with a full and untroubled faith in the ethicopolitical and epistemological agenda of nationalism. (2) Cultivate nationalism strategically, that is, use it politically without necessarily accepting its entire mandate.[24] (3) Attempt a return to one's own indigenous past in spite of the intervening colonialist-nationalist epoch. This return itself could be coded in two ways: (a) embark on the return as though colonialism-nationalism had not happened at all; and

(b) retrace the histories of colonialism-nationalism in a spirit of revisionism—read these histories "against the grain"—as a necessary precondition for one's own authentic emergence.[25] (4) Envision the diaspora as an effective way of disseminating the legitimacy of the nationalist form itself.

I am not particularly persuaded by the first two options. Accepting nationalism wholesale at the present global conjuncture seems unwise and quite risky. Let us remind ourselves that the postcolonial predicament is being played out during an anomalous historical period when nationalisms are back with a vengeance all over the world. But it is strange that this should be happening at a time when nationalism stands discredited theoretically and epistemologically. How does the political need for nationalism coexist with the intellectual deconstruction of nationalism? I would argue that the only, and the inescapably compelling, rationale for the legitimacy of nationalism is the plight of the Palestinian people: a people without a sovereign home. For the rest of the world both to enjoy nationalism and at the same time to spout a deconstructive rhetoric about nationalism in the face of Palestinian homelessness is downright perfidious and unconscionable.[26] But that apart, looking around the world, it is not immediately clear how the nationalist urge is functioning in different arenas. Although there is a general trend of secession, separatism, and, in the Eastern European context, Balkanization, it is not obvious if these are majoritarian or minoritarian movements. Is nationalism being rejected as an agent of repressive unification, or is it being upheld along racial and ethnic lines? Clearly, there is a fierce and passionate return to prenationalist allegiances, and the burden of the thesis is that for all these years nationalist unity has been a mere veneer, a thin lid trying to conceal the long-suppressed violence and resentment within.[27] In many instances, it is ironic that even the term "nationalism" should be used, as in "ethnic nationalism".[28] One would imagine that, if anything, "ethnicity" would be a powerful counterstatement to the modernist discourse of nationalism. But on the contrary, what we are finding is that even movements that are pitted against nationalism are using the language of nationalism in their very act of resistance. We thus have ethnic nationalism squaring off against nationalism; what is left untouched is the morphology of nationalism. This is clearly an indication of the extent to which nationalism has dominated the political scene for the last two hundred years or so. It has reached a point where projects of legitimation have become unthinkable except in nationalist terms: nationalism has become the absolute standard for the political as such. As a result, even the most ferocious counterhegemonic collective practices are forced to take on the discredited form of nationalism.

The second scenario where nationalism is to be practiced strategically for purposes of political legitimation falls very much under the same trap. The very idea of espousing nationalism for public-political causes perpetuates an already existing inner-outer split into a chronic schizophrenia.[29] As Partha Chatterjee has argued, in such a situation nationalism becomes a male preserve and "women" are punished into becoming the vehicles of a pure interiority that takes the form of a double deprivation ("Nationalist Resolution," 238–39). Women are effectively excluded both from the history of the "outside" and that of the "inside"—yet another instance of women being used as pawns in a male game of paranoia.[30] Moreover, such an internalized Manichaean doubleness eventually celebrates the symptom itself as the cure. The cure (within nationalist terms) becomes viable only if we accept the distinction that Fanon makes between an official nationalism presided over by the indigenous elite and a genuine populist national consciousness.[31] But the Fanonian hope, when viewed through Partha Chatterjee's lenses, sounds naive precisely because it does not identify the very epistemic form of nationalism as part of the problem.

The politics of the "return" and of the diaspora, however, are full of possibilities. Although there are significant overlaps between these two alternatives, I will take them up one at a time. The very necessity of the "return" is posited on a prior premise: the realization that to be a postcolonial is to live in a state of alienation, alienation from one's true being, history, and heritage. The "return" takes the form of a cure, or remedy, for the present ills of postcoloniality. The "return" also raises the important issue of "false consciousness" and the problem of "real-historical consciousness" versus "virtual historical consciousness." Postcolonial subjectivity is made to choose between its contemporary hybridity as sedimented by the violent history of colonialism and an indigenous genealogy as it existed prior to the colonialist chapter. The mandate of the return is based on the following diagnosis: the modern-nationalist postcolonial identity is erroneous, inauthentic, not one's own; hence the need for correction and redirection. I would caution against facilely dismissing this option as "fundamentalist" or nostalgic. The return does not have to be based on either notions of ontological or epistemological purity. The return is a matter of political choice by a people on behalf of their own authenticity, and there is nothing regressive or atavistic about people revisiting the past with the intention of reclaiming it.[32] The problem comes up when revisionist identities are held up as primordial and transcendentally sanctioned and not as historically produced. As I have already indicated, the "returns" that I am talking about are all the results of narrative invention. The dilemma then is not between two pure identities (Western or indigenous), but between two different narratives and their intended teleologies. The dilemma is this: in which narrative should the postcolonial subject be launched on its way to identity? But before the launching can be initiated, there is a prior methodological problem to be resolved: how to deal with present history and its immediate prehistory? Should the location of present history be invested in critically, or should it be strategically bypassed and neglected?

We are faced with two kinds of postcolonial returns: the subaltern route that revisits colonialist-nationalist historiographies oppositionally and nonidentically[33] and the indigenous path, with its strong countermemory or forgetfulness of matters colonialist and nationalist.[34] What is interesting to observe is the extent to which the originary assumptions of each project determine, by way of a theoretical apriorism, what is possible within the project. Subaltern historiographies as undertaken by Ranajit Guha, Dipesh Chakraborty, and others are in keeping with the classic subaltern program as enunciated by Antonio Gramsci. The six-phase program acknowledges that subalternity is necessarily mixed up with the historiographies of the dominant mode and that the production of subaltern identity has to go through (albeit critically and adversarially) dominant discourses before it can seize its agency as its own. The subaltern path to self-recovery lies through histories of negative identification where the subaltern consciousness identifies itself in terms of "what it is not." Its alienation from its self comes to an end when it succeeds in articulating its own hegemonic identity.[35]

Although this is not my present concern here, I would like to mention in passing that the epistemological status of "alienation" is double-coded. As Gayatri Chakravorty Spivak has contended powerfully, alienation is both a political and a philosophical phenomenon. In the political-Marxian sense, alienation is a negative state corrigible through revolutions. But alienation in a philosophic sense (and this is something that Spivak develops in her work[36] as she reads the subaltern project "against the grain" and, in doing so, submits the project of alienation-remediation, in the political sense, to interrogation by poststructuralist readings of alienation in a philosophical sense, that is, alienation as incorrigible) when understood deconstructively admits of no final correction. Hence Spivak's insistence that the political project of subalternity undertaken in the scrupulosity of political interest must be interrupted by the radical theme of "cognitive failure." Will the subaltern subject ever arrive at its true identity, or is its narrative fated to eternal deferral? What is the point at all in undertaking the subaltern political project when it cannot be philosophically validated? What indeed is the gain if the subaltern project, too, is predetermined to failure and its failure is nothing but an allegorical instantiation of the thesis of "cognitive failure"?

Theorists of indigeny would point out that subalternity is not an inherent state of being or a historically objective condition, but very much a matter of narrative production.[37] In other words, the alignment of postcoloniality with subalternity is not natural. A so-called subaltern text may well be an indigenous text that warrants a different historiography. We are now back to questions of interpretive authority and widely divergent narrative epistemologies. Even the grand thesis of philosophic alienation, viewed from this perspective, sounds suspect, for after all, why should the philosophical valence of alienation be allowed to contain and dominate the political semantics of alienation? Moreover, why should the epistemological project be "radically other" and therefore heterogeneous with the realities of the political program? What is at stake in privileging the epistemological as the ultimate pedagogical deconstructor of political naïveté? And even more pertinently, the indigenous theorist might well ask: why does the general-philosophical question get narrativized through Hegel-Marx-Derrida (Spivak, *In Other Worlds*, 202–15)? Isn't it more than likely that the indigenous political project is quite capable of articulating its own philosophy, its own epistemology of the "subject"? As we can see, we have come back to the same old issues: the separation of theories of knowledge from acts of political independence, and the specificity of parameters of solidarity. The danger with subaltern theory refracted through poststructuralist perspectives is that it, too, privileges Western theory and therefore insists that radical deconstructive critiques have no place for solidarity or constituency unless solidarity itself is conceptualized as a congeries of traveling interruptions and transgressions, that is, as perennial transactional readings among vastly different subject positions. Committed to the utopianism of high theory, these readings privilege perennial crisis as the appropriate historical content of postcoloniality. A further objection that could be raised by advocates of indigeny is the following, and this very much concerns the statements that Spivak makes in one of her interviews that there can be no such thing as indigenous theory: how is one to know if and when the subaltern project has succeeded in subverting dominant historiographies and has ushered in its own hegemony (*Postcolonial Critic*, 69)? Where is the guarantee that subalternity will not be totally lost in complicity with the dominant historiographies, especially given (and this is true not of the Gramscian program but of poststructuralist versions of Gramsci) the overdetermination of the political by the philosophical? Also, the claim that "there is no indigenous theory" makes no particular sense except within the subject-positional conjuncture from which it is made.

Perhaps the problem here is twofold: (1) the nature and the politics of location and (2) (this brings us back to my critique of culturalism early on in the essay) the "intellectual/critical" nature of the whole enterprise. Drawing on the work of Michel Foucault, Spivak cautions us against using the term "subject position" romantically as a surrogate term for the freedom of the self. If anything, subject positions are "assigned" and not freely chosen. It is de rigueur for any kind of subject-positional politics to take its own positionality as constitutive of the politics: in other words, the variations or inflections brought about by one's specific positionality as an academic intellectual are not epiphenomenal to some primary originary politics. To put this in Gramscian-Foucauldian terms, the very organicity of one's politics is subtended and professionally produced by one's specific positionality. Even more broadly speaking, there can be no access to macropolitics except through micropolitical mediations. By this logic, a postcolonial critic-academic-intellectual's sense of constituency is split, crosshatched, anything but unitary. Invested as she is in academic-disciplinary practices, the postcolonial intellectual would be dishonest to seek a direct cathexis with postcolonial identity politics in abeyance of her specific subject-positional location.

Is this way of accounting for one's subject position politically progressive, or is it in fact an admission and perhaps even an ironic glorification of the powerlessness of specific intellectuals beyond their immediate specialist domain?[38] With the worldliness of macropolitics "always already" mediated and spoken for by their professionalism, the postcolonial-specific intellectuals have little else to do except invest in their subject positions self-reflexively and autocritically.

In an essay that addresses the political production of knowledge in universities, Jacques Derrida calls for "protocols of vigilance and radical self-reflexivity" by way of politicizing the university (3–20). Derrida's assumption here is that the academic site of knowledge, by producing a critical second-order or metatopical awareness of itself, will have become political. While I do applaud this move of locating politics in professionalism, I still find Derrida's formulation inadequate. What is missing in this formulation is a sense of the university's relationality with other sites. For Derrida's (and by extension, Spivak's) formulation to work, the disinterested autonomy of the university as a site has to be endorsed as a first principle. Thus, when Derrida expresses the desire for producing a radical "other" critique that will be truly heterogeneous with the object of the critique, he is in fact utterly privileging the academic mode of labor.[39] There is an unwarranted confidence that somehow the ability of the critique "to think thought itself" will result in the emergence of a different cultural politics. The simple questions are these: How could anything have changed when the site remains the same? How can an intrainstitutional revolution connect with anything "outside" when the "outside" itself is conceptualized as the result of an institutional mode of production? There is a narcissistic circularity to the whole process, and the result is the glorification of the institution's accountability to itself, although in this instance the accountability is of the deconstructive persuasion. The object of my critique here is a certain poststructuralist smugness about autocritiques and rigorous protocols of self-reflexivity. The purpose of self-reflexivity should be persuasion, and persuasion should result in change, and change is too significant to be adjudicated by merely institutional-professional norms. Unless autocritiques succeed in establishing a different relationality with "the world," they are exercises in a vacuum, sans cause, sans constituency. Such a single-minded dedication to one's professional formation in fact belies what is most promising in the politics of location: that locations can recoordinate themselves macropolitically through persuasion and in response to the imperatives of other locations. For example, the formation known as African studies may and can rethink or modify its project in response to Latin American critiques of colonialism. But this dialogue cannot take place if the emphasis is merely on methodologies and protocols. In aligning "location" obsessively with the micropolitical discourses of professional knowledge, Derrida and Spivak in fact end up immobilizing locations and subject positions. And paradoxically, the professional site, in not traveling, becomes the home of a methodological universalism.[40]

In much of the work on postcoloniality, the emphasis is on the postcolonial critic and the postcolonial intellectual. I have no problem with this provided the terms "critic" and "intellectual" are problematized. As I have tried to demonstrate in the last few pages, the mediation of the intellectual-critic becomes the master mediation with a mandate of its own. Well might one ask why other positions and locations such as "being a taxpayer," "being a union leader/social activist," or "being a parent" are denied the dignity of being mediations in their own right. What about forms of knowledge produced from other sites? In addition to the culturalism tacit in "intellectuality" and "criticism," these terms, when understood as poststructuralist coinages, pose a different kind of problem. The critic-intellectual is divorced from the politics of solidarity and constituency. The critic is forever looking for that radical "elsewhere" that will validate "perennial readings against the grain," and the intellectual is busy planning multiple transgressions to avoid being located ideologically and/or macropolitically.[41] In this particular context postcoloniality as constituency, when pressured by metropolitan theory and its professionalism, is allegorized too easily and is made to forget "the return" aspect of its teleology. From an indigenous perspective, this "return" is doomed from the start. How is a "return" possible when the critic's allegiance to the *detour* is more compelling than her commitment to the return? The teleologically minded (or ends-oriented) indigenous theorist would insist that the "return" requires a different path altogether, a path that does not recuperate the historical realities of colonialism and Westernization. The difference between the two returns lies in their very different readings of the means and ends of the project. Each of the returns is underwritten by a different telos.

It is quite clear that there cannot be any one normative articulation of postcoloniality that is nation-centered or centered around the return or the diaspora. Postcoloniality at best is a problematic field where heated debates and contestations are bound to take place for quite a while to come. My point here is that whoever joins the polemical dialogue should do so with a critical-sensitive awareness of the legitimacies of several other perspectives on the issue. In other words, it would be quite futile and divisive in the long run for any one perspective, such as the diasporic, the indigenous, or the orthodox Marxist, to begin with the brazen assumption that it alone has the ethicopolitical right to speak representatively on behalf of "postcoloniality." Such an assumption can only take the form of a pedagogical arrogance that is interested more in correcting other points of view than in engaging with them in a spirit of reciprocity. No one historical angle can have a monopolistic hold over the possible elaborations of the "postcolony," especially during times when master discourses in general—for example, modernity, nationalism, or international Communism/Marxism—are deservedly in disarray.[42] Alhough this may sound a little too irresponsibly allegorical, I would venture to say that "postcoloniality" as a field could well be the arena where inequalities, imbalances, and asymmetries could historicize themselves "relationally," an arena where dominant historiographies could be made accountable to the ethicopolitical authority of emerging histories.[43] The kind of noncoercive and justice-based universalism that Samir Amin envisions in his book, *Eurocentrism*, may well call for a versatile and multivalent postcoloniality rooted differently in different histories (136–52).

Among the many heated dialogues that are taking place under the tentative aegis of postcoloniality, there is none more frustrating than the exchange between "diasporic" and "resident" voices. The exchange invariably centers around questions of authenticity and perceptions of "insideness" and "outsideness." Who has got it right, the insider or the outsider? Who speaks for the majority, the insider or the outsider? Unfortunately, what could develop into a productive dialogue often never goes beyond the preliminary moves of self-authentication and credentials presentation. It would seem at first glance that the "resident" position is representative and representational, that is, that it speaks for and on behalf of the majority of Indians or Pakistanis or Nigerians, for example, who live within their respective nation-states, whereas the diasporic voices by virtue of their travel and/or deracinatedness are postrepresentational: they do not add up to a viable constituency. There are a number of problems here. First, there is an untested assumption that majoritarianism equals moral-political authority, that minoritarian voices are either exceptional or elitist. In our own times, such knee-jerk adjudications of right and wrong will just not do: if anything, what is challenging in the present historical conjuncture is the very task of differentiating authentic hegemony from mere dominance. There are regional situations where the majority is dominant-repressive and other situations where the minority represents top-down oppression. A programmatic position that associates minorities with virtue and moral outrage and majorities with tyranny, or vice versa, is insensitive to the actual nuance of history. The complex critical task is to analyze the various processes of majority and minority interpellations as they occur in different geopolitical locations (Appadurai, 5–17).

Second, the claim that "insiders" are more representative is a specious claim. There are several "insides" within any given postcolonial nation-state, and any monolithic use of the "inside" as authentic space is dangerous. Besides, the equation of the insider with the political correctness of the majority is a gross ideological falsification, for it would have us believe that a hegemonic totality has indeed been produced through political processes, a totality that has earned the right to speak for the plenitude of the nation-state. But as Homi Bhabha and others have argued, nationalisms in general are a compelling symptom of the noncoincidence of the "performative" with the "pedagogical" ("Dissemination"). An unproblematic use of geopolitical space as either "in" or "out" also authorizes a facile forgiveness of insider elitisms and oppressions. "Differences within" are consequently not acknowledged as forms of political being.

Finally (and this to me is quite serious), almost by fiat, certain positions vis-à-vis the sovereignty of the nation-state are preemptively identified as erroneous and/or inappropriate. This is indeed a deadly formal procedure that ensures that certain articulations will not even be read as "historical contents" because they arise from positions that are inherently incorrect. Thus the diasporic takes on nationalism are virtually depoliticized and dehistoricized in one fell epistemological edict. To put it colloquially, "I will not listen to you because of where you come from." Such die-hardism is hardly helpful when diasporas and nationalisms are engaged the world over in the task of reciprocal constitution and invention. Is the diaspora the tail that wags "nationalism," or is "nationalism" the primary body that wags the diaspora? That is a question that cannot be answered through recourse to unilateral declarations of authority and privilege.

Lest I be perceived as a diasporic zealot, let me add in explanation that what I am arguing for is a mutual politicization. Just as much as I have been contending against the morphology of national identity as basic or primary and the diasporic as secondary or epiphenomenal, I will also assert that the diaspora does not constitute a pure heterotopia informed by a radical countermemory. The politics of diasporic spaces is indeed contradictory and multiaccentual. I will begin, then, with specific critiques of the diaspora before I offer my preferred versions of the politics of the diaspora. First, within the intellectual-culturalist contexts that define the production of discourses like the present essay, there is the temptation to read the diaspora as a convenient metaphorical/tropological code for the unpacking of certain elitist intellectual agendas. The diaspora, for example, offers exciting possibilities for the intellectual who has always dreamed of pure spaces of thought disjunct from ideological interpellations and identity regimes. The diaspora as the radical non-name of a nonplace empowers the intellectual to seek transcendence through exile and an epiphanic escape from the pressures of history. As such, the diaspora holds possibilities of a "virtual theoretical consciousness" sundered from the realities of a historical consciousness. This virtual consciousness may well be a form of uncorrected false consciousness. What could I mean by "false consciousness"? Let me explain: the context of the diaspora has the capacity to exacerbate the disharmony between utopian realities available exclusively through theory and agential predicaments experienced in history. Thus, given the alienated spatiality of the diaspora, one can both belong and not belong to either one of two worlds at the same time. To the diasporic sensibility, it is easy to practice a perennial politics of transgression in radical postponement of the politics of constituency. To put it differently, traveling or peripatetic transgressions in and by themselves begin to constitute a politics of difference or postrepresentation. Belonging nowhere and everywhere at the same time, the diasporic subject may well attempt to proclaim a heterogeneous "elsewhere" as its actual epistemological home.[44]

Now I would argue that such a self-understanding on the part of the diasporic subject is purely mythical and allegorical. In history, the conditions of the diasporic subject are indeed quite "other." The hyperrealization of the diaspora as a pure countermnemonic politics of its own is admissible only if we concede without qualification (1) that poststructuralist theories of "dissemination" are the natural expressions of diasporic subjectivity whereby the epistemology of poststructuralism and the politics of the diaspora become "one" without any mediation, and (2) that the historiographies of difference have effected a break from identitarian productions of historical consciousness. Neither of these claims is defensible. The poststructuralist appropriation of the diaspora aestheticizes it as an avant-garde lifestyle based on deterritorialization (hence, the frequent offensive and unconscionable use of the Palestinian diaspora as pure allegory), and poststructuralist historiographers of the diaspora are indeed guilty of mendacity, for their celebration of "difference" is completely at odds with the actual experience of difference as undergone by diasporic peoples in their countries of residence.[45] My diagnostic reading is that in these instances, high metropolitan theory creates a virtual consciousness as a form of blindness to historical realities. The metropolitan theory of the diaspora is in fact a form of false consciousness that has to be demystified before the diasporic condition can be historicized as a condition of pain and double alienation.

To consider, then, the diaspora as "the history of the present" within the *longue durée* of colonialism-nationalism: if nationalism in a deep structural sense is the flip side of colonialism, and if the diaspora is "nationalism's significant Other," how is the diaspora related to colonialism? This question takes on even greater complexity when we consider the fact that the diasporas we are talking about are "metropolitan diasporas," that is, diasporas that have found a home away from home in the very heartland of former colonialism. And this home away from home is full of lies and duplicities. A diasporic citizen may very likely find economic betterment in the new home, but this very often is allied with a sense of political-cultural loss. If the diasporic self is forever marked by a double consciousness,[46] then its entry as legitimate citizen into the adopted home is also necessarily double. Thus in the American context (the so-called nation of nations context, as Walt Whitman saw it) of ethnic hyphenation, the passage into citizenship is also a passage into minoritization. The African-American in her very citizenship is "different" and thus rendered a target of hyphenation in pain and in alienation. The utopian response to this predicament (one favored by Homi Bhabha) would be to privilege the moment of passage as a perennial moment of crisis, as though crisis were a constituency by itself. Arguing against Bhabha, I would maintain that the ethnic diasporic self is in fact seeking validation as a constituency. As I have elaborated in chapter 3, there is a place for "postethnicity," but such a place cannot be disjunct from ethnic spaces or their polemical negotiations with the putative mainstream identity. The ethnic cannot be transcended or postponed unless and until ethnicity has been legitimated, both within and without, as historiography.[47] The perennial crisis mode plays too easily into "dominant traps" and their attempts to undo and deny ethnicity. Furthermore, as Jesse Jackson reminded Michael Dukakis (that although they may now be on the same boat, they have come to the United States on different ships), there are ethnicities and ethnicities, and the difference often is the racial line of color.[48]

I agree that the diasporic location is by no means that harmonious representational space characterized by a one-to-one correspondence between self and constituency, between experienced worldliness and cognitive worldview. As Maxine Hong Kingston and many others have demonstrated, the diasporic/ethnic location is a "ghostly" location where the political unreality of one's present home is to be surpassed only by the ontological unreality of one's place of origin.[49] This location is also one of painful, incommensurable simultaneity: the Chinese/Indian past as countermemory and memory (depending upon one's actual generational remove from one's "native" land) coexists with the modern or the postmodern present within a relationship that promises neither transcendence nor return. Does this mean that the diasporic location marks an epochal spot that announces the end of representation? Does the diaspora express a liminal, phantasmal, borderline[50] phenomenology inexpressible within the representational grid? I would respond, most certainly not. Sure enough, diasporan realities do show up the poverty of conventional modes of representation with their insistence on single-rooted, nontraveling, natural origins. But this calls for multidirectional, heterogeneous modes of representation and not the premature claim that "representation no longer exists." I do not see how representation "can no longer exist" until the political "no longer exists," and I for one must admit that I do not know what "the postpolitical" is all about. The much-vaunted obsolescence of representation also oversimplifies the phenomenon of the diaspora by equating it with that of metropolitan deracination. There is a strange signifying system of equivalence operating here in the name of theory: diaspora = metropolitan deracination = loss of "where one came from" = loss of historical perspectivism = the removal of "interestedness" from the realm of the "political" and, finally, the realization of politics as a kind of unsituated anarchism. Needless to say, what is shored up as the immutable transcendent signified through this play of signifiers is the metropolitan will to meaning as effected by metropolitan avant-garde theories and methodologies. But in actuality, the diasporic self acquires a different historicity and a different sense of duration within its new location that is neither home nor not-home.[51] Rather than glorify the immigrant moment as a mode of perennial liminality, the diasporic self seeks to reterritorialize itself and thereby acquire a name.

I believe that there is something to be gained in naming the diasporic self or subject as the ethnic self. Whereas the term "diaspora" indicates a desire to historicize the moment of departure as a moment of pure rupture both from "the natural home" and "the place of residence," the ethnic mandate is to live "within the hyphen" and yet be able to speak. Whereas the pure diasporic objective is to "blow the hyphen out of the continuum of history," the ethnic program is to bear historical witness to the agonizing tension between two histories (Benjamin). Informed exclusively, almost obsessively, by "the countermemory" and the utopian urge to focus only on second-order or metatopical revolutions, metropolitan theories of the diaspora tend to make light of the tension between "past history" and "present history." I would even go so far as to say that "disseminative" articulations of the diasporic predicament are an attempt to realize theory as an allegorical prescription for the ills of history.

The repoliticization of the diaspora has to be accomplished in two directions simultaneously. First of all, and this is in accordance with the requirements of the politics of location, diasporic communities need to make a difference within their places/nations/cultures of residence. This cannot be achieved unless and until the metropolitan location itself is understood as problematic and, in some sense, quite hostile to "ethnicity." The use of location by diasporic/ ethnic (I am using the two terms interchangeably in light of my earlier recommendation that the diasporic be named as the "ethnic") communities has to be "oppositional." In other words, "mainstreaming" is not the answer at all.[52] If "ethnicity" is to be realized both as an "itself" and as a powerful factor in the negotiation of the putative mainstream identity, it must necessarily be rooted in more than one history: that of the present location and that of its past. I am not suggesting for a moment that the ethnic self indulge in uncritical nostalgia or valorize a mythic past at the expense of the all-too-real present, but rather that it engage in the critical task of reciprocal invention. Particularly, in the American context, it is of the utmost importance that a variety of emerging postcolonial-diasporic ethnicities (Asian-American, Latina, Chinese-American, Chicano, and so forth) establish themselves "relationally" with the twin purpose of affirming themselves and demystifying the so-called mainstream. But this task is unthinkable unless ethnicity is coordinated as a "critical elsewhere" in active relationship with the status quo. These "emerging relational ethnicities" may be said to be interpellated in more than one direction: there is (1) the affirmation of "identity politics" inherent in each historically discrete ethnicity; (2) the relational cultivation of each ethnicity in response to other coeval ethnicities;[53] (3) achieving common (and not identical) cause with those deconstructive metropolitan identity productions that stem from within the dominant histories; and (4) opposing perennially dominant historiographies that resist change and ethicopolitical persuasion.

I can anticipate a vociferous objection here, namely, "Is it appropriate to use one's origins (such as Indian, Korean, Chinese, or Zimbabwean) in a purely strategic way? For example, isn't the "Africa" in "African-American" different from the "African" in "African"? Doesn't an ethnic awareness of "Africanness" within the American context somehow distort and misrepresent "Africanness" as understood as an "inside" reality within Africa? Is "ethnicity," then, a mere invention, whereas "native realities" are natural? How then do we decide which is the real India, the real Nigeria, and so on? I have a number of responses. First of all, it is not at all clear that African or Indian or Nigerian reality even within its "native place" is undifferentiated or indivisible. Second, the fortuitous coincidence of a historical reality with the place of its origin does not make that "reality" any more "natural" than other realities that have traveled or been displaced through demographic movements. Reality from within is as much a production or invention as realities that straddle two or more spaces. Third, the invention of realities are the result of perspectival imaginings, and each perspective is implicated in the polemics of its own positionality.[54] Fourth, diasporas are too real and historically dense in our own times to be dismissed as aberrations. Finally, any discussions of nation-centered formations without reference to diasporic movements and vice versa are really not worthwhile: a more rewarding task would be to read the two versions relationally and to locate and identify intersections of both consent and strong dissent, for neither version has the authority to speak for the other or to speak for nationalism or postcoloniality.

In conclusion, I would like to return to the politics of the "post." Much as I critique the use of "postcoloniality" as a floating signifier, in the final analysis my own take on the term is "double" since I do wish to retain for it a sense of open spatiality for the occurrence of coalitional transformations. This may not be a "big deal" in the home country, but to me and many others in the diaspora, the politics of solidarity with other minorities and diasporic ethnicities is as important and primary as the politics of the "representations of origins." It is in this sense, then, that I am in favor of the allegorization of the "postcolonial condition": that the allegory be made available as that relational space to be spoken for heterogeneously but relationally by diverse subaltern/oppressed/minority subject positions in their attempts to seek justice and reparation for centuries of unevenness and inequality.[55] Diasporic communities do not want to be rendered discrete or separate from other diasporic communities, for that way lies co-optation and depoliticization.[56] To authenticate their awareness of themselves as a form of political knowledge, these communities need to share worldviews, theories, values, and strategies so that none of them will be "divided and ruled" by the racism of the dominant historiography.

I cannot end this essay without reference to the other "p.c.," that is, the much publicized "political correctness," for the two "p.c.'s" are indeed interconnected in the public imagination. "Postcoloniality" (and here I am talking about it as an academic formation in a certain relationship to cultural studies) is often presented as a haven for terrorists and tenured radicals who are out to destroy Western civilization itself. Laughable and unconscionable as this charge is (much like the nonexistent phenomenon of "reverse discrimination"), postcolonial intellectuals should respond to it firmly and aggressively. This response is not even thinkable unless we think of postcoloniality as everyone's concern, its ethicopolitical authority a matter for general concern and awareness and not the mere resentment of a ghetto.[57] It is important for postcolonials of the diaspora to reject patronage, containment, and ghettoization and to insist rigorously that their internal perspective is equally an intervention in the general scheme of things. To put it in terms that might best appeal to academic departments of Western literature, teaching Conrad without teaching Chinua Achebe is as much bad faith as it is bad scholarship.

Notes

1. For a sustained discussion of the term "postcoloniality" from several different perspectives, see *Social Text* 31/32 (1992), a special issue on postcoloniality.

2. I am using the terms "project" and "formation" as elaborated by Raymond Williams in his posthumously published *The Politics of Modernism*.

3. I may be perceived here as guilty of using the term "West" in a monolithic way. Although I admit that the West itself is full of "differences within," I would insist that the West as a global political effect on the non-West has indeed been the result of colonialist-imperialist orchestration, that is, it has spoken with one voice.

4. For a critique of glib celebrations of democratic-capitalist triumphalism, see essays by Neil Larsen, Barbara Foley, and R. Radhakrishnan in the "remarx" section, *Rethinking Marxism* 5, no. 2 (Summer 1992): 109–40.

5. For probing analyses of postcoloniality in the context of imperialism, colonialism and neocolonialism, see *Social Text* 31/32 (1992), the special issue on postcoloniality—in particular, essays by Gyan Prakash, Ella Shohat, Anne McClintock, and Madhava Prasad. See also Aijaz Ahmed, *In Theory*, for a number of provocative position statements on theory, Marxism, nationalism, cultural elitism, and the diasporic intellectual.

6. Chandra Talpade Mohanty discusses the issue of "methodological universalism" and other related issues concerning subject positionality in her essay "Under Western Eyes," in *Third World Women and the Politics of Feminism*, ed. Mohanty, Russo, and Torres, 51–80.

7. It is ironic that in recent years American trade policy statements call for the deterritorializations of national spaces by the flow of capital and, at the same time, bemoan the surrender of American jobs to cheap labor overseas. On the theme of "denials within the West," see Akhil Gupta, "The Reincarnation of Souls and the Rebirth of Commodities."

8. For a sustained discussion of the organicity or the lack thereof of intellectuals, in the context of Antonio Gramsci and Michel Foucault, see chapter 2 in this volume.

9. Transcendence usually suggests some sort of cartographic reconfiguration and liberation. For two very different uses of cartography, the one imperialist-colonialist and the other postcolonial, see Joseph Conrad's *Heart of Darkness* and Amitav Ghosh's *The Shadow Lines*. See also Nuruddin Farah's *Maps*.

10. For a discussion of the "return" and its relationship to the "postcolonial *detour*," see Vivek Dhareshwar.

11. For rich and politically suggestive uses of space in post-Marxist geography, refer to the works of Edward Soja and Neil Smith.

12. For an original reading of the relationship between nationalism and imperialism, see Gauri Viswanathan's "Raymond Williams and British Colonialism" and her book *The Masks of Conquest*.

13. I refer here to the growing body of work of such postcolonial/subaltern scholars as Partha Chatterjee, Ashis Nandy, Vandana Shiva, and Dipesh Chakraborty, each of whom, in her own way, problematizes received historiographies. Also see *The Invention of Tradition*, ed. Hobsbawm and Ranger.

14. This idea of a critical inventory is elaborated brilliantly by Antonio Gramsci, *The Modern Prince and Other Writings*, 59.

15. Among the many publications on the Rushdie affair, I would single out the following essays: "Editors' Comments: On Fictionalizing the Real"; Sara Suleri; Gayatri Chakravorty Spivak, "Reading *The Satanic Verses*"; Tim Brennan; and Aamir Mufti. For general information on the many global receptions of *The Satanic Verses*, see Lisa Appignanesi and Sara Maitland, eds., *The Rushdie File*.

16. On the question of the objectivity of the text and the interpretive authority of different reading communities, see Stanley Fish.

17. This search for the third space is characteristic of so much contemporary ethnic and postmodern fiction: Maxine Hong Kingston, Toni Morrison, Jamaica Kincaid, and others.

18. Amitav Ghosh's *The Shadow Lines* effectively thematizes notions of "authenticity" and "invention" in a way that accounts for political agency without at the same time resorting to doctrines of epistemological and/or ontological purity.

19. For a radical critique of Western science and reason in the context of Indian life and culture, see *Science, Hegemony and Violence: A Requiem for Modernity*, ed. Ashis Nandy, in particular, essays by Claude Alvares, Shiv Visvanathan, Vandana Shiva, and Jatinder K. Bajaj.

20. There is a hymn from the *Rig Veda* that captures a similar idea: "Let noble thoughts come to us from every side."

21. Edward W. Said's "Traveling Theory" takes up this vital question of the modification of theory through travel from one geopolitical location to another.

22. See chapter 7, "Cultural Theory and the Politics of Location," in this volume.

23. For a historically sensitive analysis of the locationality of the "post," see Anthony Appiah, "Is the 'Post' in Postcoloniality the Same as the 'Post' in Post-Modernism?"

24. For a powerful critique of a developmental nationalism, see Madhava Prasad's essay in *Social Text* 31/32 (1992).

25. See Dhareshwar for an interesting elaboration of a postcolonial detour by way of poststructuralist epistemology.

26. Edward Said's numerous recent essays on the Palestinian intifada remind us of the pitfalls of a purely allegorical mode of thinking that is divorced from geopolitical realities. See, for example, "An Ideology of Difference," *Critical Inquiry* 12 (Autumn 1985): 38–58; "On Palestinian Identity: A Conversation with Salman Rushdie," *New Left Review* 160 (November–December 1986); "Intifada and Independence," *Social Text* 22 (Spring 1989); and "Representing the Colonized: Anthropology's Interlocutors," *Critical Inquiry* 15 (Winter 1989): 205–25.

27. For a rigorous and brilliant analysis of the many reconstituted forms of nationalism, see Arjun Appadurai, "Disjuncture and Difference in the Global Cultural Economy."

28. Ernest Gellner's book on nationalism is a useful guide to the many kinds of nationalism that have been active during this century.

29. See Partha Chatterjee, "The Nationalist Resolution of the Woman's Question"; see also chapter 9, "Nationalism, Gender, and the Narrative of Identity," in this volume.

30. For an in-depth study of the manner in which the woman's question in the context of *sati* is marginalized, see Lata Mani, "Contentious Traditions." For a global sense of women's issues in a third world context, see Chandra Talpade Mohanty's introduction to *Third World Women and the Politics of Feminism*, 1–47.

31. See Frantz Fanon's *The Wretched of the Earth* for an optimistic articulation of national consciousness. See also Neil Lazarus, *Resistance in Postcolonial African Fiction*, and Mowitt, "Algerian Nation: Fanon's Fetish."

32. Toni Morrison's *Beloved* and Gayl Jones's *Corregidora* are two powerful and moving fictional attempts at "the return" to one's own history.

33. The entire subaltern project initiated by Ranajit Guha poses this question of the subaltern's "own identity" in complex historiographic terms.

34. Friedrich Nietzsche's *The Use and Abuse of History* is a seminal text that deals with questions of historical forgetting and remembering. See also Michel Foucault, "Nietzsche, Genealogy, History."

35. Antonio Gramsci's formulation of the subaltern agenda is absolutely fundamental in this regard. For a simultaneously postcolonial and poststructuralist take on the subaltern, see Spivak, "Subaltern Studies: Deconstructing Historiography."

36. For further discussion of Spivak's work, see Lazarus, *Hating Tradition Properly*, and my book *Theory in an Uneven World*.

37. For an interesting understanding of the nature of the subaltern text, see Poonam Pillai.

38. Edward Said's notion of worldliness, which permeates his book *The World, the Text, the Critic*, is an attempt to call into question the narcissistic arrogance of specialist knowledges.

39. In significant opposition to Derrida, Foucault would question the adequacy of institutional-scientific productions of knowledge. See Foucault, *Power/Knowledge*.

40. For further discussions of intellectuality in a worldly context, see Bruce Robbins, ed.

41. In contrast to this notion of "criticism against the grain," indigenous Indian (Sanskrit *rasa*) aesthetic theory stresses the importance of the critic's empathy/*sahridaya* with the text.

42. Aijaz Ahmed's *In Theory* is an attempt, unsuccessful in my reading, to reestablish the claims of a dogmatic Marxism in the area of developmental nationalism.

43. For a sustained, historically responsible and brilliant discussion of historiography, see Ranajit Guha, "Dominance without Hegemony and Its Historiography."

44. Ghosh's *The Shadow Lines* is an interesting study of the location and its bearing on one's worldview. Ghosh also raises the question of "imagined reality" in relationship to inhabited realities.

45. The journal *Diaspora* is a recently established magazine whose primary focus is the cultural politics of various diasporas in relation to themselves and their "home" cultures.

46. For example, Maxine Hong Kingston's *The Woman Warrior*, with its double-conscious narrative, refers to both "American ghosts" and "Chinese ghosts" in the context of immigration and naturalization.

47. For an early, memorable account of the boundaries of ethnicity, see Ralph Ellison's *Invisible Man*.

48. W.E.B. Du Bois astutely remarked that race indeed has been the dividing line in our own times. Recent happenings in this country and elsewhere testify to the truth of his statement. See also Anthony Appiah's essay on Du Bois in *Race, Writing and Difference*.

49. For a thought-provoking discussion of diasporic reality vis-à-vis the reality of the place of origin, see Rey Chow. The fiction of Amy Tan also dramatizes this issue.

50. See Gloria Anzaldúa's *Borderlines/La Frontera*.

51. For notions of "home" in the context of the postcolony, see *Public Culture* 4, no. 2 (Spring 1992) and 5, no. 1 (Fall 1992).

52. See Mohanty, "On Race and Voice . . ."; also see Henry A. Giroux, "Post-Colonial Ruptures and Democratic Possibilities."

53. For the concept of coevalness, see Johannes Fabian, *Time and the Other: How Anthropology Makes Its Object*.

54. See my essay "Postmodernism and the Rest of the World," *Organization* 1, no. 2 (October 1994): 305–40. See also Julie Stephens, "Feminist Fictions: A Critique of the Category 'Non-Western Woman' in Feminist Writings on India," and Susie Tharu, "Response to Julie Stephens," both in *Subaltern Studies VI*, ed. Guha, 92–125 and 126–31.

55. Samir Amin and Neil Smith, among others, have theorized the notion of unevenness in geopolitical relationships.

56. A case in point here is the ethnic predicament in the United Kingdom: during Thatcher's rule, ethnicity was successfully minoritized and ghettoized. See Stuart Hall, *The Hard Road to Renewal*.

57. Kumkum Sangari and Sudesh Vaid, in their introduction to *Recasting Women*, quite astutely claim for feminist historiography both a "special interest" and a general or total valence.

References

Ahmed, Aijaz. *In Theory*. London: Verso, 1992.
Amin, Samir. *Eurocentrism*. New York: Monthly Review Press, 1989.

Anzaldúa, Gloria. *Borderlands/La Frontera: The New Mestiza.* San Francisco: Spinster/ Aunt Lute, 1987.

Appadurai, Arjun. "Disjuncture and Difference in the Global Cultural Economy." *Public Culture* 2, no. 2 (Spring 1990): 1–24.

Appiah, Anthony. "Is the 'Post' in Postcoloniality the Same as the 'Post' in Post-Modernism?" *Critical Inquiry* 17 (Winter 1991): 336–57.

———. "The Uncompleted Argument: Du Bois and the Illusion of Race." In *Race, Writing and Difference,* ed. H. L. Gates, 21–37. Chicago: University of Chicago Press, 1986.

Appignanesi, Lisa, and Sara Maitland, eds. *The Rushdie File.* Syracuse, N.Y.: Syracuse University Press, 1990.

Benjamin, Walter. "Theses on the Philosophy of History." In *Illuminations,* ed. and intro. Hannah Arendt, trans. Harry Zohn, 253–64. New York: Harcourt, Brace and World, 1968.

Bhabha, Homi K. "Dissemination: Time, Narrative, and the Margins of the Modern Nation." In *Nation and Narration,* ed. Homi K. Bhabha, 291–322. New York: Routledge, 1990.

Brennan, Tim. "Rushdie, Islam and Postcolonial Criticism." *Social Text* 31/32 (1992): 271–76.

Chatterjee, Partha. "The Nationalist Resolution of the Woman's Question." In *Recasting Women: Essays in Colonial History,* ed. Kumkum Sangari and Sudesh Vaid, 233–53. New Brunswick, N.J.: Rutgers University Press, 1990.

———. *Nationalist Thought and the Colonial World.* London: Zed, 1986; Minneapolis: University of Minnesota Press, 1993.

Chow, Rey. *Woman and Chinese Modernity.* Minneapolis: University of Minnesota Press, 1991.

Conrad, Joseph. *Heart of Darkness.* Oxford and New York: Oxford University Press, 1984.

Derrida, Jacques. "The Principle of Reason: The University on the Eye of Its Pupils." *Diacritics* 13 (Fall 1983): 3–20.

Dhareshwar, Vivek. "Toward a Narrative Epistemology of the Postcolonial Predicament." *Inscriptions* 5 (1989): 135–57.

Dworkin, Dennis L., and Leslie G. Roman, eds. *Views beyond the Border Country: Raymond Williams and Cultural Politics.* New York: Routledge, 1993.

"Editors Comments: On Fictionalizing the Real." *Public Culture* 2 (Spring 1989): i–v.

Ellison, Ralph. *The Invisible Man.* New York: Random House, 1952.

Fabian, Johannes. *Time and the Other: How Anthropology Makes Its Object.* New York: Columbia University Press, 1983.

Fanon, Frantz. *The Wretched of the Earth.* Trans. Constance Farrington. New York: Grove Press, 1968.

Farah, Nuruddin. *Maps.* London: Pan Books, 1986.

Fish, Stanley. *Is There a Text in This Class?: The Authority of Interpretive Communities.* Cambridge, Mass.: Harvard University Press, 1980.

Foley, Barbara, Neil Larsen, and R. Radhakrishnan. "Remarx." *Rethinking Marxism* 5, no. 2 (Summer 1992): 109–40.

Foucault, Michel. "Nietzsche, Genealogy, History." In *Language, Counter-Memory,*

Practice: Selected Essays and Interviews, ed. and intro. Donald F. Bouchard, trans. Donald F. Bouchard and Sherry Simon, 139–64. Ithaca, N.Y.: Cornell University Press, 1980.

———. *Power/Knowledge: Selected Interviews and Other Writings,* ed. and trans. Colin Gordon. New York: Pantheon Books, 1980.

Gellner, Ernest. *Nations and Nationalism.* Oxford: Blackwell, 1983.

Ghosh, Amitav. *The Shadow Lines.* London: Bloomsbury, 1988.

Giroux, Henry A. "Post-Colonial Ruptures and Democratic Possibilities." *Cultural Critique* 21 (Spring 1992): 5–39.

Gramsci, Antonio. *The Modern Prince and Other Writings.* Trans. and intro. Louis Marks. New York: International Publishers, 1968.

Guha, Ranajit. "Dominance without Hegemony and Its Historiography." In *Subaltern Studies VI,* ed. Ranajit Guha, 210–39. Oxford University Press, 1989.

Gupta, Akhil. "The Reincarnation of Souls and the Rebirth of Commodities: Representations of Time in 'East' and 'West.'" *Cultural Critique* 22 (Fall 1992): 187–211.

Hall, Stuart. *The Hard Road to Renewal.* London: Verso, 1988.

Hobsbawm, E., and T. Ranger, eds. *The Invention of Tradition.* Cambridge and New York: Cambridge University Press, 1983.

Jones, Gayl. *Corregidora.* New York: Random House, 1975.

Kingston, Maxine Hong. *The Woman Warrior.* New York: Knopf, distrib. Random House, 1976.

Lazarus, Neil. *Hating Tradition Properly.* Forthcoming.

———. *Resistance in Postcolonial African Fiction.* Yale University Press, 1990.

Mani, Lata. "Contentious Traditions: The Debate on Sati in Colonial India, 1790–1833." Ph.D. diss., University of California, 1989.

Mohanty, Chandra Talpade. "On Race and Voice: Challenges for Liberal Education in the 1990's." *Cultural Critique* 14 (Winter 1989–90): 179–208.

Mohanty, Chandra Talpade, A. Russo, and L. Torres, eds. *Third World Women and the Politics of Feminism.* Bloomington: Indiana University Press, 1991.

Morrison, Toni. *Beloved.* New York: Knopf, distrib. Random House, 1987.

Mowitt, John. "Algerian Nation: Fanon's Fetish." *Cultural Critique* 22 (Fall 1992): 165–86.

Mufti, Aamir. "Reading the Rushdie Affair: An Essay on Islam and Politics." *Social Text* 29 (1992): 95–116.

Nandy, Ashis, ed. *Science, Hegemony and Violence: A Requiem for Modernity.* Tokyo: United Nations University; Delhi: Oxford University Press, 1990.

Nietzsche, Friedrich. *The Use and Abuse of History.* Indianapolis: Bobbs-Merrill, 1949.

Pillai, Poonam. "Theorizing the Margins." Ph.D. diss., University of Massachusetts at Amherst, 1993.

Prasad, Madhava. "On the Question of a Theory of (Third World) Literature." *Social Text* 31/32 (1992): 57–83.

Public Culture 4, no. 2 (Spring 1992).

Public Culture 5, no. 1 (Fall 1992).

Radhakrishnan, R. "Postmodernism and the Rest of the World." *Organization* 1, no. 2 (October 1994): 305–40.

———. *Theory in an Uneven World.* Oxford: Blackwell, forthcoming.

Rig-Veda Sanhita. Trans. H. H. Wilson. New Delhi: Cosmo, 1977.
Robbins, Bruce, ed. *Intellectuals: Aesthetics, Politics, Academics.* Minneapolis: University of Minnesota Press, 1990.
Said, Edward W. "Traveling Theory." In *The World, the Text, the Critic,* 226–47. Cambridge, Mass.: Harvard University Press, 1983.
Sangari, Kumkum. "The Politics of the Possible." In *The Nature and Context of Minority Discourse,* ed. David Lloyd and Abdul JanMohamed, 216–45. Oxford University Press, 1990.
Shohat, Ella. "Notes on the 'Post-Colonial.'" *Social Text* 31/32 (1992): 99–113.
Smith, Neil. *Uneven Development.* Oxford: Blackwell, 1984.
Social Text 31/32 (1992). Special issue on "postcoloniality."
Soja, Edward W. *Postmodern Geographies: The Reassertion of Space in Critical Social Theory.* London: Verso, 1989.
Spivak, Gayatri Chakravorty. *The Post-Colonial Critic: Interviews, Strategies, Dialogues.* Ed. Sarah Harasym. New York: Routledge, 1990.
———. "Reading the Satanic Verses." *Public Culture* 21 (Fall 1989): 79–99.
———. "Subaltern Studies: Deconstructing Historiography." In *In Other Worlds: Essays in Cultural Politics,* 197–221. New York: Methuen, 1987.
Suleri, Sara. "Whither Rushdie." *Transition* 51 (1991): 198–212.
Viswanathan, Gauri. *The Masks of Conquest.* New York: Columbia University Press, 1989.
———. "Raymond Williams and British Colonialism: The Limits of Metropolitan Cultural Theory." In *Views beyond the Border Country,* ed. Dworkin and Roman, 217–30, 336–39.
Williams, Raymond. *The Politics of Modernism: Against the New Conformists.* London and New York: Verso, 1989.

9 / Nationalism, Gender, and the Narrative of Identity

In a recent essay entitled "The Nationalist Resolution of the Women's Question," Partha Chatterjee elaborates the complex relationship between women's politics and the politics of Indian nationalism. His point is that while the women's question "was a central issue in some of the most controversial debates over social reform in early and mid-nineteenth century Bengal," this very issue disappeared from the public agenda by the end of the century. "From then onwards," Chatterjee observes, "questions regarding the position of women in society do not arouse the same degree of passion as they did only a few decades before. The overwhelming issues now are directly political ones—concerning the polities of nationalism." Chatterjee concludes that "nationalism could not have resolved those issues; rather, the relation between nationalism and the women's question must have been problematical."[1] Although these critical comments are made in the highly specific context of Indian nationalism in the nineteenth century, they express a general truth concerning the relationship among different forms and contents of political struggle and the problems that emerge when any one politics (such as "the women's question") is taken over and spoken for by another politics (such as nationalism).[2]

The conjuncture wherein the women's question meets up with nationalism raises a number of fundamental questions about the very meaning of the term "politics." Why is it that the advent of the politics of nationalism signals the subordination if not the demise of women's politics? Why does the politics of the "one" typically overwhelm the politics of the "other"? Why could the two not be coordinated within an equal and dialogic relationship of mutual accountability? What factors constitute the normative criteria by which a question or issue is deemed "political"? Why is it that nationalism achieves the ideological effect of an inclusive and putatively macropolitical discourse, whereas the women's question—unable to achieve its own autonomous macropolitical identity—remains ghettoized within its specific and regional space? In other words, by what natural or ideological imperative or historical exigency does the politics of nationalism become the binding and overarching umbrella that subsumes other and different political temporalities?[3] For according to Chatterjee, the ideology of nationalist politics in its very specificity acts as the normative mode of *the political as such*, and "the imagined community" of nationalism is authorized as the most authentic unit or form of collectivity. Consequently, the women's question (or the *harijan* question, or the subaltern question . . .) is constrained to take on a nationalist expression as a prerequisite for being considered "political." Faced with its own repression, the women's question seems forced either to seek its own separatist political autonomy or to envision other ways of constituting a relational-integrative politics without at the same time resorting to another kind of totalizing umbrella.

The questions that I've already raised lead to still others, which will be posed here in all their political and epistemological generality: What does it mean to speak of "one" politics in terms of an "other"? How is a genuinely representative national consciousness (and here I have in mind the distinction that Frantz Fanon draws between the official ideology of nationalism and nationalist consciousness) to be spoken for by feminism and vice versa? Is it inevitable that one of these politics must form the horizon for the other, or is it possible that the very notion of a containing horizon is quite beside the point?[4] Can any horizon be "pregiven" in such an absolute and transcendent way? Isn't the very notion of the horizon open to perennial political negotiation? Since no one politics is totally representative of or completely coextensive with the horizon, should we not be talking about the ability of any subject-positional politics to inflect itself both regionally and totally? In other words, isn't the so-called horizon itself the shifting expression of equilibrium among the many forces that constitute and operate the horizon: gender, class, sexuality, ethnicity, and so on? If one specific politics is to achieve a general significance, it would seem that it has to possess a multiple valence, that is, enjoy political legitimacy as a specific constituency and simultaneously make a difference in the integrated political or cultural sphere. Without such access to an integrated cultural politics, any single subject-positional politics risks losing its interventionary power within that total field.

In their vigorously argued introduction to the volume *Recasting Women:*

Essays in Colonial History, Kumkum Sangari and Sudesh Vaid advance the cause of feminist historiography toward "the integrated domain of cultural history." Claiming that "feminist historiography may be feminist without being, exclusively, women's history," they go on to say that "such a historiography acknowledges that each aspect of reality is gendered, and is thus involved in questioning all that we think we know, in a sustained examination of analytical and epistemological apparatus, and in a dismantling of the ideological presuppositions of so called gender-neutral methodologies." Carefully avoiding the pitfalls of both separatism and academicism that are only too ready to embody feminist historiography as a separate discipline based on a gender-coded division of labor, Sangari and Vaid contend that "feminist historiography rethinks historiography as a whole," and in this sense make feminist historiography "a choice open to all historians." Such a choice is understood, however, not "as one among competing perspectives" but rather "as a choice which cannot but undergird *any* attempt at a historical reconstruction which undertakes to demonstrate our sociality in the *full* sense, and is ready to engage with its own presuppositions of an objective gender-neutral method of enquiry."[5]

There is so much being said in these passages that I wish to unpack some of it in detail before describing nationalism as a subject amenable to deconstructive investigation. In speaking for a particular feminist historiography, it would seem that Sangari and Vaid empower it in a double-coded way,[6] that is, feminist historiography is made to speak both representationally and postrepresentationally.[7] In other words, the articulation and the politicization of gender as an analytic category belong initially with feminism narrowly conceived as exclusively women's questions, but do not and cannot merely stop with that. If indeed gender is a necessary category in the context of cultural and historical and political analysis, how can its operations be circumscribed within the narrow confines of its origins? Just as the elaboration of "class" is in some sense intrinsic to the history of Marxism but is by no means exclusively Marxist, "gender" has a particular placement that is local and specific to "women's questions" but is by no means merely a regional concern.[8] Feminist historiography is representational in the sense that it speaks, by way of gender, for those questions and concerns that stem from women's issues initially, but in doing so it understands "gender" as a category that is much more comprehensive in its scope. In this sense, feminist historiography speaks postrepresentationally, activating the category of "gender" beyond its initial or originary commitment to merely one special or specific constituency. This point needs emphasis, for as we have already seen in the context of nationalism, it is precisely because the women's question was kept from achieving its own form of politicization that it was so easily and coercively spoken for by the discourse of nationalism, whereas with the arrival of gender as a fully blown historical-cultural-political-epistemic category, the women's question (which in and by itself was not yet a *politics*, but merely a constituency by description) is renamed and transformed as feminism. From this point on, feminist projects are interpellated by feminist ideology and not just covered under other and alien ideologies of patronage, amelioration, and redemption. But as has been observed already, this move in itself does not go far enough; true, it succeeds in politicizing the women's question in terms of its own ideology, but this very politics runs the danger of limiting itself as a form of "micropolitics."

Sangari and Vaid's formulation of the project of feminist historiography is refreshingly different from (and more far-reaching than) a number of current poststructuralist, radically subject-positional versions.[9] Unlike many of these versions that seem happy to accept their positional separateness and difference, Sangari and Vaid's elaboration of the project boldly and relevantly raises questions concerning the "full" and "total" rethinking of historiography as such. In opening up feminist historiography in a way that concerns all historians, it would appear that they are surrendering the specificity of the feminist project to other grand theories and ideologies. But a close reading of their text tells us something entirely different: the very openness of the "choice" is conceptualized as a form of historical and political inevitability. For the choice is not just any choice, or even one among many possible choices, but a choice that cannot but be made. In repudiating the very notion of gender neutrality, they integrate the category of gender into every aspect of reality; and in opening gender out to all historians, they make it impossible for other historians (who, for example, historicize along axes of nationality, class, race, and so on) not to integrate the feminist imperative within their respective projects. To put it differently, the field of historiography as such is made to acknowledge the reality of the feminist intervention as both micropolitical and macropolitical. In my reading, Sangari and Vaid forward the very strong claim that the feminist project cannot be considered complete or even sufficient unless it takes on the project of the "feminization" of the total field of historiography as such.[10] So much of poststructuralist feminism, rooted in epistemologies of relativism and difference, renounces global and macropolitical models on the basis of "epistemological purity," but Sangari and Vaid's analysis points out that such theories in themselves cannot be devoid of global projections and commitments. The category of "gender" in its particularity resonates with a general or universal potential for meaning (why else would it be a category?), and the task is not to eschew universality or globality in favor of pure difference or heterogeneity, but to read and interpret carefully the many tensions among the many forms of "particular-universal" categorical claims.

If we now put together the critical trajectories of Chatterjee's essay and Sangari and Vaid's historiographic agenda, we find ourselves confronting, with problematic urgency, the question we started out with: how is any one politics to be spoken in terms of another politics? If feminism or nationalism are expressions of "particular-universal" ideologies, and if furthermore, each of these ideologies (from its own specificity) makes general claims on the entire social formation, how are we to adjudicate among these relativist discourses, none of which is legitimate enough to speak for the total reality? As I have suggested, the strategy of locating any one politics within another is as inappropriate as it is coercive. If that is the case, then from what space or within what domain does any historiography speak? Neither strategies of radical separateness nor those of hierarchic and organic containment do justice to the relational nature of the "absent totality" whose very reality, according to Ernesto Laclau and Chantal Mouffe, is "unsutured."[11] The task facing the many subject positions and their particular-universal ideologies is that of envisioning a totality that is not already there. Nationalist totality, we have seen, is an example of a "bad totality," and feminist historiography secedes from that structure *not to set up a different and oppositional form of totality, but to establish a different relationship to totality*. My objective here, as I loosely conflate Sangari and Vaid with Laclau and Mouffe, is to suggest both that no one discourse or historiography has the ethicopolitical legitimacy to represent the totality, and that the concept of "totality" should be understood not as a pregiven horizon but as the necessary and inevitable "effect" or function of the many relational dialogues, contestations, and asymmetries among the many positions (and their particular-universal ideologies) that constitute the total field.

A model that sees hegemony articulated among multiple determinations obviously poses serious representational problems. If the categories of gender, sexuality, nationality, or class can neither speak for the totality nor for one another but are yet implicated in one another relationally, how is the historical subject to produce a narrative from such a radical relationality, a relationality without recourse? For once we accept the notion of relational articulation, two consequences follow: (1) inside/outside distinctions become thoroughly problematized and displaced (for example, the idea of a feminist or an ethnic or a class-based historiography pursued entirely from within itself becomes highly questionable), and (2) the conception of relationality as a field-in-process undermines possibilities of establishing boundaries and limits to the relational field; in other words, relationality turns into a pure concept, an end in itself.

So when Sangari and Vaid make *their* transformative claims on behalf of feminist historiography it is not immediately clear if by "feminist historiography" they mean Indian feminist historiography or postcolonial feminist historiography or subaltern feminist historiography or third world feminist historiography. There is a certain lack of situatedness, a certain rejection of the politics of location (in Adrienne Rich's sense of the term), in the manner in which "feminist historiography" resists being located in terms of Indianness, subalternity, postcoloniality, and so on. But clearly, judging from the general thrust of their essay, they do mean to situate feminist historiography in the specific context of colonial and nationalist history. So in this sense, feminist historiography cannot become its own pure signifier, nor can it avoid the project of interpreting itself in relation to other given discourses and ideologies. Thus, in seeking to recast women against the backdrop of colonial history, Sangari and Vaid enact an oppositional relationship between their discourse and colonial history and, by extension, nationalist history. In a similar vein, the entire school of South Asian subaltern historians intentionally revises colonialist and nationalist historiographies, seeking all along to expose patterns of "dominance without hegemony" in these discourses.[12] This sense of historical specificity bounds and gives determinate shape to a project that would otherwise remain a rarefied and contentless exploration of relationality as such. What helps these historians in negotiating the boundaries among feminism, colonialism, nationalism, capitalism, Eurocentrism, metropolitanism, and so on, is their commitment to the production of a critical history that has to acknowledge "realities" in the very act of challenging and discrediting them. In directing the revisionist deconstructive energies of gender and subalternity at colonialist and nationalist historiographies, these historians acknowledge the force of a prior placement, what we could term "the assigned nature" of their subject position. By thus taking a critical Gramscian inventory of their own historical positions, they deal with nationalism earnestly rather than dismissing it outright as a failed and flawed phenomenon: the history of nationalism is not easily bypassed just because it has been the history of a failure.[13]

But why study nationalism at all, especially at a time when avant-garde, metropolitan theory has passed the verdict that like "the voice," like "identity," like "representation," nationalism is or should be dead? There are several reasons why nationalism must continue to be studied:

1. Like all complex historical movements, nationalism is not a monolithic phenomenon to be deemed entirely good or entirely bad; nationalism is a contradictory discourse and its internal contradictions need to be unpacked

in their historical specificity. The historical agency of nationalism has been sometimes hegemonic although often merely dominant, sometimes emancipatory although often repressive, and sometimes progressive although often traditional and reactionary.

2. While banished by certain theories, nationalism is back today with a vengeance all over the world. Western theorists cannot in good faith talk any more about the ugly and hysterical resurgence of nationalisms "out there and among them," as if "here and among us" nationalism is a thing of the past. The unification of the two Germanies in Europe, the breakup of the Soviet Union into fifteen national republics, and the current suppression of Chechnya by Russia have brought nationalism and the national question back into the very center of the historical stage. Neither the deracinating multinational or international spread of capitalism nor the Marxist theoretical assimilation of the national question within an internationalist Communism has been able to do away with the urgencies of the imagined communities of nationalism. Right here in the United States (which would seem to have surpassed the nationalist threshold of universal history), we witnessed televisual images of jingoistic self-celebration during the U.S. bombing of Libya. And all along, political commentators and media reporters were condemning the madman Qaddafi and the violent behavior of the Libyan zealots "out there."

3. The international community of nations continues to bear the shame and guilt of not yet acknowledging the Palestinian right to nationhood and self-determination. The Palestinians continue to be submitted to and brutalized by the duplicitous international consensus (spearheaded largely by the United States) that refuses to listen to the Palestinians because they are not yet a nation and at the same time frustrates their every attempt to become a nation.

4. And finally, stalemates such as the Salman Rushdie affair and the international impasse over Iraq's Saddam Hussein demonstrate yet again the poverty of a so-called international but in fact Western metropolitan framework when applied to other and different forms of collective identity.

It is with these polemical pointers that I would like to resume my analysis of the problems of nationalism; the particular structure that concerns me here is the dichotomy of the inside/outside that nationalist discourse deploys with telling effect. My point here is not to condemn or endorse in toto the politics of "inside/outside," but rather to observe the strategic and differentiated use of this dichotomous structure within nationalism. For instance, are we evaluating the Rushdie affair from within the spaces of Western secularism or from someplace else? Are we viewing the conduct of Arab politics from within the Arab nationalist umbrella, or from within an Arab but nonnationalist umbrella, or from yet another site? Our very mode of understanding is implicated in our mode of partisanship, and our mode of partisanship is an expression or function of our location—what that location includes and excludes. Inside/outside perceptions are indeed very much alive, and there is no transideological free space of arbitration to adjudicate among multiple nonsynchronous boundaries.

The particular instance of Indian nationalism makes use of the inner/outer distinction as a way of selectively coping with the West, and it is not coincidental that the women's question is very much a part of this dichotomous adjustment. Here again, by mobilizing the inner/outer distinction against the "outerness" of the West, nationalist rhetoric makes "woman" the pure and ahistorical signifier of "interiority."[14] In the fight against the enemy from the outside, something within gets even more repressed, and "woman" becomes the mute but necessary allegorical ground for the transactions of nationalist history. I turn again to Partha Chatterjee, who describes this effect in scrupulous detail. Chatterjee observes that nationalism could neither ignore the West completely nor capitulate to it entirely: the West and its ideals of material progress had to be assimilated selectively, without any fundamental damage to the native and "inner" Indian self. In other words, questions of change and progress posed in Western attire were conceived as an outer and epiphenomenal aspect of Indian identity, whereas the inner and inviolable sanctum of Indian identity had to do with home, spirituality, and the figure of Woman as representative of the true self. As Chatterjee puts it:

> Now apply the inner/outer distinction to the matter of concrete day-to-day living and you get a separation of the social space into *ghar* and *bahir*, the home and the world. The world is the external, the domain of the material; the home represents our inner spiritual self, our true identity. The world is a treacherous terrain of the pursuit of material interests, where practical considerations reign supreme. It is also typically the domain of the male. The home in its essence must remain unaffected by the profane activities of the material world—and woman is its representation. *And so we get an identification of social roles by gender to correspond with the separation of the social space into* ghar *and* bahir. (Emphasis added)

Chatterjee goes on to say that once "we match the new meaning of the home/world dichotomy with the identification of social roles by gender, we get the ideological framework within which nationalism answered the women's question."[15] The rhetoric of nationalism makes use of gender from its own ideological perspective and frames women narrowly in the way that feminist historiography, as articulated by Sangari and Vaid, soundly rejects. Like any framework whose finitude is the representation of its own limited and ideologically biased interests, the nationalist framework, too, thematizes its own priorities: the selective appropriation of the West and the safeguarding of one's essential identity. Unfortunately, in authorizing such a schizophrenic vision of itself, nationalism loses on both fronts: its external history remains hostage to the Enlightenment identity of the West while its inner self is effectively written out of history altogether in the name of a repressive and essentialist indigeny. And Woman takes on the name of a vast inner silence not to be broken into by the rough and external clamor of material history. Chatterjee's reading of the nationalist paradigm makes us acutely aware that the postcolonial project and its many narratives are still in search of a different political ethic or teleology (if that term is still permissible), one that is underwritten neither by the Western subject of Enlightenment nor by a reactionary and essentialist nativism. It is important to notice how nationalist ideology deploys the inner/outer split to achieve a false and repressive resolution of its identity. Forced by colonialism to negotiate with Western blueprints of reason, progress, and enlightenment, the nationalist subject straddles two regions or spaces, internalizing Western epistemological modes at the outer or the purely pragmatic level, and at the inner level maintaining a traditional identity that will not be influenced by the merely pragmatic nature of the outward changes. In other words, the place where the *true* nationalist subject *really is* and the place from which it produces historical-materialist knowledge about itself are mutually heterogeneous. The locus of the true self, the inner/traditional/spiritual sense of place, is exiled from processes of history while the locus of historical knowledge fails to speak for the true identity of the nationalist subject. The result is a fundamental rupture, a form of basic cognitive dissidence, a radical collapse of representation. Unable to produce its own history in response to its inner sense of identity, nationalist ideology sets up Woman as victim and goddess simultaneously. Woman becomes the allegorical name for a specific historical failure: the failure to coordinate the political or the ontological with the epistemological within an undivided agency.

In his book *Nationalist Thought and the Colonial World*, Partha Chatterjee addresses in great depth the political-epistemological predicament faced by nationalism. Nationalism, Chatterjee submits, should result in a double decolonization. Mere political decolonization and the resultant celebration of freedom, however momentous, does not by itself inaugurate a new history, a new subject, and a new and free sense of agency.[16] It is of vital importance that nationalist thought coordinate a new and different space that it can call *its* own:

a space that is not complicit with the universal Subject of Eurocentric enlightenment, a space where nationalist politics could fashion its own epistemological, cognitive, and representational modalities. The break from colonialism has then to be both political and epistemological. The nationalist subject in its protagonistic phase of history (as against its antagonistic phase, when the primary aim was to overthrow the enemy) has to break away from the colonial past, achieve full and inclusive representational legitimacy with its own people—the many subspaces and the many other forms and thresholds of collective identity (such as the ethnic, the religious, the communal)—and fashion its own indigenous modes of cultural, social, and political production in response. Can nationalism as commonly understood fulfill these obligations?

The problem with nationalism, in Chatterjee's view, is that it sustains and continues the baleful legacies of Eurocentrism and Orientalism. The received history of nationalism argues for two kinds of nationalism: Eastern and Western.[17] By the logic of this Us-Them divide,[18] Western nationalisms are deemed capable of generating their own models of autonomy from within, whereas Eastern nationalisms have to assimilate something alien to their own cultures before they can become modern nations. Thus in the Western context, the ideals of Frenchness, Germanness, or Englishness—national essences rooted in a sense of autochthony—become the basis of a modernity that reroots and reconfirms a native sense of identity. On the other hand, Eastern nationalisms, and in particular "third world" nationalisms, are forced to choose between "being themselves" and "becoming modern nations," as though the universal standards of reason and progress were natural and intrinsic to the West. In this latter case, the universalizing mission is imbued with violence, coercion, deracination, and denaturalization. We can see how this divide perpetuates the ideology of a dominant common world where the West leads naturally and the East follows in an eternal game of catch-up in which its identity is always in dissonance with itself.

The real tragedy, however, is when postcolonial nationalisms internalize rather than problematize the Western blueprint in the name of progress, modernization, industrialization, and internationalism. This process seems difficult to avoid, since the immediate history of these nations happens to be Western and there are no easy ways available to reclaim a pure and uncontaminated history prior to the ravages of colonialism. Even if such recovery were possible, it would serve only to render the postcolonial nation hopelessly out of sync with the "international" present of modernity. How inevitable is this scenario? Is nationalism, then, "always already" corrupt and defective in its agency? Whatever the answer may be in the long run, Chatterjee reminds us that it is crucial for the postcolonial subject to produce a critical and deconstructive knowledge about nationalism. Only such a critical knowledge will help us identify and elaborate the complicity of the nationalist project with that of the enlightened European subject. It is on the basis of such knowledge that postcolonial subjects can produce a genuinely subaltern history about themselves and not merely replicate, in one form or another, the liberal-elitist narrative of the West. And it is in this context that Chatterjee makes a sharp distinction between what he calls the "problematic" of nationalism and the "thematic" of nationalism.

Drawing on the work of Edward Said and Anouar Abdel-Malek and routing it through the phenomenology of Sartre and Merleau-Ponty and the structural Marxism of Althusser, Chatterjee makes his unique contribution to our understanding of the two terms: thematic and problematic. His purpose is to "make a suitable distinction by which we can separate, for analytical purposes, that part of a social ideology . . . which asserts the existence of certain historical possibilities from the part which seeks to *justify* those claims by an appeal to both epistemic and moral principles." The distinction takes the following form. The thematic "refers to an epistemological as well as ethical system which provides a framework of elements and rules for establishing relations between elements; the problematic, on the other hand, consists of concrete statements about possibilities justified by reference to the thematic." Applying this distinction to nationalist ideology, Chatterjee finds that "the problematic of nationalist thought is exactly the reverse of that of Orientalism." The only difference is that whereas in Orientalism the Oriental is a passive subject, in nationalism the object has become an active "subject," but one that remains captive to categories such as "progress," "reason," and "modernity," categories that are alien to him or her. Rather than being acted upon by these categories from the outside, this new subject internalizes them. Within such an ideological interpellation (which does not spring from the history of the postcolonial subject), the subject thinks that his or her subjectivity is "active, autonomous and sovereign." "At the level of the thematic, on the other hand," continues Chatterjee, "nationalist thought accepts the same essentialist conception based on the distinction between 'the East' and 'the West,' the same typology created by a transcendent studying subject, and hence the same 'objectifying' procedures of knowledge constructed in the post-Enlightenment age of Western science." The result is a constitutive contradictoriness in nationalist thought: its daring political agenda is always already depoliticized and recuperated by the very same representational structure that nationalist thought seeks to put in question. Hence, as Chatterjee concludes, the inappropriateness of posing the problem of "social transformation in a post-colonial country within a strictly nationalist framework."[19]

If we accept Chatterjee's analysis (I for one find it eminently persuasive), we have to conclude that the nationalist problematic preempts the nationalist thematic. The thematic of nationalism in a postcolonial country is constrained to remain a mere instantiation of a generalized nationalist problematic developed elsewhere. In other words, the processes and the procedures of the post-Enlightenment project are made to become the hallmark of the nation-building thematic in the postcolonial country. The post-Enlightenment telos begins to function as a free-floating signifier seeking universal confirmation. What remains concealed in such a false universalization is of course the fact that Western nationalism itself took shape under highly determinate and limited historical circumstances. In Chatterjee's terms, the thematic, justificatory rhetoric of Western nationalism is naturalized as an integral part of the very algebra of *nationalism as such*. In instantiating without historical relevance the second-order history of nationalism developed elsewhere, postcolonial nationalism forfeits its own thematic agenda. If in Western nationalism the thematic and the problematic are reciprocally and organically grounded, in the case of post-colonial nationalism the thematic and the problematic remain disjunct from each other.

What it all comes down to is the betrayal by nationalism of its own "inner" realities. Obsessively concerned with the West and other forms of local elitism, nationalism fails to speak for its own people; on the contrary, it suppresses the politics of subalternity. Paralyzed by the ideological view of its inner reality as merely a bulwark against excessive Westernization, nationalism fails to historicize this inner reality in its own multifarious forms. The very mode in which nationalism identifies its inner identity privileges the externality of the West, and the so-called inner or true identity of the nation takes the form of a mere strategic reaction formation to or against interpellation by Western ideologies. This inner self is not allowed to take on a positive and hegemonic role as the protagonist or agent of its own history. Nationalism as a mode of narration thus fails both to represent its own reality and to represent its own people.[20] The ideological disposition of nationalism toward its people or its masses is fraught with the same duplicity that characterizes its attitude to the women's question. To elaborate this thesis in the Indian context, I turn now to Chatterjee's critical analysis of the two great leaders of twentieth-century India, Mohandas Karamchand Gandhi and Jawaharlal Nehru and their very different orientations toward people's politics: Gandhi (the father of the nation), who is Indian and of the people, and Nehru (Gandhi's beloved protégé), the modern intellectual trying to bridge a nationalism of the people and a progressive internationalism based on Western reason, science, technology, and industrial-economic progress.

One of the first moves Gandhi makes on his return to India from South Africa is to repudiate the urban politics practiced by the Indian National Congress. Gandhi locates his politics in the villages of India, where the majority of India's population resides (and this is basically true even today). He seeks an active common denominator with the people of India, he changes his attire, his very mode of living, so that he can become one with the people. And this is not merely a vote-catching political stunt but Gandhi's vision of India: it is in the villages that India is to be experienced and discovered. It is in this context that the discovery of India becomes a major theme in nationalist history. Where and what is the real India? Sure enough, it exists, but how is it to be known? From what perspective is the real India to be represented so that the representation may be unified, inclusive, even total? How is national consciousness to be generated when it does not yet exist as such? The problem here is that the narrative cannot preknow its subject, which has itself to be the product of the narrative. The question that Gandhi raises is: Whose narrative is it going to be? The answer is certainly the "people's," but the term "people" covers a wide spectrum of positions, identities, and bases. How should nationalism forge from these many "subidentities" a unified identity to work for the common national cause?[21]

It is in this spirit that the discovery of India is undertaken, albeit differently, by Gandhi and Nehru. To dwell just a little longer on the semantics of the term "discovery," this theme presupposes that a certain India exists already waiting to be touched, known, and narrativized. In a narratological sense, the real India can only be the a posteriori effect of the narrative process, but ontologically, the reality of India is prior to the narrative. In other words, not any and every narrative can claim to be the signifier of the real India. Also, the criterion of reality serves two purposes: first, of demystifying the existing urban-elitist versions of India and second, of securing an ethicopolitical alignment between the knowledge produced about the real India and the sociopolitical transformations that are to follow on the basis of such knowledge. The Gandhian thesis is that no worthwhile plan of action can be based on a knowledge that is spurious and nonrepresentative. The people of India become the subject of the independence movement, and Gandhi's political ethic is to empower the people in a way that will enable them to lead themselves.

But a number of problems and contradictions arise here. Are the people the means or are they the end in the nationalist struggle? The contradiction lies in the fact that the unification of the people is going to be undertaken not in their own name, but in the name of the emerging nation and the nation-state that is to follow. The subaltern valence of the people has to be reformed as a prerequisite for their nationalization. The people thus become a necessary means to the superior ends of nationalism. The masses can neither be bypassed (for they are the real India) nor can they be legitimated qua people. And here, Gandhi's and Nehru's visions vary. Gandhi's advocacy of the people carries with it their full moral force. His model of independent India makes the people the teachers, and leaders such as himself become the pupils. Hence Gandhi's stern refusal of progress as an end in itself, and his rejection of all indices of growth and prosperity developed in the West. Hence, too, his insistence on decentralization, simple modes of production, and the ethic of self-sufficiency and his moral indictment of capital, accumulation, greed, and the systemic proliferation of want and desire. We must also remember that Gandhi was a rare leader who, in the name of the people, prescribed that the glorious Congress Party that had won India its independence should self-destruct once the aim of independence was achieved. But this of course was not to happen.

Jawaharlal Nehru's perspective on the masses of India is quite different. His discovery of India is much more ambivalent and doubt-ridden. He passionately admires the way in which Gandhi spontaneously establishes rapport with the people and becomes "one of them." But he often doubts whether he himself is capable of such organic identification with the masses.[22] Here then is Nehru in *The Discovery of India*:

> India was in my blood and there was much in her that instinctively thrilled me. And yet, I approached her almost as an *alien critic*, full of dislike for the present as well as for many of the relics of the past I saw. To some extent I came to her via the West and looked at her as a friendly *Westerner* might have done. I was eager and anxious to change her outlook and appearance and give her the garb of modernity. And yet doubts rose within me. Did I know India, I who presumed to scrap much of her past heritage? (Emphasis added)[23]

A number of interesting tensions are played out here between India and her loving patriot. First, there are visceral references to "instinct" and "blood" whose strength has nothing whatsoever to do with Nehru's rational and theoretical understanding of India. Second, India figures both as a transcendent and marvelous identity awaiting ecstatic comprehension and as malleable raw material awaiting transformation by an act of production. A kind of mystical essentialism confronts a certain secular constructionism. While the present, the past, and the future of India are imperfectly aligned, the present through which India is being perceived is both the pure moment of nativism/indigeny and the contaminated perspective underwritten by the West. And finally, there is an aporetic tension between Nehru's strong visions on behalf of India and his uncertainties about his knowledge of India. Is it conceivable that Nehru, the architect of modern India, may in fact *not know* his country?

It is from such a divided consciousness that Nehru attempts to account for the "spellbinding" agency of Gandhi. It is somewhat surprising that Nehru's viewpoint comes very close to Marx's devaluation of the "idiocy of rural life." Yet Nehru is divided in his response, at once touched and disheartened if not intimidated by the Indian peasant. On the one hand, intimate exposure to the peasants and "their misery and overflowing gratitude" fills him "with shame and sorrow, shame at [his] own easy-going and comfortable life and [the] petty politics of the city which ignored this vast multitude of semi-naked sons and daughters of India."[24] But on the other hand, there is Nehru's strong and almost ruthless evaluation of the peasants as "dull certainly, uninteresting individually," and of their need "to be led properly, controlled, not by force or fear, but by 'gaining their trust,' by teaching them their true interests."[25] The vexing question is how to mobilize the masses in this nationalist-modernist cause. And the answer seems to be Gandhi.

In Partha Chatterjee's words: "On reading the many pages Nehru has written by way of explaining the phenomenon of Gandhi, what comes through most strongly is a feeling of total incomprehension." Gandhi becomes the voice of the people, a voice that is powerful, persuasive, legitimate, and yet inscrutable in its spellbinding effectivity. This voice intervenes successfully in the history of India precisely because it speaks for the masses, yet this very voice is considered misguided. Gandhian economics, Gandhian sociology, all of Gandhi's blueprints for independent India are all wrong, but Gandhi is the one who can inspire the masses; leaders like Nehru have the right facts, the right models for India's development, but are "powerless to intervene" in the history of the Indian masses. Gandhi thus becomes that mystical and incomprehensible genius exclusively responsible for India's independence, and yet Nehru has no hesitation in declaring that once *swaraj* is achieved, Gandhi's fads must not be encouraged. The affirmative project of building India finds itself thoroughly disconnected from the ethicopolitical modality of the independence movement. In a strange way, Nehru's understanding of Gandhi's historical agency lines it up with the "otherness" and the "unreason" of peasant consciousness, whereas the future of modern India becomes identified with the rationality of Western thought.

Nationalism is thus valorized as an inaugural moment precisely because it is also a project of deracination from an unreasonable prehistory. As Chatterjee sums it up:

> And so the split between two domains of politics—one, a politics of the elite, and the other, a politics of subaltern classes—was replicated in the sphere of mature nationalist thought by an explicit recognition of the split between a domain of rationality and a domain of unreason, a domain of science and a domain of faith, a domain of organization and a domain of spontaneity. But it was a rational understanding which, by the very act of its recognition of the Other, also effaced the Other.[26]

In a real sense, then, the subject of nationalism does not exist. Conceived within this chronic duality, the nationalist subject is doomed to demonstrate the impossibility of its own claim to subjecthood. With the inner and the outer in mutual disarray, the nationalist subject marks the space of a constitutive representational debacle.[27]

The project that the subaltern historians are engaged in is the production of a subaltern critique of nationalism: a critique both to liberate those many spaces foreclosed within nationalism and to enable a nonreactive, nonparanoid mode of subjectivity and agency in touch with its own historically constituted interiority: a prey neither to the difference of the Western subject nor to the mystique of its own indigenous identity. In opening up new spaces, "the critique of nationalist discourse must find for itself the ideological means to connect the popular strength of the people's struggles with the consciousness of a new universality, to subvert the ideological sway of a state which falsely claims to speak on behalf of the nation and to challenge the presumed sovereignty of a science which puts itself at the service of capital."[28] Clearly, such a critique undertaken in the name of subalternity has to bear many different signatures within a universal and relational space, a space very much like the one invoked by Sangari and Vaid's feminist historiography.

Notes

1. Partha Chatterjee, "The Nationalist Resolution of the Women's Question," in *Recasting Women: Essays in Colonial History,* ed. Kumkum Sangari and Sudesh Vaid (New Delhi: Kali for Women, 1989), 233. This collection has since been reprinted as *Recasting Women: Essays in Indian Colonial History* (New Brunswick, N.J.: Rutgers University Press, 1990).

2. For a spirited articulation of the need to realize the women's question as its own autonomous form of politics, see Shulamith Firestone, *The Dialectic of Sex* (New York: Bantam Books, 1970).

3. I am using the term "temporalities" here as developed by Chandra Talpade Mohanty in her essay, "Feminist Encounters: Locating the Politics of Experience," *Copyright* 1 (Fall 1987): 40.

4. Fredric Jameson argues in *The Political Unconscious: Narrative as a Socially Symbolic Act* (Ithaca, N.Y.: Cornell University Press, 1981) that Marxism does and should continue to operate as the ultimate semantic horizon within which other political struggles are to be located. But the very notion of any single ideology operating as a containing horizon is deeply problematic. For a poststructuralist critique of Jameson's position, see my essay "Poststructuralist Politics: Towards a Theory of Coalition," in *Postmodernism/Jameson/Critique,* ed. Douglas Kellner (Washington, D.C.: Maisonneuve Press, 1989), 301–32.

5. Sangari and Vaid, "Recasting Women: An Introduction," in *Recasting Women,* 2-3.

6. For an insightful account of the double-coded nature of postcolonial narratives, see Kumkum Sangari, "The Politics of the Possible," *Cultural Critique* 7 (Fall 1987): 157–86.

7. For an in-depth discussion, in the context of Michel Foucault and Antonio Gramsci, of the implications of representational and postrepresentational politics, see chapter 2 in this volume.

8. I am referring here to a growing body of work by such feminist theorists as Gayatri Chakravorty Spivak, Teresa de Lauretis, Nancy Fraser, Linda Nicholson, Chandra Talpade Mohanty, Donna Haraway, and many others who elaborate gender both as a specific domain and as a general category of experience within the body politic.

9. My point here is that whereas postcolonial strategies of the politics of location are eager to take on macropolitical and global issues, Western conceptions of subject-positional politics (practiced in the manner of a Foucault or a Deleuze) tend to overlook global and macropolitical concerns. As Edward Said points out, there is a certain asymmetry that governs the relationship between discourses emanating from the world of former colonizers and those that rise from the world of the formerly colonized; see his essay "Intellectuals in the Post-Colonial World," *Salmagundi* 70–71 (Spring–Summer 1986): 44–81.

10. The tension between the local valence and the general or total valence of any constituency is illustrated powerfully in the American context, where "ethnicity" plays a constitutive role in the shaping of American identity. The concern of each ethnic group is both to legitimate its own form of ethnicity and to influence the general platform where different ethnic groups renegotiate the nature of American identity.

11. See Ernesto Laclau and Chantal Mouffe, *Hegemony and Socialist Strategy,* trans. Winston Moore and Paul Cammack (London: Verso, 1985).

12. See Ranajit Guha, "Dominance without Hegemony and Its Historiography," in *Subaltern Studies VI: Writings on South Asian History and Society,* ed. Ranajit Guha (Delhi, Oxford, and New York: Oxford University Press, 1989), 210–309.

13. For an important exchange about nationalism as a threshold in the development of a transnational and nonessentialist feminism, see the essays by Julie Stephens and Susie Tharu in *Subaltern Studies VI.*

14. In much the same way, Freudian psychoanalysis makes feminine sexuality "unknowable" without raising the question of knowledge itself as a gender-inflected category. French feminists such as Luce Irigaray, Hélène Cixous, Julia Kristeva, and

Catherine Clément have raised the question of a feminine epistemics/*écriture* both within and without the economy of psychoanalysis.

15. Chatterjee, "The Nationalist Resolution," 238–39.

16. See Gayatri Chakravorty Spivak, "Reading *The Satanic Verses*," *Public Culture* 2, no. 1 (Fall 1989): 79–99, for a suggestive distinction between "subject formation" and "agency formation."

17. See John Plamenatz, "Two Types of Nationalism," in *Nationalism: The Nature and Evolution of an Idea*, ed. Eugene Kamenka (London: Edward Arnold, 1976), 23–36. The body of work on nationalism is too rich and complex to be fully represented, but here are a few significant (and of course, problematic) contributions: Benedict Anderson, *Imagined Communities: Reflections on the Origin and Spread of Nationalism* (London: Verso, 1983); John Breuilly, *Nationalism and the State* (Manchester: Manchester University Press, 1982); Horace B. Davis, *Toward a Marxist Theory of Nationalism* (New York: Monthly Review Press, 1978); Ernest Gellner, *Nations and Nationalism* (Oxford: Blackwell, 1983); Elie Kedourie, *Nationalism* (London: Hutchinson, 1960); Anthony D. Smith, *The Ethnic Origin of Nations* (Oxford: Blackwell, 1986); Kumari Jayawardena, *Feminism and Nationalism in the Third World* (London: Zed Press, 1986); E. J. Hobsbawm, *Nations and Nationalism since 1780* (New York: Cambridge University Press, 1990); and Partha Chatterjee, *Nationalist Thought and the Colonial World* (Delhi: Oxford University Press, 1986).

18. See Satya Mohanty, "Us and Them: On the Philosophical Bases of Political Criticism," *Yale Journal of Criticism* 2, no. 2 (Spring 1989): 1–31.

19. Chatterjee, *Nationalist Thought and the Colonial World*, 38–39.

20. For a brilliant and varied discussion of the complicated relationship between nationalism and narration, see Homi K. Bhabha, ed., *Nation and Narration* (London and New York: Routledge, 1990), in particular the essays by Homi K. Bhabha, Tim Brennan, Doris Sommer, Sneja Gunew, and James Snead.

21. The rise of Hindu fundamentalism, the destruction of the Babri Masjid, violence against Muslims, and other related events point up the crisis of nationalism in India. The authority of the nation-state in itself does not guarantee the realization of an inclusive national consciousness.

22. Here I use the term "organic" as developed by Antonio Gramsci in his essay, "The Formation of Intellectuals," in *The Modern Prince and Other Writings*, trans. Louis Marks (New York: International, 1957), 118–25.

23. Jawaharlal Nehru, *The Discovery of India* (New York: John Day, 1946), 38.

24. Jawaharlal Nehru, *An Autobiography* (London: Bodley Head, 1936), 52.

25. Nehru as quoted in Chatterjee, *Nationalist Thought and the Colonial World*, 148.

26. Ibid., 150, 153.

27. For a complex reading of the nature of representation in the postcolonial context, see Homi K. Bhabha, "Signs Taken for Wonders: Questions of Ambivalence and Authority under a Tree outside Delhi, May 1817," *Critical Inquiry* 12, no. 1 (Autumn 1985): 144–65.

28. Chatterjee, *Nationalist Thought and the Colonial World*, 170.

10 / Is the Ethnic "Authentic" in the Diaspora?

My eleven-year-old son asks me, "Am I Indian or American?" The question excites me, and I think of the not-too-distant future when we will discuss the works of Salman Rushdie, Toni Morrison, Amitav Ghosh, Jamaica Kincaid, Bessie Head, Amy Tan, Maxine Hong Kingston, and many others who have agonized over the question of identity through their multivalent narratives. I tell him he is *both* and offer him brief and down-to-earth definitions of ethnicity and how it relates to nationality and citizenship. He follows me closely and says, "Yeah, Dad [or he might have said "*Appa*"], I am both," and a slight inflection in his voice underscores the word "both," as his two hands make a symmetrical gesture on either side of his body. I am persuaded, for I have seen him express deep indignation and frustration when friends, peers, teachers, and coaches mispronounce his name in cavalier fashion. He pursues the matter with a passion bordering on the pedagogical, until his name comes out correctly on alien lips. I have also heard him narrate to his "mainstream" friends stories from the *Ramayana* and the *Mahabharatha* with an infectious enthusiasm for local detail, and negotiate nuances of place and time with great sensitivity. My son comes back to me and asks, "But you and Amma [or did he say "Mom"?] are not U.S. citizens?" I tell him that we are Indian citizens who live here as resident aliens. "Oh, yes, I remember we have different passports," he says and walks away.

At a recent Deepavali (a significant Hindu religious festival) get together of the local India Association (well before the horrendous destruction of the Babri

Masjid by Hindu zealots), I listen to an elderly Indian man explain to a group of young first-generation Indian-American children the festival's significance. He goes on and on about the contemporary significance of Lord Krishna, who has promised to return to the world in human form during times of crisis to punish the wicked and protect the good. During this lecture, I hear not a word to distinguish Hindu identity from Indian identity, not a word about present-day communal violence in India in the name of Hindu fundamentalism, and not even an oblique mention of the ongoing crisis in Ayodhya. In a sense, these egregious oversights and omissions do not matter, for the first-generation American kids, the intended recipients of this ethnic lesson, hardly pay attention: they sleep, run around, or chatter among themselves, their mouths full of popcorn. I do not know whether I am more angry with the elderly gentleman for his disingenuous ethnic narrative or with the younger generation, who in their putative assimilation do not seem to care about ethnic origins.

I begin with these two episodes because they exemplify a number of issues and tensions that inform ethnicity. I imagine that the main problem that intrigued my son was this: How could some*one* be both *one* and something *other*? How could the unity of identity have more than one face or name? If my son is both Indian and American, which *one* is he *really?* Which is the real self and which the other? How do these two selves coexist and how do they weld into one identity? How is ethnic identity related to national identity? Is this relationship hierarchically structured, such that the "national" is supposed to subsume and transcend ethnic identity, or does this relationship produce a hyphenated identity, such as African-American, Asian-American, and so forth, where the hyphen marks a dialogic and nonhierarchic conjuncture? What if identity is exclusively ethnic and not national at all? Could such an identity survive (during these days of bloody "ethnic cleansing") and be legitimate, or would society construe this as a nonviable "difference," that is, experientially authentic but not deserving of hegemony?

The Indian gentleman's address to his audience of first-generation Indian-Americans raises several insidious and potentially harmful conflicts. First it uses religious (Hindu) identity to empower Indian ethnicity in the United States, which then masquerades as Indian nationalism. What does the appeal to "roots and origins" mean in this context, and what is it intended to achieve? Is ethnicity a mere flavor, an ancient smell to be relived as nostalgia? Is it a kind of superficial blanket to be worn over the substantive U.S. identity? Or is Indianness being advocated as a basic immutable form of being that triumphs over changes, travels, and dislocations?

The narrative of ethnicity in the United States might run like this. During the initial phase, immigrants suppress ethnicity in the name of pragmatism and opportunism. To be successful in the New World, they must actively assimilate and, therefore, hide their distinct ethnicity. This phase, similar to the Booker T. Washington era in African-American history, gives way to a Du Boisian period that refuses to subsume political, civil, and moral revolutions under mere strategies of economic betterment. In the call for total revolution that follows, immigrants reassert ethnicity in all its autonomy. The third phase seeks the hyphenated integration of ethnic identity with national identity under conditions that do not privilege the "national" at the expense of the "ethnic." We must keep in mind that in the United States the renaming of ethnic identity in national terms produces a preposterous effect. Take the case of the Indian immigrant. Her naturalization into American citizenship simultaneously minoritizes her identity. She is now reborn as an ethnic minority American citizen.

Is this empowerment or marginalization? This new American citizen must think of her Indian self as an ethnic self that defers to her nationalized American status. The culturally and politically hegemonic Indian identity is now a mere qualifier: "ethnic." Does this transformation suggest that identities and ethnicities are not a matter of fixed and stable selves but rather the results and products of fortuitous travels and recontextualizations? Could this mean that how identity relates to place is itself the expression of a shifting equilibrium? If ethnic identity is a strategic response to a shifting sense of time and place, how is it possible to have a theory of ethnic identity posited on the principle of a natural and native self? Is ethnicity nothing but, to use the familiar formula, what ethnicity does? Is ethnic selfhood an end in itself, or is it a necessary but determinate phase to be left behind when the time is right to inaugurate the "postethnic"? With some of these general concerns in mind, I would now like to address the Indian diaspora in the United States.

This chapter began with a scenario both filial and pedagogic. The child asks a question or expresses some doubt or anxiety and the parent resolves the problem. The parent brings together two kinds of authority: the authority of a parent to transmit and sustain a certain pattern generationally and the authority of a teacher based on knowledge and information. Thus, in my response to my son, "You are both," I was articulating myself as teacher as well as parent. But how do I (as a parent) know that I know? Do I have an answer by virtue of my parenthood, or does the answer have a pedagogic authority that has nothing to do with being a parent? In other words, how is my act of speaking for my daughter or son different from a teacher speaking for a student? Is knowledge *natural,* or is it a questioning of origins? In either case, is there room for the student's own self-expression? How are we to decide whether or not the "conscious" knowledge of the teacher and the "natural" knowledge of the parent are relevant in the historical instance of the child/student?

Let's look at yet another episode as a counterpoint to my teacherly episode with my son. During the last few years, I have talked and listened to a number of young, gifted Indian children of the diaspora who, like my son, were born here and are thus "natural" American citizens. I was startled when they told me that they had grown up with a strong sense of being exclusively Indian, and the reason was that they had experienced little during their growing years that held out promise of first-class American citizenship. Most of them felt they could not escape being *marked* as different by virtue of their skin color, their family background, and other ethnic and unassimilated traits. Many of them recited the reality of a double life, the ethnic private life and the "American" public life, with very little mediation between the two. For example, they talked about being the targets of racial slurs and racialized sexist slurs, and they remembered not receiving the total understanding of their parents who did not quite "get it." Sure, the parents understood the situation in an academic and abstract way and would respond with the fierce rhetoric of civil rights and antiracism, but the fact was that the parents had not gone through similar experiences during their childhoods. Although the home country is indeed replete with its own divisions, phobias, and complexes, the racial line of color is not one of them. Thus, if the formulaic justification of parental wisdom is that the parent "has been there before," the formula does not apply here. Is the prescriptive wisdom of "you are both" relevant?

Within the diaspora, how should the two generations address each other? I would suggest for starters that we candidly admit that learning and knowledge, particularly in the diaspora, can only be a two-way street. The problem here is more acute than the unavoidable "generation gap" between students/young adults and teachers/parents. The tensions between the old and new homes create the problem of divided allegiances that the two generations experience differently. The very organicity of the family and the community, displaced by travel and relocation, must be renegotiated and redefined. The two generations have different starting points and different givens. This phenomenon of historical rupture within the "same" community demands careful and rigorous analysis. The older generation cannot afford to invoke India in an authoritarian mode to resolve problems in the diaspora, and the younger generation would be ill advised to indulge in a spree of forgetfulness about "where they have come from." It is vital that the two generations empathize and desire to understand and appreciate patterns of experience not their own.

What does "being Indian" mean in the United States? How can one be and live Indian without losing clout and leverage as Americans? How can one transform the so-called mainstream American identity into the image of the many ethnicities that constitute it? We should not pretend we are living in some idealized "little India" and not in the United States. As Maxine Hong Kingston demonstrates painfully in *The Woman Warrior*, both the home country and the country of residence could become mere "ghostly" locations, and the result can only be a double depoliticization. For example, the anguish in her book is *relational*; it is not exclusively about China or the United States. The home country is not "real" in its own terms and yet it is real enough to impede Americanization, and the "present home" is materially real and yet not real enough to feel authentic. Whereas at home one could be just Indian or Chinese, here one is constrained to become Chinese-, Indian-, or Asian-American. This leads us to the question: Is the "Indian" in Indian and the "Indian" in Indian-American the same and therefore interchangeable? Which of the two is authentic, and which merely strategic or reactive? To what extent does the "old country" function as a framework and regulate our transplanted identities within the diaspora? Should the old country be revered as a pregiven absolute, or is it all right to invent the old country itself in response to our contemporary location? Furthermore, whose interpretation of India is correct: the older generation's or that of the younger; the insider's version or the diasporan?

These questions emphasize the reality that when people move, identities, perspectives, and definitions change. If the category "Indian" *seemed* secure, positive, and affirmative within India, the same term takes on a reactive, strategic character when it is pried loose from its nativity. The issue then is not just "being Indian" in some natural and self-evident way ("being Indian" naturally is itself a highly questionable premise given the debacle of nationalism, but that is not my present concern), but "cultivating Indianness" self-consciously for certain reasons; for example, the reason could be that one does not want to lose one's past or does not want to be homogenized namelessly, or one could desire to combat mainstream racism with a politicized deployment of one's own "difference." To put it simply, one's very being becomes polemical. Is there a true and authentic identity, more lasting than mere polemics and deeper than strategies?

Before I get into an analysis of this problem, I wish to sketch briefly a few responses to the home country that I consider wrong and quite dangerous. First, from the point of view of the assimilated generation, it is all too easy to want to forget the past and forfeit community in the name of the "free individual," a path open to first-generation citizens. As Malcolm X, Du Bois, and others have argued, it is in the nature of a racist, capitalist society to isolate and privatize the individual and to foster the myth of the equal and free individual unencumbered by either a sense of community or a critical sense of the past. As the Clarence Thomas nomination has amply demonstrated, the theme of "individual success" is a poisoned candy manufactured by capitalist greed in active complicity with a racist disregard for history. We cannot afford to forget that we live in a society that is profoundly antihistorical, and that leaders represent us who believe that we have buried the memories of Vietnam in the sands of the Gulf War, which itself is remembered primarily as a high-tech game intended for visual pleasure. We must not underestimate the capacity of capitalism, superbly assisted by technology, to produce a phenomenology of the present so alluring in its immediacy as to seduce the consumer to forget the past and bracket the future.

The second path is the way of the film *Mississippi Masala*, reveling uncritically in the commodification of hybridity. The two young lovers walk away into the rain in a Hollywood resolution of the agonies of history. Having found each other as "hybrids" in the here and now of the United States, the two young adults just walk out of their "prehistories" into the innocence of physical, heterosexual love. The past *sucks*, parents *suck*, Mississippi *sucks*, as do India and Uganda, and the only thing that matters is the bonding between two bodies that step off the pages of history, secure in their "sanctioned ignorance," to use Gayatri Chakravorty Spivak's ringing phrase. What is disturbing about the "masala" resolution is that it seems to take on the question of history, but it actually trivializes histories (there is more than one implicated here) and celebrates a causeless rebellion in the epiphany of the present. Just think of the racism awaiting the two lovers. In invoking the term "masala" superficially, the movie begs us to consume it as exotica and make light of the historical ingredients that go into making "masala." My point here is that individualized escapes (and correspondingly, the notion of the "history of the present" as a total break from the messy past) may serve an emotional need, but they do not provide an understanding of the histories of India, Uganda, or the racialized South.

What about the options open to the generation emotionally committed to India? First, it is important to make a distinction between *information about and knowledge of India* and an *emotional investment in India*. What can be shared cognitively between the two generations is the former. It would be foolish of me to expect that India will move my son the same way it moves me. It would be equally outrageous of me to claim that somehow my India is more real than his; my India is as much an invention or production as his. There is more than enough room for multiple versions of the same reality. But here again, our inventions and interpretations are themselves products of history and not subjective substitutes for history. The discovery of an "authentic" India cannot rule over the reality of multiple perspectives, and, moreover, we cannot legislate or hand down authenticity from a position of untested moral or political high ground.

Second, my generation has to actively learn to find "Indianness" within and in conjunction with the minority-ethnic continuum in the United States. To go back to my conversations with the younger generation, it is important to understand that many of them confess to finding their "ethnic Indian" identity (as distinct from the "Indian" identity experienced at home) not in isolation but in a coalition with other minorities. It is heartening to see that a number of students identify themselves under the third world umbrella and have gone so far as to relate the "third world out there" and "the third world within." (I am aware that the term "third world" is deeply problematic and often promotes an insensitive dedifferentiation of the many histories that comprise the third world, but this term when used by the groups that constitute it has the potential to resist the dominant groups' divide-and-rule strategies.)

My generation is prone, as it ages, to take recourse to some mythic India as a way of dealing with the contemporary crises of fragmentation and racialization in the United States. Instead, we could learn from first-generation Indians who have developed solidarity and community by joining together in political struggle. The crucial issue for the older generation here is to think through the politics of why we are here and to deliberate carefully about which America they want to identify with: the white, male, corporate America or the America of the Rainbow Coalition. In cases where economic betterment is the primary motivation for immigration into the United States, and especially when these cases are successful, it is easy to deny the reality of our racially and *color*fully marked American citizenship. Even as I write, communities are targeting schoolteachers with "foreign" accents for dismissal.

Third, it is disingenuous of my generation to behave as though one India exists "out there" and our *interpretation of India* is it. This is a generation both of and distant from India, therefore the politics of proximity has to negotiate dialectically and critically with the politics of distance. We may not like this, but it is our responsibility to take our daughters and sons seriously when they ask us, Why then did you leave India? I believe with Amitav Ghosh (I refer here to his novel *The Shadow Lines*) that places are both real and imagined, that we can know places that are distant as much as we can misunderstand and misrepresent places we inhabit. As Arjun Appadurai, among others, has argued, neither distance nor proximity guarantees truth or alienation. One could live within India and not care to discover India or live "abroad" and acquire a nuanced historical appreciation of the home country, and vice versa. During times when the demographic flows of peoples across territorial boundaries have become more the norm than the exception, it is counterproductive to maintain that one can only understand a place when one is in it. It is quite customary for citizens who have emigrated to experience distance as a form of critical enlightenment or a healthy "estrangement" from their birthland, and to experience another culture or location as a reprieve from the orthodoxies of their own "given" cultures. It is also quite normal for the same people, who now have lived a number of years in their adopted country, to return through critical negotiation to aspects of their culture that they had not really studied before and to develop criticisms of their chosen world. Each place or culture gains when we open it to new standards.

In saying this I am not conceding to individuals the right to rewrite collective histories that determine individual histories in the first place, nor am I invoking diasporan cultural politics as a facile answer to the structural problem of asymmetry and inequality between "developed" and "underdeveloped" nations. My point is that the diaspora has created rich possibilities of understanding different histories. And these histories have taught us that identities, selves, traditions, and natures do change with travel (and there is nothing decadent or deplorable about mutability) and that we can achieve such changes in identity intentionally. In other words, we need to make substantive distinctions between "change as default or as the path of least resistance" and "change as conscious and directed self-fashioning."

Among these mutable, changing traditions and natures, who are we to ourselves? Is the identity question so hopelessly politicized that it cannot step beyond the history of strategies and counterstrategies? Do I know in some abstract, ontological, transhistorical way what "being Indian" is all about and on that basis devise strategies to hold on to that ideal identity, or do I—when faced by the circumstances of history—strategically practice Indian identity to maintain my uniqueness and resist anonymity through homogenization? For that matter, why can't I be "Indian" without having to be "authentically Indian"? What is the difference and how does it matter? In the diasporan context in the United States, ethnicity is often forced to take on the discourse of authenticity just to protect and maintain its space and history. Would "black" have to be authentic if it were not pressured into a reactive mode by the dominance of "white"? It becomes difficult to determine if the drive toward authenticity comes from within the group as a spontaneous self-affirming act, or if authenticity is nothing but a paranoid reaction to the "naturalness" of dominant groups. Why should "black" be authentic when "white" is hardly even seen as a color, let alone pressured to demonstrate its authenticity?

Let us ask the following question: If a minority group were left in peace with itself and not dominated or forced into a relationship with the dominant world or national order, would the group still find the term "authentic" meaningful or necessary? The group would continue being what it is without having to authenticate itself. My point is simply this: When we say "authenticate," we also have to ask, "Authenticate to whom and for what purpose?" Who and by what authority is checking our credentials? Is "authenticity" a home we build for ourselves or a ghetto we inhabit to satisfy the dominant world?

I do understand and appreciate the need for authenticity, especially in first world advanced capitalism, where the marketplace and commodities are the norm. But the rhetoric of authenticity tends to degenerate into essentialism. I would much rather situate the problem of authenticity alongside the phenomenon of relationality and the politics of representation. How does authenticity speak for itself: as one voice or as many related voices, as monolithic identity or as identity hyphenated by difference? When someone speaks as an Asian-American, who exactly is speaking? If we dwell in the hyphen, who represents the hyphen: the Asian or the American, or can the hyphen speak for itself without creating an imbalance between the Asian and the American components? What is the appropriate narrative to represent relationality?

Back to my son's question again: True, both components have status, but which has the power and the potential to read and interpret the other on its terms? If the Asian is to be Americanized, will the American submit to Asianization? Will there be a reciprocity of influence whereby American identity itself will be seen as a form of openness to the many ingredients that constitute it, or will "Americanness" function merely as a category of marketplace pluralism?

Very often it is when we feel deeply dissatisfied with marketplace pluralism and its unwillingness to confront and correct the injustices of dominant racism that we turn our diasporan gaze back to the home country. Often, the gaze is uncritical and nostalgic. Often, we cultivate the home country with a vengeance. Several dangers exist here. We can cultivate India in total diasporan ignorance of the realities of the home country. By this token, anything and everything is India according to our parched imagination: half-truths, stereotypes, so-called traditions, rituals, and so forth. Or we can cultivate an idealized India that has nothing to do with contemporary history. Then again, we can visualize the India we remember as an antidote to the maladies both here and there and pretend that India hasn't changed since we left its shores. These options are harmful projections of individual psychological needs that have little to do with history. As diasporan citizens doing double duty (with accountability both here and there), we need to understand as rigorously as we can the political crises in India, both because they concern us and also because we have a duty to represent India to ourselves and to the United States as truthfully as we can.

Our ability to speak for India is a direct function of our knowledge about India. The crisis of secular nationalism in India, the ascendancy of Hindu fundamentalism and violence, the systematic persecution of Muslims, the incapacity of the Indian national government to speak on behalf of the entire nation, the opportunistic playing up of the opposition between secularism and religious identity both by the government and the opposition, the lack of success of a number of progressive local grassroots movements to influence electoral politics—these and many other such issues we need to study with great care and attention. Similarly, we need to make distinctions between left-wing movements in India that are engaged in critiquing secularism responsibly with the intention of opening up a range of indigenous alternatives, and right-wing groups whose only intention is to kindle a politics of hatred. Diasporan Indians should not use distance as an excuse for ignoring happenings in India. It is heartening to know that an alliance for a secular and democratic South Asia has recently been established in Cambridge, Massachusetts.

The diasporan hunger for knowledge about and intimacy with the home country should not turn into a transhistorical and mystic quest for origins. It is precisely this obsession with the sacredness of one's origins that leads peoples to disrespect the history of other people and to exalt one's own. Feeling deracinated in the diaspora can be painful, but the politics of origins cannot be the remedy.

Time now for one final episode. Watching Peter Brooks's production of the Hindu epic *Mahabharatha* with a mixed audience, I was quite surprised by the different reactions. We were viewing this film after we had all seen the homegrown TV serials *The Ramayana* and the *Mahabharatha*. By and large, initially my son's generation was disturbed by the international cast that seemed to falsify the Hindu/the Indian (again, a dangerous conflation) epic. How could an Ethiopian play the role of Bheeshma and a white European (I think Dutch) represent Lord Krishna? And all this so soon after they had been subjected to the "authentic version" from India? But soon they began enjoying the film for what it was. Still, it deeply upset a number of adults of my generation. To many of them, this was not the real thing, this could not have been the real Krishna. My own response was divided. I appreciated and enjoyed humanizing and demystifying Krishna, endorsed *in principle* globalizing a specific cultural product, and approved the production for not attempting to be an extravaganza. On the other hand, I was critical of some of its modernist irony and cerebral posturing, its shallow United Nations–style internationalism, its casting of an African male in a manner that endorsed certain black male stereotypes, and finally a certain Western, Eurocentric arrogance that commodifies the work of a different culture and decontextualizes it in the name of a highly skewed and uneven globalism.

Which is the true version? What did my friend mean when he said that this was not the real thing? Does he have some sacred and unmediated access to the real thing? Is his image any less an ideological fabrication (or the result of Hindu-Brahmanical canonization) than that of Peter Brooks? Did his chagrin have to do with the fact that a great epic had been produced critically, or with the fact that the producer was an outsider? What if an Indian feminist group had produced a revisionist version? Isn't the insider's truth as much an invention and an interpretation as that of the outsider? How do we distinguish an insider's critique from that of the outsider? If a Hindu director had undertaken globalizing the Hindu epic, would the project have been different or more acceptable or more responsive to the work's origins? But on the other hand, would a Western audience tolerate the Indianization of Homer, Virgil, or Shakespeare? Questions, more questions. I would rather proliferate questions than seek ready-made and ideologically overdetermined answers. And in a way, the diaspora is an excellent opportunity to think through some of these vexed questions: solidarity and criticism, belonging and distance, insider spaces and outsider spaces, identity as invention and identity as natural, location-subject positionality and the politics of representation, rootedness and rootlessness.

When my son wonders who he *is,* he is also asking a question about the future. For my part, I hope that his future and that of his generation will have many roots and many pasts. I hope, especially, that it will be a future where his identity will be a matter of rich and complex negotiation and not the result of some blind and official decree.

References

Ahmad, Aijaz. *In Theory.* London: Verso, 1992.
Amin, Samir. *Eurocentrism.* New York: Monthly Review Press, 1989.
Anderson, Benedict. *Imagined Communities: Reflections on the Origin and Spread of Nationalism.* London: Verso, 1983.
Anzaldúa, Gloria. *Borderlands/La Frontera.* San Francisco: Aunt Lute Books, 1987.
Appadurai, Arjun. "Disjuncture and Difference in the Global Cultural Economy." *Public Culture* 2, no. 2 (1990): 1–24.

Bhabha, Homi K., ed. *Nation and Narration.* New York: Routledge, 1990.
Chatterjee, Partha. *Nationalist Thought and the Colonial World: A Derivative Discourse.* Delhi: Oxford Univeristy Press, 1986.
Chow, Rey. *Woman and Chinese Modernity: The Politics of Reading between West and East.* Minneapolis: University of Minnesota Press, 1991.
Dasgupta, Sayantini. "Glass Shawls and Long Hair: South Asian Women Talk Sexual Politics." *Ms.* 3, no. 5 (March–April 1993): 76–77.
Dhareshwar, Vivek, and James Clifford, eds. *Inscriptions* 5 (1989).
Ghosh, Amitav. *The Shadow Lines.* London: Bloomsbury, 1988.
hooks, bell. *Black Looks: Race and Representation.* Boston: South End Press, 1992.
Jayawardena, Kumari. *Feminism and Nationalism in the Third World.* New Delhi: Kali for Women, 1986.
Kingston, Maxine Hong. *The Woman Warrior.* New York: Knopf, 1976.
Kishwar, Madhu. "Why I Do Not Call Myself a Feminist." *Manushi* 62 (1990): 2–8.
Lloyd, David, and Abdul JanMohamed, ed. *The Nature and Context of Minority Discourse.* New York: Oxford University Press, 1990.
Manushi 74–75 (double issues, January/February, March/April, 1993).
Mohanty, Chandra Talpade. "On Race and Voice: Challenges for Liberal Education in the 1990s." *Cultural Critique* 14 (Winter 1989–90): 179–208.
———, ed. *Third World Women and the Politics of Feminism.* Bloomington: Indiana University Press, 1992.
Morrison, Toni, ed. *Race-ing, Justice, En-gendering Power.* New York: Pantheon, 1992.
Mufti, Aamir, and John McClure, eds. Special issue on postcoloniality. *Social Text* 31/32.
Mutman, Mahmut, and Meyda Yegenoglu, eds. *Inscriptions* 6: "Orientalism and Cultural Differences."
Nandy, Ashis, ed. *Science, Hegemony and Violence: A Requiem for Modernity.* Oxford: Oxford University Press, 1988.
Radhakrishnan, R. "Culture as Common Ground: Ethnicity and Beyond." *MELUS,* 14, no. 2 (Summer 1987): 5–19.
———. "Postcoloniality and the Boundaries of Identity." *Callaloo* 16, no. 4: (Fall 1993): 750–771.
Rosaldo, Renato. *Culture and Truth: The Remaking of Social Analysis.* Boston: Beacon Press, 1989.
Rushdie, Salman. *Imaginary Homelands.* New York: Penguin, 1992.
Said, Edward W. *Culture and Imperialism.* New York: Knopf, 1993.
———. *Orientalism.* New York: Vintage Books, 1978.
Sangari, Kumkum, and Sudesh Vaid, eds. *Recasting Women: Essays in Indian Colonial History.* New Brunswick, N.J.: Rutgers University Press, 1990.
Shiva, Vandana. *Staying Alive: Women, Ecology and Survival in India.* Delhi: Kali for Women, 1988.
Sunder Rajan, Rajeswari, ed. *The Lie of the Land: English Literary Studies in India.* Oxford: Oxford University Press, 1992.

11 / Conjunctural Identities, Academic Adjacencies

To begin with an anecdote: the other day I had gone to a newly opened Thai restaurant with an Indian friend, a fellow Thai food enthusiast. The decor and atmosphere were excellent, and there was perceptible bonding among the owner, the waitress, and us as Asian-Americans of the diasporic-ethnic persuasion. The lunch itself was so-so; we had partaken of much better Thai lunches at comparable restaurants. As we asked for the check, there was further pleasant conversation; and then she, the owner, asked us: How was the food? After a fleeting mutual glance we responded, "Good, it was very nice." Both of us instantly felt we had been less than honest. My friend had even asked me during the meal if it would be within our mandate to suggest a few alterations to the chef: the vegetables a little crisper, the curry blended just a bit differently. Yet none of this was communicated, and, remember, we had been asked.

Why hadn't either of us offered our opinions, our critiques? Was it just the preference not to commit oneself, not to offend? Clearly, there was the question of who we were vis-a-vis Thai food: surely we had had Thai food on innumerable occasions; but we are not Thai, so how capable are we of evaluating the "authenticity" of Thai food? The fact that as impassioned cosmopolitan restaurant junkies we had had the Thai cuisine experience does not necessarily confer on us the kind of critical insider expertise necessary for an act of evaluation.[1] Moreover, where is the guarantee that cosmopolitanism is a desirable platform for comprehending ethnic nuances?

Had this been an Indian restaurant, would we have felt more free to have been vocal?

I begin with this episode, and the questions that I have generated around it, with the intention of opening up a substantive thematic space where we can discuss the relationship between identity and expertise.[2] Is this relationship mutually constitutive, or hierarchically tilted toward either of the terms? What is the relationship between "Thai" as existential-ontological space and "Thai" as performative practice or category of expertise? It would seem that on the one hand "identity" exists as a specific and determinate anteriority that enables and legitimates certain expert representational practices; and on the other, it is these very expert practices that in effect constitute the anteriority-effect of identity.[3] Indeed, Thai or Indian practices of identity-styling can be evaluated with reference to a framework called "Indian" or "Thai," but at the same time this framework itself is nothing but the consolidated-negotiated effect of heterogeneous and contradictory practices. If identity itself is radically informed by heterogeneity, how then are distinctions to be made between one kind of heterogeneity and another?

When my friend and I refrained from critical comment, perhaps we were concerned that such a comment would call into question the very ethnic ontology of both the food and its maker. It would perhaps have amounted to an outsider saying: Your Thai practices have not added up to an authentic Thai identity. How then is the "other" to have a say in a situation where her expectations are simultaneously valid and irrelevant—valid since in a sense identity is always intended for the other, and irrelevant since the "other" is ontogenetically extrinsic to the "self"? The incommensurability that I am trying to adumbrate lies in the relationship between identity-practice as expertise, and therefore as something externalizable (whereby Self and Other become structural positions and locations, not essences), and identity-presence as something inherent and therefore irreducible, autochthonous and nongeneralizable.[4] What is open to question and criticism is the performative aspect of identity, but hiding behind the performative is the ontological authority of a name: the name and its agential control over the performance.[5] Between "being Indian" and "practising Indian" there lies a space of semantic openness that is neither ideologically free nor ideologically consummate: a space where "name" and "agency" problematize each other. The issue that I am attempting to raise has to do with the relationship of identity to methodology, of constituency to epistemology, of macropolitical solidarity to micropolitical specialist practices, and of organic solidarity to specific intellectuality."[6]

Before I undertake to analyse Asian-American studies as project-and-formation, perhaps a little more is in order about "disciplinarity," "representation," and "production." When I was invited to be part of this project of envisioning a certain future for Asian-American studies, I felt delighted and honored as though I had been interpellated both with respect to my specific disciplinary formation (postcoloniality, poststructuralism, and the relationship between the two) and with reference to my larger and more inclusive solidarity with minority discourses in general and with Asian-America in particular. I am an Asian-American as well as a third world citizen, but I am not in Asian-American studies. My sense of ethnicity is based on my being an Asian-American *here* (though there is a lot more to me than can be covered under the rubric "Asian-American"), and yet I have theorized ethnicity at the intersection of poststructuralism and postcoloniality. So, who am I by virtue of my macropolitics of location, and who am I by virtue of my subject-positionality as a specific-academic and expert intellectual? Furthermore, how well do I understand the relationship between these two dimensions or mediations, and how can I clinch the two into one overarching sense of constituency? Do categories like "postcolonial," "poststructuralist," "Asian-American," "Pakistani," and the like, all work in the same way? Do they belong to the same order of indexicality? When I call myself Asian-American, am I making a representative identity claim on behalf of a certain group, or am I announcing the legitimacy of a certain institutional formation called Asian-American studies, or am I assuming that the institutional logic of Asian-American studies will be subsumed thoroughly, without remainder or contradiction, by Asian-American macropolitical identity? What is the difference between the statements, "I am a poststructuralist" and "I am an Asian-American"? How does the copula ("to be") work in each case? This fraught relationship of identity to methodology takes on an even sharper significance in the context of the institutional-academic production of knowledge.

A representational model is also a representative model. A representational model raises concerns such as adequacy, fidelity, authenticity, historical veracity, spokespersonship, inclusiveness, and so on. This move from the epistemological to the political is based on the reality of some unifying ideology that is presumed to have effected the generalization of *a* perspective by way of the ideological production of a collectivity. It is in this sense that the heterogeneous lived realities of peoples are mobilized and hegemonized *in the name of* nationalism, Hindutva, Islam, the proletariat, and the like. In other words, the representational model achieves success by way of the prescriptive singularity of the name that supposedly speaks for the "differences within." How is the One forged out of the many? Does the One speak for the many? These are questions that have been discussed with great passion in the impressive literature on nationalism.[7] There is no representation without "naming" (Asian-America as a name creates a certain interrelationship among the parts that constitute it), and "naming" as a process is symptomatic of a tension between epistemology and politics. If radical epistemology insists on a deconstructive and open-ended process, politics advocates strategic closure. As the Asian-American presence grows stronger in numbers, the question arises: How and in what forms should this presence be felt within the American body politic? Should Asian-America slip into all-America without tension, opposition, or friction in an exemplary "model minority" fashion, or should Asian-America raise its own questions and concerns even as it factors itself into the national equation called "America"?

Furthermore, isn't there the need to create a new and different language for the articulation of these concerns and issues? I would recommend that unless minority experiences are backed by their own independent epistemic claims, these experiences will get parsed coercively within the assimilationist syntax presided over by a dominant all-America. Unless minorities craft their experiences into their own forms of knowledge, they will always be vulnerable to cooptation by the epistemic categories of the dominant discourse. Clearly, minority knowledges are neither "pure" nor separatist; instead, they take the form of a double or multiple consciousness that dislodges the regime of the dominant One, which for my purpose here is the *Western* or the Eurocentric One.[8]

As specific-academic intellectuals, knowledge is our concern both in a specialist as well as in an organic sense. Minority intellectuals have to take the knowledge game very seriously and simultaneously sniff at it with rigorous suspicion. In an overall global context where the question "What is knowledge?" seems to have been settled definitively well before subaltern peoples and cultures were even asked to participate, subaltern/minority intellectuals need to play the knowledge game in a deconstructive "double-session": both reactively and proactively. They have to engage deconstructively with the fait accompli of dominant knowledges even as they legitimate their own subjugated knowledges. Rather than be seduced by the avant-gardism of metropolitan epistemologies, they need to develop criteria to differentiate between empowering and alienating knowledges, between knowledges that one can call one's own through the exercise of collective agency and those that call for the sacrifice of subaltern agency in the name of metropolitan success and acceptability. The institutional-academic formations of ethnic/minority knowledges will have to do better than merely canonize themselves and follow the road to success already paved by the dominant discourse: capitalist, patriarchal, Eurocentric. They will have to seek a different modality of knowledge (not just the usual winner-take-all, zero-sum games) and unless and until they revolutionize the rules by which the knowledge game is played, they will only serve to strengthen the regime of universal dominance undertaken in the name of the advanced and all-knowing West.

If knowledge is partly representation, it is also a production. The production model transgresses representational norms in the following ways: the authority of the original has no ontological primacy or priority over the actual production; the intelligibility of the object (such as Asian-America) is itself the constituted function of the act of production; the production adds something new that is not already there in the original object; the production model calls into question the synchronicity of the original object and thus opens it up to the differential plays of diachrony; and finally, the production model also raises the question of ideological perspectivity and interest and thus disallows the normative sovereignty of the original object. All these implications have a very special salience in the context of diasporan production that both acknowledges and problematizes "origins." To put it differently, diasporan projects can be mnemonic, provided the mnemonic itself is conceptualized as the product of a countermemory.

Will the ideology of Asian-America be single or plural? Will it be capitalist, nationalist, hybrid, hyphenated, Marxist, post-Marxist, ethnic or postethnic, gendered, sexualized? Whatever the eventual response, the historical reality of Asian-American studies cannot be thought of outside the framework of global asymmetry: the framework of a world structured in dominance. The fundamental issue confronting the conceptualization of Asian-America is that of ethnic hyphenation. Dwelling in the hyphen is not a matter of neutrality or of benign participation in the conjuncturality of "equal" histories. It is a mandate to acknowledge coevalness between two histories as well as a call to redress the existing imbalances between the two histories.[9] In other words, an activist-interventionist agency has to be coded into the very being of Asian-American studies. Dwelling in the hyphen is neither to be romanticized in the name of "free" individual choice, nor is it to be registered as a freefloating hybridity devoid of historical baggage. So, at the risk of sounding ideologically shrill, I will raise the question, "Which Asian-America?" in a theoretical vein, rather than as a bland descriptive query.

There is a need to make a distinction between "Asian-America" as a mere demographic census marker and "Asian-America" as a political-epistemic category. I am interested in the ideological production of Asian-America along certain lines, and not in Asian-America as a quietist, benign, and noninterventionist category that represents all Asian Americans. My emphasis here is that Asian-American intellectuals, scholars, and teachers should take up the responsibility of creating, molding, and bringing into being a certain kind of bloc known as Asian-America (here I am espousing a Gramscian model of the intellectual as leader/persuader/activist), and not throw up their hands in despair and/or neutrality. I realize Asian-Americans can be conservatives, Republicans, mainstream assimilationists, fierce capitalist-individualist-consumer fetishists, and all-American to the point of denying ethnic origins. Now, those are not my fellow Asian-Americans; the Asian-America that I am thinking of is neither nativist nor natalist, but an ideologist perspective that will have to be critical of mainstream America, of capitalist individualism, of Orientalism and Eurocentrism, and in deep solidarity with gay, lesbian, feminist, minority activist movements, and with the third world even though that world is not *here*. It is from such a point of view that I recommend that the hyphen-as-space be polemicized/militarized to call into question the motif of monothetic citizenship and render America vulnerable and accountable to the rest of the world.[10] Too often one hears the argument that since we have been *here* for generations now the significance of the *there* (wherever there might be in Asia or Africa, but Euro-America is a different matter altogether) dies, atrophies away for lack of context and relevance. It is as though Africa and Asia are not worthy epistemic domains in themselves; they can only be part of a traditional and nonmodern memory that can be obliterated in and through the process of Americanization.

It must be quite clear by now that I look on hyphenation in a favorable light. Not only am I contending that there are hyphenated identities, but also that such identities should produce knowledges that are hyphenated; for any other morphology does not have the capacity or the legitimacy to speak for hyphenated identities and hyphenated experiences. So, how does the hyphen speak, and how is the hyphen to be produced subjectively and agentially rather than be embraced and/or accepted as a given condition?[11] I begin with the assertion that the hyphen can speak only when it produces itself conceptually, theoretically, categorically. Ethnic hyphenation is indeed a cliche in the history of American identities. What I am suggesting, however, on behalf of the hyphen is something quite other. My point is that in the diasporan context, the hyphen should be produced as a theoretical category that is not to be owned by or normatively deployed by any one hyphenated constituency. In acknowledging the existential-epistemic alterity of the hyphen, both Asia and America are radically derealized in the name of an emerging heterogeneous historiography. The hyphen is also the *topos* that stages the ongoing differential conversation between the nameability of the diaspora and the perennial namelessness of the *diaspora as such*[12] The historicity of the hyphen warrants a different historiography, and dwelling in the hyphen, between identity regimes, necessitates a different narratoiogy. Betweenness and conjuncturality ought to be enfranchised as modes of legitimate being before the hyphen can speak. How is the hyphen, whether graphically expressed or understood, in Asian-America to be historicized, to be produced? The *hyphen as such* in Asian-America has to do double duty and coordinate the Asian experience without resort to hierarchical maneuvers or identity coups. American identity is not something consummate to which an Asian flavor is being added, nor is Asia something more real than the mystifying and often discriminating contemporaneity of the United States of America. These options do not do justice to the complete coevalness of Asia with America as witnessed by the hyphen in all its double vision. There is indeed an America prior to hyphenation by the Asian immigrant experience, and indeed an Asia that has not traveled to America; but the hyphen both acknowledges these anterior relatives and de-and reterritorializes them in the context of the hyphen-as-relationality and relationality-as-hyphen.[13] The critical-semantic significance of the hyphen lies in its capacity to demand that so-called discrete, autonomous, or absolute histories be read and interpreted relationally, that is, with reference to other histories. Indeed relationality is so much at the heart of the hyphen that it represents relationality as such, and with the autonomous advent of the hyphen, there is no History, nor are there separate histories, but histories cross-hatched in relationality.[14] If the accountability of the hyphen to itself escapes the identitarian claims of both Asia and America (i.e., in a sense both Asia and America are reterritorialized given the emergent historicity of the hyphen), is the hyphen then neither an "insider" nor an "outsider" to either constituency, doubly "out" and doubly "in" in a Mobius-strip like dimensionless dimensionality? If from the point of view of hyphenation, America and Asia are "always already" mediated by each other, how do we get at any reliable and, need I say, "authentic" representations of and on either side of the hyphen? It would seem that here again the hyphen derails canonical notions of the One, and faithfulness to origins. From the point of view of Asian-America then, can Asia be invented and imagined at will, strategically or otherwise, and indiscriminately instrumentalized in the service of the history of the present, the history of the hyphen/the diaspora?

Sau-ling Cynthia Wong, in her essay "Sugar Sisterhood: Situating the Amy Tan Phenomenon" (1995) makes an excellent contribution to our understanding of the rhetoric of authenticity: what she calls "authenticity effects" and "authenticity markers."[15] Reading the Amy Tan phenomenon symptomatically, Wong situates "authenticity" between self and other, between the history of the self and anthropology. Making a distinction between authenticity-itself and authenticity markers, Wong problematizes any transparent valorization of authenticity. The questions raised are (as I travel with Wong's insights into other related directions): Can there be authenticity without authenticity-effects and authenticity markers? Who is the authenticity for, the self or the other? Is authenticity-to-oneself a contradiction in terms, redundant, and is it different from authenticity-for-the-other? In a perceptive double-reading of Tan's use of Chinese "material," Wong tells us that certain features, whether these be the use of Chinese names or references to Chinese customs or lexical borrowings from Chinese, function for the white Western reader as "authenticity markers" whether or not they are reliable vehicles of authenticity. Driving a critical wedge between authenticity as content and authenticity as practice (for the other), between authenticity as verifiable and authenticity as autotelic style, Wong's essay knocks at an important question: Is identity thinkable/assumable/practicable without the normative notion of authenticity?

Authenticity functions on more than one level, the easiest to adjudicate being "facticity." In the essay, Wong corrects a few errors; and these are factual errors, literal misreadings of Chinese letters, words, etcetera. It turns out that even the evocative phrase "sugar sisterhood" is an instance of *meconaissance,* and yet it works, albeit erroneously. Thus, for example, an Asian-American scholar could be corrected, even reprimanded, by a Chinese specialist for getting a nuance wrong, and yet, I would not like to think that it is somehow intrinsic for the "insider" to "know it right."[16]

This issue has to do not just with facticity, however, but also interpretive authority. Yet how does one legislate interpretive authority given that the order of interpretation is not the same as the order of meaning or truth? One could of course say that certain modes of interpretation are specified within a tradition whereas certain others, though not without merit or interest, are not *within* that tradition. Thus we can distinguish among Confucian, Buddhist, and Taoist readings of Chinese texts, and say, postmodern or New Critical interpretations of the same texts. Besides, there have always been critical projects, from within a tradition, that have sought to revise, reform, and even revolutionize that tradition.[17] Battles among interpretations then are part of a constructivist epistemology where the relative merits and demerits of different constructions or constitutive interpretations cannot be settled through an appeal to the transcendent ontology of the Object. Yet choices are made, immanently perhaps, among different constructions based on interests, criteria, tastes, and the like.

Beyond the factual and the interpretive levels, there is a third level that has to do with the totality or the holistic integrity of any culture or tradition. Within a culture, there are all sorts of intricate metonymic and synechdochal relationships between qualities and states of being between parts and wholes; and these relationships are not "iterable" unless the entire structure is repeated either in the same context or in a different context. If it is a different context, then perhaps purists would expect the orthodox, normative canonical practice of that total structure, that is, the identical repetition of that structure, to nullify the alienating effect of a new and different context; by this logic one could say that Chinatown or Little India should be cultivated in active abeyance of their immediate American contemporaneity: but does this make sense, for why should a repetition be identical? Cannot iterability be dissipative rather than conservative of identity? Furthermore, what about the context in which the repetition is achieved? By holistic logic, details, such as the Japanese tea ceremony, or the Indian tradition that one should not stretch one's feet in the direction of elders, cannot be deracinated from their context and then derided or critiqued. While many of these caveats do have a protectionist purpose, i.e., protectionism against hostile misrecognition by dominant and/or antagonistic groups, they also serve to come down harshly, even punitively, against what I would like to call "the diasporization of identity." Chinatowns and Little Indias are interpellated by a double logic: on the one hand, the authority internal to the repetition and on the other, the dissemination of this very authority in alien and different contexts. The logic of dissemination is reducible neither to the value of the past, its rectitude within its own temporality, nor to the no-holds barred opportunism of the present moment: it can only be embodied as an ongoing form of historical noncoincidence of the "before" in the "after."

It is a little too naive to expect that the "Asia" in Asian studies and the "Asia" in Asian-American studies are/should be identical. There are determining connections, and relationships between the two. Both "Asias" are constructed and not natural, and both carry historical density as well as urgency. The "Asian" in Asian studies is not necessarily authentic whereas the "other" Asia is merely "hybrid." My contention is that both "hybridity" and "authenticity" are forms of history, and neither is free of the taint of strategy and ideology: there are several morphologies of history, and no one morphology is by definition more historical than another. The diasporan take on Chinese nationalism, for example, has a historicity of its own and this sense of history within the diaspora should not be construed as any less dense, real, or representative than the resident Chinese nationalist production.

We must also not forget that articulations from within ethnic/diasporan hyphenation propose a different object of study altogether. The interests that inform Asian studies and Asian-American studies are different. Built into the Asian-American experience of Asia is the diasporan context, the diasporan perspective: if you will, the historicity of the diaspora as well as the historicity of hybridity. This diasporan historicity is not something secondary or epiphenomenal that one can bracket off comfortably before proceeding to study Asia objectively, as though from its own perspective. Diasporic displacement is an autonomous theme in itself, *and* it acts as a critical/hermeneutic perspective from which the country of origin is seen in a certain light.

Diasporan historiography raises the second-order issue of mediation and mediatedness as an autonomous epistemological issue and thus complicates any attempt at enjoying an immediate relationship with whatever lies on either side of the hyphen: a pre-post-erous situation where the self-reflexive production of "mediation/mediatedness as meaning" postpones and problematizes the objective status of those realities and histories *of which* the diaspora is itself a *mediation*. I will allow myself to say, infelicitous as it may sound, that diasporan historicity functions in a double mode: as *mediation as such*, and as *mediation of*. The problem is to relate the two within a sense of constituency.

A term that comes to mind in this context is one that is often used in the Indian diasporan community: ABCD, that is, American-Born-Confused-Deshis (where "deshis" signifies national citizens of the country of origin). The assumption here is that these folks don't really know India except in the form of bits and pieces, rumors and myths, all resulting in confusion. There is then identity by birth (American), which does not seem to matter except as a matter of fact, and there is the deshi affiliation that is perhaps affective and value-laden, but an affiliation founded on confusion, half-knowledges, and putative values. The ABCD population sample is representative or expressive of a fatuous form of hybridity that is neither here nor there, anchored neither here nor there, clueless in superficial ambivalence.

As someone who values hybridity as a semantically rich state of being posited on the possibility of global heteroglossia, I would reformulate ABCD to spell "Americans Because Conjunctural Diasporans."[18] It is not America versus the diaspora and ethnic hyphenation, it is not ethnic separatism, and it is not American identity as the ideological resolution of the unfinished citizenship inherent in diasporic ethnicity. Most importantly, the purpose of the formulation is to read conjuncturality into the very heart of "identity." To state this in the context of my entire discussion of the identity politics of the hyphen, the ethic of the hybrid is to work on both sides of the hyphen, to divest itself of monoradical modes of belonging and inaugurate "ambivalence" as a positive existential category. The Asian-American objective should be to announce and implement dialogism and reciprocity of influence such that the Asianization of America will be perceived as equally valuable as the reterritorialization of Asia in America. To live as an ABCD, then, is to realize the centrality of the conjuncture within the very heart of identity.

Whether it is Asian America or any other hyphenated community, the diasporan experience raises one big unsettling question that is rarely raised amidst the pragmatics of functional citizenship: Who are we? Diasporan theory does not emanate from a secure source of being, and it is not an attempt to consolidate through knowledge what is already obvious and axiomatic in the living experience. The living and the telling, the experiencing and the meaning-making happen simultaneously much like a radical existential script that begins to exist only when the screen is lifted and the lights turned on. The hyphen has to speak to exist, and given the ambivalence of the diaspora, it is not always clear who the addressee is: all of America, Asia, only Asian-America? The identity question, "Who am/are I/we?" constitutes the diasporic epistemological domain; in other words, indeterminacy and the immanent undecidability of identity are the cornerstones of diasporic studies, as also the challenge, "how to proceed from I to 'we.' " It is not a situation where epistemological investigations are authorized in the name of a preexisting identity secure in its normativity. The very reception and the production of identity are performed interhistorically and not within the representative plentitude of a single intetpretive community. Might not an Amy Tan, as against a Chinese writer living in China and visiting the United States of America, say that the American audience that Sau-ling Cynthia Wong identifies as external to Chinese valences is very much internal to Amy Tan's sense of being? Furthermore, just as the "America" in "Asian-America" is not meant only for endorsement and celebration, so too with the "Asia." An Asian-American will and should have the intellectual freedom to dislike, reject, and critique aspects both of America and Asia. The ability to embody an identity and be part of a collectivity means nothing unless it also includes the capacity and the expertise to critique the very ground one occupies. Solidarity without critique is either a straitjacket or an empty shibboleth.

With this connection between critique and identity in mind, I reach the final segment of my essay that has to do with the adjacencies that have developed among the several disciplines that constitute the humanities. Should methodology be pure and totally intrinsic to the "truth" of the object of study? Or is it okay for methodology to be creatively interdisciplinary, even be nothing more than bricolage? Firmly grounded in the belief that methodologies should be broad-based, interdisciplinary, and heuristically open-ended, I would assert that the macrology (as well as the teleology) of Asian-American studies has room for a variety of practitioners. There is not and cannot be a single methodology that is immanently coextensive with the field called "Asian-American studies." As history tells us time and time again, even revolutionary knowledges and truths are not born with their own pristine ex nihilo modalities and procedures. Emergent knowledges take the "given" and shape it to their ends through the exercise of political will. Just as the political effectivity of an individual or group is measured both in terms of its ability to define itself and the effects of such self-definition on others who inhabit the social space, so too with academic formations.

Postmodernism and Asian-American studies. Following up on Cornel West's formulation that African-American postmodernism is not the same as Lyo-tardian, Baudrillardian, or Euro-postmodernism, I would say that Asian-American studies, too, has and can establish its own mediated relationship to postmodernity and not lose itself in the process. What are some of the themes in postmodernism that are germane and perhaps even helpful to Asian-American studies? Two motifs that on the surface seem hostile: the death of representation, and the death of authorial voice. Many minority theorists have noted (myself included) with indignation the cynicism with which Eurocentric "high theory" announces the end of representation and the death of the author at the very moment when subjugated and formerly colonized peoples have begun finding their voices and their modes of self-representation. Brilliant as this critique is, there is another side to this story. Distinctions need to be made between just and dominant representations. The postmodernist critique of representation is also a critique of dominance and of the inherence of dominance in erstwhile forms of so-called universalism — Eurocentrism in particular. Given the history of representation, minority and subaltern constituencies need to cultivate critical ambivalence toward the politics of representation: on the one hand, insist on the right for self-representation and on the other, resist programmatic univocality. Both postmodernism and poststructuralism produce deconstructive insights from within the dominant location, and with Edward Said, I would like to believe that there is a strong case to be made for cooperation across asymmetries between deconstructive knowledges of the West and the emerging knowledges of the Rest. The postmodern critique of univocity needs to be understood with its corollary: the celebration of multiplicity, heterogeneity, hybridity.

As for the death of the author's voice, again there is another side to it: the denaturalization of the voice opens up the meaning of the text/ experience to its own imagined historicity. It also shows the way toward decanonization when the canon becomes dominant, and demonstrates usefully how "voice" and "canonicity" are not natural, but rather ideologically fraught. Equally useful is the manner in which the denaturalization of the voice promotes a critical attitude toward discourses of authenticity based on exclusion and the foreclosure of heterogeneity.

Poststructuralism and Asian-American studies. Poststructuralism at its best is informed by the Benjaminian insight that every document of civilization is also a document of barbarism. The fact that Asian-America or, for that matter, any constituency, is victimized or subjugated at a particular moment in history does not absolve it of the will to dominance. Subjugated cultures in particular are prone to internalizing dominance unless they are vigilant, and there is the practice of widespread dominance even within the solidarity of minority and subaltern groups. Asian-America is thus both outside dominant America even as it is part of that structure. The project of realizing itself in its own way is not disjunct from the project of "turning the dominant pages in a certain way."[19] Even in the case of minority formations where knowledge production is and should be closely related to the ideology of the politics of representation, every effort should be made to maintain both the heterogeneity as well as the openendedness of the thinking process so that political solidarity will not come in the way of the production of transgressive and autocritical knowledge.

Postcoloniality and Asian-American studies. It is ironic that the dimension that has made postcoloniality unpopular with traditional Third World scholars is the very thing that makes it sympathetic to Asian-American studies, i.e., the focus on the diasporan location. Here are some overlapping concerns: hybridity and the politics of hybridity, the travails and attractions of metropolitan double-consciousness and ambivalence; a certain critical interest as well as distance from the development of discourses of "post-ality"; simultaneous attention to the intersectional nature of identity politics (race, class, gender, and sexuality); critique of nationalist discourses and the inadequacy of the "imagined community" of nationality; and finally, issues confronting "origins" and revisionist renditions of history. Also significant is the manner in which postcoloniality has succeeded in befriending and instrumentalizing varieties of poststructuralist practice (a theoretical alliance that has already spawned a number of controversies and anxieties) and in the process has served to highlight the issue of "traveling theory": of how theory in traveling can be renamed and reclaimed heterogeneously.

Finally, as one of the more recent entrants into the disciplinary areas called ethnic studies, Asian-American studies needs to do all it can to foster a coalitional mentality among minority formations.[20] As the African-American experience teaches us, many of these problems and crises have arisen before: the wheel does not have to be invented over and over again. I mention this only because there are occasions where, even in the field of theoretical productions, minorities skirmish over the questions of "who created the concept first?" and "who is bypassing whose prior authority?" and "who, in a blatantly cavalier fashion, is refusing to acknowledge prior contributions and prior battles?" At a time when multiculturalism is being invoked with such surpassing ease by administrators, corporations, and creators of commercials, it behooves Asian-American studies, along with other minority discourses, to wrest the initiative from these colonizing promoters and endorsers of multiculturalism and to empower the flow of heterogeneous knowledges as forms of persuasion that will transform the status quo and the "business as usual" mentality of the dominant corporate regime. Creating a space between discourses of a dehistoricized and superficial hybridity and the languages of essentialized authenticity, hyphenated knowledges have the honor as well as the hardship of elaborating an ongoing ethico-political coalition of what Lani Guinier (1994) calls "like minds, not like bodies." For it is to be hoped that minority knowledges as forms of persuasion will work differently from dominating knowledges and begin to imagine a relational world that has retired once and for all the model of "the winner take all" and the cultural politics of conquest.

Notes

1. For more on the nature of cosmopolitan identity, please see Robbins and Cheah 1998.

2. For a thought-provoking elaboration of the space between expertise and cultural identity, see Said 1983.

3. No one has theorized the performative more rigorously than Judith Butler. See in particular *Gender Trouble* (1990) and *Bodies That Matter* (1993).

4. I refer here to Lacanian psychoanalysis that posits that the unconscious is structured like language and effects the de-essentialization of the Self.

5. For more on the performative nature of identity in the context of nationalism and diasporan hybridity, see Bhabha 1994.

6. For a detailed discussion of the Foucauldian specific intellectual and the Gramscian organic intellectual, see my chapter, "Towards an Effective Intellectual: Foucault or Gramsci?" in this book.

7. See in particular Parker et al. 1992; Bhabha 1992; and Chatterjee 1986 and 1993.

8. For a powerful inaugural statement of double-consciousness, see W. E. B. Du Bois's *The Souls of Black Folk* (1996; 1903) also, see Paul Gilroy's *The Black Atlantic* (1993). For a recent memorable application of Du Bois in the South Asian context, see Vijay Prashad, *The Karma of Brown Folk* (2000).

9. See Amin 1989 and Anzaldua 1987 for multilateral universalism and "betweenness," respectively. See Johannes Fabian, *Time and the Other* (1983), for an enabling evaluation of coevalness.

10. For a postcolonial critique of postmodernism, see my essay, "Postmodernism and the Rest of the World" (Radhakrishnan 1994).

11. This question is intended in the same register as Spivak's "Can the Subaltern Speak?" (1988).

12. For more on diaspora as a mode of intellectuality, see Rey Chow. Also see Sau-ling Cynthia Wong's influential essay, "Denationalization Reconsidered" (1995) and Kandice Chuh's "Transnationalism and Its Pasts" (1996).

13. See Deleuze and Guattari 1986 for notions of re- and deterritorialization.

14. See Mohanty 1989.

15. See Sau-ling Cynthia Wong 1995.

16. As Amitav Ghosh demonstrates brilliantly in *The Shadow Lines*, if facts and details are learnable any-where, they are also learnable every-other-where. Of course, the degree of immersion in the material may be of varying levels of intensity and organic belonging.

17. Chandralekha's ambitiously intellectual revisionist renditions of Bharata Natyam are a good example of an indigenous critique of one's own tradition.

18. For a powerful and persuasive theorization of hybridity, see Nestor Garcia Canclini, *Hybrid Cultures* (1995).

19. See Derrida 1981.

20. See Jan Mohamed and Lloyd 1991.

12 / Diaspora, Hybridity, Pedagogy

What does it mean to teach in the diaspora? What does it mean to teach the diaspora as a domain with its own kind of autonomy? How is the authority of pedagogy realized or decentered in the diaspora? If indeed, the phenomenon of "the generation gap" is further vivified and exacerbated in the diaspora, what can one say about who is teaching and who is learning, and from whom? What sorts of dialectic/dialogic/differential transfers are possible between the position of the student and that of the teacher? What do terms like "young" and "old" mean in the context of the diaspora and its history of the present? Is it indeed possible to conceive of diasporan pedagogies as pedagogies of immanence? Should hybridity be valorized as the appropriate content of the diaspora, and if so, how is hybridity to be simultaneously embodied, represented, and adjudicated? How should a merely "given or symptomatic" hybridity be differentiated from an erudite and self-reflexive hybridity? These are some of the questions that I wish to elaborate in this essay.

Scenario 1. The Dakshinamurthy motif

Chithram vata tharor moole, vruddhaha sishyaha gururyuvaha.
Gurosthu maunam vyakyanam, sishyaha chinna-samshayaha.

This Sanskrit shloka may be translated thus: "In the southeast corner under the tree, the picture of students who are aged and the teacher who is young. The discourse of the teacher is silence, and the students are rid of their doubts."

In this celebrated verse that thematizes pedagogy from an unusual perspective, the teacher is a singular youth expressive of divinity, and the knowledge-seekers are old and sagacious men. The discourse of the teacher takes the form of silence, and the effect of such a pedagogy is that the student-seekers are rid of their doubts. In this brief frieze of a scene, nothing is transacted, and yet everything is transacted. To be more precise, everything is transacted precisely because nothing is transacted. As I undertake my brief critical analysis of this scene, just a couple of avowals: one, I might well be guilty of conflating notions of immanence and transcendence from two different epistemological traditions, one eastern and the other western; and secondly, I will indeed be guilty of using the Dakshinamurthy motif as a traveling secular motif rather than as a Hindu theme. In other words, when I comment on "the discourse of silence" or "silence as discourse", it will not be in line with spiritual or Advaitic notions of numinous or unmediated access to the Real.

Why am I haunted by this motif? To start with, this frieze of the young god-teacher and the aged human students functions as a prolegomenon to the actual scene of teaching. It is a spectacle of meta-pedagogical self-reflexivity that in effect mirrors what is going on within the pedagogical frame: the riddance of doubts by way of the discourse of silence. Subject positions are announced, the genealogy as well as the pedigree of the participants is recognized, and their respective ontologies are identified. It is the performative moment par excellence, in all its irreducible intransitivity. And, strangely, even eerily, nothing follows. The frieze is the immaculate narrative, and the pre-pedagogical performativity is the pedagogical imperative in all its awesome plenitude. Questions of methodology as discourse and that of epistemology as material perspectivism is magisterially bypassed in the name of a self-evident ontology that obviates representation. In the sheer immanence of ontology-as-answer, the knowledge issue is laid to rest in silence, by silence, as silence. As I have suggested already, my critical position would be to insist that ontological immanence works not as unmediated transparency, but by way of an intentional "absenting" of epistemology as question. What is at work here is something like a Heideggerian *Gelassenheit* or "a letting be": a productive listening by the students that enables the silence of the answer: the answer as silence. In other words, the efficacy of silence as answer is, from my poststructuralist perspective, not the celebration of a primordial ontology where the answer is the question and vice versa, but rather, the thematization of a chronic pedagogy that will not allow authority to rest either with the position of the teacher or that of the student. My secular rendition of this motif would read it as the representation of a learning process that is perennially uncertain and contingent.

What then is the connection with the diaspora? Often, very often as a matter of fact, as a diasporic parent and intellectual who writes about the diaspora, I am transfixed and cathected by an untenable and contradictory desire. I would like to represent the diaspora but only through questioning representation as such. And, I would rather be represented by the diaspora since I am of it, though perhaps not as exclusively as my son and his generation. How then does one garner the credentials to be worthy of representing the diaspora, and at the same time, submit to be interpellated by the very phenomenon that is the object of one's pedagogical desire? The diasporic situation generates in me the perverse impulse to want to be student-and-teacher, offspring-and-parent simultaneously. To put it in personal terms, I want to practice quietness, suspend discourse and learn from my son and his generation, even as the desire to teach him immeasurably wells up within me. Perhaps, with that statement I have made my deconstructive intention clear: to implicate the teacher in the non-innocence of silence, and to critically randomize the impact of age and experience on the process of generating knowledge.

As a diasporic parent/intellectual, how do I get out of the way even as I am in it, paving it? On the contrary, how can I as a professional "pedagogue" not focus on the teleology of pedagogy? Clearly, pedagogy cannot be non-directed, non-authoritative. Perhaps, given the doubleness of the diasporic situation, direction and authority can be split, doubled, reversed, and re-reversed? But how is the "authority" of a bilateral pedagogy achieved, instrumentalized? Finally, what does it mean "to learn", "to learn from", to "learn from the parent", and "learn from one's progeny"? "I do anticipate the question: Why introduce the diaspora in some rare and exemplary manner when all that we are talking about is a generic generational problem? The answer is that often the diaspora, as it intervenes between the immigrant-generation and the first-generation, transforms an intra-historical form of difference into an inter-historical register. For example, in the diaspora, what could be considered as a sign of inter-Indian difference has to be construed simultaneously as an Asian-American form of difference.

A different look at the same scenario. What does it mean to learn from youth, and what is the connection between youth culture and diasporan knowledge? Why is youth privileged: its ontology, its mode of being, its temporality? Under what epistemic conditions does the expression of youth become the expression of contemporaneity, the embodiment of the eternal present? Mortality can be metaphorically deferred, conquered as much by the perpetuation (eternalization) of old or middle age as by the immortalization of youth. Yet, even divinity is figured as youth that knows by virtue of itself and *ergo* communicates through its sheer embodiment.

For my purposes, the Dakshinamurthy scenario raises the following question: Are there two kinds of knowledge? Clearly the aged students do not constitute a blank slate. In fact, they know enough to entertain doubts: doubts that are clarified by the sheer ontological presence of youth as divinity. It is interesting to note that in the Dakshinamurthy motif, the hierarchy of pedagogical authority is dealt with in ambivalence. There is the superiority of old age based on the historical reality of process. It has experienced much more "becoming" than youth. But age has doubts that need to be set at rest. In the mutual interpellation that happens between the two parties, it is the hierarchically underpowered figure of the youth that achieves eminence by "masquerading" as divinity. It is as though there is a mode of being (dwelling ontologically if you will, after Heidegger) that when captured at an essential moment can embody knowledge fully and transparently. To put it in contemporary terms, the temporality of youth by "being with it" establishes its truth claims, whereas the temporality of old age suffers from the agonies and the incertitudes of representational poverty. Nobody wants to be old whereas youthfulness is valorized and entertained poignantly through recall and nostalgia. As William Wordsworth would maintain didactically throughout his Prelude, the trick is: how to revisit and idealize youth as the immanent fount of wisdom and knowledge?

This brings me back to my earlier question: Are there two schools, two pedagogies, two knowledges? When reality is invoked in the name of an ineffable answer and in the body of youth conceived as divinity, what happens to that other knowledge riddled with doubts? The Dakshinamurthy motif may be read as temporality's answer to itself. But who is producing this silence as knowledge within the duality of the teacher and the taught, the young and the old, the divine and the secular, the ontological and the epistemological? To put it in the diasporan context, does the spectacle of youth offer itself as the appropriate text of the diaspora: a text characterized by relative alterity *vis a vis* the old?

Often my son, from whom I have learned quite a bit already, will tell me as he introduces me to a new cultural phenomenon: "Appa/Dad, please just listen, don't prejudge." As I listen to him I do understand that he is pointing out to me the relative differences between our respective "origins", between "where we come from". It is only after I acknowledge his radical unknowability to me that I can begin to negotiate the terms that will make him intelligible to me. In other words, he is "what I cannot be or know". And this is a tantalizing situation. Certain new locations, subject-positions, modes of address and listening need to be imagined if a two-way pedagogy is to be inaugurated. What will the youth learn from the wise old men, even as the old men constitute the youth as subject and object of study? To paraphrase Hans-Georg Gadamer: in this diasporic exchange, whose truth and whose method, and to fine-tune it some more: who is truth and who is method?[1] If method is not to be co-opted within the primary sovereignty of truth, then the only way the two generations in the diaspora can produce understandings of each other is through an initial reciprocal opacity. My son is indeed the other and I am "his" other: not essentially, but coevally and therefore negotiably. My point here is that the self-other effect is the result of a historical process, not the *fait-accompli* of transcendental philosophy.

To make diasporan learning work multi-directionally, it is vital that meta-pedagogical reflexivity from either side not be mastered in the name of pedagogical efficiency or functionalism. How can I learn from diasporic youth which is far from being divine and self-assured, and is in fact fallible as the avatar of the ABCD (American Born Confused Deshi)? Two interrelated confessions here as I begin. First, in some deep unethical manner, in my pedagogical context I find myself fantasizing and wanting to be my student, but endowed with my reflexive consciousness. In other words, I want not to intervene; for if I intervened I would only be "treating" "ABCD-ness" as corrigible symptom, rather than constituting it as a domain worthy of my seeking. In a strange way, the hybrid alterity of that generation is sexy, exciting. I desperately want to allegorize the condition of that generation even as I am eager to alleviate, assuage, and cure the confused-ness of that condition. I want to abnegate my pedagogical responsibility; I want to switch rules and implore my son to teach me at that very moment when he is in need of my pedagogical intervention. My pedagogical ethic is in schizophrenia.

Second, I must confess that I am a little annoyed and disappointed with the way in which diasporic studies has been hijacked by the mnemonic imperative. What about remembering and forgetting, what about Foucauldian counter-memory and its contradictory commitment to history?[2] Why should diasporic studies be trivialized by the need for authentic homes and single roots and origins?[3] Is not the historical sense conditioned both by the return motif to as well as the flight from the past motif? Frankly, my impulse, when confronted by a diasporic student who needs epistemology as ontology, knowledge as comfortable home, is to tell her that I live in the world of fractious and contested representations that postpone and problematize "homeliness". There is no home except by way of a critical and historically aware imagination.[4]

I realize that my student's historical starting point, and *ergo* her quest too, is different from mine. But my general formal point is that whatever one's starting point, resident or diasporic, migrant or naturalized, hegemonic or subaltern, home is not to be fetishized as immaculate arrival or history coded purely as return or plenary memory. So, what does all this mean? Simply this. As the older teacher I need to offer my historicity as symptomatic body to the diasporan gaze even as I read the diasporic body diagnostically. Maybe I need an acronym like ABCD: perhaps SSBDA (Seemingly Secure But Deeply Ambivalent) to characterize my situation. I too am of the diaspora and even when I was not, geographically speaking, my attitude to my home was ambivalent. I both liked it and wanted to run away from it. Diaspora is of the mind, not a mere superficial effect of physical movement.

Scenario 2

In this scenario, I am watching a youth show where a group of first generation Indian/Asian-American (what is not in a name?) youth is performing a variety of events: dance, music, skits. Every item, one way or the other, highlights and foregrounds the reality that these are ABCDs, less frequently FOBs: the fresh-off-the-boats who have just arrived in the USA on student visas. I see ontology in performance here. These young men and women are carving out a social space for themselves where they can, in amateurish fashion, raise the question of who they are as hybrids. Labels like ABCD and FOB are invoked quite matter-of-factly, and without pathos, as historical markers. They are indeed connecting with other similarly placed youth and they are all creating a public sphere through performance. Their skits and plays do include parent characters who are understandably portrayed as necessary but also somewhat irrelevant, alterior, and different. In these skits and vignettes, the older generation does not understand since they are differently located within the Indo-American continuum: their India and their America are different. The sense I get is that these young folk are not looking for enlightenment and clarification from their elders who will somehow demystify the ABCD condition and produce an "authentic" identity within the Asian-American "hy-phen".

I realize that they are requesting to be heard both by themselves and by their elders. They are insisting that their diasporic immanence and their stranded hybriditics are audible, and indeed worthy of audition. Though it is true that they would like to address their ABCD-ness through appropriate knowledge channels, they are not prepared to identify or recognize their

ABCD-ness as an exclusively pathological symptom to be remedied by parental care and expertise. They are indeed claiming these labels, ironically and literally, as their particular moments of passage into history. They are claiming their belatedness as belatedness, that is, as a Derridean supplement that does not always look to the original text for its self-validation.[5] On the contrary, they are parading their immanence as sound and spectacle: they are speaking their hybrid selves without a clear understanding of what or whom they are "speaking for." They are in immanent process, on their way to representation; and in this path, the parental generation is often a block, a hindrance, and a nuisance. In their stories we are rendered "different," and requested to see ourselves as they see us.

Looking at it transferentially, I find myself asking whether in my diaspora I am really all that sure of who I am or whom I speak for (and here I will not for a moment entertain the strategy of national flag-waving: neither the tricolor nor the stars and stripes) and indeed if there is anything in my self-reflexive ontological erudition that can address their identity issues, their representative and representational confusions and ambivalences. This brings to mind an incident from the movie *American Desi* where an ABCD young man insists that the pronunciation of his name not be corrected. In other words, he is happy to have his name butchered and mispronounced by mainstream America, and he is ashamed of his ethnic heritage. What is more, he wants to be intelligible to the dominant discourse at any cost.

I want to do a double take on this: first, the predictable and the "correct" response that here indeed is a benighted youth waiting and wanting to be whitewashed and brainwashed by mainstream America. No question here but that this youth needs knowledge about both cultures so that he does not become a two-way racist and idiot. I would be delighted to sit him down and lecture him. But this is not all, for there is more to the historical situation of the benighted youth. I wish to point out that the young man's pigheaded insistence symptomatically raises a different question: a meta-theoretical question about cultural rectitude. Just as the label ABCD works both as a state of confusion to be perennially rectified by ongoing knowledge about both cultures *and* as a legitimate and viable point of entry into history, here, too, the will of the youth to will knowledge a certain way has a double dimension. It is not merely a matter of "corrigibility", for we do need to get into the question of how this young man's will is taking a certain direction, however perverse.

To put it concretely, the parents of this youth need to acknowledge and respond to the reality of a racist America where "exotic" names are laughed at, racialized, and orientalised. The idea that the young man would resort to such unabashed self denigration is indeed pathetic and reprehensible, but he is trying to survive against heavy odds.[6] The parental generation needs to understand

1. that they too are living in the same America where their son is ashamed of his ethnic name,
2. that he is "here" and not "there" because the parents decided to migrate,
3. that the parents themselves and their generation are facing similar problems in their double-conscious lives in America: problems that persist beyond the efficacy of traditional solutions,
4. that the youth's generation is definitely and insightfully *on* to the problems confronting the parents' generation,
5. that this applies to intellectual-radical left-wing parents like me, that no amount of theoretical-programmatic pedagogy of anti-racism, sexism, homophobia is going to work like a mantra in an actual instance of embarrassment, harassment, or racialization in the youth's life, and
6. that all of these issues need to be confronted with searing and rigorous candor both intra-and inter-generationally without either generation pulling rank or youth: in other words, no Dakshinamurthys, old or young.

Therefore, when I watch the youth program and respond to its bland and amateurish contemporaneity, I am torn. I want to step in and tell them things: sit them down and lecture to them, inviting dialogue in the process. But on the other hand, I want to see them unpack their historicity, unencumbered by me, and watch carefully how my generation is being identified and named in their history. In a strange way, as a son who had to run away from his tradition and is still doing so in some selective ways even as he is reclaiming that tradition in other and revisionist ways, I desire deeply to be present in their story as an "absence", to be remembered countermnemonically and not with representational fidelity. My point is simple: even as they militarize their ethnicity sometimes to resist mainstream racism, and at other times, repress it for the sake of bland acceptance by the mainstream, they need to transcend the unutterable poverty of strategic identity politics and of a purely reactive-paranoid identity formation as well as the abjection politics of assimilation. They need to "imagine with precision"[7] new spaces of representation where remembering and forgetting will take place critically, and in a differential relationship to each other.[8]

Scenario 3

There is a scene in the diasporic Indian film *East is East*, where the song "Inhee logon ne" from the movie *Pakeezah* is playing in an immigrant Islamic house in London, and a first generation daughter, a young woman, is dancing western style to this song as she is sweeping the floor *a la* Mary Poppins: an absolutely seductive moment of iconic immanence. It is a moment that negotiates the gap between "speaking" and "speaking for": phenomenologically and non-didactically. In this hybrid moment, the *Pakeezah* icon has traveled and not traveled at the same time: the "original" moment is being repeated non-identically in the diaspora, and the Mary Poppins response is both "improper" and exquisite in its aesthetic randomness/contingency. Now to my didactic use of this scene. How much do we need to know in the diaspora before we know that we know?[9] This is both a general question about the prolegomenon *vis a vis* the main text, and a special question concerning the discontinuous continuity of the diaspora.

Let us say then that the young woman in the movie has no cognizance of the original moment in *Pakeezah*. To what extent would the epiphany of the moment be spoiled or impoverished by the lack of this awareness? If the diaspora is the history of the present, and if the present is the sedimentation of several traces of the past, how full or exhaustive should such an inventory be?[10] Is not there always the problem of an infinite intertextual regress? What if the *Pakeezah* moment is itself a *deja vu,* a reminder of an earlier and yet earlier prototype? To me who knew the earlier moment it was pleasurable to put it *sous rature*[11] and indulge theatrically in the immanence of the diasporic moment and its counter-mnemonic possibilities. If the young woman is not even aware of the earlier history of that song, then there is no question of the counter-memory at all. There is no memory in the first place. In conflating my response with the experience of the young woman in the movie, I would then be guilty of a certain exoticism: the desire to experience myself as alterity and absence within the diasporic moment. I have to confess that there is a kind of *frissons* in the experience of de- and re-territorialization as the earlier moment is seduced and hybridized in the repetition. This diasporic repetition loses all ostensive and representational significance as it points to neither me nor not-me. Strangely, the same "I" that would insist, on a political register, that every act of "speaking" go through the ordeal of recognizing who it is "speaking for," at this hybrid juncture is swayed and seduced by the sheer immanence as well as the intransitivity of the "speaking" *sans* the "speaking for" . At that aesthetic moment I have the intense desire to occupy that frame "in absence," with my historical consciousness parsed as counter-memory. Now does this lead to knowledge, and whose?

As Said had argued brilliantly in his *Beginnings,* there are beginnings and beginnings, and starting points and starting points. A secular beginning is one that in the very act of inaugurating and instrumentalizing itself in relationship to a particular narrative project is aware of its own contingency with respect to other possible beginnings. There is no beginning that is transhistorical. The catch here is one is both born into history and at the same time initializes history by one's birth. As Rosa Burger in Nadine Gordimer's *Burger's Daughter* learns, everyone has to internalize history in accordance with and not in abeyance of one's point of entry, and at the same time not be complicit with a subjectivist historiography.[12] It is both, not either/or. How is the objectivity of history given subjectively to each individual: that is the troublesome question. There has to be a perspectival/ subjectivist mis-recognition of the given-ness of history before any attempt can be made to "get history right." In the diasporan case, there are two histories that we need to get right, that is, get them right in all their interconnectedness.

The diasporan generation is repeating in its own way the objective given-ness of both American and Indian history. Without a doubt, as an immigrant-naturalized diasporan parent/ intellectual/ teacher, I have a role to play that cannot but be didactic and ideological. There really is no *laissez faire* pedagogy; the real difference is between open, self-reflexive pedagogies and self-naturalizing pedagogies. I would insist that my students/sons and daughters read Romila Thapar, Madhu Kishwar, Kumkum Sangari, Ashis Nandy, Partha Chatterjee, Veena Das, Gail Omvedt, Ranajit Guha and the Subaltern collective on the one hand; and on the other, immerse themselves in the works of Ronald Takaki, Howard Zinn, Noam Chomsky, Glenn Omatsu, Lisa Lowe, Rey Chow, Angela Davis, Bell Hooks, Chandra Talpade Mohanty, Sunaina Maira, Vijay Prashad, and others.

But, despite such pedagogical solicitude on behalf of the next generation, one has to acknowledge that any repetition of history as performance is both *a repetition and a repetition of.*[13] Though there is a relationship of representational fidelity to "the original," this is a pseudo-procedural obligation, which is not necessarily content driven. Furthermore, as we all know, the original will and must get dislodged, and its authority relativized by repetition, that is, with reference to the history of the present. The repetition has to care of itself, transitively and immanently, even as it aligns itself responsibly with the "origin/s", both American and Indian. Here is the rub. Why does one remember the past? Clearly, for multiple reasons: for a certain wholeness, for reasons of continuity so that wrongs and injustices may be redressed, for reasons of the future as there can be no future except by way of the past mediated and spoken for by the present, to be remembered in mourning and not in melancholy so that life can go on, for the legitimate fear that a consumerist and super-capitalist USA will forget, and forget with impunity, and *because the past is useable, or, it has to be made useable.*[14]

Once we concede that the significance of history has something to do with its usefulness, we have already acquiesced in an opportunistic/pragmatic historiography. This automatically means that certain pasts, though real, are not useable; and what is more, the historical subject is not always in a position to dictate what is useable and what is not. Let us take the example of the travel of the legend of Fa MuLan to San Francisco, CA.[15] The question that Maxine Hong Kingston asks is not about the authenticity of the legend, but rather about its usefulness in San Francisco. Will a myth that belongs "there" work "here"?[16] I shall shelve for the moment the question whether the legend worked even there. If the legend is a significant part of one's past as charm, as talisman, as strategy, and if it does not work here for reasons beyond one's control, should the diasporic subject

1. abandon/forget that legend without compunction and *ergo* cut off all connection with the Chinese past,
2. look to hybridize and contextualize the past in relationship to the present context,
3. keep agonizing, and flagellate itself with the questionable diagnosis that the legend is not working because one is not authentically Chinese enough as filiation has now given place to affiliation and dissemination,
4. cultivate a rigorous schizophrenia such that the legend will be part of one's inner spiritual-cultural-Chinese self while out there some other principle will be made to work,[17]
5. go all out with full consciousness towards martyrdom by insisting in the efficacy of the legend despite all evidence to the contrary, or,
6. critique the host/mainstream culture for its racist/ethnocentric hostility towards new immigrants and new "others?"

This partly is the diasporic problem with history. Indeed, ideally speaking, the Indian or the Japanese or the Chinese past, given all the dramatic celebration of internationalism and globalization, should be useable wherever and whenever, but such alas, is not reality! Quite to the contrary, shedding a certain register of the past purely on pragmatic/opportunistic grounds works towards being anointed as the model minority, and eventually crowned as all-American.[18]

So where lies the answer? I have been arguing for a while now that the way towards an answer lies in the critical cultivation of double-consciousness: not as a label forced on ethnics/diasporans/immigrants, but as a pro-active, and agentially realized mode of being.[19] Here, I do not mean double-consciousness as "content," but rather as a critical "signifying practice" with the potential to re-identify and re-articulate problems and questions. One of the first imperatives of such a re-identification is that in the diasporan context it is neither possible nor advisable to maintain compartmentalized distinctions between intra- and inter-historical dimensions. For example, the negotiation of Indian identity is not to be achieved within some irrefragable inner sanctum, and then taken out for a public walk to meet up with the American sphere. Nor is the American side of the hyphen to be thought of as a perfect pragmatic program untouched by ethnicity. The very purpose of double consciousness is to confound the inside-outside distinction, to "contaminate" white all-America with ethnicity and challenge Indian or old world assumptions with the politics of location. Clearly, there is good and bad in both cultures. Rather than focus on identity politics which in the ultimate analysis is always divisive and "othering" of some difference, double-consciousness should dwell seriously on the politics of representation and its shifting coalitional parameters.

Scenario 4

If one of the outcomes of the ABCD syndrome is a bland Americanization based on ethnic self-loathing and self-racialization, the other possibility, which is a binary reflection of the former, is the blind and fanatical cultivation of the separatist-ethnic self in opposition to dominant racism, and in isolation from other minority discourses. There is a moment in the movie, My *Son, the Fanatic* where the secular father is in shock when confronted by his son who has chosen the Islamic "fundamentalist" path in response to a racist Britain that disrespects Islam. The father in turn turns "secular fundamentalist" and loses his flexibility, his secular cool. The son asks significantly, "Now, who is the fundamentalist?" As I conclude this essay I would like to focus on the rich and ambivalent semantics of that simple question asked by the diasporic son of the immigrant father.

The diasporic situation drives homes the fact with ruthless honesty that all identities are imagined and reactive or strategic. In other words, to echo Nietzsche somewhat, in a perspectival world that is structured in dominance, the values that we claim for our particular "ism" are nothing but the naturalized effects of positions adopted in a conjuncture of conflict and resistance where we militarize ourselves to resist some dominant predatory other. Clearly, Hinduism, and Islam, and Secularism are intrinsically value-coded, but this very intrinsic value-code is occasioned historically as a polemic. Thus, secularism is conceived as an antidote to the ills of pre-modern communalisms, and at a later postcolonial moment the "return to one's own *dharma*"[20] functions as a corrective to the modernist-secularist denigrations of pre-communal worldviews and ontologies. The problem, then, is how to imagine honest and non-paranoid spaces where one can question the complex complicities between "pure identities" and "strategic identities" in the name of a multilateral politics of representation. I am not for a moment denying the possibility that in some sequestered haven each "ism" might possess its intrinsic value; but all we have to go by are the historical paths taken by these different "isms" in the real world where there has been such an intermixing of histories, for a variety of reasons. Just as the history of human intentionalities can be accessed only through the actual historical forms that these intentionalities took, the histories of identities and their embeddedness in their respective "isms" cannot be judged with reference to some ideal history that never happened, either.

To return now to the question, "Now, who is the fundamentalist?" Each of the words in the sentence is characterized by ambivalence: the kind of ambivalence that presides over the relationship between nouns and pronouns, between "place markers" and "place fillers/contents." Hence, the syntax necessitates a simultaneous double-coding. The "now" makes an ostensive reference to the phenomenological eternal present, but at the same time invites interpellation. Which "now" is the one in question: the nationalist now, the diasporic now, the Islamic or the secular now? The indeterminacy/undecidability of the "now" is dangled both as an *a priori* and as a formal possibility to be broken open by historical agency. The same goes for the pronominal openness of the "who": which who and under what circumstances? Any "one" could occupy that position; it all depends on historical circumstantiality, the polemical constructedness of the conjuncture. The "is" as a temporal verbalization of the infinitive "to be" is always already marked by the undecidable tension between the possibilities of predication and the determinacy of a particular predication; just as the definitive exemplarity of the definite article "the" cannot at all anticipate the noun to follow. As for "fanatic", that too points to the possibility that the fanatic could be Hindu, Muslim, Sikh, Christian, Secular, or the ultimate utopic/dyslopic anti-fanatic who wants to put an end to all fanaticisms, unaware meanwhile of his own complicity in the underlying logic of binarity. In this context, both father and son have to acknowledge a mutual pathology as well as a shared etiology. Each position mirrors the other, and it is this mirroring that needs to be re-symbolized.

The legitimacy of the history of the present is both form- and content-driven, and the relationship of the two is neither predictable nor governable within a given horizon. So, "who is who?" under what epistemological and political conditions? Who is the teacher, and who the student? One of the significant insights that the diaspora offers is that identities and subjectivities are positional and therefore ontological, and not the other way around. The algebraic indeterminacy of the subject position is variously occupied under shifting historical conditions that refuse the aegis of a single horizon. Conjunctural by definition, diasporan subjectivities can be interpreted with other subjectivities that are not necessarily of the same horizon. The singular challenge of the diasporic situation is that there is no preexisting historical-temporal horizon; the horizon has to be coordinated simultaneously with the creation of the contents that are to be historicized within the horizon. Thus the question, "Now, who is the fundamentalist?" is being posed within an indeterminate and hyphenated horizon, and not exclusively within a Pakistani, British, secular, or Islamic horizon. It then follows that the ethico-political valences of any of these systems are determined polemically, i.e., not neutrally or disinterestedly. These valences cannot be understood and appreciated without reference to the historical conditions that engendered them in the first place. The son, in the movie, embraces Islam not ideally, but in polemical response to the racialization of his brown identity in a racist Britain. Were he living in Pakistan, who knows what axiology he would gravitate towards. My point is not that value systems such as Islam, secularism, nationalism have no intrinsic worth, but rather that the historical practice of these systems are polemically determined. In other words, no communalism, then no secularism; no white racism, then no militant ethnic separatism. The conditions under which the father is interpellated by secularism and the conditions under which the son identifies his father's secularism as a form of fundamentalism occur, are not automatically intelligible to each other. The diasporic condition would insist that these different histories ought to be studied with reference to each other, as immanent critiques of themselves and of each other. Both the certitudes of filial belonging and the guarantees of pedagogical sovereignty are dislocated in the diaspora.

To return one final time to the Dakshinamurthy motif as I conclude my essay: it is in the staging of the silence as the prolegomenon to the pedagogical moment that I am interested. I am no believer in the plenitude of silence or in the primordiality of silence. In the diasporan situation, before any pedagogical transaction can even begin to take place between parent offspring, between the teacher and the student, there needs to be a meta-pedagogical staging of pedagogical possibility. Within such a critical and distantiating performativity, the two concerned horizons have the obligation to un-name themselves in the presence of each other and acquire the courage to entertain questions as possible answers. The teacher's silence has to be produced by the rigor of the student's passion, and the student's educability has to rest squarely on the radical self-questioning of the teacher: neither the old leading the young nor youth invigorating the old, but a cross-hatched temporality of the perennial present, i.e., not forever young or forever old, but forever "forever," the time of the teacher and the time of the student transcended by the immanence of the pedagogical moment.

Notes

1. Here I refer to Hans-Georg Gadamer's groundbreaking henneneulic work *Truth and Method*, inspired by Heidegger.

2. Michel Foucault's notion of the "counter-memory", as developed in his essay, "Nietzsche, Genealogy, History" offers significant ways of investing in history (139-164). Equally important is the category of "subjugated knowledges" as elaborated by Foucault in his essays on Power and Knowledge.

3. See *Theorizing Diaspora*, eds. Jana Evans Braziel and Anita Mannur, Blackwell 2003.

4. Amitav Ghosh, *The Shadow Lines*. Delhi: Ravi Dayal Publishers, 1988.

5. I refer here to the concept of "the dangerous supplement" as developed by Jacques Derrida in his Of *Grammatology*.

6. I can remember an incident from my childhood as a "Madrasi Tamil" in New Delhi when my parents had taken me out, dressed in a "veshti" to visit an uncle and aunt who were staunch "Delhi Tamils". The aforesaid uncle and aunt reprimanded my parents for having dressed me and parading me in public in New Delhi in ethnic Tamil attire.

7. Amitav Ghosh develops the strategy of "imagining with precision" in THE SHADOW LINES. See also, R. Radhakrishnan, *Theory in an Uneven World for* more on this strategy.

8. Nietzsche's memorable formulation of the relationship of remembering to forgetting takes place in his work, *The Use and Abuse of History*.

9. See my essay, "We are the World, but Who are We, and How do We Know?" in *Rethinking Marxism:* 94-110.

10. Both Antonio Gramsci and Jacques Derrida elaborate the notion of traces, or the trace: Gramsci in a decidedly political manner whereas Derrida's approach is by way of eviscerating metaphysics of the dominance of presence.

11. The strategy of "sous rature" employed by Derrida in his *OfGrammatology* has its origins in Heidegger.

12. See Nadine Gordimer, *Burger's Daughter*, and my extended treatment of (his work in the last chapter of *Theory in an Uneven World*. 124-130.

13. For more on the theme of repetition, by way of Giles Deleuze, see Michel Foucault, "Theatrum Philosophicum" in *Language, Counter-Memory, Practice*. 165-196.

14 Adrienne Rich's poem, "Diving into the Wreck" explores the Ihcmc of historical revisionism with tremendous political and aesthetic passion.

15. See Maxine Hong Kingston, *The Woman Warrior*.

16. For more on authenticity and the politics of the "here," and the "there," see essays by R. Radhakrishnan and SauLing Wong.

17. For a memorable reading of the highly gendered inner-outer divide in the context of postcoloniality, see Partha Chatterjee's essay in the collection, *Recasting Feminism*, eds.

Kumkum Sangari and Sudesh Vaid. See also R. Radhakrishnan, "Nationalism, Gender, and the Narrative of Identity", in *Nationalisms and Sexualities,* eds. Andrew Parker et al. 77-95.

18. See *The State of Asian America,* ed. Karin Aguilar-SanJuan, and *Orientations,* eds. Kandice Chuh and Karen Shimakawa.

19. See Du Bois, "The Souls of Black Folk" for the initial articulation of "double consciousness," and Paul Gilroy's *The Black Atlantic* and Vijay Prashad's *The Karma of Brown Folk* for further elaborations.

20. See Madhu Kishwar's essay with the same title in *Manushi.*

References

Aguilar-SanJuan, Karin. *The State of Asian America.* Boston: South End Press, 1994.

Barthes, Roland. "To write: Intransitive Verb," in *Textual Strategies*, ed. Josue V. Harari. Ithaca, NY: Cornell University Press, 1979.

Benjamin, Walter. *Illuminations,* trans. Harry Zohn. New York: Harcourt, Brace and World,1968.

Chatterjee, Partha. "The Nationalist Resolution of the Woman's Question" in *Recasting Feminism.* eds. Kumkum Sangari and Sudesh Vaid. New Brunswick, NJ: Rutgers University Press, 1990.

Chuh, Kandice and Karen Shimakawa, eds. *Orientations: Mapping Studies in the Asian Diaspora.* Durham, NC: Duke University Press, 2001.

Derrida, Jacques. *Of Grammatology,* trans. Gayatri Chakravorty Spivak. Baltimore, Maryland: John Hopkins University Press, 1974.

Du Bois, W.E.B. *The Souls of Black Folk.* New York: Penguin Books, 1996.

Evans Braziel, Jana and Anita Mannur, eds. *Theorizing Diaspora.* Oxford: Blackwell 2003.

Foucault, Michel. "Theatrum Philosophicum," in *Language, Counter-Memory, Practice,* trans. Donald E. Bouchard and Sherry Simon. Ithaca, NY: Cornell University Press, 1977: 165-196.

Foucault, Michel. "Nietzsche, Genealogy, History," in *Language, Counter-Memory, Practice,* trans. Donald E. Bouchard and Sherry Simon. Ithaca, NY: Cornell University Press, 1977.

Gadamer, Hans-Georg. *Truth and Method,* trans. and ed. Garrett Barden and John Camming. New York: Seabury, 1975.

Ghosh, Amitav. *The Shadow Lines.* Delhi: Ravi Dayal Publishers, 1988.

Gilroy, Paul. *The Black Atlantic.* Cambridge, MA: Harvard University Press, 1992.

Gordimer, Nadine. *Burger's Daughter.* Harmondsworth: Penguin Books, 1979.

Kingston, Maxine Hong. *The Woman Warrior.* New York: Knopf, 1976.

Kishwar, Madhu. "Why I Do Not Call Myself A Feminist." *Manushi* 62 (1990): 2-8.
Nietzsche, Friedrich. *The Use and Abuse of History,* trans. Adrian Collins. Indianapolis, IN: Bobbs-Merrill: 1949.
Prashad, Vijay. *The Karma of Brown Folk,* Minneapolis MN: University of Minnesota Press, 2000.
Radhakrishnan, R. "Nationalism, Gender, and the Narrative of Identity." *Nationalisms and Sexualities,* eds. Andrew Parker et al. New York: Routledge, 1991.
Radhakrishnan, R. "We are the World, but Who are We, and How do We Know?" *Rethinking Marxism* 14.3 (2002) : 94-110.
Radhakrishnan, R. "Conjunctural Identities, Academic Adjacencies," in *Orientations: Mapping Studies in the Asian Diaspora:* 240-63.
Radhakrishnan, R. *Theory in an Uneven World.* Oxford: Blackwell 2003.
Rich, Adrienne. "Diving into the Wreck," in *Diving into the Wreck, Poems 1971–1972.* N.Y. and London: W.W. Norton & Co 1973.
Said, Edward and Daniel Barenboim. *Parallels and Paradoxes: Explorations in Music and Society,* ed by Ara Guzelimian. London: Bloomsbury, 2003.
Said, Edward W. *Beginnings.* New York: Basic Books, 1975.
Wong, Sau-ling Cynthia. "Sugar Sisterhood": Situating the Amy Tan Phenomenon." In *The Ethnic Canon: Histories, Institutions, and Interventions,* ed. David Palumbo-Liu. Minneapolis, MN: University of Minnesota Press, 1995: 174-210.

Index

ABCD (American Born Confused Desi), 224, 234, 235
Acheve, Chinua, xvi, 178
Africa, 177
African-American, 177, 204
agency: in Gramsci, 48–49; and post-coloniality, 163
agency formation, 142
Ahmad, Aijaz, xv, xxiv
alienation, 167
Althusser, Louis, xiii, 5–7, 10–11, 14
American Desi, 236
Amin, Samir, xxvii, 171
Appaduria, Arjun, 172
Asian-American, 204, 215, 217, 220, 221
asymmetry, 146–47
authenticity, 162, 211, 215, 222

Bakhtin, Mikhail, 70, 93
Barthes, Roland, xviii, xix, 3–4
Benjamin, Walter, 19
Benston, Kimberly, 68–69
Bhabha, Homi K., 158, 172, 174

boundary 2, xiii
Burger's Daughter (Gordimer), xxi, 120, 123, 127–28, 239

Camus, Albert, xx, 38
canon, 105
Chakraborty, Dipesh, 148, 167
Chatterjee, Partha, xxiii, 147, 185, 192, 199
Christian, Barbara, 88–89
Cixous, Hélène, 87
class, 56–59, 187
Cogito, xiv, xv, xviii
colonialism, 156, 158. 166
common ground, 59, 81, 89
countermemory, 39, 176
Critical Inquiry, 81, 86–87
cultural studies, 139

Dakshinamurthy, 230, 233
Das, Veena, 137
decanonization, 115
deconstruction, xiv, xviii, xxi, 97
Deleuze, Gilles, 34–35, 39

de Man, Paul, 106–8
Derrida, Jacques, xiii, xiv, xix, 17–19, 110, 170
Dhareshwar, Vivek, 150
diaspora, xx, xxiv, xxv, 159, 165, 173, 206, 230
diasporic subjectivity, xiii
differe(a)nce, xx
difference, 42, 48, 62, 71–72, 84
difference in identity, 58, 84
discontinuity, xvii
double consciousness, xxi
doubleness, xxii, 77
Du Bois, W. E. B., 40, 205, 207

Eagleton, Terry, 124
East is East, 237
ecriture, xv
epistemology, xv, xvii, xxi, 2, 216
essentialism, 136, 162, 211; strategic, xxvi
ethicopolitical, the, 2, 164
ethnicity, xxii, 63–65, 90–91, 176, 217
Eurocentric Enlightenment, xiv
Eurocentrism, xx, 136, 194, 220

Fanon, Frantz, 186
Felman, Shoshana, 103
feminism, xxv, 121, 129, 186
feminist historiography, 187–88
FOB(fresh off the boat), 235
Foucault, Michel, xiii, xiv, xx, 9, 20, 28, 31, 36–37, 39, 66
Freire, Paulo, xiii, 109
Freud, Sigmund, xxiii, 11, 44
fundamentalism, 241

Gandhi, Mohandas K., xxiii 163, 196–97
Gates, Henry Louis Jr., 84, 86, 88
gender, 187–88
generation gap, 206
Ghosh, Amitav, 209
Gordimer, Nadine, xxi, xxii, 120–22, 125–29

Gramsci, Antonio, xx, 28, 46–50
Guha, Ranajit, 147
Guinier, Lani, 228

Hall, Stuart, 28–29
hegemony: in Gramsci, 50, 55, 58
Heidegger, Martin, xiv, 52
hybridity, xx, xxv, 159–62, 224, 230, 231

identity, xviii, 27, 71–72, 75, 77; ethnic, 62, 90, 216
identity politics, xiii, 176, 227
ideology, 11–13; critique of, 13
in-betweenness, xiii
intellectual, 30, 35–36; organic, 51, 67; postcolonial, 170; specific, 46

Jackson, Rev. Jesse, 28–30, 72–74, 82
Jameson, Fredric, xiii
JanMohamed, Abdul, 120

King, Martin Luther, 40
Kingston, Maxine Hong, xxiii, 175, 207

Lacan, Jacques, xxiii
Laclau, Ernesto, 29, 55–57
Location, xviii
logocentrism, 72
Lord, Audre, xxii

Macherey, Pierre, 5
Mahabharatha, 203, 212
Malcolm X, 207
Mani, Lata, 149–50
Marx, Karl, 7–8, 44, 58
Marxism, 6, 7, 14, 134; structuralist, 4, 8
May 1968, 35, 38, 134
McDowell, Deborah E., 71
Meese, Elizabeth, 120–24, 129
Mignolo, Walter, xviii
minority, intellectuals, 52, 217
modernism, xv
Mohanty, Chandra Talpade, 149–50

Mouffe, Chantal, 29, 55–57
My Son, The Fanatic, 241

Nandy, Ashis, xvii, xxv
narrative, 119, 166
nationalism, xxii, xxiii, 164–65, 174, 190–91; Indian, 185
Nehru, Jawaharlal, xxiii, 163, 196–99
Nietzsche, Friedrich, 12, 18, 20
Nixon, Rob, 137
nostalgia, 4, 204

Ontology, xv, 231
Orientalism, 194, 220

Pakeezah, 237, 238
Passage to India (Forster), 122
pedagogy, xxiii, xxiv, xxv, 96–98; critical, 114; poststructuralist, 101; radical, 113
politics of location, 148–50, 168
post-, the, 76–77, 157, 177
postcoloniality, xviii, xix, xx, xxii, 149, 155–56, 164, 217, 227
postcolonial subjectivity, 166
postmodernism, xv, 226
poststructuralism, xviii, xix, xx, 138, 217, 227
poststructuralist politics, 55, 63
psychoanalysis, 11; Lacanian, 16

race, 80–82
Rainbow Coalition, 27–28, 56, 74, 83
representation, xx, xxii, 31, 35–36, 39, 41–42, 140, 217, 219
return, 166, 170
Rushdie, Salman, 160–62

Said, Edward W., xvi, 36–37, 51, 85, 125, 145–46

Sangari, Kumkum, xviii, 161, 187–90
Sartre, Jean-Paul, 38
Sassoon, Anne Showstack, 50–51
Satanic Verses (Rushdie), 159
secularism, 160, 212, 243
self-reflexivity, 170
Shohat, Ella, 157
Smart, Barry, 45
Socrates, 98, 101–3
Socratic method, 100–101
Spanos, William V., xiii
Spivak, Gayatri Chakravorty, xiii, xviii, xx, 10, 37, 42, 56, 148, 167–69, 208
structure, 3–6
subaltern identity, 167
subject, 1–2, 8–10, 12–14, 33
subject formation, 142
subject position, xiv, 27, 120, 127, 130, 169
subjugated knowledges, 32

Tan, Amy, 221, 222
theory, xiii, xiv, xvii, xx, xxi, 5–6, 8, 19, 21, 27, 35, 92–93; indigenous, 168; metropolitan, 174; subaltern, 168
third world, 157, 209
turn, the linguistic, xiv

Vaid, Sudesh, 187–88

Washington, Booker T., 205
West, Cornel, 63–64
Western individualism, 48
Williams, Raymond, 133–35, 137–42, 144–47
women's question, 185, 188
Wong, Sau-Ling Cynthia, 221
worldliness xvi, xviii, xix